THE
ARMED CITIZEN

THE
ARMED CITIZEN

EDITED BY JOSEPH B. ROBERTS, JR.

A PUBLICATION OF
THE NATIONAL RIFLE ASSOCIATION OF AMERICA

BOOK SERVICE

ISBN 0-935998-56-X
Library of Congress Catalog Card Number 89-061009
Printed in the United States

Published by the
National Rifle Association of America
1600 Rhode Island Avenue, N.W.
Washington, D.C. 20036

George Martin, Executive Director, NRA Publications
Frank A. Engelhardt, Dep. Director & Book Service Manager
Michael A. Fay, Manufacturing Director
Harry L. Jaecks, Art Director

CONTENTS

PREFACE

Through the years it has been frequently suggested that a compilation of entries from "The Armed Citizen," a column devoted to reporting citizens' use of firearms in legitimate self-defense, that appears in each month's edition of *American Rifleman* magazine, would be a welcome book. Here, at last, is that book—196 pages of it—its publication mandated by both the demands of the times and of NRA's membership.

Before the task of assembling a book of Armed Citizen entries had progressed very far, we were confronted with the urgent need to limit the amount of material. There is sufficient material, still unassembled, to fill a second volume, and perhaps a third. The immediate question, thus, was . . . how to select the material for this volume, and how to edit it?

We decided, first, not to *select* the material that we have published. Editors of *American Rifleman* over a period of five decades have already *selected* items for publication from the abundance of material submitted each month. So, instead of selecting we devised a scheme by which four or more alternative columns from each year of publication have been set aside and reprinted just as they appeared in the magazine. In the same vein, we did not edit the material. It is reprinted word for word, just as it was originally printed—almost.

In reading through the columns of Guns vs. Bandits (all of which have been reprinted) we found not-infrequent references to the race, ethnic or national origin of a victim or a criminal—usually the latter. It was a common editorial practice, in the 1930s, to report such information. Such a report, nowadays, is not merely uncommon, it is downright unacceptable—which is as it should be. Therefore, we omitted references to race or origin, or substituted words like "man" or "bandit." And we were able to confirm a suspicion of long standing, that behavior, and not the color of a man's skin, or where his parents came from, identifies criminality. We left in the national origin of one victim, victimized primarily because of his nationality. We also left in the word "vigilante," for in the *American Rifleman* of the 1930s, vigilantes were citizens banded together in the face of a present threat who defended themselves against that threat, then disbanded—a militia, if you please, as the framers of our Constitution and Bill of Rights intended it.

Beyond that, the job was simple, extract the material according to the scheme, assemble it (and correct a few spelling errors), then turn the package over to our art and production staffs for the Herculean task of putting it into print. It is they, the artists and producers, not the editor, who do the real, hard work. And this editor thinks that they have done it handsomely.

Joseph B. Roberts, Jr.

INTRODUCTION

During the decades the *American Rifleman* has published The Armed Citizen column, thousands of incidents of law-abiding Americans using firearms to halt or prevent crime have appeared in the magazine. The total could have been much higher. Given editorial space constraints, only a portion of the newspaper clippings dutifully sent in by NRA Members each month can be printed. The editors who select and edit the items that appear in The Armed Citizen do so with one goal in mind. They seek to present to our readers an accurate and balanced portrayal of what happens when American gun owners, in the absence of law enforcement protection, seek to defend themselves, their families and their property.

As you read the pages that follow, bear in mind that the incidents depicted are the very small tip of a very large iceberg. Upon reading Paul Blackman's article, you will discover, however, that the size and formation of this iceberg have been explored.

Historically, criminologists have ignored the defensive use of firearms in America and the resultant effect on crime. This changed in 1988 with the publication of Dr. Gary Kleck's study, "Crime Control Through the Private Use of Armed Force." Dr. Kleck estimates that firearms are used defensively one million times each year in the U.S. He also concludes that more than 98% of these incidents involve neither woundings nor killings. The mere presence of a firearm is an effective deterrent.

Dr. Kleck's important study and common sense tell us that criminals fear armed citizens. What neither can tell us is—why do some editorial writers and politicians?

William F. Parkerson, III
Editor
American Rifleman

CHAPTER 1
A HISTORY OF "THE ARMED CITIZEN"

BY WALTER J. HOWE

For more than sixty years, *The American Rifleman** (official publication of the National Rifle Association) has included all sorts of editorial references to civilians using firearms to protect themselves and other persons and property. Regular monthly reports of incidents in which armed civilians killed, wounded, apprehended or chased off assailants began in the January 1932 issue of the *Rifleman* under the heading Guns vs. Bandits. It varied in size from one column to two pages during the more than seven years that it was a regular *Rifleman* feature.

Guns vs. Bandits consisted principally of excerpts from newspaper accounts of incidents in which police and civilians used firearms to protect lives put in jeopardy by assailants. Guns vs. Bandits last appeared in the November 1939 issue of the *Rifleman*. NRA records are silent as to why Guns vs. Bandits was discontinued, but examination of issues of the period suggests the feature was eliminated during an extensive redesign of the entire *Rifleman* format. Moreover, although the *Rifleman* was not abandoning its 'keep and bear arms' reporting, all possible magazine space was needed for a changed editorial emphasis that would prepare NRA members for a new challenge—their role in the fast approaching World War II.

During World War II and for some years following, the NRA, thru *Rifleman* editorials, continued to champion the law abiding citizen's right to use firearms for every legal purpose. But the *Rifleman* included very little hard copy demonstrating that civilians were indeed using firearms to drive off life-threatening assailants. This conspicuous void remained until the September 1958 issue when The Armed Citizen feature was introduced.

When I was appointed editor of the *Rifleman* in late 1953, I compiled a list of format changes and features to be added as more advertising revenue

would allow for more editorial pages. My list included features I knew were needed, plus the features requested by the NRA Executive Director speaking for the Board of Directors.

At that time and for the next several years, as the *Rifleman* editorial content underwent critical scrutiny and significant change, a Guns vs. Bandits type feature was never even thought of. However, the editorial content changes and the addition of more ads in various sizes necessitated format changes. It was these changes which generated a need for one-and two column editorial features having definitive identity in title, content and appearance—something the interested reader could count on to appear regularly and to reinforce or challenge his belief on a particular subject matter. Thus was The Armed Citizen born.

It first appeared in the September 1958 issue as a one column unit consisting of a bold headline, an introductory explanatory paragraph and five items. Three of the five armed citizens were men, two were women. There were six assailants involved in the five incidents. Three were killed, one was wounded, one was apprehended and one fled. Three incidents took place in stores and two in homes. Four of the five citizens used handguns while the fifth used a rifle. Each item showed the source and date of the newspaper report from which the item had been digested.

I bylined the first Armed Citizen column because, had there been significant opposition to The Armed Citizen concept from credible sources, then the Editor, rather than the Association, would have been the guilty one.

In the October 1958 issue, another editor-bylined Armed Citizen column appeared. The five items included the newspaper name but not the date of publication. Otherwise the presentation was in every way similar to that in the September issue. The ten items required for the September and October issues exhausted the backlog of suitable clippings for The Armed Citizen. Accordingly, the November 1958 issue did not include the feature.

The Armed Citizen was resumed as a feature in the December 1958 issue. It had six items, and in

The American Rifleman was for decades the title of the NRA's Official Journal. Several years ago the "The" was dropped leaving *American Rifleman*. In this background, for brevity, the single word *Rifleman* is used.

1

only one incident did the citizen fire a gun. In none of the incidents were the assailants shot. The column was not bylined. It was now established as a regular feature of the NRA's Official Journal, with the following notice at the bottom of the column: "MEMBERS—Please send all such newspaper clippings to: Editor, *The American Rifleman.*"

Inviting NRA members to send clippings to the Editor was necessary. Years of experience had shown that very few appropriate newspaper clippings were received routinely, except for those few times when a spectacular incident received national coverage. To put together the best possible Armed Citizen each and every month demanded that the pool of clippings be large and national in scope.

Unlike the predecessor Guns vs. Bandits feature which included digests of incidents in which both law enforcement officers and private citizens used guns to thwart criminal activity, I determined tht the Armed Citizen feature would recount the actions only of civilians*. My reason, for this determination was that accounts of police officers using firearms to combat criminals, while newsworthy, did little to reinforce one of the basic tenets of private firearms ownership—that, in the absence of sworn officers, on the scene, it is the duty of private citiens to uphold and defend the law. The Armed Citizen, by reporting only civilian activity, promotes this notion, and NRA's belief that . . . "every law-abiding citizen is entitled to the ownership and legal use of firearms . . ." in apposition to the often-expressed (by anti-gun groups) idea that only organized police units and formal military organizations have a proven need for guns.

Although The Armed Citizen was well received by *Rifleman* readers from the very first, over the years this feature has not been without its critics. While I was *Rifleman* editor, a few letters came from NRA members faulting the feature because they saw it as condoning situations which were at odds with NRA safe gun handling and proper gun storage rules. Stronger criticism came from a small number of non-NRA members—newspaper writers and educators, plus those who were obviously just plain anti-gun. In essence, these critics saw publication of The Armed Citizen items as an endorsement of irresponsible and possibly illegal use of firearms, and concluded that such endorsement might encourage others to do the same.

As *Rifleman* editor, I responded to each letter dealing with The Armed Citizen content. If the safety aspect of having a firearm in a home or place of business was at issue, NRA safety literature went along with the letter of reply.

*While the expression Armed Civilian is more precise than Armed Citizen, the latter is a well established term and cannot be discarded. Accordingly, in this background, Armed Citizen is descriptive of an individual who is neither a sworn law enforcement officer or a serviceman under arms.

If the critic declared The Armed Citizen to be morally wrong or that it sensationalized shootings, etc., the response included one or more of the following points, in tone and detail appropriate to the critics tack:

● That reporting relevant information is an essential and legitimate function of publications, and if the censorship inclinations of persons who declare "that type of material should not be published" were followed, the remaining meager content of the nation's best information sources would be uninformative and vapid.

● That The Armed Citizen items are less sensational, digested versions of accounts which have already appeared in newspapers.

● That only the victim of a criminal confrontation can determine how he or she can best cope with the situation, which at times involves more than one assailant.

● That just as anyone is free to elect *not* to defend himself, each person has the right—some say a duty—to defend himself within the law.

● That the person who elects to use a firearm in one way or another, must bear the consequences of the action.

At the time (mid-1966) I departed as Editor of the *Rifleman,* there was much activity in Congress—and throughout the nation—to enact tough gun laws. And despite what one reads from time to time today, the anti-gun sentiment was powerful and had been building since the shooting of President Kennedy in 1963. Everyone who was in close touch with the situation knew that any untoward "gun happening" would mean a new Federal gun control law. Anyone who wasn't very concerned with the "bad image" (trite words but descriptive) that guns had, was whistling in the dark—or just didn't know how to read the winds.

The "gun happening" occurred twice in 1968 and the new laws came. Many things, including the firearms industry and the NRA were forced to walk and talk a bit more softly for awhile. The Armed Citizen was affected, too.

Although a quick glance at the contents of thirty years of The Armed Citizen does not show it, the column has bent to both external (public attitudes) and internal (NRA) pressures. The best examples of this can be found in the early 1970s—during an announced period in which no injuries were to have been reported — and in the years since 1977, in which both a full page of material and a permanent spot in the magazine — on the page preceding the NRA Executive Vice President's column — were mandated. Other changes, more subtle, have occurred as successive editors of the *Rifleman* have applied their own sense of what is needed. These changes are mirrored in changes to the preamble to the column that have been made over the years. So that they may be better examined, these introductory paragraphs are reproduced here, in chronological order, preceded (and in one instance followed) by my comments.

SEPTEMBER 1958

The original heading very clearly explained why people sometimes have no logical alternative to using firearms for protection. It also pointed out that the NRA's official publication, the *Rifleman*, had digested the material from accounts which had already been made public in the identified newspapers.

"Law enforcement officers cannot at all times be where they are needed to protect life or property in danger of serious violation. In many such instances the citizen had no choice but to defend himself with a gun. Below are accounts of recent instances digested from newspaper clippings sent in by NRA members."

SEPTEMBER 1968

In April 1968, Dr. Martin Luther King was assassinated by rifle fire and in June 1968 Senator Robert Kennedy was assassinated by handgun fire. The Federal Gun Control Act of 1968 became effective, and several states and cities enacted new—and in some cases, broad base—gun control laws. All levels of Government had, for several years, been under intense public and press pressure to "do something about the firearms problem." The September 1968 issue of the *Rifleman* includes more than a dozen pages of packed copy describing proposed and enacted gun control legislation, along with a review of the press (editorial and advertising) comments on the firearms problem. Understandably, The Armed Citizen was omitted from the April, July and August 1968 issues of the *Rifleman*, and when it was resumed in the September issue, the heading included figures from an analysis which showed that in some 38% of the encounters, The Armed Citizen displayed, but did not fire, his gun. This is how it was explained:

"An analysis of The Armed Citizen for 5 years, 1963-1967, recently revealed that the mere presence of a firearm prevented crime, without the firing of a shot, in 121 incidents. In 112, a would be assailant was killed and in 92 others he was wounded. Shooting as a rule cannot be justified, it should be emphasized, except where crime constitutes an immediate, imminent threat of violence to life or limb, or in some circumstances, property. Above accounts are from newspaper clippings sent in by NRA members."

MARCH 1969

Despite the September 1968 heading, incidents involving killing and wounding of assailants continued to be included in issues for the remainder of 1968. The Armed Citizen feature was omitted from the January and February 1969 issues, but was resumed in March with the heading changed in wording but not in thrust:

"A five year analysis recently revealed that the mere presence of a firearm, without firing a shot, prevented crime in more than a third of the cases

reported in The Armed Citizen. Shooting usually can be justified only where crime constitutes an immediate, imminent threat to life or limb, or in some circumstances, property. The above accounts are from clippings sent in by NRA members."

APRIL 1970

The entire Editorial page was comprised of eleven Armed Citizen incidents. In four of the encounters, warning shots were fired by the armed citizen but none of the assailants were wounded or killed. In the other seven incidents the armed citizen displayed a firearm but no shots were fired. The page carried a large-type headline, "The Armed Citizen—And Not A Scratch." Below that banner appeared the following explanation:

"Some advocates of handgun confiscation have asserted repeatedly that the possession of firearms by private citizens endangers the owners more than criminals who attack them. Like most persons familiar with firearms, we doubt this. Yet this mistaken statement appears in a staff report of the National Commission on Causes and Prevention of Violence, in which personal protection by firearms is termed 'largely an illusion' and 'rarely effective' in urban homes.

"Here, on the contrary, are many instances, taken at random from the news, where a firearm in private hands averted or halted a crime without anyone being shot. Many more such instances could be given in which the mere sight of an armed, determined citizen ended a crime attempt on the spot. In such cases, it often proves unnecessary to fire a shot."

MAY 1970

Despite the closing sentence in the April 1970 declaration, above, and the thrust of the new heading in the May issue, in two of the ten May incidents, warning shots were fired. Note also the declaration that "The Armed Citizen hereafter will consist only of cases in which crimes were halted without casualties." This "no casualties" policy remained in force for eleven continuous issues—until the April 1971 issue in which two incidents involved casualties. In subsequent issues, reports of woundings and killings of assailants by armed citizens have continued to be the rule rather than the exception. Even in the May 1970 issue—and subsequent issues—there were incidents in which not only warning shots were fired, but also shots which were intended to be more than warnings, but missed the fleeing assailant.

"We are now demonstrating through The Armed Citizen one of the most important and most overlooked facts about firearms—that their mere presence often deters crime without the firing of a shot. To emphasize this, The Armed Citizen hereafter will consist only of cases in which crimes were halted without casualties. NRA members are asked to send instances of this kind from newspapers or official police reports, giving the name, place and

3

date of publication, or reprt and name of sender. Address Armed Citizen, NRA, Washington, D.C. 20036.'' At the bottom of the two columns of incidents appeared a new tag line: *"Anyone is free to quote or reproduce the above as all of the information comes from published or official sources.''*

JUNE 1970

The following explanation first appeared in the June 1970 issue and continued thru to the April 1971 issue.

"NRA members are asked to send instances of this kind from newspapers, giving their own names and the name, place and date of publication, or to send official police reports, including name of sender.''

APRIL 1971

The following explanation for The Armed Citizen first appeared in the April 1971 issue and has continued to the latest issue of the *Rifleman*.

"Mere presence of a firearm, without a shot being fired, prevents crime in many instances as shown by news report sent to The Armed Citizen. Shooting usually can be justified only where crime constitues an immediate, imminent threat to life or limb, or in some circumstances, property. The accounts are from clippings sent in by NRA members. Anyone is free to quote or reproduce them.''

The Armed Citizen — whether referring to the column or to the book — does do one thing, and it always has. It contradicts, totally, the false contention that armed resistance to crime is futile. It puts paid, with its reports of wounded and deceased criminals, to the antigunners' idea, that it is usually the citizen, not the criminal, who gets hurt. It proves that in the face of an armed and determined citizenry crime really does not pay.

ABOUT THE AUTHOR:

Walter J. Howe, of Fairfield, Conn., whose historical monograph on The Armed Citizen appears here, is the originator of that column as it is currently published in *American Rifleman*.

Howe, a gunsmith, writer, editor, and forensic ballistician, was recruited from his position as managing editor of Management Methods Magazine, by NRA's then-executive staff director, Gen. Merritt Edson, in 1953, to assume the editorship of the American Rifleman. He had previously worked as a gunsmith, an Army Ordnanceman (during World War II), and on the editorial staffs of Sporting Goods Dealer and Hunting & Fishing magazines. He remained at NRA, as editor of *American Rifleman* from October 1953 until June 1966.

Upon his departure, Howe returned to Management Publications, Inc., by then a group of which he was part owner. When Management Publications dissolved, in 1968, he joined Sturm, Ruger, Inc., first as a consultant, then as full time staff and director of production. He remained with Ruger until his retirement in 1984.

Today, W.J. Howe keeps busy primarily as a consultant on firearms product liability, and with an occasional writing project.

CHAPTER 2
THOUGHTS ON AN ARMED CITIZENRY

ARRESTS BY THE ARMED CITIZEN: LEGAL AND MORAL CONSIDERATIONS
By David I. Caplan, Ph.D., LL.B.

In recent years, American courts have been curtailing the rights of both police and civilians to make arrests. As noted in the prestigious legal encyclopedia *Corpus Juris Secundum, A Complete Restatement of the Entire American Law As Developed by All Reported Cases:*

> "The increasing concern of the courts for the protection of personal rights has led to new restrictions on the right to make arrests without a warrant." (C.J.S., Vol. 6A, preface, p. v, 1975 ed.)

As an illustration, in a 1977 Massachusetts court case, adjudicated in the absence of a state statute dealing with citizens' arrests, the lawfulness of such an arrest was determined by the common law (purely judge-made rules in the absence of legislation, based upon Anglo-Saxon jurisprudence). A homeowner had shot his pistol at two burglars escaping from a drugstore across the street at about 2 o'clock in the morning when nobody was inside the store. The burglars had failed to stop running away even after having been ordered to halt by the homeowner. Both burglars were wounded by the shots. The homeowner was convicted by a jury of assault and battery with a dangerous weapon. On appeal, the Supreme Judicial Court of Massachusetts reversed the conviction on the ground that under common law a citizen had been fully justified in using even deadly force where necessary to arrest a fleeing felon, and that deadly force had in fact been necessary to stop the fleeing burglars in that case, burglary being a felony. By "deadly force" the Court meant force intended or likely to cause death or great bodily harm. The Court advised, however, that this was the last time it was going to rule this way on the permissible circumstances where deadly

force would be justified; and that in the future the rule of law in Massachusetts would be that a person who used force to arrest a fleeing felon who had committed a crime only against property, like the burglary of the drugstore when nobody was inside, would not be considered legally justified in using deadly force to make the arrest. In essence, the court warned that in the future a citizen who acted in the same way as the homeowner had acted in that case could be validly convicted of assault and battery if the fleeing burglars were wounded, and of murder if they were killed.

According to the Massachusetts Supreme Court, this new rule of law, restricting the right to make a citizen's arrest, was necessary in order to set new limits on the use of deadly force as a guard against "the dangers of uncontrolled vigilantism and anarchistic action . . . and in the interest of curbing the promiscuous use of firearms," (*Commonwealth* v. *Klein,* 372 Mass. 823; 363 N.E. 2d 1313, 1317, 1320.) The Massachusetts Supreme Court announced that this new rule, a "somewhat subtle requirement of the law" in its own words (*id.,* 1320), was to apply only in future cases simply because of the admittedly unexpected nature of such a drastically novel restriction on the traditional right of the citizen to use force in making an arrest, as well as because of the obvious law-abiding intent of the homeowner; he had called the police when he had first seen the burglary in progress, before he attempted the citizen's arrest.

The Massachusetts Supreme Court further stated, however, that if a burglary involved a *dwelling* house, then the threat of death or great bodily harm to the victim of the burglary "should be presumed, whether or not it was shown that there were actually occupants in the house at the time of the crime" (*id.*, 1319, n.9), and that then the citizen would still have the right to use deadly force if necessary to arrest the fleeing felon. The Court's somewhat broad language on the use of deadly force to apprehend burglars of a dwelling house should be tempered by the fact that some states by statute prohibit the use of deadly force against a fleeing felon by a private citizen regardless of the circumstances. On the other hand, a very similar rule to that found in the Massachusetts *Klein* decision had also been announced by the Supreme Court of Pennsylvania just nine years earlier, in 1968, the Pennsylvania Court further noting that capital punishment no longer existed for burglary or robbery as it had at early common law. (*Commonwealth*, v. *Chermansky*, 430 Pa. 170, 242 A. 2d 237, 32 A.L.R. 3d 1072.)

It is relevant to note that a parallel tendency, restricting the use of firearms in effecting arrests by police officers of fleeing felons (or even aggressive felons), has been developing in the courts and major police departments across the nation. Legislatures, however, do not necessarily follow this tendency. For example, the Legislature of New York State in 1968 expanded the previously more restrictive rule in that State on the legal justification for the use of deadly force by a private citizen, by allowing him thereafter to use even deadly force when he reasonably believed such force is necessary to "effect the arrest of a person who has committed murder, manslaughter in the first degree, *robbery*, forcible rape or forcible sodomy, and who is in immediate flight therefrom." (Penal Law of New York, §35.30, subdivision 4; emphasis added.) In New York, as in other States, a "robbery" is defined as the use, or threat of immediate use, of *any* physical force upon another person in furtherance of a wrongful taking of property. However, under the same New York statutory law, even a homeowner is not allowed to use deadly force to arrest a burglar fleeing from the homeowner's dwelling unless the burglar had actually committed at least one of the above enumerated crimes, of "murder, manslaughter in the first degree, robbery, forcible rape or forcible sodomy, and is in immediate flight therefrom." (*Id.*)

At any rate, the judicial tendency is in the direction of imposing more restrictions against the use of deadly force in making citizens' arrests. In formulating these new restrictions, however, the courts do not even discuss the value of the relative simplicity of earlier common-law rules governing citizens' arrests and the advantage of such simplicity for quick and easy guidance, to enable law-abiding citizens to conform their conduct to law when they are under the pressure of split-second decision-making on the permissible use of force in effecting a citizen's arrest. Nor do the courts discuss the social value of the more liberal earlier doctrines on the legal rights of citizens to make arrests as a deterrence against violent crime. However, one possible reason courts are restricting the right to use deadly force in making citizens' arrests stems

from the tendency of modern legislatures to create numerous *malum prohibitum* type offenses—that is, crimes without any morally evil quality to them, such as those created by the Gun Control Act of 1968—and to punish these offenses as felonies.

There is little doubt that these new restrictions against making citizens' arrests are based on the theory that arrests are the job of the police as much as possible, if not exclusively. One of the troubles with this theory is, however, that the police themselves are also being subjected to all sorts of new restrictions against the use of deadly force in making police arrests. More specifically, the nation's 15 largest cities have issued guidelines and regulations curbing the police in the use of their own firearms both in self defense and in arresting fleeing violent felons. (N.Y. Times, Oct. 12, 1980, p. 61: "Directive on Deadly Force Angers Philadelphia Police.") Even gun control advocate, Robert J. McGuire, who served as Police Commissioner of New York City, 1977-1983, complained that these guidelines had caused "an enormous increase in the number of cops being wounded, shot at, and killed." (Sunday News Magazine, May 17, 1981, p. 34).

The trend in curbing the use of force by police and civilians in making arrests is further based in substantial part upon the social philosophy of downgrading "property rights" in favor of "personal rights" (as though there were a sharp line of distinction between them). This downgrading of "property rights" of law-obedient victims, in favor of "personal rights" of law-breaking violent criminals, may well be responsible, at least in part, for the present violent crime wave directed against persons as well as property. It is but a small step for the emotionally and ethically undisciplined criminal mind, especially in the value-changing times of today, to go from the idea that if one can get away with taking someone else's property by stealth, without dire consequences, then one can likewise get away with taking someone else's property by personal confrontation. Moreover, the problem of violent crime is made worse by the fact that overt acts of aggression, which were formerly effectively dealt with, are now unchecked by prompt interpositions of citizens' arrests, which are being deterred both by the courts and by the popular media in this anti-hero era. However, as Robert Sherrill notes in his book *The Saturday Night Special*, all violent crime waves in America have been put down by direct citizen action.

Lest any reader worry about "vigilantism" or "taking the law into one's own hands," let us not forget that a citizen's arrest is both a private right and a "public duty." The general rule of law in the United States still is: "It is the right and duty of a private person to apprehend one who has committed a felony in his presence, either at the time of its commission or upon immediate pursuit." (5 Amer. Jurisprudence 2d Series, §35, p. 727.) Of course, in an increasing number of states deadly force may be used to effect such an arrest for a felony only if the felony involves the threat of death or great bodily harm, and in other states deadly force is prohibited by statute in all cases of fleeing felons. Moreover, the reader should realize that no matter how sincerely a person may believe that his or her use of force for self defense or citizen's arrest was morally and legally justified by the facts and circumstances, the judge or jury with the benefit of 20-20 hindsight may adjudge otherwise. In other words, a citizen who uses force, especially deadly force, had better be clearly in the right and had better be able to convince the judge and jury likewise. Nevertheless, a citizen's arrest properly executed under proper circumstances remains a civic duty just as it was under the old common law of England.

As the great 18th century English jurist Sir William Blackstone wrote in his famous and authoritative treatise on the common law, *Commentaries on the Laws of England*:

> "Any private person that is present when any felony is committed, is bound by the law to arrest the felon; on pain of fine and imprisonment, if he escapes through the negligence of the standers by." (4 *Comm.* ★292-293.)

Although it is extremely unlikely these days that anyone would suffer any penalty for failing to make a citizen's arrest even of a felon, and although the extent to which force may be used in making such an arrest has been somewhat restricted in modern law, nevertheless, the citizen's arrest remains a fundamental bulwark for civilization.

The problem of "vigilantism" arises only when the citizen goes further and conducts a mock "trial" or "execution" of the arrested felon, even when there is ample time and opportunity safely and successfully to deliver the felon to the proper authorities. After all, when a criminal confronts a victim with physical violence, the criminal is the one who has taken the law into his hands. It then becomes the right, if not duty, of the victim or his rescuer to take back that law and keep it in his own hands. Otherwise the victim is no longer law-obedient but becomes criminal-obedient.

It is therefore of fundamental importance not to confuse the criminal assailant's taking the law into his hands with the assaulted victim's keeping it in his own hands. These clear delineations must be maintained at all times—lest good and evil likewise be equated, and lest society lose all its moral force by failing to make and maintain vitally needed moral distinctions so essential to civilization.

ARMED CITIZENS AND CRIME CONTROL
BY PAUL H. BLACKMAN, Ph.D.

ONE of the most popular features in the *American Rifleman* is "The Armed Citizen" column, a listing of a tiny fraction of the incidents in which citizens use their privately owned firearms for protection. Only those incidents reported to the police, and covered in local newspapers, are highlighted in the column.

How widespread is the use of firearms by citizens for their self-defense? Data from diverse studies indicate that firearms—particularly, handguns—are used for protection in hundreds of thousands of incidents each year. Now, after years of research, a criminologist from Florida State University has published the most thorough estimates on the prevalence of defensive use of guns by Americans. The study—"Crime Control Through the Private Use of Armed Force" by Professor Gary Kleck—was published as the lead article in the February 1988 issue of *Social Problems*.

Dr. Kleck notes that although criminologists have long ignored the issue of guns for protection, they do study how "routine activities" may impact on crime and crime control. He notes that, with half of all American households and a quarter of retail businesses keeping firearms, "gun ownership must surely be considered a very routine aspect of American life and of obvious relevance to the activities of criminals." Nonetheless, Dr. Kleck adds, "victimology scholars have largely ignored victim gun ownership and use. [Yet] victim gun use may be one of the most serious risks a criminal faces."

Dr. Kleck's study focuses on: (1) the frequency and nature of private citizens' defensive uses of firearms against criminals; (2) the effectiveness versus risk of such actions; and (3) the potential deterrent impact on crime of defensive gun ownership and use.

Primary sources for the study are national and state surveys on gun ownership and use, on victimization and protective measures taken, and on local

7

studies on "justifiable" and "excusable" (self-defense) homicides. Dr. Kleck also weighs what he calls "quasi-experimental" cases of deterrence, such as the well-known example of Orlando, Florida, where women purchased firearms and attended safety classes on gun use in response to an increase in rapes. As a result, incidences of rape and burglary dropped dramatically.

Although several national surveys all suggest relatively small percentages of the nation's 60 million gun owners are using their firearms for protection, Dr. Kleck notes that the figures represent a "large number of actual uses." He estimates that "there were about 645,000 defensive uses of handguns against persons per year, excluding police or military uses." In addition, Dr. Kleck made projections on the uses of long guns, based on the numbers of households keeping long guns vs. handguns primarily for protection. Added together, Dr. Kleck estimates "that guns of all types are used for defensive purposes about one million times a year," and that "guns of all types are used substantially more often defensively than criminally." Most of these uses do not involve firing the gun, much less injuring the criminal.

"Although shootings of criminals represent a small fraction of defensive uses of guns, Americans shoot criminals with a frequency that must be regarded as remarkable by any standard," says Dr. Kleck. The criminologist notes that the FBI's so-called "justifiable homicide" data miss most killings of criminals by civilians because of technical reporting reasons. Using those data as suggestive and local studies as a means of estimating how many *actually* occur, Dr. Kleck estimates that annually, "gun-wielding civilians in self-defense or some other legally justified cause" kill between about 1,500 and 2,800 felons—or 2½ to seven times as many criminals as are shot dead by police.

Insofar as citizens protect themselves from criminals, Dr. Kleck estimates "there were about 8,700-16,600 non-fatal, legally permissible woundings of criminals by gun-armed civilians" annually, and "the rest of the one million estimated defensive gun uses, over 98% involved neither killings nor woundings but rather warning shots fired or guns pointed or referred to."

National gun prohibitionists claim that firearms owned for protection are "generally useless and even dangerous to the victim. . . ." Using victimization surveys commissioned by the U.S. Department of Justice, Dr. Kleck puts that contention to rest, finding that "for both robbery and assault, victims who used guns for protection were less likely either to be attacked or injured than victims who responded in any other way, including those who did not resist at all. Only 12% of gun resisters in assault and 17% in robberies suffered any kind of injury. After gun resistance, the course of action least likely to be associated with injury is doing nothing at all, i.e., not resisting. However, passivity is not a completely safe course either since 25% of

robbery victims and 27% of assault victims who did not resist were injured anyway.

Significantly, Dr. Kleck notes that the victimization surveys actually exaggerated the association of injury with gun-resistance since the surveys generally fail to ask whether the injury occurs after and because of resistance or whether the injury occurred first. In a supplemental questionnaire, however, it was found that most injuries to armed resisters preceded their resistance: "For cases involving both robbery and attack, forceful self-protection actions never preceded attack . . . even among the minority of cases where forceful self-protective acts were accompanied by attacks on the victim, few incidents support the contention that the victim's defensive action provoked the attack."

In addition to preventing injury to the intended victim of a violent crime, the data Dr. Kleck analyzed "show that victims who resisted robbers with guns or with weapons other than guns or knives were less likely to lose their property than victims who used any other means of resistance or who did nothing." As Dr. Kleck puts it in his study: "When victims use guns to resist crimes, the crimes usually are disrupted and the victims are not injured."

Criminologists generally believe, Dr. Kleck notes, that "punishment deters as its certainty, severity and celerity (promptness) increase," and "the maximum potential severity of citizen self-help is far greater than legal system responses to crime." And, obviously, the promptness of punishment, in the form of being shot, is much faster than the criminal justice system: "victims almost always use guns defensively within minutes . . . , the average celerity of even arrest is much lower than for citizen gun use, while the celerity of conviction and punishment is lower still."

Dr. Kleck believes that the well-known Wright-Rossi survey of armed felons underestimates the number of criminals who admit that they had avoided committing some crimes for fear that their intended victims were armed or carrying guns. According to Dr. Kleck, "given that being 'scared off' by a victim is not the sort of thing a violent criminal is likely to want to admit, incidents of this nature may well have been underreported, if [reported] at all. . . . These results, therefore, may reflect a minimal baseline picture of the deterrent potential of victim gun use."

Looking at instances where publicity over gun purchases and training was associated with dramatic declines in crime, Dr. Kleck writes that "these natural quasi-experiments . . . do support the argument that routine gun ownership and defensive use by civilians has an ongoing impact on crime, . . . an impact which is intensified at times when prospective criminals' awareness of potential victims' gun possession is dramatically increased. Gun training programs are just one source of increased awareness: publicity surrounding citizen gun use against criminals would be another." And he notes how crime dropped dramatically following Bernhard

Goetz's shooting of four robbers in the New York subways—a "quasi-experiment" whose results were muddied by the fact that, in addition to a well-publicized gun use, there was also an increase in police manpower on the subway trains.

Burglars devote considerable effort to avoid occupied dwellings at least partly because so many residences in the United States are armed, according to Dr. Kleck. He quotes from a study which found that several burglars "reported they avoided late-night burglaries because it was too difficult to tell if anyone was home, explaining, 'That's the way to get shot.' " In addition, Dr. Kleck notes that victimization surveys in at least three other countries "indicate that in countries with lower rates of gun ownership than the United States, residential burglars are much more likely to enter occupied homes, where confrontation with a victim is possible."

There are several advantages to the American burglar's fear of confrontation. Most importantly, "The nonconfrontational nature of most [American] burglaries at least partly accounts for the infrequency of associated deaths or injuries. . . . Because victim gun ownership is partly responsible for the nonconfrontational nature of burglary, it is therefore to be credited with reducing deaths and injuries by its deterrent effects. The benefit is enjoyed by all potential burglary victims, not just those who own guns, since burglars are rarely in a position to know exactly which households have guns and thus must attempt to avoid confrontations in all their burglaries."

Dr. Kleck's conclusions address the implications of his research for crime-control policy. He, basically, suggests that policies aimed at reducing gun ownership among the law-abiding would be good for criminals but bad for the country generally. Dr. Kleck argues persuasively that "gun use by private citizens against violent criminals and burglars is common and about as frequent as arrests, is a more prompt negative consequence of crime than legal punishment, and is more severe, at its most serious, than legal system punishments. Victim gun use in crime incidents is associated with lower rates of crime completion and of victim injury than any other defensive response, including doing nothing to resist. Serious predatory criminals say they perceive a risk from victim gun use which is roughly comparable to that of criminal justice system actions, and this perception appears to influence their criminal behavior in socially desirable ways."

Nonetheless, Dr. Kleck adds "We cannot pre-cisely calculate the social control impact of gun use and ownership any more than we can do so for the operations of the legal system . . . rates of commercial robbery and residential burglary might be far higher than their already high levels were it not for the dangerousness of the prospective victims."

In conclusion, Florida State University's Kleck believes that "[Measures] applying equally to criminals and noncriminals are almost certain to reduce gun possession more among the latter than the former . . . there would be little direct crime control benefit to be gained by reductions in gun possesion among non-criminals. . . . Consequently, one has to take seriously the possibility that 'across-the-board' gun control measures could decrease the crime-control effects of non-criminal gun ownership. . . ."

Just as Professors Wright and Rossi were forced to conclude that some restrictive gun laws might make things worse by spurring criminals to commit more and more dangerous robberies without guns, or more dangerous assaults using potentially deadlier large handguns (instead of the so-called "Saturday Night Special") or with long guns instead of handguns, so Professor Kleck's study leads him to conclude that restricting guns among the law-abiding may simply encourage criminals, particularly burlars, and limit the beneficial impact of the armed citizen on crime control in the United States.

EDITOR'S NOTE

Dr. Gary Kleck is an associate professor at the Florida State University School of Criminology in Tallahassee. His research has focused on firearms for a dozen years, since he was a University of Illinois graduate student working with Professor David J. Bordua on patterns of firearms ownership, use and regulation in Illinois and on his dissertation, "Homicide, Capital Punishment, and Gun Ownership."

A specialist in research methodology, Dr. Kleck has authored or co-authored several articles on firearms and the "gun control" issue. His studies generally undermine the various assumptions of advocates of restrictive firearms laws and include a definitive academic rebuttal. of the myth of the so-called "Saturday Night Special." He is currently working with Dr. Bordua on a study of private firearms ownership in the U.S.

Even though his research does not show restrictive firearms laws to be either necessary or beneficial, Dr. Kleck supports a "permissive" licensing system for all firearms on the assumption it would not interfere with private ownership. He is opposed to gun schemes directed exclusively at handguns, including licensing.

CHAPTER 3
THE BEGINNING

NOVEMBER 1931

ONE MORE INSTANCE OF ARMED RESISTANCE

In direct refutation of the declaration of certain sincere but misguided officials that armed citizen resistance to banditry is futile comes a report from Sharpsville, Indiana, where the bank was held up on the afternoon of May 2.

Following the retreat of the bandits with the bank cash, one Edrite Parks, member of the Kokomo N. R. A. Club and cashier of the robbed bank, grabbed the bank's .45 Colt pistol and opened fire on the bandit car as it backed away from the curb. The car was pierced by six bullets, one of the two through the windshield, seriously wounding the driver in hand, arm and shoulder.

Mr. Parks is an excellent small-bore rifle shot and one of the most enthusiastic members of his rifle club. It is evident he has plenty of courage, and takes violent exception to the theory of passive submission to armed thugs. In honor thereof the Kokomo N. R. A. Club members held a banquet and special meeting and presented Mr. Parks with a "Reward of Merit" gold medal, the meeting being called to order with a special gavel made from one of Park's .45 A. C. P. bullets recovered from the riddled car abandoned by the bandits.

DECEMBER 1931

BANDITS FEAR ARMED RESISTANCE

The fear of being confronted with the same "tool" with which he was menacing a prospective victim sent a hold-up man scurrying without accomplishing a "job" which he undertook in Denver, Colo., on the night of October 7.

J. T. Stein was putting his car in his garage when he suddenly found himself covered with a pistol and his money demanded. The voices awakened Stein's mother. She went to a window and asked what was wrong. Stein hesitated to explain. The mother thought she understood.

"Just a minute," she called to him, "I'll get your gun."

Once more the stick-up man made his demand and then, still unsuccessful, he took to his heels and was out of sight before his near-victim's mother reappeared at the window.

CHAPTER 4
GUNS vs. BANDITS—1932 to 1939

1932

JANUARY 1932

GUNS VS. BANDITS

Attempting a holdup of a fur store in Chicago on November 18, two men, both reputed to have criminal records, were shot and killed, which brought to 60 the total number of bandits who met death since January 1, 1931, at the hands of private citizens and police officers, citizens killing 26 and police, 34.

Sixty instances in one city of the usefulness of guns as a defense against the criminal!

Frank Ebertsch, 24, temporary manager of the Edgewood office of the American District Telegraph Company, responded to a burglar alarm sounded from the store by the proprietor. As Ebertsch entered the place, one of the robbers rushed at him but fell with a bullet in his abdomen. Ebertsch was struggling with the other man when Policeman Michael Trainor arrived just in the time to prevent the wounded man from shooting Ebertsch. The officer then killed the second man.

In St. Louis, Gregory Dowling, 29, vice-president of the Midland Savings Bank, frustrated a robbery of the bank by killing two bandits and wounding a third. The attempt to rob the bank was made at noon on November 12 when Dowling was alone.

One of three men who had robbed the Hazleton (Idaho) State Bank was killed on November 9 by a posse and two of his accomplices were captured. The stolen money was recovered.

FEBRUARY 1932

Bandit killings by police and private citizens in Chicago during 1931 had mounted to 70 on December 26. Thirty-nine were killed by police, 26 by citizens and 5 by private watchmen. More than 150 bandits were wounded by police and citizens in the same period of time.

Three youths, armed with two revolvers and a rifle, were wounded and captured after robbing the First National Bank, Allendale, Ill., on December 23. The group of citizens who responded to an alarm sounded from the bank and accomplished the arrests were almost 100 per cent N. R. A. members. Two farmers, who had been warned the young thieves were heading in the direction of their home, aided materially, using their guns freely in the face of the fire of the youthful bandits after the latter's car had been wrecked. Bayard P. Leeds, assistant cashier of the bank and crack shot of the local rifle club, effectively used a shotgun against the bandits.

In Philadelphia, Pa., Mrs. Gladys Blumner prevented the escape of a man charged with shooting another on December 7 when she shot him in the shoulder as he was fleeing over house roofs.

Laden with $1,000 payroll money, George Gerlach, a drug store employee, was leaving a Cleveland, Ohio, bank on December 5 when he was told by two gunmen to "stick 'em up." Instead, he drew his own pistol and fired a little too quickly for the bandits. One bandit was killed by him while the other escaped.

One of three bandits was shot and killed after an unsuccessful attempt to rob the Bank of Edwards, Jackson, Miss., on December 5. When the robbers entered the bank, the cashier sounded the burglar alarm. A volley of shots was their reception as they emerged from the bank.

MARCH 1932

All good citizens should buy a gun, get a permit, and, if held up by a bandit, use it, and when gunmen realize they may get what they don't hesitate to give, banditry will cease. This opinion came from Judge Harry S. McDevitt, of Philadelphia, in an address before the Fathers' Association of Cheltenham Township School at Elkins Park, Pa., on January 14.—*From a newspaper report.*

13

THE ARMED CITIZEN

Hold-ups of small stores cannot be stopped by police or law, but only by individual storekeepers arming themselves or having arms where they can quickly get their hands on them. This advice was given before the men's class of the Pawtucket, R. I., Congregational Church, on January 24, by Judge Lellan J. Tuck, formerly of the 10th District Court.—*From a newspaper report.*

"Citizens of Denver: Don't let Hoodlums Bluff You—Fight!" Under this editorial headline that had a feature place in the January 22 issue of the *Denver* (Colo.) *Post,* this exhortation was given: "Answer stick-ups and kidnappers with hot lead. That's the proper medicine. If you haven't a gun, yell as loud as you can. . . . Don't submit weakly to any hoodlum, no matter if he does have a gun. Not one out of ten of these stick-ups and kidnappers will shoot if resisted. . . . Now is the time to show the criminal world that Denver men and women will not submit to intimidation from any ruffian. Suppose your assailant does shoot. Better go down fighting to protect your life and property than to submit to kidnapping and be hauled away to be tortured and maybe killed like a dog!"

At Stanwood (Iowa) on February 22 Vigilantes killed one robber and wounded and captured another after the pair had held up the Union Trust and Savings Bank. The bandits fired at four Vigilantes who were behind a truck used as a barricade across a highway. The Vigilantes answered with a volley that was more effective.

A dream that his store was being robbed was interrupted when W. H. Marshall, grocer, of Knoxville, Tenn., was aroused by a knock at his door. It was a friend to tell him that his store really was being robbed. The two hurried to the store and, as they approached, they heard men running from the store. Marshall decided to wait in the store for a possible return of the robbers. After fifteen minutes, the door was stealthily opened and Marshall fired. One man dropped, mortally wounded. His alleged accomplice was later arrested. This instance occurred January 22.

What was described as an attempted hold-up and assault at a filling station near Erie, Pa., on January 28, was frustrated when the owner, F. L. Burden, seized a gun and held the two robbers at bay until the arrival of state police.

Opening fire when warned by his wife of an attempted robbery, Harry Kirkwood frustrated a robber in his store in Erie, Pa., on January 17. The robber escaped but it was believed that two of Kirkwood's shots took effect.

In Columbus, Ohio, on January 22, John Wirtz, proprietor of a malt store, shot and killed one of two bandits who attempted to rob his place. While believed wounded, the other robber escaped.

Two of four youths who were alleged to have attempted a hold-up of the butcher shop of David Cubbage at Etna, Pa., on January 30, were wounded by shots fired by Cubbage after one of the men had fired at him while his nephew was grappling with another of the intruders. The two who escaped without harm from the bullets were later captured.

Instead of holding up his hands when commanded by two bandits on January 9, R. E. Kemp, Newark, Ohio, yanked out his gun and fired, wounding one of the men in the abdomen. The two intruders fled but the wounded one was later captured when he stopped at a home and requested that a doctor be called. Kemp was wounded by one of the hold-up men's bullets.

With $3,000 on them, John Renn, 60, and Joseph Stoeckel were driving from a bank in Chicago on December 19 when they were forced to the curb by a car bearing five bandits. Two of the bandits, carrying guns, alighted, but Renn and his companion opened fire. The three who remained in the car drove off and the other two, after exchanging shots with their near-victims, managed to escape, but without any loot.

Two robbers were ransacking the drug store of Albert Blank in Cleveland, Ohio, on January 23, while they had the druggist, his wife and clerk lined up against a wall with their hands above their heads. Taking advantage of a momentary lowering of a pistol in the hands of the one who had them "covered," Blank quickly drew a pistol from his shoulder holster and fired. He wounded one of the robbers and held the other under threat of his gun until police arrived.

Ignoring a threat to "get out of the way or I'll plug you," James Lawrence, 67, a tenant in a Cleveland, Ohio, apartment house, fired, while engaged in a struggle with one of two men found in the basement of the building on January 16, and killed him. The second man escaped. Burglars had broken into the building three times.

Four bandits, three armed with revolvers and the fourth carrying a machine gun, fled from the Metropolitan State Bank, Chicago, on November 17, when John Brenza, president, fired on them. They escaped just before police arrived in answer to an alarm sounded by Miss Helen Kuphas, assistant cashier.

A night manager of a garage in San Antonio Tex., was on duty early in the morning of November 27 when a bandit entered, switched off the lights and slugged him into almost unconsciousness. However, the near-victim, Sandy Wolff, was able to draw his pistol and fire. The hold-up man hurriedly departed.

While fleeing with $1,000 loot from the State Bank of Keyesport, Ill., on December 21, a hold-up man was shot and wounded by John Carver. An alarm had been sounded and the bandit was trying to escape a posse when Carver appeared on the scene.

APRIL 1932

In a pistol battle in front of the B. M. Behrends Bank, Juneau, Alaska, on January 23, Guy McNaughton, cashier, shot and seriously wounded a robber and recovered from him $3,000 he had taken from G. E. Cleveland, assistant cashier of the bank. The robber carried two pistols.

Accosting a suspiciously-acting man in San Bernardino, Calif., on the night of November 26, 1931, Police Officer George A. Pickett was fired upon. The two then exchanged shots, the officer firing six and his attacker eight, and at one time the officer's gun stuck and he had to take refuge in a doorway. While five of the officer's shots took effect in the man, the latter continued his resistance and the officer had to "rush" him and take his gun from him. The man died several days later.

On the night of February 16, two robbers were shot and killed in Cleveland, Ohio. One was killed with a shotgun when he and two companions were holding up a grocery store. The other was killed by Joseph Svara after he had robbed Svara.

When a bandit tried to rob the Universal Shoe Store in Chicago on the night of March 1, he was shot by the manager, Anton Zaleski, but escaped.

In Bono, Ark., on February 24, two robbers, who obtained $3,300 in a holdup of the People's Bank, were both wounded by pursuing citizens. Both were captured and the money recovered.

Policeman Philip Igoe was guarding a store in Chicago on the night of February 9 when a bandit crept up behind him and pressed a pistol against his back. The officer quickly whirled about, drew his gun and shot the bandit dead. An accomplice of the killed robber fled.

MAY 1932

Two men were shot and killed in Mill Creek, Okla., on March 9 in an attempt to rob the First National Bank of that place. They were shot down by citizens as they emerged from the bank.

In a gun duel with an intended victim, one of two bandits was fatally wounded near St. Paul, Minn., on February 28. Carleton Bourdeaux, 20, a carrier for a Minneapolis newspaper, had used his car to help the bandits get a truck, later discovered to have been stolen, from a ditch. After the truck was back on the road, one of the holdup men drew a pistol and, when Bourdeaux hesitated about submitting to robbery, he fired but missed. Bourdeaux then fired, mortally wounding the man.

When Edward S. Tucker, a storekeeper in Nash, Ohio, showed no signs of alarm over being threatened with a pistol, but rather went to the rear of the store and got his rifle, a bandit abandoned his robbery plan and hurriedly left the place.

After he had been held up by two bandits in his store in Wichita, Kans., on April 2, P. G. Jacobsen opened fire on the car in which the two men were making a getaway. The result was that one of the holdup men was killed.

One of three men who attempted to hold up a wholesale grocery store in Detroit on April 4 was shot and probably fatally wounded by police.

A bandit leader was shot and killed in an unsuccessful attempt to hold up the exclusive Embassy Club in Miami, Fla., on February 27. Three accomplices were critically wounded. The holdup was frustrated by police.

One of three bandits who boasted they "were out to kill a cop" was killed in a pistol battle with police in New York on February 20. The bandits had stolen an automobile from a garage.

Citizens of Waveland, Ind., battled seven bank raiders on February 6 for nearly an hour and finally drove them off after the gunmen had wrecked the Waveland State Bank with dynamite.

A burglar, fired upon by Clinton Fogelsang in Kewanee, Ill., on February 7, promptly desisted from his attempt to break into Fogelsang's store and fled.

JUNE 1932

While Arthur Cash was putting his automobile in his garage in Urichville, Ohio, on April 22, two men accosted him, one covering him with a revolver and the other hitting him over the head with a club. Mr. Cash, instead of submitting, drew his own revolver and fired, severely wounding one of the men. The second of the bandits was later captured.

Attempting to break into a department store in Piqua, Ohio, on April 27, a man was shot by Harry Foreman, night watchman at the store. A revolver and a blackjack were found on the man.

Two brothers were fatally wounded when they attempted to rob a grocery store in Evansville, Ind., on April 30. Entering the store, the bandits demanded the contents of the cash register. Charles Burton, the manager, answered their command by firing both barrels of a shotgun into one of the men and then mortally wounded the other with a pistol.

In an attempted holdup of a store operated by Charles Greenstein in Cleveland, Ohio, on April 16, a robber was shot and killed by the storeman.

In Niles, Ohio, on April 15, two youths entered a filling station operated by C. R. Freeman and told the owner to "reach for the skies." Freeman obeyed, but as the two bandits left the place he procured his revolver and opened fire, seriously wounding one of the men.

THE ARMED CITIZEN

Two bandits, their faces smeared with grease, were thwarted by J. C. Dubois, cashier of the bank, in an attempt to rob the Asheville (Ala.) Savings Bank. As the men parked their car in front of the institution and one alighted carrying a sawed-off shotgun, Mr. Dubois secured his pistol and opened fire. The men immediately retreated.

Three bandits, two of them armed, fled from the Smith County Bank at Taylorsville, Miss., on April 14 when Z. Hester, the teller, ducked below his cage and opened fire. They escaped in a waiting automobile.

Two bandits were thwarted in an attempted holdup of a store in Chicago when the janitor, Charles Gunderson, 65, defied their revolvers and opened fire with a shotgun. Each of the bandits fired a shot at Gunderson but missed.

Pursuing a bandit machine in Chicago on April 7, Policeman Bernard Bukowski fired while his wife loaded his gun for him, despite flying bullets from the fleeing robbers. Finally, the officer and his wife forced the bandit car to the curb and captured three men, who, together, with a fourth man arrested later, confessed to 20 robberies. The bandits were making their getaway after a robbery when the officer and his wife started the chase.

In an attempt to hold up O. E. Price in his grocery store and filling station in Corinth, Miss., one of two holdup men was shot. One of the men covered Mr. Price with his revolver but the latter, rather than submit, procured his own gun and commanded the armed bandit to drop his weapon. As the weapon reached the floor, the second bandit grappled with a customer for its possession and was wounded in the struggle.

Five pistol shots fired by Ross McFarland, proprietor of a drug store in Portland, Oreg., on April 4, rid the city of a bandit who had been conducting a series of raids on drug stores. Mr. McFarland is described as "a veteran of many holdups but until this time always the loser." The bandit was armed and had his revolver cocked and ready to shoot.

After they had robbed the People's Bank in Bono, Ark., of $3,300 on February 24, two bandits were felled by bullets fired by pursuing citizens and Officer Jim Coward who had been warned by Luther Barnes after he suspected a robbery when he saw the men enter the bank.

In Seattle, Wash., following an epidemic of holdups, merchants decided to take matters in their own hands and not depend upon the police for protection of their cash. A report of March 15 states that "instances where merchants have 'shot it out' with gunmen in Seattle have been increasingly noticeable, in most cases the bandits being driven off, wounded or killed."

Three armed gunmen held up the drug store of William Krop and Nicholas Kirinic in Chicago on April 12. As the bandits were getting into an automobile, Kirnic fired and wounded one of the men, who was dragged into the car by his accomplices.

Police of Portland, Ore., checking over their records as spring brought to an end the annual major drives against crime, reported five bandits slain and several others wounded. The city's experience was that robbers are brave enough when their victims quietly submit, but their courage fails when the would-be victims produce weapons of their own and "fight it out." According to Detective Captain Harvey A. Thatcher, the records show that after each encounter in which a robber was fatally wounded other holdup men withdrew to their lairs for several days.

In Portsmouth, Ohio, City Manager F. E. Sheehan has appointed W. L. Compton, active in the "Y" pistol and revolver work, to the task of training the police officers in markmanship and has also asked an inspection of and report on the arm carried by each officer and how it is kept. Two Portsmouth officers have been killed by thugs in the past four years but in the future the gunmen will be met with a draw as quick as their own and marksmanship which is likely to be superior. The city manager's move has won the support of the best citizens of the community.

When one of two robbers pulled a revolver on him in an attempt to hold up his gas station near Lewisburg, Ohio, on March 10, Luther Bixler knocked the gun from his hand and quickly procured his own weapon and shot the man. The men fled in an automobile but were captured when the machine was wrecked.

One of four bandits was shot in the right temple by Isadore Weinberg after a holdup of Weinberg's place of business in Chicago on April 3. Weinberg shot through a hole in a partition in his store as the bandits were leaving the place.

After four bandits had robbed the State Bank of Burlington, Ill., on March 1, John Meyers procured a gun from a hardware store and fired on them as they were fleeing in an automobile. One shot hit the driver and seriously wounded him but the bandits, another taking the wheel, escaped.

A robber was wounded and captured in Chicago on March 12 after he and two companions had held up a grocery store. Arthur Coates, 16, a clerk in the store, shot the bandit as he was leaving the store. On the same day, Henry Ahaus, who operates a grocery store in Chicago, drove off two bandits with his revolver. Both robbers were wounded and captured. It was the second robbery visit the same men had made to the store.

Awakened by crashing glass in his store in Worthington, Ky., on April 8, F. B. Potter opened fire. One of three youths fell mortally wounded while his two companions escaped.

JULY 1932

Commenting on the routing by Margaret Rappa, 23, of an armed bank burglar in Chicago and suggesting a Carnegie medal award in her case, an editorial in the Los Angeles *Daily News* had this to say: "This heroic conduct by a girl is one that might be imitated with good results by the opposite sex. There would be fewer robberies and holdups if thugs were sure to be met with stiff, red-blooded resistance. Unfortunately, in some states the average citizen is deprived of the right of self-defense by laws which make it almost impossible for an honest man to carry a gun. These are useless statutes that clutter our books and that make mockery of civil rights."

In Greensburg, Ind., Mrs. W. S. Cooke routed and shot a kidnapper who attempted to drag her 12-year-old daughter from bed. The woman used a .22-caliber rifle.

Finding that armed resistance confronted them when they attempted to rob the Bronx County (N.Y.) Trust Company on May 17, six bandits fled. A bank guard and one of the bandits were wounded. The bandits escaped in an automobile piloted by a seventh man.

When he saw his father's life jeopardized by a knife in the hands of a man who had been detected stealing in the Barkett store in Shreveport, La., on May 8, 10-year-old Sammy Barker procured his father's .32-caliber revolver and shot and critically wounded the man while he was grappling with the elder Barkett.

One of four bandits who attempted to hold up the Clody Flower Shop in Chicago was killed and a second one wounded on May 8. The slain bandit was an ex-convict. Edward Clody, 63, and his son, Laurent, 39, were the ones who frustrated the robbery with pistol fire.

Robbery of a service station in Bethel Township, near Pittsburgh, Pa., was frustrated May 20 when a patron of the station fired a revolver shot as the robber was fleeing. The bullet struck the bandit causing him to stagger and drop the money he had stolen, but the man escaped.

Guns blazed as three robbers emerged from the First State Bank of Morris (Okla.) on May 27. One of the men was killed and another apparently critically wounded. Miss Claire Aggas, bookkeeper in the bank, was taken along by the robbers as a shield and was wounded in the exchange of gunfire. The wounded bandit escaped in an automobile and his unharmed companion fled on foot.

Matt Gardner, who operates a filling station at Elyria, Ohio, accomplished the capture of his twelfth burglar on May 27 when one of three youths surrendered after Gardner had fired three shots. Gardner rushed to his filling station when awakened by his home-made burglar alarm.

Fired upon and slightly wounded by a youth who had been acting suspiciously about a road stand in Frontenac, Kans., Officer Leon Delamaide shot and killed him May 16. Delamaide, an ex-service man, was substituting for a sick officer.

In San Francisco on May 11, Lee On prevented a robbery of his Chinese restaurant when he seized a pistol and fired, the two would-be robbers hurriedly retreating.

One of three robbers was slain when he and his companions attempted to rob the grocery store of Joseph Franz in Gary, Ind. Franz had been forced into a rear room, but he secured his revolver and repelled the robbers with the one fatality.

Two men entered the restaurant of Thomas R. Miller in Los Angeles May 23. Miller opened fire and the men fled to their automobile. The restaurant man so riddled the car with bullets that the would-be robbers took to their heels to escape.

Instead of "putting up his hands," Loren Springer grabbed his shotgun and fired at two bandits when they attempted to rob an inn near Danville, Ind., on May 7. One of the robbers was wounded. The two who entered the inn had two accomplices waiting in an automobile.

Held up by two men, Paul D. Northrup, proprietor of a service station in Los Angeles, Calif., started shooting, though he himself was under fire. The robbery was not consummated and no one was injured.

When two men broke into a home in an isolated section near Montgomery, Ala., while only two women, were in the house, there happened to be a small-caliber rifle and plenty of ammunition at hand. The result was that the men gave up their plans and fled under fire. Mrs. P. H. Crawford and a Mrs. Nelson were the two women.

Two bandits who tried to hold up M. Bertone, cafe proprietor of Los Angeles, on May 23, instantly took flight when Bertone made use of his gun.

Two bandits were killed May 31 in Chicago during an attempt to rob Earl Riley in his delicatessen store. Riley surprised them by grabbing his pistol and firing, the shot killing one of the men. As the fatally wounded man fell he fired, but the bullet struck and killed his accomplice instead of Riley.

When a man attempted to rob him of $1,230 in Hot Springs, Ark., on May 31, W. A. McWright, 55, shot and fatally wounded him.

Thirteen criminals had been killed by citizens and 18 by police in Chicago up to May 11. Last year 45 were killed by police and 28 by citizens. Praising the police and citizens, Mayor Cermak stated: "I wish there was some appropriate way of recognizing the fortitude of a citizen who shoots it out with a desperado, especially in instances like that of a 17-year-old girl (Marie MacLaughlin), who, while under fire, brought down a holdup man. The community should mark such persons for distinction for their part in ridding the city of its diminishing criminal element."

William C. Keim, prominent Beverly Hills (Calif.) real-estate man, saved himself from robbery early May 22 when he shot two men, who were accompanied by two women, when they attempted to hold him up while he was driving near Encino, Calif. One of the men and his woman companion were later arrested. "If fathers would learn how to handle guns and shoot them and teach their children how to shoot, there would be fewer holdups," Keim expressed himself. "I began to teach my boys how to shoot when they were 6 years old. If those thugs had confronted my boys instead of myself, the results would probably have been the same. An armed bandit is a cowardly creature when he looks into the barrel of another man's gun."

Although twice wounded, a Union City (N. J.) restaurant proprietor, James Markstein, shot and killed a bandit May 24 and put two accomplices to rout. Despite that he was "covered," Markstein refused to "put up his hands," instead getting his pistol and firing.

Three gunmen climaxed a series of gasoline station holdups in Long Beach, Calif., with a gun fight during which the bandit leader was killed after a police officer had been wounded in the leg. The fatal bullet was fired by Sergt. Clyde Allen of the Long Beach force.

On the night of May 18, two bandits entered a filling station at Wilmot, Ark. The watchman, L. C. Foster, opened fire when they refused to halt. The men escaped but left behind a stolen car loaded with stolen merchandise.

In a holdup of the store of Stanley Likritz in Chicago on June 2, one of two bandits unwittingly let his trigger finger slip and fired a shot that struck an employee in the leg. A customer, Allen Michalski, quickly seized a chair and felled the nervous gunman and Likritz seized the pistol. That ended the robbery attempt.

AUGUST 1932

Robbers, in the fourth time in eight days to hold up the barbecue stand of C. D. Allen and his son, Carl, in Memphis, Tenn., on June 26, were driven off when the younger Allen seized a revolver. The place has been held up 15 times in 7 years.

BURGLAR, CAPTOR GET EQUAL FINES UPON ARRAIGNMENT

The next time that James D. Chalmers, 27 years old, 215 West Utica Street, encounters an intruder in his home in the early morning hours he probably will invite him to sit down and have a cup of coffee and lecture him on the futility of crime in an effort to have him go about his business.

Early yesterday Chalmers was confronted with the problem of how to get rid of an unwelcome guest who had forced his way into his home through a rear window. He decided to be as rough as his guest, according to police, and poked a revolver against the man's ribs and held him at bay while he called the police.

It was not long before Lieut. William E. Downey and Patrolman William J. Schneider arrived and took charge of things. They lost no time in arresting the visitor, Francis J. Boyle, 24 years old, 699 Elmwood Ave., on a charge of unlawful intrusion. Then they began talking things over with Chalmers and learned that he had no license for his weapon. So guest and host were taken to the Cold Spring station together.

Boyle, when arraigned in city court yesterday before Judge Clifford J. Chipman, pleaded guilty to being an unwelcome guest and was fined $25. And Chalmers, the hero, was informed by Judge Chipman that his exhibition of bravery would cost him $25 also. He pleaded guilty to illegally possessing firearms.—*Buffalo Courier-Express.*

Mayor George A. Hahn, of the village of South Chicago Heights, Ill., made effective use of his pistol when a bandit car drew alongside his automobile on a deserted stretch of road near Chicago on June 23. His shots killed one of the three bandits and the other two fled.

Disregarding personal danger when commanded to stop, the mayor stepped on the accelerator. The bandits fired on him but he returned the fire. Neither he nor Mrs. Court Kraemer, a neighbor, who was riding with him, was injured, while Mayor Hahn had the experience of seeing one of his bullets bring to an end the life of one of the thugs.

In an attempt to rob the store of A. Glenn Overbey, in Franklin, Tenn., on June 18, one of four men was seriously wounded by the store proprietor, who is a veteran of the World War and commander of the Franklin Post, American Legion.

An attempt to rob the Quality Meat Market in Hoopestown, Ill., on June 1, was abandoned by four burglars when a load of shot came in their direction. The shot was fired by a bakery employe.

Dr. Herman T. Reinecke, of New York, secretary of the Board of Missions of the Presbyterian Church, used a pistol in an endeavor to halt bandits who had broken into his father-in-law's drug store in Chicago on June 6 but the robbers made good their escape.

"What we need is not so much drastic laws to prevent the sale of weapons as quick and punitive sentences for criminals who carry them."—From editorial in *Philadelphia Public Ledger*.

Three young gunmen who attempted to hold up the drug store of Louis F. Porter, Medford, Mass., fled when Porter snatched his gun from a shelf and threatened to fire. The bandits made their getaway in an automobile.

A gun frightened off two men and a woman who attempted to break into the garage of Mrs. Ben Kohner in Waverly, Ohio, on June 12. Edgar Pyle was the one whose use of the pistol drove the would-be robbers away.

A man, alleged to have been attempting to enter the home of Jack Larkin in Pekin, Ill., on June 6, was shot and killed by Larkin.

In a gun battle staged in the darkness of a Long Beach (Calif.) grocery store on June 23, a burglar suspect was shot and wounded by Officer J. W. Johnson and his accomplice was captured.

One of three men, while driving away after paying a robbery visit to the Aux Sable (Ill.) cabin of Mr. and Mrs. Frank Simon, of Joliet, was killed instantly on June 30 by a shotgun charge fired by Thomas Wells, who had been awakened by the stir. Two of the men escaped in the darkness. The slain robber was later identified as the driver of the machine in which five bandits rode when they robbed the Spring Valley City Bank several months previously.

Awakening early in the morning of April 17, Rudolph F. Grosskpof, of Indianapolis, found a robber in his room. He reached for his pistol and fired. The intruder fell dead. Grosskopf's wife and young son were in the same room at the time.

An armed, masked bandit was shot and killed by Mrs. Myrtle Gairnese, of San Francisco, as he fled from her home after robbing her of $30 shortly after midnight June 29. It was the second time the same bandit had robbed Mrs. Gairnese within a week.

The crack of a pistol was enough to assure one of three robbers who attempted to enter the grocery store of Leon Joseph, in Kansas City, Mo., on May 22, that he had been shot. His two accomplices fled but the man lay on the floor and groaned. An examination revealed he only imagined one of the bullets fired by Joseph had struck him. However, the attempted robbery was a failure, due to the grocer's prompt action with his pistol.

SEPTEMBER 1932

One of two bandits was wounded in an attempted holdup of the Ambassador Hotel, San Francisco, on July 8, by Alfred Nelson, manager of the hotel. The bandits left without any loot.

Patrick Smith, 24, of 3050 Third Avenue, entered a restaurant at 2789 Eighth Avenue at 3.30 a. m. yesterday and barked at the waiter, "Hands up." Glen Daniels, the waiter, grabbed a revolver from the bread box and retorted, "Hands up yourself." Smith turned and ran.

Daniels and a policeman pursued Smith for two blocks before the fleeing holdup man fell with a slight bullet wound on the side of his head.

Smith, who had no gun and had held his hand in his coat pocket to create the impression that he was armed, was held without bail on a charge of attempted robbery.

Daniels was complimented for his quick action by Magistrate Farrell, but was paroled for hearing Monday on a charge of violating the Sullivan law. The revolver did not belong to him.—New York *Herald-Tribune,* July 15, 1932.

When a man entered his drug store in Chicago on August 1 and nervously asked for a telephone slug, B. Z. Harrison suspected a holdup was in sight so he dropped his pistol in his pocket. Shortly after, a second man entered flourishing a revolver. Harrison was ready and his first shot struck the gunman in the forehead, killing him. The first bandit, who had remained in the telephone booth, made his escape.

Held up by two armed and masked gunmen while he was driving from Dallas to Nacogdoches, Tex., on August 4, T. K. Irwin, a Dallas lawyer, shot and critically wounded one of the men. The uninjured man then took refuge in a clump of bushes and fired on the attorney but caused no damage.

In a holdup of a cafe in Los Angeles on July 22, a bandit was shot and probably mortally wounded by H. J. Deering, a special police officer. The bandit, "covering" the customers and employees with his gun, had looted the cash register and was rifling the pockets of the men in the restaurant when Deering quietly pulled out his gun and fired.

Ordered to stick up his hands in an attempted holdup of his confectionery store in Youngstown, Ohio, on July 9, Nick Conti, 42, ignored the command and instead opened fire on the two armed men. One of the men was killed and the other escaped in a waiting automobile.

Confronted by an armed and masked bandit at 1 o'clock in the morning of July 9, W. J. Lyons, 71, an attendant at a filling station on the edge of Kokomo, Ind., decided to fight it out with his gun rather than submit. The result was that the holdup man was killed.

Two sheriff's deputies saved themselves from being choked to death by three convicts on July 15 by making good use of their guns. One of the convicts was killed and the other two critically wounded. The deputies were taking the men to court when the attack was made.

When three bandits attempted to hold up Mr. and Mrs. C. E. Stoner, of Santa Monica, Calif., on July 17, as they emerged from their garage after putting their car away, Stoner drew forth his pistol and fired. One of the men left a trail of blood extending three blocks.

After killing a police officer in Elwood, Ind., on July 6, a man was shot six times and fatally wounded by Detective Kenneth Horstman, of Muncie, Ind., who was in Elwood investigating a robbery. Before he died, the bandit confessed a number of robberies.

While robbing the general store of Harry Jones in Janesville, Ill., on July 11, three bandits were fired on with shotguns by Jones and T. M. Stanberry, who were across the street from the store at the time. The robbers fled, scattering loot behind them. Blood stains on the floor indicated that at least one of the men had been struck.

In a battle with two holdup suspects on July 24, R. J. Harsha and C. H. Haller, police officers of Portland, Oreg., killed one of the men and wounded the second, who, however, was able to make his escape.

Discovering a man attempting to break into his home in Chicago on July 18, J. M. Johnson shot the intruder, who turned out to be an ex-convict, in the right shoulder and made him an easy arrest for the police.

Stealing gas from parked automobile to fuel an automobile which they had stolen, two youths were fired on by Charles Cooper, a druggist of Princeton, Ind. One of the youths immediately surrendered, while his accomplice made his getaway. Cooper got off only one shot before his gun jammed, a condition of which, however, the two thieves were not aware.

Two robbers quickly abandoned their plans to rob a wholesale grocery store in Hattiesburg, Miss., on July 19, when B. J. Lee, a member of the fire department, fired on them when he saw them entering through a window which had been broken in a previous robbery.

Two of three bandits were shot and probably mortally wounded by Adam Bijou, whom they had picked out as a victim, in New York on July 20. Entering the pharmacy where Bijou is a clerk, two of the bandits seized the man while the third "covered" him with a pistol. Bijou wrenched himself loose, drew his pistol from his holster and fired. While two of the holdup men crumpled to the floor, the third escaped. Bijou had a permit to carry the gun so was saved from the Sullivan law.

A Montana posse shot and killed two bank robbers on July 10, after a holdup of the Security Bank and Trust Company of Bozeman, Mont. The bandits fell into a trap and were killed after a gun duel.

Two youths suffered gunshot wounds on July 26, when Sylvester Midgett, Flat Rock, Ill., caught them attempting to steal gasoline from a shed on his farm.

A burglar fled from a sorority house in Urbana, Ill., on July 28 when the matron, awakened by the creaking of the stairs, fired on him in the dark.

OCTOBER 1932

Holdups have become rather commonplace in Los Angeles, but there is one factor that is playing a telling part in the campaign against the hoodlums: the armed citizen whose nerve and aim have spelled defeat for many of the stickup men.

"Witsell Ord, a bank manager of slight stature but firm jaw, braved odds of death stacked against him this afternoon and shot and killed two members of a bandit 'mob' which attempted to rob a Bank of America branch," the *Los Angeles Herald-Express* related on August 24.

It was a particularly nervy act on the part of Ord for he was "covered" by one of the bandits when he suddenly drew open a desk drawer, grabbed a .45-caliber pistol and, despite that his robber-guard started firing first, he succeeded in mortally wounding two and was himself uninjured.

Seven bandits were involved. Of these, two were killed, four were jailed and one, at last reports, was still being sought by police. The *Los Angeles Examiner*, under a headline which said the killing "Bares Parole Abuse," charged that one of the slain men had "obtained his freedom through California's lax parole system."

Another recent instance in the West Coast city: Luther Thompson, a service-station operator, was held up by two men on August 21. Instead of complying with their demand to turn over the proceeds of the day's business to them and despite that he was under threat of a gun, Thompson made for his own pistol and opened fire, critically wounding one of the men.

Then on September 8, a robber was shot and killed in a running gun battle with police after he had been caught in a trap when he attempted to rob a chain-store market.

Instead of complying to a command to "put up his hands," under threat of a revolver, Albert Lay, of near Hillsboro, Ill., got his shotgun and, without any shots being fired, scared off his two molesters.

Roy Benosky, proprietor of a fruit stand near Toledo, Ohio, frustrated a holdup on August 12 when he reached for his unloaded revolver as two men sought to rob him. The two holdup men fled to their machine and escaped.

B. G. Kidd, of Knoxville, Tenn., drove off a prowler who attempted to break into his home, firing three shots at the would-be robber, on August 9.

"A burglar frightened Mrs. James Noel in her apartment early today and the police came and arrested her husband.

The reason was that he joined in the search for the burglar with a small pistol, for which he had no permit, in his hand.

"Magistrate Ford held him for Special Sessions in West Side Court today on a charge of violating the Sullivan law."—*New York Sun*, August 24.

Commenting on the foregoing item, a New York citizen writes in: "Freedom for the crook; tyranny, injustice and oppression for the honest citizen who lacks political 'pull' to get a permit to defend himself against politicians and other burglars. What kind of a President would the man make who deliberately permits such outrages to continue and is directly responsible for continuance of this iniquitous injustice and unconstitutional deprivation of a 'free' citizen's rights and privileges? How long must we stand this?"

In Dierks, Ark., J. L. Kenner, vice-president of the Bank of Dierks, who learned about firearms during the World War, wounded two of three bandits who robbed the bank on August 23, causing the three to surrender an hour later after a posse of officers overtook them. Kenner, who made his expert rating in the war, started firing as the bandits drove off from the bank with the bank cashier as a hostage.

One man was killed, another was not expected to live and a third was arrested after a holdup of Nicholas Molnar, a farmer, living 2 miles from Ringoes, near Trenton, N. J., on August 21. Molnar, as he was entering his home ostensibly to comply with the demands of his attackers for $500, was fired upon and then he returned the fire with a shotgun, hitting two of the men and causing them to surrender. The robbers were armed with a sawed-off shotgun and a revolver.

Isaac W. Turner, White Plains, N. Y., shot into the air when he suspected the "business" of a man who had clambered up the fire escape of an apartment building where he lives. Uncertain as to whether the man was a tenant who had forgotten his key, Turner did not aim to hit but the shot fired had the effect of sending the prowler scampering for safety and abandoning his apparent robbery attempt. Mr. Turner is a member of the N. R. A., a pistol shot of note and was active a few years ago in helping in the formation of the Westchester County Police Revolver Association.

When three men who had held up a gasoline station in Memphis, Tenn., on August 23, returned to get a cap that was dropped in the raid which netted them nothing, R. V. Adams, who had been beaten on the trio's first visit, seized his pistol and fired, killing one of the men. Adams first called to the men to stop but they ignored his order.

A bandit tried to raid the home of Orion Torrence in Gibson City, Ill., on August 8, but was frustrated by the prompt action of Mr. Torrence, who surprised him thrusting a revolver against his ribs and telling him "to travel." The man joined two companions in a machine outside the house, the three making their escape.

Three armed bandits robbed a grocery store in Marion, Ohio, on August 20, but their escapade sent all three to a hospital with bullet wounds suffered at the hands of Ashworth Stover, manager of the store. They were captured 5 miles from the city by Police Chief W. E. Marks 25 minutes after the crime had been committed.

Commenting editorially on the affair, the *Marion Star* lauded Stover for an "effective contribution to the campaign against lawlessness, especially the steadily growing operations of armed robbers."

On May 24 a lone bandit held up the Merrimack State Bank at Merrimack, Wis., and when he was captured within three hours after the robbery, it was found he had one bullet lodged in his shoulder and three minor flesh wounds, the result of the markmanship of the vigilantes who gave pursuit. The machine he used had 23 bullet holes in it, both rear tires were shot up and the gasoline tank was perforated. He started a 35-year prison sentence 48 hours after the burglary.

"As they [the bandits] become bolder they are ignoring the factor of numbers. Apparently they are concluding that a crowd, however large, can be cowed by a show of force, and that the chance individual who happens to be armed and is ready to resent robber orders is negligible. . . .

"Robbery is now aggressive in this country to the point that it has extended the contempt it has long felt for the forces of law to the public itself. And America is going to find that these murderers, the pets of sob artists and official pardon boards, will force the fighting."—From editorial in *Wichita* (Kans.) *Eagle*, July 28.

A movement to write into the Nebraska statutes a "gun permit" law has been started by business men of Grand Island with the idea of providing defense for civilians against outlaws. The law would be fashioned principally after the Iowa law which sanctions the issuance of permits to carry pistols to citizens of peaceable, sober habit, good character and of reasonable proficiency with weapons.

J. E. Risden, Bureau of Investigation, Department of Justice, Des Moines, Iowa, has advised the sponsors of the Nebraska movement, in regard to the Iowa law, that he personally feels every law-abiding citizen should be permitted to carry a gun for practically all the crooks are armed at all times. It is pertinent that daylight holdup insurance for banks in Iowa is only $1 per $1,000 while in Nebraska the rate is $4.80.

THE ARMED CITIZEN

DECEMBER 1932

A 17-year-old boy, Kenneth Anderson, routed four robbers with a shotgun near Racine, Wis., on September 9. One of the bandits was wounded and was carried away by his accomplices. The men had attempted to hold up the place of business of Kenneth's father, one of the men taking a position at the door armed with a sawed-off shotgun. Kenneth happened to be in the rear of the place when he heard the command, "Hands up," and he immediately procured the shotgun and fired.

Betty Hoffman, 15, was alone in her home in Glendale, Calif., on October 17 when she heard a noise in the bathroom. She secured her .25-caliber pistol, crawled to the bathroom door and saw a man climbing in the window. She fired and the man made a getaway.

Held up for the second time in three weeks, George Sunderland, 45, night watchman of a service station in Southington, Conn., shot and fatally wounded one of two bandits while the other escaped. Sunderland was covered by a gun when he suddenly reached for his own weapon and fired.

An attempt by two men to hold up Henry Layman, confectioner, in Woodburn, Ore., on September 13, resulted in Layman's sending one of the bandits to a hospital with a shotgun wound, though the other escaped. The wounded man, who said he had spent practically all his life in jails and reformatories, had held up Layman with a pistol.

In commenting on the foregoing incident, the *Woodburn Independent* had this to say, in part:

". . . . we believe that if everybody resolved to defend himself and his property with a revolver and carried that resolution into effect, the greater part of our crime problem would be solved almost over night. And we are inclined to think, further, that no other solution will ever prove adequate. Just as good government depends on the vigilance and intelligence of the individual voter, so the enforcement of the law and protection of property rests on the individual citizen."

When a man attempted to break into his garage, Tony Novak, Chicago, fired two shots at him. The would-be robber fled without accomplishing his burglary purpose.

With a pistol which he kept handy for such occasions, Col. R. Thomas Gowenlock, Lake Forest, near Waukegan, Ill., prevented a robbery of his home on September 21—the two burglars fleeing when the colonel opened fire.

An attempt by three men to hold up a grocery store in Portsmouth, Va., on September 17, was frustrated by D. N. Allsbrook, the store manager. Mr. Allsbrook fired three shots and the bandits fled without further ado, one falling, possibly struck by a bullet, but managing to escape.

Two bandits who paid C. H. Vickery, of Los Angeles, a visit on September 21 may carry bitter reminders of their escapade. Mr. Vickery, robbed of $23, used a high-power rifle on the holdup men as they fled and believes he wounded one or both of them.

"This is one of the best deterrents in the world to major crimes." Thus spoke Police Chief R. E. Steckel, of Los Angeles, as he revealed that between July 1, 1931, and September 14, this year, 21 bandits had been killed and 21 others wounded by police and citizens in Los Angeles.

One of five men who held up and robbed the Bradley State Bank, Bradley, Ill., on September 16, was wounded by Ross Faltsider, but the robber, though he lost his bag of loot, was carried away by his companions. Faltsider happened to be in the post office next to the bank and when he realized a holdup was in progress he secured a gun from the postmaster.

In a holdup of an attendant at an oil station in Chicago on September 1, a bandit was shot and killed. The attendant, under threat of a gun, reached into his pocket and drew out $18 and handed it to the holdup man—then he reached into his pocket again, drew out a revolver and fired with perfect effect.

"It's open season on burglars, holdups and bank robbers, with no bag limit.
"Police Chief Hooper so declared today, adding an offer of free use of the police-target range to any organized group whose members desire to take advantage of the open season. This offer applies particularly to bank employes.
"Renewal of the invitation to use the range was made as a result of the attempt made yesterday to rob the savings department of the Old National Bank."—From the *Daily Chronicle*, Spokane, Wash., September 16.

In an attempt to hold up an oil station in Peoria, Ill., on September 17, a man was mortally wounded by Alvin H. Shelby, who operates the station. As the holdup man pointed a revolver at him, Shelby thrust it aside, grabbed his own pistol and fired.

"A succession of tragic errors resulted in the murder of a Huntington, L. I., constable and the wounding of a theatre's private policeman and the capture of one of 5 empty-handed holdup men yesterday. . . . The constable perished because he didn't know how to throw the safety catch of an automatic pistol. The theatre policeman was wounded when he rushed upon the outlaws with the self-same pistol in his pocket rather than in his hand."—*New York Daily News*, September 26.

An instance that forcibly drives home the need of training for those whose duties call for enforcement of the law!

One bandit was killed and his companion thought mortally wounded on September 29 in an attempted holdup of an inn near Woodland, Calif., by Marvin Conway, a patron at the inn. A third bandit was captured.

Instead of heeding a command to "stick 'em up," Carl Dooley, wholesale house manager in Cleveland, Ohio, drew a gun and killed one man and seriously wounded another.

An attempted holdup led to the death of the bandit at the hands of his intended victim, John Zuetcher, in Kenton, Ohio, on October 21. Zuetcher fired when commanded to hold up his hands.

In Portland, Oreg., on October 11, Mrs. Donald Bailey prevented a robbery of her home by sending a bullet in the direction of the intruder, who promptly fled.

Disregarding shots aimed in their direction, T. L. Jolliff, teller, and Lewis Bress, manager, of a branch of the Virginia National Bank in Norfolk, Va., prevented a robber's attempted holdup of the bank, though the robber escaped, on October 27.

"You've armed every outlaw in Texas but you haven't armed a single conscientious citizen," District Judge Clark M. Mullican declared before a meeting of the Lubbock County (Tex.) Bar Association on October 17.

Stating that he carries a gun for self-defense, Judge Mullican asserted it was time that every citizen had one, that every merchant should equip employes with guns and that citizens should cooperate with the law enforcement officers. While attacking regulation of firearms, the jurist condemned indiscriminate carrying of weapons.

Lubbock county is aroused over its crime problem and the meeting of the bar association at which Judge Mullican set forth his attitude took place two nights after an assistant manager of a grocery store had been killed by a bandit.

The career of a Texan wanted for bank robbery and murder and involved in the $2,000,000 Rondout (Ill.) train robbery of 10 years ago, was ended in Oklahoma City, Okla., on October 17 by Police Officer Jerry Campbell. Under arrest and in charge of Campbell, the man drew a pistol and fired but the officer thrust his gun aside in time to save himself and then drew his own pistol and killed the robber.

JANUARY 1933

A young bandit eluded ten squads of detectives during a speedily-conducted series of holdups only to meet death at the hands of Michael Kriegler, 63, Englewood, Ill., who saved his bakery shop from looting with one fatal shot at the holdup man, who was armed.

When two armed bandits entered his store with the usual command on November 26, Frank Ohler, Toledo (Ohio) druggist, backed away and, despite fire from the holdup men's guns, drew his own pistol and killed one of the men. Ohler had the same experience last January and, as in the more recent instance, killed one of two thugs who attempted to hold up his store.

As a tribute to Ohler's courage, The Toledo Safety Club had him as its honor guest and he received a vote of thanks from the police department.

Bernard J. Kennedy, target shooter, sent one of four bandits to his death in Akron, Ohio, on November 12.

Kennedy is a druggist in the Stein Pharmacy in Akron. Two of the quartet of bandits entered the store, took $75 from the cash register and, taking a rifle from the counter, ordered Kennedy outside, but Kennedy did not move. Mary Heindl, clerk, passed a revolver to Patrick Murphy who was in the store. Murphy fired and the bandits made a speedy exit. Kennedy then relieved Murphy of the weapon and emptied its contents into the bandits' automobile as it was driven away.

Two robbers were shot and killed by Joseph Palermo, former army officer, as they attempted to hold up Victor Diesing, 71, in his drug store in downtown St. Louis November 26. Both bandits were identified as ex-convicts.

After an afternoon of target practice, Jay Wilcox, a salesman, was visiting in Robertson's Drug Store in Phoenix, Ariz., on November 19, when a bandit, who had previously robbed another store, entered. Wilcox had laid his pistol on a counter and so was unable to offer any resistance when the gunman ordered all to a rear room.

As the bandit was taking his departure, however, the salesman made a dive for his pistol, braving several shots from the robber's gun. He followed the holdup man, firing at him. Two days later the man's body was found in an automobile camp, the victim of two bullets from the salesman-marksman's gun.

The incident inspired an editorial in the *Arizona Republic*, Phoenix, from which we quote:

"Good shooting, Mr. Wilcox! His presence at the scene of a holdup was quite opportune. He put the county to the expense of burying a dead bandit, but that is less than the cost of sending him to the penitentiary. *This instance has almost caused us to revise a life-long view against the sale of concealed weapons.* In this country or in most parts of the country, the law is a futile one without any pretense of enforcement . . .

"If all citizens were armed and trained to shoot there would be fewer holdups."

1933

THE ARMED CITIZEN

Darting to a gun when a bandit was concentrating on scooping up money, J. E. Quisenberry, cashier of the Hiwassee bank at Charleston, Tenn., opened fire and frustrated consummation of the robbery attempt.

Ignoring pistols in the hands of two bandits who entered his drug store in Chicago on November 2, Vincent A. Corcoran fought it out with the gunmen and dropped one of them with a bullet.

An armed holdup man left the grocery store of Frank Cerre in Peoria, Ill., on November 8, without any loot as a result of Cerre's quick action in procuring his gun and firing.

Seeing the rays of a flashlight in the general store of Ed Holloway in Gilson, Ill., on November 23, Claude McCoy, a nearby resident, secured his shotgun and routed the burglars.

Opening fire, Fred Stilkler, on November 27, frightened off burglars who had entered his garage at Shobonier, Ill.

John Kohney, chef, thwarted a robbery of the Granada Cafe, Rockford, Ill., on October 22 by his quick resort to his gun, the intruder fleeing without accomplishing his purpose.

After eight robberies had been committed over a short period of time, the village of Donnelly, Minn., secretly organized a number of its citizens into a vigilance group which, on October 9, brought about the downfall of two youths who had broken into the Donnelly Mercantile Company store. A dozen or more citizens, arriving on the scene armed with rifles and shotguns, secured the immediate surrender of the two robbers.

Commenting on the affair, the Morris (Minn.) *Sun* said editorially: "It can be taken for granted that any community would be highly immune from robberies of most varieties if it was known that a group of men skilled in the use of shotguns and rifles was ready to give instant response to an alarm."

Two bandits were shot and severely wounded in a gun battle with Sheriff E. J. Welter and a group of deputies who surprised them in the act of holding up a filling station near Ottawa, Ill.

"If more of us were proficient with the intelligent handling of a gun and used it when circumstances demanded and kept it in a well guarded place when it was not intended to be used, the simple practice of virtually having a vigilance committee with practically every law-abiding citizen enrolled under the banner would discourage the wanton, cowardly night prowlers in a remarkably short time and America would soon be able to raise the head which is now kept bowed in shame because we have allowed crime and her criminal agents to overrun and to control the country almost without a struggle."—Pomeroy (Ohio) *Tribune-Telegraph.*

Use of a gun saved the Isador Sprietler service station in Evansville, Ill., from robbery on October 14. While the burglar escaped, his bullet-perforated hat, found afterward, gave evidence of the narrow escape he had from the shots.

While in the act of robbing a store in White Heath, Ill., on October 1, one man was shot and captured while his accomplice managed to escape.

One bandit was shot and killed but his confederate escaped after a gun battle on the main street of Corning, Iowa, on September 21. The two men had held up Henry Webster, 60, one striking him on the head with a blackjack, when Webster drew his automatic pistol and started firing.

Awakened by hearing the threat, "Don't move or I'll kill you," as she lay in bed, Mrs. Emma L. Smith, who conducts a grocery store in Kansas City, Kans., reached under her pillow, got her revolver and fired, wounding the burglar, on October 8.

Luther Bixler, 70, a service station attendant near Lewisburg, Ohio, shot and killed one of two holdup men when faced with a gun in an attempted robbery of the station on November 7.

Harry Graham, manager of a grocery store in Portland, Oreg., cowed a holdup man with his revolver and was not compelled to fire a shot when he brought his weapon into sight. The holdup man's "gun" turned out to be a cap pistol.

In an attempted holdup of a bank in Boley, Okla., on November 23, three gunmen were killed after they had slain the president of the institution. The robbers were killed by the guns of the assistant cashier and officers.

One of four bandits was killed by the rifle fire of Jesse L. Hughes, Fort Worth (Tex.) cafe proprietor in an attempted holdup in Fort Worth on November 27.

FEBRUARY 1933

Sixty-three bandits and other criminals were slain by police and citizens in Chicago during 1932. Police accounted for 37 on the list of the dead and citizens and private watchmen accounted for 26. Nine police officers, beaten to the draw by men committing crimes or resisting arrest, fell. "The criminals have come off decidedly second best in 1932," the *Chicago Daily Tribune* notes.

Formation of a corps of night-riding vigilantes has been advocated by former Attorney General Albert Ottinger to drive gangsters out of New York City. Mr. Ottinger has declared, according to reports, that he will recommend a provision in the New York City charter, soon to undergo revision, for a force of 10,000 trusted, public-spirited citizens to wage relentless warfare against the underworld.

24

Two bandits abandoned an attempt to hold up a drug store in Marion, Ohio, on December 29, when the proprietor, John W. Chrispin, defied a pistol in the hands of one of the men, obtained a shotgun and let go a load of shot at them when a bullet fired at him from close range went wild.

"Issuance of extra ammunition to all policemen and reopening of the department's target range, closed several weeks ago in the city's economy program, today was Safety Commissioner William F. Durnan's reply to a new outbreak of gasoline station holdups."—*Rochester Times-Union*, December 15.

In Atlanta, Ga., according to reports coming from that city, 200 business men are arming themselves and keeping on the lookout on the streets as aides to the police in a civic drive to stop bandits.

Advocating repeal of the state's law against the carrying of concealed deadly weapons, Chief of Police Robert E. Whelan, Kansas City, Mo., urges on the State Legislature: "The criminal element pays no attention to the law. The law should be repealed so that the ordinary citizen will have the right to carry firearms for their protection. If criminals knew their intended victims might be armed, they might hesitate to attempt a holdup."

Lawrence S. Howe, former senior detective sergeant, Chicago police department, had this recommendation to make in an article, "Will Los Angeles Inherit Chicago's Gangsters?" which appeared in the *Los Angeles Times* magazine section of December 4:
"It is illegal to carry concealed weapons. I believe this law should be repealed! Let every law-abiding citizen carry a gun. But make the penalty extreme for any known criminal, for any man ever convicted of a crime, to carry a gun. Make it a felony. If a known criminal or ex-convict is found with a gun in his possession, whether concealed or not, send him to the penitentiary. Criminals would dread a law of that kind. And few of them can do their best work without a gun."

Two bandits were routed with one shot by Mrs. Fordyce Adams, after her husband had been slightly wounded by one of the bandits, in an attempted holdup of Forest Inn, near Kenton, Ohio, on December 14.

Although covered with a gun, Andrew Burgdorf, attendant at a filling station at Pontiac, Mich., shot and killed a bandit and captured one of his four companions December 13 as they tried to hold up the station.

Drawing a revolver instead of surrendering after an attempted burglary in Pulaski, Wis., a robber was shot and killed by Mike Blochowiak as Al Kubiak, town marshal, tried to wrest the gun from the robber in a hand-to-hand tussle.

After breaking into a store in Milford, Ohio, on December 29, a burglar, armed with a revolver, was shot and killed by Marshal J. L. Pierson.

First knocking down one of three holdup men with his fist and then racing for a pistol which, however, failed to fire and permitted the men to escape, Arthur C. Brown frustrated a robbery of his filling station near Jefferson, Ohio, on October 6.

A bandit was slain December 29 by Emory Rowland, attendant at a gasoline station in Des Moines, Iowa, in an attempted holdup of the gas station. Seven shots entered the bandit's body.

Two armed bandits fled from the store of Tilden Riley and E. B. Riley, owners of a grocery store in Hamilton, Ohio, on December 23, when one of the brothers ran to his office and procured his gun while the other grappled with one bandit. One of the holdup men was shot by E. B. Riley. The two brothers received the commendation of Police Chief John C. Calhoun.

As he left the Blakely store in Benton, Ill., after having held up the owner and a customer on December 23, a bandit was wounded three times by the storeman and was captured.

A youthful gunman was wounded and his companion captured by J. W. Pogue, who operates a tea room in Chattanooga, Tenn., on December 7. Pogue came from the rear of the place with his pistol when attracted by the voices of the two men and his wife, who had served them before a gun was "pulled" on her by one of the men.

The night watchman for a pool room in Carterville, Ill., routed two men who tried to break into the place on December 28. The watchman fired several shots which convinced the robbers it was better to abandon the "job."

Attempting to hold up a laundry at 670 North State Street, Chicago, on January 4, a bandit was shot and probably fatally wounded by Edward Jones, son of the proprietor, who was attracted from a rear room by the screams of his sister.

MARCH 1933

On December 15, Chris Sorensen, manager of a grocery store in Malden, Mass., shot and wounded a man who had robbed the store.

In an attempted holdup of a service station in Memphis, Tenn., a bandit was seriously wounded by J. A. Scott, manager of the station.

Three bandits made a hasty getaway from a cafe in Kansas City, Kans., on January 1, when Frank Swearinger, the proprietor, started into a rear room for his revolver.

THE ARMED CITIZEN

Harold Koehler, 17, a member of the Lakewood (Ohio) Junior Rifle Club, proved the worth of his junior training in marksmanship when he brought down a bandit who had robbed his filling station. As the bandit left with instructions to the boy to keep his face to the wall, Harold instead procured a pistol and fired at the man. The first shot, fired at 10 feet, felled the holdup man who, however, recovered himself and ran. Then a second shot fired at 50 feet again brought the fleeing man to earth but once more he recovered and ran. Several days later the twice-wounded man was brought to a hospital and died. Only the jamming of his pistol prevented Koehler from making more prompt disposal of the bandit.

Drawing his own revolver when held up by two men after he had emerged from his garage, Louis V Poulson, secretary of the Middlesex (N. J.) Building and Loan Association, caused the highwaymen to flee on January 10. Both bandits were armed and fired on Poulson but failed to hit him.

One bandit was killed and another critically wounded in Cleveland on January 29 by Tuchi Tasa, a restaurant owner, who claimed the men attempted to rob him.

Alone with her six small children in her home near Nashville, Tenn., Mrs. C. W. Sharp shot one of two robbers who sought to force an entrance into her home on January 5.

An attempted robbery of the Charles Schwam store at Bartlett, Tenn., was frustrated January 13 by J. T. Goin, night watchman, who shot and fatally wounded one of the two robbers. The second robber escaped.

John H. Zetsche, owner of a delicatessen store in New York City, foiled the sixth attempt to hold him up when he shot it out with a bandit on January 8, wounding the intruder three times.

David Taylor, Denver, who had never before handled a pistol, killed one of two holdup men who sought to rob passengers on a bus passing through Kansas City, Mo., on January 10. Taylor fired only one shot. The slain bandit's accomplice escaped.

After he had held up and robbed an attendant at a service station in Portland, Oreg., on January 8, a man was shot and killed by Lawrence Vance, the attendant.

One of two men who attempted to hold up Ed and Curtis Wells on a road near Conroe, Tex., on January 13, was seriously wounded by the intended victims of the holdup. The second highwayman escaped.

Robbers fled from an oil company office in Continental, Ohio, on January 17, when Cliff Worline fired on them.

Stealing gasoline from a parked automobile in Watsonville, Calif., a man was surprised by George Covell and held at bay with a revolver until the arrival of police. The man was an ex-convict on parole and had previously tried to break into Mr. Covell's residence. Two accomplices were also captured.

In Los Angeles, Harry Lytle, a Pacific Electric conductor, probably mortally wounded one bandit and caused a second to flee on December 27. One of the holdup men leaped on Lytle's back without warning while the other jammed what turned out to be a toy pistol against his back. Lytle jerked the first bandit over his head, drew his own revolver and fired.

A robber who held up the Bank of Gray Summit, Mo., on December 23, surrendered when confronted by the rifles and shotguns of a posse of townsmen.

In an attempted robbery of the Carmine (Tex.) State Bank on January 11, a bandit was slain by W. A. Plueckhahn, assistant cashier of the bank.

Charles Norman, attendant at a filling station at Kansas City, Kans., frustrated a holdup on January 26 by drawing his own revolver and firing after two shots had been fired at him by the two holdup men.

When he returned to his home on December 19, S. B. Morgan, Kansas City, Kans., found a prowler ransacking his house. He procured a pistol from a neighbor, and the robber, confronted by the weapon, surrendered.

Following a holdup of the Shawnee (Kans.) Savings Bank on December 7, vigilantes captured two of the three bandits in a gun battle and Capt. T. J. Higgins, of the Kansas City, Mo., police, later shot and captured the third man in Kansas City.

As Tom Anest ascended the steps to his home in Portland, Oreg., on January 16, he was commanded by two bandits to "stick 'em up." Instead of obeying, Anest pressed the trigger of a revolver in his pocket. One shot struck one of the bandits but with the aid of his companion he made his escape.

In Kilgore, Tex., L. H. Suggs shot and killed a man who tried to rob him as he sat with his wife at their tent home on January 8. Two pistols were found on the body of the holdup man.

Engaging in a gun battle with three men who attempted to hold up the Kempton (Ind.) State Bank on January 7, George Richman, cashier, prevented the robbery. It was believed one of the bandits was wounded though he succeeded in escaping.

H. D. Brown, cashier of the Spring (Tex.) State Bank, prevented robbery of the bank by shooting it out with the two holdup men on January 7. The men fled when Brown returned fire from the guns of the bandits.

Clarence E. Fox was at the Commercial and Savings Bank, Berea, Ohio, on January 12 when it was held up by two bandits. He first notified police from a nearby drug store telephone and then returned to the bank to battle the armed holdup men. He grappled with one, wresting one of the man's two pistols from him, and with the seized pistol he shot the bandit twice, causing his capture. The other bandit escaped.

Three armed bandits, who entered the Fagerberg grocery store in Rockford, Ill., on December 29, with drawn pistols, fled when Harry Fagerberg greeted them with gunfire.

One of two men who robbed the Security Bank of Wingate, Tex., on December 22 was shot and killed and his accomplice was seriously wounded by the cashier of the bank.

An attempt to hold up James Peacock in his meat market in Chicago terminated fatally for a 27-year-old bandit. Carrying an automatic and shielding his face with one hand, the bandit entered the store and fired one shot, hitting his intended victim on the hand, when Peacock reached for his own revolver. Then fleeing from the place, the holdup man was hit by two of three bullets fired by Peacock and several days later he died. Just ten minutes before, the gunman had held up another man. A coroner's jury commended Peacock on his action.

In Newark, N. J., John Posner, manager of a grocery store, drove off two bandits when he fired upon them. It was believed one of the bullets took effect in one of the holdup men.

Four of six men interviewed by the "Inquiring Reporter" of the *New York Daily News* answered "Yes" to the question: "Do you think holdup men would be less desperate and less numerous if the Sullivan law were repealed?"

"The Sullivan law makes it difficult for law-abiding men to obtain firearms with which to protect their families in their own homes."—*New York Evening Journal,* January 25.

"Those who study the record of the Sullivan anti-pistol law in New York State must agree that regardless of theory its effect is to arm the crooks and disarm all honest men."—Bridgeport, Conn., *Telegram.*

"The Sullivan law is defective in that it makes it difficult for law-abiding citizens to obtain firearms or to keep them on their premises. The law should be changed to differentiate between permits for revolvers that may be carried on the street and those to be kept in homes and places of business. . . . If burglaries and banditry in homes are to be curbed citizens must be enabled to protect themselves."—*Brooklyn Daily Eagle,* January 23.

"Col. Calvin Goddard, Director of the Crime Detection Laboratory of Northwestern University: 'Our laws against permitting self-respecting adults to carry guns are one reason for our terrific crime wave.'"—*Golden Book Magazine,* January.

County Judge Leigh D. Van Woert, sitting at Oneonta, N. Y., has given decision holding that the 1931 amendments to the Sullivan law are invalid. The amendments require that applicants for pistol permits be photographed and finger-printed and at the same time cancelled all existing permits, requiring all pistol owners to apply for new permits.

"It is to be hoped that police and sportsmen's organizations, working together for a standard law that protects the good and punishes the bad, may succeed at Albany this year. Justice supports their cause."—From editorial in the *Schenectady Gazette* approving change in Sullivan law.

APRIL 1933

Two convicts in Folsom Prison, California, turned amateur gunmakers in their desperation to effect an escape and, despite the close surveillance kept over prisoners, constructed weapons that were so workable that one of the convicts shot and killed himself with his gun when the plot failed. The attempted getaway was made February 27.

The barrels of the guns were made from a hollow steel drill, 7/8 of an inch in diameter, which the convicts stole from the quarry where they worked. The drill was rimmed to give it a 1/2" bore and cut into two sections. Pipe handles were fitted, making the guns appear like automatics. The barrels were hinged to the handles like a break-down revolver to permit loading and extraction. Tiny springs were devised to operate an improvised firing pin and triggers were attached. The cartridges were laboriously contrived from tin, with match heads tamped in for explosive and lead fitted into the end for bullets. Percussion caps were used to fire them.

Armed with the pistols, the two prisoners had captured six guards but their trap for the warden, whom they wanted to use as a shield in their flight, failed. One of the men surrendered but the other placed his home-made weapon to his head and fired, ending his life.

Confronted with guns in the hands of two men who entered his office on February 16, Dr. James A. Owen, Cleveland, Ohio, reached for his own pistol and opened fire after one of the bandits fired at him but missed. One of the holdup men was captured with one wound in his right leg, two wounds in the right side and two fingers shot off. His accomplice escaped, leaving a trail of blood. Dr. Owens, who is chairman of the board of trustees of Wilberforce University and served as a captain in the Medical Corps overseas during the World War, had kept a revolver in his office ever since he was robbed nearly two years ago.

THE ARMED CITIZEN

Milt Pittman, of Columbus, Nebr., does not claim to be quite so adept with his pistol as he is with his rifle but he demonstrated his coolness with the handgun when he saved himself from a holdup on February 19. He drove off two bandits with a small automatic pistol after having had to shoot out the windshield of his car. The men escaped unharmed but later two men suspected as the bandits were arrested.

Stephen Marsh, 19, killed one bandit and seriously wounded another after they had held up his mother's restaurant in Peoria, Ill., on February 14.

One of three bandits was shot and killed on February 10 in an attempted holdup of the Madison Department Store in Chicago. Thomas Pavlakes, joint owner of the store, was the wielder of the gun that frustrated the robbery. A number of shots were fired by the holdup men without doing any damage.

Appearing on the scene as two gunmen were holding up her husband in his store in San Francisco on February 26, Mrs. Catherine Nilan procured her husband's revolver and leveled it at the holdup men, who promptly fled from the place.

After holding up Mr. and Mrs. Elmer Pierson at their filling station near Decatur, Ill., on March 1, a youth was shot and wounded by Mr. Pierson, who procured his pistol while the bandit was attempting to make his getaway in the Pierson automobile.

Jim S. Doyle, 50-year-old blacksmith of Spencer, Okla., shot and killed one of four bandits emerging from the Spencer State Bank on February 2.

Two bandits were shot and critically wounded by Capt. V. J. Fleming, of the sheriff's office, in an attempted holdup of the Rio Hondo Country Club, Downey, Calif., on February 13. A third bandit fled.

Three bandits fled from a branch of the Sixth National Bank, Philadelphia, Pa., on February 15, when a 62-year-old watchman, James Andrews, fired on them from an armor-plated "pill box" commanding the entrance to the bank. Scurrying from the place, the men turned and fired but caused no damage.

Refusing to comply with shouted commands to halt, a bandit was shot and killed by radio police officers in Los Angeles, on March 3. The officers were J. F. McCarthy and B. H. Phelps.

An ex-convict was shot to death by Nat Rogers, a farmer, near Bardstown, Ky., on December 13 after the man and his brother had kidnaped a taxi-driver and driven off with him to stage a robbery.

In Buffalo, N. Y., a bandit was shot and seriously wounded by Patrolman Thomas Wright while attempting his third holdup.

A bandit was shot and killed by James L. Russell, cashier, in an attempted holdup of the United States National Bank in San Diego, Calif., on February 15.

A bandit was shot and fatally wounded by L. R. Billings, cashier of the McFarland National Bank, Bakersfield, Calif., on February 25.

When bandits fled after holding up a groceryman neighbor, Charles Hassig, a druggist, Kansas City, Kans., opened fire on them with his moose rifle, killing one of the bandits and wounding and causing the capture of the second.

Drawing his pistol after being held up by two men in Newark, N. J., on February 26, David Gordon shot and is believed to have wounded one of the men but both succeeded in escaping in an automobile.

At the point of a pistol, Joseph A. Klein, general manager of the National Surety Company, drove three robbers from his home in Philadelphia, Pa., on February 9.

One bandit was killed and another seriously wounded by Michael Santaniello, a provision merchant of East Boston, Mass., in an attempted holdup on February 22.

Kidnaped and then threatened with attack, a 16-year-old Chicago high school girl saved herself when she picked up the man's rifle and held him under threat. The man was captured.

E. C. Butler, visiting the store of E. D. Eason in Los Angeles, frustrated a robbery of the store by three armed bandits on February 14 when he grabbed a shotgun from behind a counter and opened fire, wounding one of the holdup men.

One of four men who were looting a freight train near Santa Ana, Calif., on February 14, was killed by Train Rider W. A. Thomas. The slain man had been sought as a train robbery suspect for some time.

In an attempted holdup of train passengers on the Southern Pacific Golden State Limited near Colton, Calif., on February 15, J. N. Caster, conductor, shot and killed the bandit after the robber had opened fire on him. The conductor died the following day of wounds suffered in the battle.

After two burglaries, Maury M. Morrison, who operates a pharmacy in Jamaica, N. Y., applied for a pistol permit but, according to his story, the police captain told him they "couldn't arm every citizen in the country." A short time later he was the victim of a third holdup. He declared that in the second robbery he "could have potted one of the bandits; I'm a former service man and know how to use a gun."

MAY 1933

"Possessing a pistol and having it handy saved a prominent citizen of St. Petersburg from being manhandled and possibly kidnaped a few nights ago. Knowledge that the occupant owns and knows how to use a pistol is the best protection many homes have. All accidents from pistols put together are as nothing compared to automobile accidents every week. Shall we, for that reason, prohibit by law the manufacture of automobiles? Full-blooded Americans claim the right of arming themselves for self-protection and of knowing how to shoot."— Editorial in St. Petersburg (Fla.) *Evening Independent,* March 11.

One robber was killed and another was wounded by Stephen Marsh, 19, of Peoria, Ill., following an unsuccessful attempt to rob Marsh's widowed mother on February 14. Two of the bandits entered the Marsh home and young Marsh early disturbed their plans by attacking one with a butcher knife. As the pair left and joined accomplices in an automobile, Marsh secured a revolver and fired on them.

Robert Duty, cashier, frustrated a robbery of the State Bank of Doddridge, Ark., on March 10, when he opened fire on the four robbers while they were endeavoring to pry open the front door of the bank.

When a man demanded money of her in her store in Montgomery, Ala., on March 11, Mrs. J. T. Jackson drew a pistol on him. He fled without further ado.

A gunman, fleeing with nearly $6,000 in cash obtained in a holdup of the Security State Bank at Woodland, Wash., was shot and critically wounded on March 17 by the bank president, C. A. Button, and was captured.

Two holdup men were shot and wounded by Truman Hayes, night operator of the station, in an attempted robbery of a service station at North Wilkesboro, N. C., on March 1. The two men were armed.

One of two bandits who attempted to hold up the Stein Pharmacy in Akron, Ohio, on March 11 was shot and killed by the druggist, Bernard Kennedy.

Opening fire with his pistol instead of handing over his money, William Novotny, proprietor of a delicatessen store in Chicago, routed five stickup men on February 28.

Fleeing after a holdup of a Toronto (Canada) bank, one of two bandits was shot in the right arm by a constable and was disabled, resulting in his capture. The thug was firing at the officer from behind a post when a well-aimed bullet caught him in the arm.

In an attempt to rob the Cedar Grove (La.) Bank on April 5, a bandit was shot and mortally wounded.

An attempt to rob the hardware store of Russell Turner in Mann's Choice, Pa., on March 24, resulted in the death of one of three bandits and the later capture of the other two when Mr. Turner opened fire on them.

One of three men who attempted to hold up Wallace Lyle at his filling station and restaurant at Huston, Pa., on March 22, was seriously wounded by Lyle. Two of the bandits were armed and commanded the proprietor to "stick 'em up," but instead Lyle whipped out his own pistol and fired.

Two armed bandits, one of them carrying a pistol in each hand, fled empty-handed from the pharmacy of G. Walter Humphrey, Evansville, Ind., when Mr. Humphrey opened fire on them from the rear of the store. One of the holdup men was thought to have been wounded.

After three successful holdups, a bandit carried his activities to the cafe of Ivan Burkett in Los Angeles from which he made a terrified exit when Burkett opened fire on him.

A bullet fired by Edward H. Felch, a one-time Alaska deer hunter and now operator of a filling station in Chicago, brought death to one of two men who robbed his station on March 20.

In Ola, Ark., on March 25, one of three robbers was killed by A. F. Hendricks, 70, a hotel proprietor, following the burglary of the Bank of Ola and the Ola post office.

"We always have attempted to legislate crime out of existence by one device or another. The outrages of murder and attempted murder, robbery and threats utilizing firearms excite a lot of people to support bans which they think would disarm all criminals. . . . Some states have tried to disarm criminals and would-be criminals by ruling out firearms. The fact that, of the millions of guns of all kinds possessed in America, the small percentage used unlawfully is about the same as all sash-weights used for murder, never occurs to the reformers."— From editorial in *The Athens Messenger,* Athens, Ohio.

"Give every citizen in Boston a gun to protect himself," City Councilor Leo F. Power declared before the Boston City Council recently. "Every store in my district," he said, "has been held up, some of them more than once, and nothing has been done about it. Nobody has been caught."

Unaware that Edward Bloom, a police officer, was in the rear of the place washing his hands, two bandits entered Edward H. Rowe's store in Ozone Park, Long Island, N. Y., and covered the proprietor with guns. The police officer walked into the store with his gun and killed one of the holdup men and wounded the other.

THE ARMED CITIZEN

Two bandits left the drug store of Louis Scalfo, Passaic, N. J., empty-handed when the druggist opened fire on them in an attempted holdup of the store on February 7.

In an attempted robbery of the service station of Joe Carter in Nashville, Tenn., an armed bandit was killed by a bullet from Carter's gun.

In an attempted holdup of a filling station at Benson, Minn., one bandit was killed and another wounded by Chief of Police S. O. Johnson.

JUNE 1933

Prepared for a holdup after having once before been the victim of a robbery, L. M. Prine, druggist, of Long Beach, Calif., shot and apparently critically wounded one of three bandits as they were leaving his store on March 15. One of the thugs held the druggist at bay with a pistol during the robbery, but as they left the place Prine went to the rear of his store and obtained a .30-caliber rifle and a pistol which he had secreted there for just such an emergency after his previous experience. A shot from the rifle caused the wounding of one of the bandits.

Henry A. Harris, California crack shot of a quarter of a century ago, captured an ex-convict who had broken into the home of a neighbor, in Oakland, Calif., on April 26. The robber put up no fight when confronted by a gun in Harris' hand and no shots were necessary.

Attempting to hold up and rob a cigar store in Long Island City, N. Y., on the night of May 9, one bandit was killed and another critically wounded by Anthony Leto, a clerk in the store. As he raised his hands in obedience to a command of the robbers, Leto pulled his pistol from his shoulder holster and opened fire, his action taking the intruders by surprise. Passing police officers arrested a third man suspected of being the driver of the bandits' ''getaway'' car.

Mrs. Martha Pepper, who operates a small grocery store in Bellingham, Wash., saved herself from loss on April 17 when she anticipated the intentions of a youth and confronted him with a revolver as he was edging his way to the cash register.

Drawing a pistol and opening fire instead of obeying the command to hold up his hands, J. C. Dubois, cashier, critically wounded one of two men who attempted to hold up the Ashville (Ala.) Savings Bank on April 11.

Two armed thugs were shot and severely wounded by Tacoma (Wash.) police on May 3 when caught in the act of staging a hold-up of a loan office. Chance arrival of Detectives Charles Brooke and Harold Thornburg, both expert with the pistol, at the store was responsible for the frustration of the robbery and wounding of the bandits.

After robbing Leon Chin at the point of a gun in Portland, Oreg., on April 3, a holdup man was shot in the leg by his victim and was captured.

While Mrs. Jud Cooper, wife of the manager of a grocery store near Tompkins' Corner, N. Y., was alone in the store, an armed bandit entered and demanded the store money, but instead she reached under the counter and obtained a pistol, whereupon the bandit promptly fled without further ado.

Darius J. Gregoire, 70, thwarted a robbery of his store in Holyoke, Mass., on May 2 by grabbing a pistol and firing upon two stick-up men, causing them to flee.

Driven into a woods by a posse armed with high-power rifles, five bandits who had held up a filling station and shot a deputy sheriff near Carrollton, Ohio, finally surrendered.

''News reports which have come to our attention in recent months show that where citizens have a reasonable chance at the average gunman, he seldom escapes. . . . The community which keeps guns handy to furnish appropriate reception for the bad men of our modern era is a wise community. Let the presence of the guns be no secret. Let the news of watchful citizens, willing to serve as hosts, travel around. Our guess is that such a community will have no serious trouble with the 1933 brand of banditti.''—From editorial in Shreveport (La.) *Times*.

SEPTEMBER 1933

''Exterminate gangsters with guns. Fight fire with fire . . . If I had my way, I would arm honest, dependable citizens and declare open war on all manner of gangsters. I would shoot on sight. If the gangsters were obliged to face the same weapons they use in menacing honest citizens, they would change their tactics.''—Police Commissioner Roche, of Buffalo, N. Y., as quoted in the Buffalo *Times*, July 11.

''Police officials should encourage use of concealed weapon permits by responsible citizens. They should see that the citizen is qualified to use a gun. Target practice clubs would be one method. . . . The citizen is embarrassed by red tape and gives up the idea of carrying a gun for protection. Knowledge that a large part of the public is armed would be an important crime restraint.''—Charles H. Stone, Assistant to the Chief of the California Bureau of Criminal Identification.

Russell Hale, cashier of the Mauston (Wis.) State Bank, frustrated a holdup of the bank on May 15 when he opened fire on 2 armed bandits with his rifle, fatally wounding one of the men and capturing the other.

"A beer salesman who thwarted the attempt of 5 thugs to take him for a ride shortly after midnight was himself arrested for possession of the .44-caliber revolver he wrested from one of his would-be kidnappers."—New York *Daily News*, June 15.

The exacting marksmanship of Isaac McCarthy, cashier of the Labette County State Bank at Altamont, Kans., on July 14, saved the bank from robbery by killing one of 2 bandits and critically wounding the other and prevented the possible kidnapping or murder of his wife who was being held as a shield by the slain bandit.

Suspicious of the 2 men, both of whom were among 11 who escaped from the Kansas penitentiary on May 30 by kidnapping the warden, McCarthy hid behind a curtain, where he had his weapons concealed, as they entered the bank. When his suspicions were confirmed, McCarthy opened fire with a shotgun, wounding one bandit. The other then seized Mrs. McCarthy, an employee of the bank, to shield himself from the gunfire and threatened to kill or kidnap her. Laying aside the shotgun because of this new situation, McCarthy, having to use extreme care not to hit his wife, brought a rifle into play and killed the holdup man instantly.

Using their guns to such good advantage that they scored six hits out of seven shots, two border patrolmen, who engaged in a pistol fight with three Mexicans who opened fire on them when caught climbing to the American side of the Rio Grande, killed two of the Mexicans and wounded the third. Neither of the patrolmen was injured. Subsequent investigation divulged that one of the Mexicans was a fugitive from justice, being wanted in New Mexico in connection with the murder of a family of seven.

Making use of his own pistol rather than submit to robbery when stopped by 2 bandits while he was motoring with his wife near Hot Springs, Ark., on June 26, W. P. Westmoreland, of Houston, Tex., killed one of the holdup men and gravely wounded the other. The bandits were both ex-convicts.

Two of 3 bandits who attempted to hold up the tavern of George Capedona in Chicago on July 17 were killed and the third fled when Peter Capedona, a brother of the owner, fired upon them with a rifle from behind a partition. Two of the bandits were armed with shotguns and the third with a pistol. The place had been held up twice previously within a period of 2 weeks.

One of 4 bandits was seriously wounded by Robert Simon, who used a shotgun, as they were leaving a shop in Chicago after having held up the place on June 10.

One bandit was critically wounded in an attempt to hold up Olin Yale, a garage proprietor, in Uniondale, Pa., on May 8, when Yale beat his 2 molestors to the draw. The second bandit fled.

When 2 bandits drew revolvers on him in a Chicago drug store on June 7, Louis Wayjay, a clerk in the store, drew forth his own gun and opened fire. One bandit fell dead while the other fled.

Although hit in the neck by a bullet from the gun of a burglar whom he surprised while ransacking his home on June 21, George A. Lyon, Jr., Peoria, Ill., fired a shot that instantly killed the intruder.

JANUARY 1934

Target practice for its employees is the answer and challenge of the Bank of America National Trust and Savings Association of Los Angeles, to the menace of bandits. Employees are shown at practice on the Los Angeles police pistol range.

"Atlanta police are in a quandary because there is nothing they can do to keep people from toting ice picks, officially declared 'the most deadly weapon used by criminals.'

"Confronted by frequent slayings at the hands of persons, wielding the lowly household implement, Chief of Police T. O. Sturdivant appealed to City Attorney James L. Mayson to find some law by which it could be classed as a deadly weapon. But Mayson gave no encouragement, pointing out anybody is free to carry a pick as he pleases unless the state legislature amends the laws.

"Police records of recent months show more people have been killed and wounded by ice picks than by pistols, razors and blackjacks."—AP report from Atlanta, Ga.

In St. Johnsbury, Vt., Mrs. Olive Jones, 79 years old and 100 pounds in weight, captured at the point of a rifle an alleged safe cracker who had eluded a posse of 100 officers, deputies and volunteers. Informed that a man had been seen entering her barn, the woman loaded her rifle, strode to the building and held the man at bay.

"Throwing the confiscated guns of gangsters into the lake was just one of the several futile operations under ordinary police methods. Depriving the killer or the potential killer of his weapon meant only that upon his release from custody he would procure a new gun. The whole system created a brisk demand for bootleg weapons. Even the anti-pistol-toting law was ineffective during the reign of terror of prohibition. A former city administration was indifferent toward crime. Petty politicians 'fixed' gun-toting cases and smoothed the paths for criminals in more serious affairs. Desperate gunmen were provided with permits to carry weapons and often wore stars, posing as deputies this or deputies that."—Chicago *Sunday Tribune*, October 15.

1934

THE ARMED CITIZEN

A dozen employees of the Edgewater Beach hotel in Chicago, including three girl cashiers, are being instructed in the use of firearms because of the many recent hotel robberies. Sgt. Ted Kuhn, former police officer, is the instructor. Eighteen revolvers, shotguns and rifles are cached in convenient places about the hotel for use in case of an emergency. William M. Dewey, managing director of the hotel, regards the training as "better than holdup insurance."

"Gangsters, thugs and hoodlums of all degrees were busy yesterday casting spurious ballots and interfering with honest balloting. . . . It was a great day for the lead pipe, blackjack and stiletto wielders. . . . 'This was my first experience with gunmen,' William M. Chadbourne, Fusion manager, said. . . . Lead pipe was used by six men who invaded Fusion headquarters and assaulted several workers. . . . Blackjacks were swung into action on Fusion workers while police looked the other way at Public School 177. . . . George Bennett, 40, was beaten by six men and stabbed on the back."—Excerpts Election Day report in New York *Herald-Tribune* of November 8.

"The trouble (with laws prohibiting pistols) is that the professional crook would find a way, through smuggling, bribery or other unlawful means, to get his gun. Even if all firearms were required to be registered it would take another army of inspectors to keep track of them. Besides, every criminal would provide himself with a good-sized arsenal before the law could be put into effect.

"Maybe the object could be accomplished the other way around—by making it compulsory for everybody to carry a gun after sundown. Then the crooks would have a less advantage."—Waynesboro (Pa.) *Record-Herald*.

"The weapon with which modern America must arm herself is moral indignation. Until we acquire the capacity to rouse public wrath against all general corruption, any private shooting we may do will only confuse the issue."—Mrs. Walter Ferguson in a column headed, "Better than Guns."

In Covington, N. Y., Mrs. Mary Simon, 36, engaged in a pistol fight with two men who attempted to hold up an automobile in which she was riding and wounded both. The men made their getaway but were arrested several hours later while receiving treatment for their wounds at a physician's office. The driver of the automobile had been slugged over the head when Mrs. Simon intervened with the pistol.

Discovered in an ice company's building in Sacramento, a bandit was shot and instantly killed while he was attempting to escape through a window, by Frank Muranaha. The bandit was the first to open fire.

Awakened at 1:30 a. m. by an intruder in her home in St. Louis, Mrs. Cora Pasley, 28, fired three shots at the man as he fled through a kitchen window and across a lawn. The house-breaker fell on the third shot but managed to arise and make his escape.

Miss Helen Barker, 25, was serving customers in a restaurant in Gilroy, Calif., on November 13, when two men entered and, at pistol point, ordered all to "hands up." The waitress, complying, contrived to move against an alarm buzzer which called the proprietor, William Economou, from the rear. Armed with a pistol, the owner entered and at his first chance drove some lead into the bandit who was holding the waitress and customers at bay while his companion was doing the searching. At the sound of the shot, the rifling bandit started to run but was brought down with a shot in the head by the restaurateur. The bandits were later identified as ex-convicts.

Frank Rauth, a New York Central Railroad detective in Cleveland, saved himself from a brutal beating, after having caught two men tunneling under tracks, only by using his pistol. One of his attackers fell mortally wounded. Rauth was being beaten over the head with a board and had one arm pinned behind him by one of his molestors before he fired.

"Patrolman Nelson Paige is a man famed as a marksman. This was much in evidence when 35-year-old Pete Douglas was brought before Recorder's Judge Henry S. Sweeney, charged with the larceny of restaurant fixtures. 'Guilty,' Douglas pleaded. 'I am very guilty, as guilty as I'll ever be. I was taking them fixtures when all of a sudden I looked up and saw officer Paige, who is a mighty fine pistol shooter, Judge. And then I looked down and said, 'Feet, stand still, we ain't going no place.' The court decided that in view of Douglas' candor he would have to serve only 30 days."—Detroit *Free Press*, November 8.

Observing two men entering the laundry at which he is the watchman in Washington, D. C., on November 23, John Wynkoop, 55, leaped on them but, suffering injuries that later required treatment at a hospital, drew his pistol and fired, killing one of the men. The second man, however, escaped.

One of two bandits who sought to hold up Samuel Janke and customers in his inn in Delaware Township, N. J., on November 29, was mortally wounded by the proprietor. A customer kicked one of the holdup men in the stomach and in the confusion Janke secured his gun and, exchanging shots with the intruders, succeeded in killing the one.

Frustrated by gunfire of P. H. Leslie, watchman, 3 bandits lost their nerve and surrendered their loot after detectives and radio patrolmen surrounded them in the Sun Building in Los Angeles on July 7 following a holdup.

When ordered to hold up his hands by a trio of bandits, Roy Allard, cashier of the Vergennes (Ill.) State Bank, replied with a shotgun charge, whereupon the holdup men fled.

". . . Probably the only way to stamp out the 'snatch' racket which has become so lucrative a business is for every person of means to have a revolver ready at hand and use it if prowlers come around the house. That is the opinion of nearly every citizen. Gangsters have had their way too long. They take advantage of the fact that the average citizen does not own a gun, and they also know that if a sleeping person is aroused during the night, he will say, 'Who is there?' And that gives the burglar plenty of time to make his exit. He also knows that, without a weapon of any kind, the only thing a person can do is to submit to the instructions of the burglar and hold up his hands. Every break is with the criminal who has the advantage of a surprise attack, a weapon and a ruthless mind which stops at nothing. Now, if Mr. Average Citizen refuses to be a sheep, surrounds himself with an arsenal if necessary, and goes to meet the enemy halfway, he will find a weak and frightened adversary who is only willing to take the risks when he holds all the high cards. This is the general opinion, and probably the only action which will successfully stamp out crime."—*Street and Smith's Detective Story Magazine.*

Because he had a gun, with which he had armed himself in trailing down and effecting the capture of a bandit who had shot and killed his brother, Michael Schwartz, Chicago, was arrested on a charge of carrying concealed a deadly weapon. Police said, however, they would intercede for him.

Three men who attempted to waylay Anthony Frumefreddo while on his way from business to his home in Brooklyn, N. Y., on October 21, abandoned their plans and made a hasty exit from the scene when their intended victim opened fire on them.

A pistol battle between a bandit and two victims in a Chicago furniture store ended dramatically when the holdup man, wounded by the store proprietors as he was leaving the place with $138 loot, sent his last bullet into his brain. The bandit's marksmanship was no match for his victims'.

"If the law-abiding men of the country were armed as are the criminals there might be an end to the reign of lawlessness. At present the criminals have weapons and prey on people who are unarmed and therefore easily overcome. . . . Shoot down the criminals when they make an attack and presently they will find that crime does not pay."—A. R. Dunlap, managing editor, St. Petersburg (Fla.) *Evening Independent.*

Opening fire when cornered by 3 officers, a bandit, whose shots missed their mark, was killed in Los Angeles.

"We believe that no legislation ever devised for the purpose—from New York's drastic Sullivan law on down—ever yet kept a really dangerous crook from arming himself. Such legislation, however, has notoriously kept honest men from possessing the firearms essential for the protection of their homes and business places. The more drastic the legislation, the heavier the handicap on honest men, as has been so well demonstrated in New York and Chicago."—Minneapolis *Journal.*

"One of the silliest laws on the books, and one of the most dangerous to public security, is the statute forbidding citizens to carry guns.

"To our notion, it is plainly unconstitutional, all the courts in the land notwithstanding. The Constitution plainly says that 'the right of the people to keep and bear arms shall not be infringed.'

"In face of this we have laws practically forbidding a man to carry a gun for protection. Do these laws stop criminals from carrying guns? Certainly not. They merely debar honest citizens from taking steps to defend themselves.

"If criminals knew that their intended victim carried a gun, and would very likely use it to defend himself, we would soon see a decrease in the shameful number of armed robberies on city streets."—From editorial in Portland (Oreg.) *News-Telegram,* February 21.

As she passed the First National Bank in Starbuck, Minn., Miss Florence Bulman was ordered by one of two bandits to "come in here" but, seeing that the man already had the bank employees and two patrons held at bay by a pistol, she defied the command and ran across the street, warning Rudy Hanson, restaurant operator, of what was taking place. When the two robbers left the bank a few minutes later, Hanson fatally wounded one of the men, from whose hands the loot fell.

FEBRUARY 1934

Called to the door of his home in San Francisco, Calif., on the night of November 20, George Bistany, director of the Fleishhacker Zoo, found three men who requested to use his telephone. When he directed them to a service station where a phone was available, one of the men flashed a gun, but Bistany, who makes a practice of carrying a pistol when answering the door, promptly started shooting and one of the men fell but was dragged away by his companions.

Thirty-three gunmen, robbers, kidnapers and automobile thieves were killed by citizens and private watchmen in Chicago during 1933, and thirty-eight were slain by police officers. As against this showing of 71 killings of bandits, fifteen Chicago policemen were killed in gun battles. The number of thugs killed by citizens and private watchmen was seven more, and by police one more, during the preceding year.

Within a half hour after two bandits had held up the Bank of Adrian, W. Va., on December 11, one was dead, the victim of a bullet from the gun of cashier Hill Stump, and the other was captured. Stump shot the one bandit after he had struck French See, assistant cashier, over the head with a revolver in the attempted getaway.

"Any private citizen has a right to use a gun in defending himself during a robbery, even to the extent of killing, and I'll refuse to sign any indictment where an attempt to prosecute is made. There was an epidemic of holdups in 1932. We gave the perpetrators of these salty sentences and the holdups ceased. Recently we have been lenient and as a result crime has increased."—District Attorney Mortimer E. Graham, of Erie, Pa., as quoted in the Erie *Dispatch-Herald*.

Following robbery of the Stockgrowers and Farmers National Bank at Wallaowa, Oreg., in October, Cliff McGinnis, who has a ranch 40 miles north of Enterprise, Oreg., saw two men who aroused his suspicions. He followed them on horseback and, leveling his rifle at them, caused them to surrender. They were the fugitive bank bandits and their capture resulted in the recovery of the money and securities.

"With gangland roaring and shooting on, what a contemplation are 'tall men, sun-crowned, who tower' above personal fear and make bandits throw away their guns!" commented the *Oregon Journal*, Portland, in editorially commending McGinnis for his act.

"In New York, Armando Infante, was brutally beaten by two thugs, who, according to police, had been promised $5,000 for killing Infante. Whoever offered $5,000 for a killing was offering too much. The late 'Big Tim' Sullivan, New York State Senator who prepared the Sullivan law to prevent carrying concealed weapons, and kept all but criminals from getting pistols, said this writer:

" 'I can have any man in New York killed for $50.' "—Arthur Brisbane, noted columnist.

American gangsters would not last five minutes in Mexico City, according to a statement of Señor Heodoro Gonzalez, head of the city's criminology department, while on a visit to Detroit. The city, he explained, is armed to combat criminals, and every Mexican has a gun and knows how to use it.

Seizing a gun when a bandit attempted to hold up his store in Los Angeles on October 20, Harry Fink took the aggressive and, in a chase, shot and seriously wounded the bandit, who had previously held up nearly a score of haberdasheries.

MARCH 1934

"The first drastic move to cope with the growing menace of organized banditry throughout the state was made last night as a result of the machine-gun slaying of two Needham policemen during the $13,900 holdup of the Needham Trust Company Friday.

"It is a plan to train the citizenry of the smaller cities and towns throughout Massachusetts in the use of firearms, arm them, and make them members of a sort of police department auxiliary, to supplement and support the present police forces in these cities and towns.

"The plan is under consideration by Brigadier-General Daniel Needham, commissioner of public safety, and District Attorney Edmund R. Drewing, of Norfolk County, in whose jurisdiction the Needham outrage was staged.

"Chief of Police Walter F. Reeves, of Swampscott, was the first to embrace the drastic plan when he sent word out to the citizens of his community that the police department needs their support and urged them to come forward and assist the police in meeting the challenge of organized banditry.

" 'We must have the cooperation of the citizens,' he declared. 'I recommend that citizens carry revolvers. I'll issue a permit to any citizen of good character, and, more than that, I'll teach him how to shoot the gun. I'll give him the benefit of my knowledge and I believe I can teach a man to shoot straight in two weeks.'

"The plan to arm the citizenry is understood to have the support of most of the police chiefs of the smaller cities and towns throughout the Commonwealth. Most of them are privately admitting now that the average police department in the state cannot hope to cope with organized banditry without active support from private citizens.

" 'If every reputable citizen were trained in the use of firearms and was equipped with a gun, the police department of the community in which he lives would feel that it may expect assistance from a trained person in the event that it is confronted with a sudden emergency that calls for assistance from outside,' Brigadier-General Needham commented."—Boston *Post*, Jan. 7.

"Illinois is going to be asked to pass a law forbidding the placing of guns in the hands of gangsters. Looking back on how effectively the Eighteenth Amendment and the Volstead law kept people from making, selling, or transporting liquor and a great many other laws that didn't seem to be obeyed very strictly, if at all, the only way to keep guns from the hands of gangsters is to wait until a new race of gangsters is born—a kind that has no hands."—From column, "A Line of Type or Two," Chicago *Tribune*.

"In Swampscott, Mass., the chief of police, Walter Reeves, is granting pistol permits to 'decent citizens' and offers to teach them how to shoot. It is probable that the chief will pick and choose his decent citizens. If so, his plan is good, and should be more widespread throughout the Commonwealth. Admitting that a person held up has little chance to get his gun, the knowledge that he has a pistol may deter many of our younger criminals from risking their pimply hides.

"Even if an armed robber does get the drop on a householder or storekeeper, the fact that other persons in the neighborhood have guns may be helpful. The holdup man cannot have the drop on all the decent citizens.

"If this community could have just about two weeks in which a stick up artist or two were killed by decent citizens every day, crime would diminish."—Boston *Traveler*, Feb. 7.

"A trio of gunmen early today held up two watchmen at Mechanics building, robbed a Massachusetts state police exhibit of shotguns, revolvers and gas bombs and escaped. The exhibit was a feature of the annual automobile show. The gunmen . . . took more than a dozen shotguns, as many revolvers and a large quantity of gas bombs of various types. The exhibit displayed all the most modern types of weapons used by police in combating crime . . ." —From AP report, dated Boston, Mass., Jan. 27.

"Congressmen and others who lean toward a law to disarm citizens in an effort to disarm criminals should look to Boston for an exceptional example of the ineffectuality of such procedure. This news story tells how a gang stole a police exhibit of guns at the automobile show. The exhibit was to demonstrate the methods of combating crime, but the criminals made a better exhibit out of it."—St. Petersburg, Fla., *Independent*.

"Bank bandits who choose Nebraska for the scene of their operations in the future will have to contend with determined, sharpshooting war veterans, pledged to halt a series of holdups that cost Nebraska banks more than $190,000 in 1933. At the call of Golden P. Kratz, of Sidney, Nebr., commander of the Nebraska Department of the American Legion, Legionnaires have banded into vigilante committees to combat the desperadoes."— UP dispatch from Lincoln, Nebr.

"The move to ban the possession of firearms has many of the characteristics of the national prohibition amendment, from the standpoint of enforcement. It would serve to disarm the honest and the law-abiding, while leaving the criminal as well armed as he is now. . . . National prohibition went at the subject of liquor in much the same way. Drys said: 'We will stop drinking by outlawing liquor by amendment,' but it didn't work."—*The Day*, New London, Conn.

"Patrolman A. J. Sweeney, former chief of police in Milford and at one time a member of the Keens Police Department, today gave law enforcement officials a tip on how to stifle crime. He would enact a law to compel every law-abiding citizen to 'tote a gun and practice until becoming proficient.'"— AP report from Peterboro, N. H., Feb. 6.

"Chief Inspector Lewis J. Valentine, who spoke last night at a meeting of the Ovington Democratic Club, Brooklyn, suggested with emphasis that citizens victimized by racketeers should protect themselves with rifles and shotguns, while he promised in behalf of the police department that 'we will stop every racket that ever hit New York.'

"Inspector Valentine did not say directly that business-men should have rifles in their homes or places of business, but he left no doubt of his meaning. Combined with the vigilance of the police, self-protection by citizens would make racketeering disappear like 'winter's snows,' he said, and he cited the Constitution to show that a man could arm himself when endangered by criminals."—New York *Herald-Tribune*, Jan. 22.

" . . . Laws are my business. By passin' a law about machine guns, I can convince a stupid public that I'm out to clean up through public officeholders. It's a great publicity, see? But what really comes of it? Through police an' elected judges, I control the whole effect except one. . . . Yes, I control every effect but one. That one I don't have to control. Laws mean somethin' only to people who obey 'em. The machine-gun laws keep machine guns out of the hands of honest people. That's all. As a gangster, I let you have them. As an honest man, the other fellow is stopped by the law. That's a sweet break for you when trouble comes along! You fight with machine guns an' let the honest guy fight back with brooms, or mebbe a stray rock if he can lay fingers to one!" —"The boss" speaking in Charles Francis Coe's story, "Repeal," in the *Saturday Evening Post*.

" . . . The alliance of organized crime with corrupt politics is the chief factor in the crime of this period in many, if not virtually all, communities. That alliance must be persistently exposed and attacked if we are to make any substantial advance in the war on organized crime."—Chicago *Tribune*, Nov. 7, 1933.

As four bandits, who had robbed him and a customer, were preparing to take their leave of his drug store in Chicago, Harry I. Star reached for his pistol and fired upon the nearest of the intruders, killing him. The four bandits were armed and used their weapons, slightly wounding a clerk who entered the store as the bandits were retreating to an automobile containing two confederates. The incident occurred the night of January 23.

"... The regulation of anything by law is effective only in-so-far as it can be enforced. If the law breaker will smuggle other things prohibited by law, how much more quickly will he smuggle firearms if he is forced to. The law, therefore, will operate only to the detriment of the law-abiding citizen and disarmament will take place only in the case of the man who would make no illegal use of the arms. ... Disarming people who will obey the law in order to make assurance doubly sure for the crooked possessor of the 'bootlegged' pistol that he will have to face none but unarmed victims brings about the greatest aid to crime that can be imagined. In making his recommendations to Congress for aid in combating organized crime, the attorney general would do well to stress other changes in a too complicated legal procedure, rather than a too hasty regulation of firearms possession. In the hands of law-abiding citizens, the small arm becomes of twofold benefit. It is a defense in time of great need and it is a necessity to one of the greatest of outdoor sports. Both are within the rights of every citizen and should not be abrogated by a rule which would reserve the rights for the underworld alone. For no law on firearms will ever disarm the underworld any more than prohibition of liquor made the same underworld dry."—The Arizona *Daily Star*, Tucson, Ariz., January 7.

When two youths, who attempted to hold up J. H. Hurl, Lents, Oreg., on January 26, found themselves looking at a gun in Hurl's hand, they lost their bravado and listened to some advice before being sent on their way.

Opening fire on Patrolman Herard Reed without effect, a robber was himself killed in the exchange of shots by the officer in Cincinnati on December 20. The dead man was identified as having been involved in three burglaries. Officer Reed is a former Marine and one of the police department's best shots.

In New York City, Theodore Souci, apartment house janitor, found a pistol and decided it was a good thing to have on hand to stop an epidemic of apartment house burglaries, which had mounted to 150 in two years. He went to a police station and told detectives of his find. A detective was detailed to go back to the house with him. After seeing the pistol, the officer arrested Souci for violating the Sullivan law, and the man who meant to do the right thing later was held in bail for court trial. "Cops Ignore 150 Robberies, Hold Victim Who Finds Gun," was the appropriate headline over the newspaper story that told of Souci's dicomforting experience.

APRIL 1934

Hearing a noise in the rear of his living quarters and barber shop in Chicago on February 12, Fred Bittner picked up his gun, leaned out a window and fired once, wounding the prowler.

Miss Margaret Borhy, a high school senior, had her first occasion to fire a pistol on March 2 when a thug held up her mother and sister in their confectionery store in Detroit. She was in the kitchen in the rear of the store when she heard noises indicating a stickup. She seized a pistol, went into the store, where she saw her parent and sister fighting with the robber, and then at her first opportunity pressed the gun against the intruder's back and fired. The man fled. A body found a half mile from the store sometime later was identified as that of Miss Borhy's victim.

Drawing a pistol on Dr. Claude C. Long in San Francisco on February 16, a man, who had a long police record, was himself shot and mortally wounded by the arrival of William J. Connell, a special officer hired by the doctor to guard his offices since a holdup last November. Although "covered" by the intruder, Dr. Long, when Connell appeared, drew his own gun and fired. The man attempted to escape but was shot down by Connell with a shotgun. A woman, an alleged accomplice, had held Mrs. Geraldine Kooey, a nurse for the doctor, at bay with a pistol on a lower floor.

"Louis Kyriazopulos is 13 years old and he lives at River Grove. But he is really a contemporary of Daniel Boone, Davy Crockett and Buffalo Bill. When underworld rats, brandishing guns, raided his daddy's restaurant the other night, Louis, in the flat upstairs, instinctively reached for the family shotgun, just as the frontier lad used to grab the long rifle from its peg over the cabin hearth when prowling redskins or road agents appeared.
"Louis of the fighting heart is in marked contrast to the 200 latter-day Americans who were lying prone upon the restaurant floor when he broke up the party and stopped the stickup.
"Congress, now mulling over faint-hearted and feeble-witted bills to encroach yet more upon the constitutional right of free men to possess arms, should read about Louis."—Chicago *News*, February 20.

Flourishing a pistol, a bandit jumped into the automobile of William Spitzel, jewelry company executive in Los Angeles on January 20, and ordered him to "throw 'em up." Spitzel declared he couldn't as he was "going to faint." The robber reached for the wheel and Spitzel, whose "faint" was only acted, grabbed the bandit's gun and killed him.

Held up by two bandits in his place of business in St. Louis on January 25, Joe Bauer elected to "shoot it out" with the intruders. The result was that one of the bandits fell dead from a bullet and the other fled while Bauer was unharmed. He had never fired a pistol, but after coming off second best in a holdup a year ago, he bought a revolver and practiced when occasion presented itself. Hence, victory for him in his second engagement with thugs.

Frank Landon, of Riverside, near Chicago, on February 18, shot and possibly fatally wounded a holdup man who boarded the automobile in which he and his wife were riding. The Landons, with Mrs. Landon driving, were driving slowly along a road between Gary and Hammond, Ill., when an automobile, in which were several men, drew alongside. Several shots were fired from the bandit car and the Landons were forced to halt. One man, flourishing a pistol, entered the rear seat of the Landon machine and directed Mrs. Landon to drive into a side road. Mr. Landon, when the intruder carelessly lowered his pistol, quickly yanked a gun from the door pocket, whirled around and fired.

In Oakland, Calif., Vendes Mann awakened to find a burglar ransacking a bureau drawer in his room. He drew a pistol from beneath his pillow and fired. The burglar fled and at one point fell as if hit but succeeded in making his escape.

Maurice Weiss, of Chicago, played an heroic part on February 24 in a battle with three burglars who attempted to drill their way into a drug store. He shot and killed one of the robbers who had slugged a police officer. The policeman wounded the second robber and the third was captured later.

Fleeing in an automobile after robbing Albert De Witt, operator of a Chicago filling station on February 2, two armed bandits were fired on by their victim, one of the robbers falling mortally wounded. The slain bandit had attempted to return De Witt's fire when the fatal bullet struck him in the chest.

Threatened for testifying against men she accused of robbing her, Mae West, movie actress, started pistol practice on the Los Angeles police range with a pistol loaned her by the police department, according to a newspaper story. It is another case of recognition of the value of a gun as a proper means of defense against the criminal.

"By forbidding the citizen to have a weapon, we doubly arm the criminal. Every man should have the right to protect himself, if he can prove conclusively that he is a decent, law-abiding citizen intent on protecting his family and his property."—Col. Calvin Goddard, director of research, Northwestern University Scientific Crime Detection Laboratory.

"Atlanta, Feb. 24.—Police Chief T. O. Sturdivant today urged Atlanta motorists to help curb wave of kidnap-bandits by 'judicious use of arms' after four more motorists were 'taken for rides' and robbed of money and their cars last night.

"Declaring 'the time has come for the public to help,' Chief Sturdivant again called on motorists 'to shoot the bandits and ask questions later. A man has no more right to jump on the running board of your car than to break into your house.'"—UP.

Myron Baker, an N.R.A. member of Fremont, Ohio, turned the tables on a youthful bandit who held him up and robbed him at a filling station at which he is an attendant on January 12. The bandit, armed with a revolver, had turned his back to get into the stolen automobile he was driving, after having secured the service station money, when Baker, quick to take advantage of the opening, drew his own gun and commanded the youth to surrender. Baker held the bandit at bay until assistance arrived. After his arrest, it was discovered the young "bad man's" gun was unloaded.

"Firearms are not the origin of criminal tendencies, nor would the forbidding of their manufacture bring about a condition wherein the criminal could not avail himself of their use. Such arms already are in existence, multiple millions of them, and to these the criminal would have access. Or he could, if he chose, manufacture his own firearm. Or procure it from a bootlegger of firearms, for there would be no lack of those who sought to profit by the opportunity. The price would go up, of course, but there would be no real scarcity of firearms for criminal employment.

". . . To forbid a lawful man the possession of firearms, broadly speaking, for no other reason than that similar firearms are employed criminally by the lawless is clearly the infringement of a natural right. It is desirable, too, as national policy, that citizens be familiar with firearms and their use. This traditional familiarity has counted heavily for the American cause in more than one conflict. It is more than probable that even now crime is held in considerable restraint through criminal fear of the possession of firearms by law-abiding people.

"There were criminals, desperate and deadly fellows, before firearms were invented. Criminality is not coeval with this type of weapon. Nor would suppression of firearms, and their restriction to military and police forces, put an end to crime—a social illness calling for quite different curatives."—Portland, (Oreg.) *Morning Oregonian*.

Police Chief Everett F. Russell, of East Bridgewater, N. Y., has invited the men of the town to join a pistol class with the understanding that when they attain a required proficiency they will be given permits to carry firearms and in case of emergency they may be called into action to assist the police officials.

"We think the laws against average citizens' carrying pistols and weapons, unless formally permitted, is a well-intentioned one but futile as well as injurious to the best interest of society. The only one who has difficulty obtaining a gun is the honest citizen."—Clifford B. Ward's column, "Abracadabra," in the Fort Wayne (Ind.) *News-Sentinel*.

"For several years machine guns and sawed-off shotguns have been the favorite weapons of the more dangerous gangster mobs. That fact seems to have been overlooked, however, by the sponsors of a group of bills pending in Congress. The avowed purpose of the bills, which contain many excessive and some ridiculous regulations, is to prevent crime by depriving criminals of their weapons. In reality they would tend to prevent the possession of arms by sportsmen and law-abiding householders, but would interfere little, if at all, with the well-armed bandit's raids upon a disarmed public.

"The measures display a particular animus toward the revolver and the pistol, and would require the labeling of all shipments of those weapons in interstate commerce. If there is any lesson in the record of recent exploits of the gangsters, it is that progress in underworld ballistics is making the pistol merely a defense weapon. It may still be used by unorganized footpads and poorly equipped police, but its greatest present value is as a means of protection in the home.

"No law-abiding citizen will quarrel with the ostensible purpose of these bills. But they would be as unenforceable as prohibition was. If real regulation of the sale of firearms and ammunition is desired in the interest of crime prevention, it should be limited to machine guns and sawed-off shotguns. It is these weapons in the hands of ruthless gangsters which constitute the real menace to public safety."—Chicago *Daily News,* February 9.

"There are some legislators now who are advocating changes in the laws to make it more difficult for people to buy firearms. Instead of hindering the gunmen, as is the good intention of the law makers, they will be simply putting stumbling blocks in the way of honest people who wish guns for legitimate purposes. There should be, instead, heavier sentences for gunmen."—Capt. Louis E. Lutz, retired drillmaster of the Boston police department.

DECEMBER 1934

POLICEMEN THANK GROCER AND THEN ARREST HIM

Man Who Trapped Forgery Suspect Lacks Pistol Permit

Three police radio cars answered an alarm from a grocery at 164 East 122nd Street and the patrolmen found the grocer, Luigi Soada, thirty-five years old, covering a man with a .22-caliber revolver. Soada explained that the man had made a purchase and then attempted to pay with a check drawn on a Kalana, Wash., bank and made out to Hans Kauppila. He had endorsed the check in the store, Soada said. The man said he was Thomas A. Mantyla, thirty-one, of 6 East 129th Street, and, according to the police, admitted he had found the check. He was arrested on a charge of forgery.

The police thanked Soada for his cooperation and then arrested him on a charge of violation of the Sullivan law. He could produce no permit for the revolver with which he captured Mantyla.—New York *Herald Tribune.*

1934 EDITORIAL COMMENTARY

APRIL 1934

SHOOTING IN THE WHITE HOUSE

Mrs. Franklin D. Roosevelt considers shooting a skill and she intends to practice on the new White House revolver range as soon as she has a chance. That's what she told her press conference today and, in answer to questions, emphasized she did not consider practice shooting in conflict with her theory that children should not be taught war by playing with tin soldiers.

The President's wife hasn't seen the range yet, installation having been made while she was absent from the White House, but she hopes it will prove useful to everyone about the mansion.

The guards and secret service men, all of whom carry pistols, will do their practice there, she said, adding she had no idea where the plan originated. It had been attributed to Mrs. Roosevelt herself.

"Can you shoot?" she was asked.

"Yes."

"Well, what do you shoot?"

"Anything I'm given to shoot."

"Isn't that against your idea not to give children warlike toys?"

Her answer was an emphatic negative. She said she wouldn't start to teach children to shoot with toy revolvers, but when they were old enough to be taught to use guns as firearms and to use them properly, then shooting became skill—a training of hand and eye.

"As well argue that teaching children to go on long hikes is teaching them to march," was the way Mrs. Roosevelt disposed of the question.

ASSOCIATED PRESS REPORT

JULY 1934

MACHINE-GUN BILL PASSES

In the closing minutes of the Seventy-third Congress, the anti-machine gun bill was enacted into law.

This bill had the approval of the National Rifle Association and will not affect the sportsman or other honest citizen.

DECEMBER 1934

GUN-EDITOR SHARPE ON ANTI-GUN LAWS

In the November issue of Dell Men's Group of Magazines, Philip B. Sharpe, in a special article on the Anti-Firearms situation sounds a warning to all gun owners. Mr. Sharpe, who is Gun Department Editor of *All Western Magazine* (one of the Dell Group) also pays tribute to the NRA's organized attack on unsound "anti" laws, stating as his opinion that the NRA method is the only successful way to combat such legislation.

The Association and fellow shooters are grateful to Mr. Sharpe for his frank and enlightening article. A few sample paragraphs:

"You sportsmen who love to hunt for rabbits, birds and upland game and waterfowl with your shotguns—

You bugs who enjoy your periodic visits to rifle or pistol range—

You collectors who have been gathering rare specimens of handguns and rifles of a by-gone age—

You homeowners who believe a revolver an excellent defense of your life and property—

You fans who love the feel of gun steel, love the balance of perfect firearms, who revel in the romance and lure of guns—

Gun lovers one and all, you are going to lose your possessions.

All this is to be done by the United States Government, State governments and local city governments. In many cases it has already happened.

Organized prohibition fanatics, their clutches pried loose from the vicious 18th Amendment, no longer able to dictate what man shall or shall not drink, have turned their energies to deprive man of his right to bear arms.

They are doing this, mind you, in the United States, a country where it is every man's heritage to own and carry guns, a country that was blasted from the wilderness by your forefathers with black powder and flintlocks, where children are taught the use and care of guns as were their fathers before them. If the nefarious end of these fanatics is accomplished it will mean just one more victory for the gangster. Crime armed vs. Citizens unarmed.

It is enough to make one think—and act!"

JANUARY 1935

The end of a five year juvenile crime trail was written in blood when Herbert Francis Mannon, 19 years of age, was wounded mortally while plundering a grocery store in Portland, Oregon, on September 23.

The youth, whose police record included escapes from the county jail at San Francisco and the Washington and Oregon reform schools, chose to fight rather than surrender and was fatally shot by the store proprietor, M. V. Wallace.

Alone in the house when she was awakened by burglars ransacking the dining room, Mrs. A. L. Willi, wife of a San Jose, Calif., policeman, ambushed three men in the backyard, routed them with six shots from her husband's revolver, and dropped one with a bullet in the side.

The wounded man's companions carried him into the street to a waiting automobile, in which they drove away. They had dropped their loot as soon as the courageous housewife opened fire.

Declaring the "United States is the easiest place in the world to rob and murder," Gov. Joseph B. Ely of Massachusetts told the Florida Bar Association that the machinery of justice needs overhauling in this country.

"The Communist," he said, "cannot injure our institutions with all his dangerous propaganda so much as the crooked lawyer and his jury-fixing."

The city of Lawrence, Mass., is to be congratulated for having good marksmen on its police force. On October 10 two of Lawrence's "shooting" officers—Maroney and Riley—appeared on the scene of an attempted poolroom holdup. Although "off duty," the officers immediately went into action by dropping to the floor behind a stove, from which point of vantage both bandits were "coolly picked off." Officer Maroney is one of the best marksmen in the state.

F. M. Williams, President of the State Bank of Byron, Minn., foiled an attempted holdup of his bank on August 29 by holding two men at the point of a sawed-off shotgun until officers arrived to make the arrests. When told "this is a stick-up," Williams dropped to the floor, grabbed a sawed-off shotgun, and slipped the gun into an opening in the bank cage partition. Both men surrendered with the plea, "Don't shoot."

A minister's son, working as a gasoline station attendant, was seriously wounded in Cleveland in an attempted holdup, but before he fell he shot and killed the holdup man.

The attendant was John Niegarth, 29 years old, the son of John R. Niegarth, of Reed City, Mich.

The robber ran around the corner of the station, and started firing at the attendant. Niegarth grabbed a revolver from his cash register and returned the fire. The robber was shot through the heart on the attendant's second shot.

1935

When a bandit entered the home of little Miss Jean Swanson, 16, in Kansas City, Mo., he pulled a gun and announced, "This is a stick-up." Jean dashed upstairs, snatched her father's revolver and came back shooting. The intruder fled. "I like to shoot," Jean explained.

Manual Garcia was sitting on his front porch in San Antonio, Tex., one evening last April when he noticed his friend, J. F. Alvardo, the corner grocer, standing behind his counter with his hands in the air. Three men were confronting Alvardo. Garcia stepped into his home, got a small rifle and returned to the porch. Then he shouted to Alvardo to lie down and started shooting. The first shot killed Francisco Martinez. The second shot dropped Manuel Reyes. The third man ran and escaped. Garcia then called police.

Protecting her home and two small children from an intruder who was attempting to enter the residence, Mrs. Jessie Armstrong, 3336 Delphos Avenue, Dayton, Ohio, fired three shots through the front door and slightly wounded the prowler, who was arrested later for being intoxicated.

Two long-term convicts escaped from San Quentin on April 26, kidnaped two police officers, and in two days traveled half the length of the state. In San Bernardino they released the officers, held up a drug store, and started out over the desert. They were met on the road by officers who turned around and gave chase.

The convicts immediately opened fire on the officers with pistols which took no effect. Just eleven shots were returned by the pursuing officers. Five shots from a shotgun blew up three tires which put the car out of control. The other six shots were from a .30-'06 Springfield in the hands of Deputy Sheriff R. S. Snedigar, all of which struck the car. The convicts were killed outright. Each had been shot through the head.

George M. Jackson, pioneer farmer of Spring Lake, in Cook County, Illinois, celebrated his 92nd birthday on June 2. The occasion was doubly significant because on that same day five uninvited visitors called upon pioneer Jackson. "We know you have saved a lot of money and we want it," they demanded. "Your information is wrong," Jackson told them, but the five men insisted on ransacking the house, paying no attention to the old man's protest. Jackson sat down in a chair by his bed to watch the search. Suddenly he reached under the pillow and pulled out the old "peacemaker" he had carried as village marshal. "This old gun has never failed me, and it's not likely to now," he sputtered angrily. "So you had better get out and get out quick." The five intruders "got," bowling over each other as they departed.

On the night of February 20 Thomas J. Martin, Placerville, Calif., police officer, received a call that John Morgan was trying to shoot and kill his family. The city traffic officer, Delbert Howe, and Martin went in answer to the call. In a letter to the N. R. A.,Officer Martin relates his experience:

"On arriving at the house I looked in the front window and saw Mrs. Morgan run from one room to the other, her husband after her. As Morgan entered the second room, he drew his gun, a .30 caliber Harrington & Richardson revolver. Mrs. Morgan ran out of the back door so I ran around the house to head Morgan off before he could shoot his wife. Howe had no gun so he remained on the front porch.

"As Mrs. Morgan ran past me Morgan fired a shot. I rushed him and demanded his gun. He started shooting, one bullet entering my left shoulder, then I could see that it was up to me to shoot it out with him. But when I went to raise my gun I found that my left arm was paralyzed. I am left-handed, and as he was raising his gun to shoot again I had no time to change hands, so I laid my hand on my left hip and raised my hip high enough to shoot him in the right groin. At the same time I received a bullet in my left chest, just over the heart, the bullet striking my police badge first, which deflected the bullet, causing it to miss the heart. By that time the shock had left my arm so I shot him through the liver and as he grabbed his stomach in his arms and pitched forward I landed another bullet in the base of his neck. Morgan died a few minutes later. I was laid up for six weeks, but I am back on the job again, just as good as ever. I was using an S. & W. .38-44.''

On March 28 there appeared on the front page of the *Milwaukee Sentinel* an editorial, "Federal Firearms Control," signed by publisher, Paul Block. The editorial favored federal control of firearms because "state laws have been found to be ineffective in keeping firearms out of the hands of criminals," and warned that "sportsmen must recognize the importance of curbing weapons in every conceivable way."

Perhaps it is only a coincidence, but in this same issue of Mr. Block's *Sentinel* there appeared on page 3 a picture and story of August Paridaens, Green Bay farmer, whose "uncurbed weapon" helped him out of a difficult situation. The story: "August Paridaens, 61-year-old farmer of Green Bay, isn't ready to surrender his cash just because four masked gunmen ask him for it. No, sir. Tuesday four bandits, neighbors of Paridaens, who have heard the report that he keeps much money in his home, decided to hold him up there. One of them, Paul Kamps, was shot to death. Another, Bert Vande Hei, was shot in the abdomen and may die. Two others, Russell Vande Hei and Fred Hock, Tuesday afternoon were sentenced from three to eight years in prison for the escapade. When they shouted: 'Your money or your life!' Paridaens got his pistol and fired twice. Two went down.''

A gray haired grandmother, Mrs. Fred Curtis, 71, was credited with wounding two gunmen whom she engaged in a pistol duel during a holdup.

The elderly woman's marksmanship resulted in the recovery of $35 loot that three bandits had taken from the cash register of her husband's drug store.

Mrs. Curtis opened fire from a back room. Her first shot dropped the bandit who was rifling the cash register. He spilled a handful of bills. The other gunman returned Mrs. Curtis' fire until one of them dropped. The two wounded men crawled and dodged from the store and the trio fled in an automobile. Neither Curtis nor his wife was hurt.

Speculating as to how much mayhem could be committed with nine pickaxe handles, Patrolman Patrick Casey of the Fields Corner station arrested two young men found possessing them at Minot Street and Gallivan Boulevard, Dorchester.

Casey in questioning the two had acted on an anonymous tip that the gang warfare which sent a number of young men to a hospital about eight months ago was about to break out again. The handles were to be passed out to gang members for use on the heads of members of a rival gang, police believe.

Albert Pullman, 29, of San Francisco, was shot and fatally wounded on May 10 by Officer Frank Winslow of the Salem police. Pullman was in the act of burglarizing the George E. Waters wholesale cigar store, 229 State Street.

The burglar was shot when, instead of lifting his hands at the command of the officer, his right hand darted towards a pocket. On his person was found a .25 caliber automatic pistol of Spanish make, with a cartridge in the firing chamber and the safety off.

Glenn Harmon, 30, Carthage, Mo., kidnap-murder suspect, was shot to death in a hand-to-hand encounter with Detective Lieutenant A. C. Stromwell of Los Angeles in a crowded café in Los Angeles.

A score of patrons fled in terror as the suspect opened fire on the officer after felling him with his fists. Two shots went wild and the suspect's gun jammed before Stromwell drew his own revolver, discharging six shots into Harmon's head and body. Death was instantaneous.

A burglar, believed to have been Will Collier of Huntington, W. Va., was shot and instantly killed in that city on November 22 by Dr. J. D. Williams in the doctor's home at 5308 Winchester Avenue. The man was shot through the heart with a .38 caliber police special revolver. Dr. Williams was promptly exonerated by a jury which held that the prowler's death was justifiable homicide.

S. Harry Silver, branch bank manager at Whittier and Atlantic Boulevards, in Los Angeles, brought his score against bandits to four when he shot and killed one and captured another. Several years ago Silver pursued and captured, single-handed, two men who had robbed the bank in his charge.

On both occasions he displayed common sense combined with courage and quick thinking. There was no foolhardy attempt to "shoot it out" in either case; in both he waited for a favorable opportunity and took immediate advantage of it. If it were possible for such a man to be placed in every bank, there would be fewer robberies.

Patrolman Russell B. Malcolm, Syracuse, N. Y. police marksman, sent two bullets into the back of a moving car, one of them nicking the driver's head, after surprising two men on the sidewalk there removing a safe from a store. Both men were arrested with their loot intact.

Making a practice of carrying a revolver in his waist during business hours, George Ayoob, storekeeper of Boston, drove off the second pair of bandits within a year on April 17. The men, one of whom flourished a pistol, fled when the store man pulled forth his weapon.

In Baltimore, two bandits who attempted a holdup in a crowded confectionery store were shot and killed by a customer, Joseph Kelly, on March 11. Kelly fired when one of the bandits ordered another man to throw up his hands.

Awakened from his sleep by a noise in the kitchen in his cafe in Los Angeles on March 9, L. E. Kelly grabbed his shotgun and fired, killing one of the two burglars.

FEBRUARY 1935

Theft of a dozen shotguns and rifles stolen from the show windows of three downtown Washington, D. C., sporting goods stores, during the Christmas holidays, caused speculation among capital police officials as to whether the robberies might have been perpetrated by gangsters seeking to replenish diminishing stocks of firearms. Stores looted included the Atlas Sporting Goods Store, and two Army and Navy Trading Companies.

Columbus, Ohio, papers recently reported a similar theft from a local National Guard Armory. The Columbus loot, valued at $229.00, included eight revolvers.

Secretary of the Treasury Henry Morgenthau, Jr., has ordered that all treasury department employees, except clerks and stenographers, must be provided with side arms and become proficient in their use. Capt. L. J. Gillman, assistant custodian of the courthouse, and Lieut. Samuel Gray of Coast Guard Headquarters were appointed firearms instructors. Certificates are to be issued.

For months W. L. Nichols, Atlanta, Ga., and his wife had practiced what to do in case of a hold-up. When two bandits entered their store, Mrs. Nichols, in accordance with often rehearsed tactics, dropped to the floor, while her husband killed one of the men and routed the other. The dead man could not be identified.

An attempted hold-up was frustrated and three bandits were captured by Carl E. Thompson, owner of a road house near Mankato, Minn., on the night of December 27th.
Brandishing revolvers immediately after entering the road house, the men demanded Thompson and his wife to "stick 'em up." Mrs. Thompson complied, but the road house owner darted for a back door and ran upstairs to get his shotgun. Firing from an upstairs window he wounded two of the trio after which the third surrendered. The three men were disarmed and turned over to the county sheriff. Both wounded bandits will recover.

When J. L. Morris, Chief of Police at Astell, Ga., was knocked down by two bandits whom he surprised trying to enter a bank from an adjoining store, he came up shooting, and killed one of his attackers. The dead man was identified as Jerry B. Munsey, of Lenoir City, Tenn. Chief Morris, who used a target revolver, said that he learned to "shoot quick" in France.

"Although our idealists seem to think they are doing a great thing when they introduce anti-firearms legislation, they are in fact putting us at the mercy of the criminal. They *are* doing a great thing—for the gangster. . . . It is high time that the leaders of these United States were made to realize that crime cannot be curbed by telling gangsters that they may not carry guns, and that the only way to curb crime is to arm the population of the country to such an extent that much crime will be left uncommitted because the criminal is afraid to unduly risk his own neck."—Elizabethtown (Pa.) *Chronicle.*

Charles Linhart, Oakland, Calif., tailor, was in the rear of his son's grocery store when he heard a strange voice: "Hands up and give me all your money." He walked into the store to find a bandit facing his son. The old man ducked behind the counter, grabbed a revolver and came up shooting. The bandit ran, but was overtaken and captured after receiving at the hands of the Linharts, what is politely known as a thorough "going over."

Daniel Kehoe, ex-cow puncher, who learned to handle guns on the plains, now operating a roadstand in New Jersey, proved to be the Nemesis of three armed and masked bandits who held him up just prior to the Christmas holidays.
Suddenly Kehoe made a dive for the largest of the three and the two went down. Afraid to shoot, two of the bandits stepped back while their companion struggled to his feet. Kehoe, however, was not beaten. He quickly crawled behind the bar and came up with a gun in his hand. Faced with a dose of their own medicine the bandits fled in panic and escaped in a waiting car.

Franklin D. Windle, 31, owner of a San Francisco service station, has always said that he would "shoot it out with any bandit any time." Unfortunately for them, the two youthful bandits who held up Windle last month either did not know about his attitude or thought Windle was boasting. The Service Station owner responded to the command to "stick 'em up," by drawing his own gun. Both bandits dropped, one dead, the other mortally wounded. "I never fired a gun so fast in all my life," Windle told police.

Edwin Busch, 32, entered the Chicago tavern of John Consigliari Christmas day and asked for a meal. It was Christmas so Consigliari locked the tavern and took Busch to a restaurant, where he ordered a hearty lunch. As he left Consigliari pressed a bill into Busch's hand and wished him a Merry Christmas. Then he visited friends. Two hours later Consigliari returned to his tavern and found Busch rifling the cash drawer. He shot and killed him.—(*Chicago U. P. Dispatch.*)

James Kain and Russell Moore, both of Akron, the latter a deserter from the U. S. Army, were shot by Vigilantes when the pair attempted to hold up a tavern near LeMars, Iowa. Kain, who was fatally wounded, died on Christmas Day. Moore (alias Rodgers) is still in a hospital but will recover. The Vigilantes, all members of the LeMars Rifle Club, opened fire from across the street when the robbers, attempting to make their escape, failed to comply with the command to halt.

Mrs. C. E. Zuspan, Fairmont, W. Va., housewife, keeps a .32 revolver in her home for self protection. She had occasion to use it on the night of December 15th when an intruder tried to gain entrance to her home. Hearing a rattling of the door-knob, Mrs. Zuspan called but got no response. The intruder continued his attack on the door, threatening to break it down if not admitted. Mrs. Zuspan then fired, intending to frighten him away, but the bullet struck the intruder—Kenneth E. Hall—in the chest and hospital attendants said he had very little chance for recovery.

The crime career of an unidentified man who held up the Sioux National Bank of Harrison, Nebr., was ended on Christmas Day by a rancher's bullet. The man, fleeing on foot after his automobile went over an embankment, was brought down by Albert Moody, rancher and a member of a hastily organized posse of business men and ranchers. The entire loot of $685.00 was found on the dead man.

DECEMBER 1935

STURGIS, N. D., March 4.—(U.P.)—An unidentified bandit was slain and another bandit wounded in a gun battle in front of the Bear Butte Valley Savings bank on March 4. A third bandit escaped.

The shooting occurred when an attempt was made to rob the bank at its opening, while a raging snowstorm obscured movements of the trio.

Police Chief Glen Rogers and Traffic Officer C. E. Peterson of Rapid City, S. D., rushed the robbers and a gun battle started. Two of the gangsters were felled and both officers were slightly wounded in the exchange of shots.

A man identified as Chance Barker of Omaha, Neb., was critically wounded in the stomach when he attempted to hold up Al W. Greenleaf, of Des Moines as Greenleaf locked up the Bonnie Cafe, 1355 Lyon St., one day last March.

Greenleaf is a member of the Des Moines Rifle Club and an expert target shot.

"I further feel that marksmanship on the part of officers is another important factor. It is my rule that every officer, including police women, of the Los Angeles force must visit the range at least twice a month and practice.

"We award extra salary for marksmanship ranks and I can assure you that our criminal element knows this and is not at all anxious to engage in gun play. We are proud of the fact that our pistol team, for more than five years, has held the national and international police championships.

"Criminals steer clear of officers who bear the reputation of being crack shots." From an article by Jas. E. Davis, Los Angeles Police Chief.

Dec. 7, 1934—Frank Windle, a filling station operator in Glendale, Calif., again proved last evening that he was too quick on the trigger for holdup men.

At about 8:45 P. M. two masked men drove in to Frank's filling station in a Chrysler sedan and jumped out with drawn guns.

Windle, who shot Stanley Groce, notorious bandit two years ago, carries a .38 service revolver on duty.

Immediately sizing up the situation when the two bandits rushed him last night, Windle opened fire, killing one of the men instantly and wounding the other seriously—*Glendale Times.*

A new law, known as the "short firearms act," went into effect on July 1 in the state of Washington. It is intended to keep pistols out of the hands of criminals. It is not easy to see how such a thing can be accomplished by fiat of law, no matter how laudable the object. If a person is intent upon the commission of a felony for which he risks hanging he is not likely to be deterred by threat of fine and imprisonment for carrying a pistol in his pocket, in a holster under his arm or in his automobile. Probably the best that can be hoped for the law is that it will give a better opportunity for punishment of yeggs who are caught in anticipation of or attempt to commit crimes—they may be sentenced for possession of prohibited arms when it would be impossible to prove attempts at crimes.

Wholesale prohibition of the possession of firearms has been proposed—if no one has guns but peace officers the theory is criminal gun play would cease. Such law, of course, would be contrary to the constitutions of the United States and the states. The right to bear arms is elemental law, and a necessity for the safety of the people against invasion or the usurpation of power within the country—history is replete with seizures of power through misuse of governmental armed forces. An Oregon statute dated 1868 provides:

"Every white male citizen of this state above the age of sixteen years shall be entitled to have, hold, and keep, for his own defense, the following firearms, to-wit: Either or any one of the following named guns, and one revolving pistol; a rifle, shotgun (double or single barrel), yager, or musket; the same to be exempt from execution in all cases, under the laws of Oregon."

Many other laws are on the books in Oregon in regard to possession and use of firearms; it is impossible for an ordinary person to be informed as to exactly what they are; probably the authorities would find difficulty in saying what is permitted and what not. The remedy is to mete out prompt and vigorous punishment for the ancient felonies, regardless of whether committed with club or gun.—*The Morning Oregonian.*

Three of seven men caught in the federal government's net were given prison sentences Saturday when they pleaded guilty to charges in connection with the theft of 74 automatic pistols from the Ninth Infantry armory last October.—*San Antonio* (Texas) *Light.*

Consternation and embarrassment gripped the police and detective departments of Knoxville, Tenn., one hot day last July when they discovered that someone invaded the police station and stole three revolvers.

A law forbidding manufacture or sale of trousers with hip pockets is advocated by Circuit Court Judge J. Henry Johnson as a remedy for homicides. "People wouldn't have such a handy place to carry a pistol," he says—*York* (S. C.) *Observer.*

ELMIRA, N. Y.—(U.P.)—As members of a modern police force, Elmira policemen would make a swell bunch of peashooters, in the opinion of the city manager.

Upon his order to assemble for target practice, the policemen lined up at the target grounds. The first patrolman had to press the trigger nine times before his revolver discharged.

Most of the other weapons were found to be rusty and dust filled, and practically useless. One captain's holster was found to be moth infested.

"Those guns are almost as good as peashooters—almost, but not quite," the manager remarked.

He issued orders for a drastic cleanup and regular target practice.

The bandit fired first with his heavy caliber gun. He missed Greenleaf.

Greenleaf's first shot from his .22 caliber target pistol wounded the gunman, who, at once, turned and fled.

Four hours later police arrested Barker. He was found lying in a bed at 1505 Lyon St.

In the efforts of law enforcement agencies to combat crime, there has to be a never-ceasing vigilance, for the tricks that the gangsters and gunmen resort to are devious and clever. One of the main objectives of the law agencies lately has been against the sources which produce guns and place them within reach of criminals. An illustration of the things which the officers encounter was given in New York the other day, when the police arrested a man who admitted that he ran a "rent-a-gun" service, by which guns were rented out to criminals for $10 a night per gun. It is almost incredible that such a situation could exist, but that and many other equally fantastic conditions will prevail the minute the vigilance of the law forces is relaxed—*Boston Post*.

The job of making better shots out of Chicago policemen has been assigned to Maj. John Bauder, director of personnel.

It is an extremely important undertaking.

In the "Old West" of glamorous tradition criminals studiously avoided certain cattle towns simply because it was known that the town marshals there could shoot fast and shoot straight.

Criminals will avoid Chicago, too, when and if the word goes out that here THOUSANDS of policemen know how to shoot fast and shoot straight—*The Chicago American*.

Portland, July 9 AP —Wounded in the leg by a police bullet, a man booked as Arthur E. White was held under guard in a hospital today on a burglary charge following his arrest near a pharmacy from which several hundred dollars worth of merchandise had been stolen. Two other men escaped. White suffered a compound right leg fracture as the bullet crashed through the bone. Most of the loot from the drug store was recovered as the fleeing robbers tossed it aside in their hurry to escape.

Glen Harmes, police Bertillon expert, said fingerprints showed that Schaeffer, alias Arthur E. White, was arrested at Pendleton for burglary on July 19, 1929, and was given a three-year prison sentence.

A burglar walked into a volley of six bullets and was apparently badly wounded when he tried to break into a tavern at 1200 North Fremont Street in Baltimore, Md. Picked up by confederates, the man was carried off in a speeding automobile.

The shooting was done by Edward Fahey, owner of the saloon, who has been staying in the place at night recently. The tavern has been entered five times in five months, and Fahey had determined to put a stop to the burglaries.—*Baltimore* (Md.) *Sun*.

1936

JANUARY 1936

LOS ANGELES, May 21 AP —A youth giving the name of Vernon Marihugh, 16, a resident of El Monte, was in a hospital today, critically wounded after an attempted hold-up.

E. W. Quay reported to police that the youth robbed him of $19. As he started to flee, Quay said he seized a pistol and fired at him. After being struck, the youth ran nearly two blocks before collapsing.

Elizabeth City, N. C. AP , April 4—Two convicts were wounded and another overcome by tear gas today as guards quelled a revolt and attempted escape by a score of long-term prisoners at the Woodville prison camp. The wounded were Woodrow Purdie, serving a 30-year sentence for murder, and Albert Hardlee, serving a life term for murder.

Mauston, Wis.—Asst. Cashier Russell H. Hale frustrated a robbery of the Bank of Mauston here Wednesday at the cost of being shot in the arm and side. He engaged one of the robbers in a gun fight from inside the vault.

Unnerved by Hale's plucky resistance, the robber leader dropped the loot he had collected and fled without a penny with his two companions.

This was Hale's second brush with stick-up men. On May 15, 1933, two robbers entered the bank. Hale dashed into the vault and grabbed his deer rifle. He leaped after them as they fled. In the ensuing street fight he killed James M. Miles and single handedly captured Irving J. Hill. Hill is serving 15 to 30 years now.

Hale was wounded in the right arm and side Wednesday. Friends took him to the hospital here. Doctors said the injury was not serious, although the bullet lodged against Hale's ribs—*Milwaukee Journal*.

Calmly firing from the floor after a bandit knocked him down, Louis Rousse, a watchman, today routed three men who broke into the United States Soft Drink Works at 1840 S. Damen Ave.

Shortly afterward Theodore Tarzan, 19, of 1951 Cortland St., was brought into the Norwegian-American Hospital, suffering from a bullet wound in his stomach—*Chicago American.*

LONG BEACH, Jan. 24 A P —A man identified by papers found in his pockets as Ted de Boiser of Shelbyville, Tenn., was shot and killed last night after he was alleged to have forced L. M. Long, service station owner, to give him the contents of the cash register under threat of a pistol.

After taking the money, the man jumped into an automobile and attempted to flee. Long grabbed a pistol and opened fire, instantly killing the man.

LOS ANGELES, Feb. 4—Defying gun fire threats of two robbers about to burglarize an Inglewood theater safe early today, J. H. Gold, 24, private patrolman, emptied his gun at them, killing one and possibly wounding the other—*Glendale* (Calif.) *News Press.*

BALTIMORE, Md., Feb. 16—Waking from a dream his store was being robbed, Samuel Winuekour, 56, sprang from bed to discover a burglar descending the stairs of his home.

He grappled with the man and the sounds of the struggle wakened Charles Owens, 61, a boarder, who shot and seriously wounded the alleged house-breaker. The intruder was later identified as Lawrence Green, 33.

With the muzzle of an automatic pistol pressed against her neck, Mrs. R. Mosso, proprietor of a cafe at 3343 Wilshire Boulevard, was opening her safe for a bandit when the match he held went out. As he struck another one she saw her chance and grabbed his gun, wresting it from him.

"He struck another one and as he did he held the pistol in front of me. I grabbed it and jerked it away from him. I turned it on him and he ran out the door with me screaming"—*Los Angeles Times.*

Burglars will show good judgment in steering clear of Glen Jernigan's drug store at Lyons, Colo. Early Tuesday morning, from his living quarters in the rear of the store, he heard somebody "kick in the front door." Getting his shotgun, which was loaded with buckshot, he watched through a window between his apartment and the store, and saw a man trying to knock the combination off the safe. Jernigan fired and, as the robber staggered across the store, fired again. One of the two robbers in the store was killed. The other was wounded and was captured later in Boulder. A shotgun is more effective than all the burglary insurance in the world in discouraging safecracking—*Denver* (Colo.) *Post.*

Three men entered the store of Salvatore Manzella at 206 Forsyth St. in New York, and held up his wife, Mrs. Anna Manzella.

Manzella, who was playing cards in the rear, threw down his cards, snatched a revolver from a cupboard and opened fire through the doorway at the intruders, one of whom at least fired back. The storekeeper's bullets killed one of the thieves, Charles Lombardi, of 511 East 116th Street, who had a card in his pocket showing that he had a relief job. The other two got away.

Two of the bullets which the holdup men fired struck Internicula and Olaivan, each of whom was wounded superficially in their right arms. A pistol from which two shots had been fired was found beside Lombardi's body. *When the police arrived they arrested Manzella on a charge of having a revolver without a permit.—N. Y. Herald Tribune.*

Four times thieves had looted the little jewelry store belonging to W. A. Rusk in Los Angeles, for a total loss of $1500, but in the early morning hours on Feb. 17 he finally got his man when he inflicted wounds upon Jerry Arbellow, alias Gerald Raymus, 28-year-old ex-convict, of 123 East Seventy-fifth Street, which caused his death a short time later in the Georgia Street receiving hospital.

On the occasion of the four previous burglaries Rusk was sleeping in his home which adjoins that of his store. But four times was four too many for Rusk, so he moved his bed into the rear of his establishment.

At 2:30 A. M. today Rusk was awakened by the sound of breaking glass in the front of his shop. Revolver in hand, he stealthily made his way to the front of the store and fired twice through the front window at shadowy forms.

Police arrested Arbellow at his home when he telephoned for an ambulance and later arrested Henry Graveson, 19, 8813 Juniper Street, and Walter Sanders, 19, of 1228 East Eighty-eighth Street, as suspected accomplices.—*Los Angeles* (Calif.) *Examiner.*

Glen Jernigan, the Lyons druggist, who shot a pair of Boulder burglars, killing one of them, deserves praise, not censure. The fellows were caught in the act and by wounding one of them there was uncovered many burglaries in Boulder county, relieving others than the men shot of suspicion of complicity in them and possible miscarriage of justice.

SAN FRANCISCO, Dec. 8 (U.P.)—Genero Beckerro, 40, San Francisco, was shot and killed today in the home of W. R. Markt.

Markt told police that he surprised a burglar in his bedroom, fired two shots in the air as the man ran, and sent a third shot at the intruder as he dashed through the front door. The bullet killed the alleged burglar identified as Beckerro.

Official reports show that Chicago police have killed eleven armed bandits so far this year. That is in line with the fighting tradition of Chicago's bluecoats.

Even more interesting, however, is the fact that, in addition to the armed outlaws slain by the police, five have been killed by private citizens in self-defense. That fact is pertinent comment on the Conners bill, now before the Illinois legislature—a bill designed to restrict ownership of arms by private citizens.

Obviously neither law nor red tape is any deterrent to the armament of criminals. Five more murderous criminals would be alive in Chicago today if the citizens had previously been deprived of their right to possess arms.—Editorial from Mar. 28 issue of *Chicago* (Ill.) *Daily News*.

A man's home is his castle and he is not only legally but morally in the right when he defends it against criminal trespassers.

The coroner's jury commended Jernigan and with its verdict law-abiding citizens will agree.—*Boulder* (Colo.) *Canero*.

"Maybe those guys will learn to lay off."

Thus spoke Thomas Steen in injured fashion, wiping his hands of the second alleged burglar he has shot in two years.

Each attempted to rob the Atlantic and Pacific Tea Company store, in Brooklyn, which Steen manages.

Latest of his victims was William Webber, 23, who was shot in the abdomen after he and two companions are alleged to have forced Steen's assistant, Thomas Finn, to the rear of the store.

Reaching into a drawer in the rear of the store where his own gun rested, Steen aimed true and fired. The robber's two companions fled.

Two years ago Steen, in shooting an intruder, had to utilize the gunman's revolver, since he had none of his own.

At his 169 High St., Brooklyn, home, he admitted he was annoyed by these unwarranted intrusions upon his time.—*The Brooklyn* (N. Y.) *Queen*.

Miami, Fla., Feb. 25 AP —Strange weapons were used in two holdups reported to police today. Max Olenick told detectives he surrendered $62 to a bandit who brandished a milk bottle. S. M. Hosring said he was robbed of $80 at the point of an ice pick.

John Dauss, who keeps a candy store at 608 South Tripp Avenue, called the Fillmore Street police last night to report that he had been robbed. "A gunman held me up, searched me, and got $125 I had in my pockets," Dauss reported. "Everything you had, eh?" sympathized the sergeant. "Well, no," replied Dauss, "not everything. He didn't find the pistol I had stuck in my belt. I always keep it as a protection against robbers."—*Chicago* (Ill.) *Tribune*.

FEBRUARY 1936

On May 8, 1933, two brothers, Samuel and George Smith of 247 45th Road, Long Island City, N. Y., killed one thug and aided in capturing two others when their store was held up. When police arrived they arrested both Smiths for possessing revolvers without a permit. This action was in conformity with New York's Notorious Sullivan Law which theorizes that citizens thru taxation pay for police protection against thugs, hence guns in the possession of citizens are of no avail and should be outlawed.

Recently the Smith brothers were brought before Magistrate August Dreyer in Long Island City Court for a hearing. The courtroom was crowded with reporters and citizens, all anxious to know what action the Court would take. Would these men—heroes in the eyes of their fellow citizens—be convicted of a felony for ridding the city of three notorious bandits? Or would the Sullivan Law rightfully suffer open condemnation by the Court's prompt dismissal of the case?

The Verdict? "Decision reserved." It was explained that Magistrate Dreyer desired to confer with police Commissioner Valentine of New York City before handing down his decision. Everybody knows Commissioner Valentine is a firm advocate of The Sullivan Law. But the Smith brothers and their sympathetic fellow citizens were nevertheless encouraged by Dreyer's statement in which he said "Any citizen who shoots and kills a bandit and then has courage enough to go through with holdup charges against two accomplices of the dead robber, sending them to Sing Sing for the Crime, should get consideration from the police and courts in return."

M. A. Wilkinson, 6131 South Michigan Ave., killed Kenlock Peques, 31 year old robber, when he discovered him in his apartment.

Nicholas Schmidt, owner of a cigar store at 5901 Irving Park Blvd., and Charles Stutter, a clerk in the store, reached for their guns instead of their money when 19-year-old Messina proclaimed himself a holdup man. Messina was killed.

Pubelo Alcala shot and fatally wounded Lozard Flores when he found him attempting to enter the rear of his home.

Frank Bamber, a watchman, killed Frank Jones when he interrupted him at a burglary.

Sam Lowe, a watchman, caught Winton Pannell while he was fleeing from a burglary at 3908 Broadway. Lowe fired and brought down the burglar.

Louis Woznick, a watchman, surprised John Dunn, 49 years old, trying to crack open a safe in the basement at 3635 Roosevelt Rd. Roznick fired and killed Dunn when he attempted to escape.

Joseph Pharms gave up his life when he fought off an attempted holdup by Nathaniel Akins. Both men were fatally wounded in the fight.

CHICAGO CITIZENS KILLED 14 BANDITS IN 1935

Fourteen bandits died in 1935 because Chicago still has a number of citizens who believe in the power of armed resistance to an attempted holdup. Twenty-seven more robbers, burglars, and automobile thieves were killed by policemen who knew how to handle their revolvers when the occasion demanded. During the three-year period ending December 31, 1935, Chicago citizens accounted for more than forty percent of the bandits who were "killed in action."

It is interesting to note that only four policemen and one citizen were fatally wounded by bandits who were met with opposition to their illegal acts.

Chicago's 1935 honor roll of private citizens follows:

Dr. Emil Miller, victim of two previous holdups, armed himself in readiness for any other would-be bandits. William Frietag, 19 years old, 2156 North Kilbourne Ave., was shot to death when he attempted to hold up Dr. Miller on the street.

George Harrington, tavern owner of 6852 South Ashland Ave., protected his property by shooting and killing Anthony Majcher, 20 years old, when he attempted a holdup.

Mrs. Marie Boksa captured George Psidda, 40 years old, 1338 West Division St., after he had burglarized her home. When Psidda made a dash for freedom before the police arrived on the scene, Mrs. Boksa cooly shot him to death.

Joseph Duranda was making a purchase in a drug store at 372 West Chicago Ave. when Michael Gilardi, 23 years old, 1135 Townsend St., entered with a companion with the intention of holding up the place. Duranda opened fire and fatally wounded Gilardi.

Nicholas Millow, a watchman, opened fire when two intruders tried to strongarm him. One of the two, Hayward Doby, 1849 Fulton St., was killed.

Rev. Edward Wainwright, minister, was at home with his wife at 3311 East 91st St. when two young bandits attempted to rob him. The minister opened fire in spite of the two-to-one odds and killed both the intruders, Charles Thomas, 25, and Wesley Streeter, 19.

Arab, Ala., AP A bank bandit lay dead yesterday, victim of a fast-moving and straight-shooting civilian.

The robber, named by Sheriff O. D. Taylor as Bill Abney of the Brindley Mountain region, entered the bank of Arab (Ala.) Tuesday, and seized $560 at the point of a pistol, escaping from the building amid an exchange of shots with Assistant Cashier Kirby Howard.

The shooting and a burglar alarm were heard by A. R. Ingram, 31, in a nearby store. He gave chase as Abney ran by the store. Guns of both cracked out and after 10 or 12 shots the robber fell mortally wounded with two bullets in his body. He died a few minutes later. Ingram was unhurt.

Philadelphia, Pa., AP—Edward Dee, smalltime gunman, thought a policeman's uniform would make a good disguise to use in holding up an armored car. He tried it last night. Today Dee and one of his companions were dead. The others fled without obtaining any loot.

It happened when H. W. Arnhold, 58, and Harry Arnhold, 38, who operate their own protective service, had drawn up before a chain store to collect the day's receipts. Dee, wearing a policeman's uniform and followed by a companion, strolled up to the car.

"Say, fella, one of your lights is out," he told the elder Arnhold. Arnhold said a glance told him differently and, an instant later, he penetrated the disguise.

Arnhold Sr. leaped at Dee, his son jumped on Dee's companion. Both the gunmen drew pistols, but the Arnholds seized the weapons and fired. Dee fell dead. His companion, later identified as Joseph Kennelley, 29, Philadelphia underworld character, staggered to an automobile and was driven away by one or more accomplices. Later he was found on the doorstep of a suburban hospital. He died this afternoon.

Harry Arnhold killed another would-be holdup in 1929, when six gunmen attempted to take his armored car.

The Times wishes John A. Robinson a merry Christmas, regardless of whether the burglar he shot five times lives or dies.

Mr. Robinson's courage and marksmanship commend him. If many householders were as ready with firearms and as accurate in aim, burglary would not be as widespread as it is.

The man who tackles a burglar assumes, naturally, that the burglar is armed, and is more or less accustomed to the idea of shooting his way through, if not actually accustomed to killing those who resist his intrusion.

In this case, a report says, Mr. Robinson opened fire when the intruder was attempting to shoot him. (The intruder Sanford Taylor—alias Herman Simpson was arrested May 10, 1935, on charges of housebreaking, which were later dismissed).

In most cases the householder who is covered by the burglar's pistol throws up his hands.

In shooting the burglar five times, Mr. Robinson did, with thoroughness the occasion made appropriate, a workmanlike job.

It is always to be hoped that the burglar who has been dealt with, by the householder, as he deserves will recover and have opportunity to amend his life. But, regardless of whether Taylor dies, congratulations to John A. Robinson!

Everyone who so acquits himself in a midnight emergency serves the public.

Frank Kowalski, first team revolver shot of the Wilmington (Dela.) Rifle & Pistol Club, and a member of their Competition Committee, recently captured a burglar single handed when a gang burglarized the filling station of the Pacific Gas & Electric Co. at Wilmington.

Mr. Kowalski, who is the service man for that company, fired one shot at the feet of a fleeing holdupper with such effect that the man promptly stopped and surrendered. Local police are credited with subsequently rounding up 5 others concerned in the matter and one of whom was reported to have been identified as a veteran of 7 previous burglaries.

The troupe has been held in $1,200.00 bail each for General Sessions Court.

For some years the Director of Public Safety and the Chief of Police of Wilmington have cooperated with local pistol and revolver shots and have provided them with an indoor range.

One good turn deserves another!

MARCH 1936

Branford, Fla., Jan. 31. AP—One man was killed, one was captured and at least one other escaped today when an attempt to rob the Branford State Bank here was frustrated by the shouts of the bank president and a volley of gunfire from hastily armed citizens.

The captured man gave his name as Fred Phillips, but authorities refused to believe him, because that was the name of the bank president who sounded the alarm. The prisoner refused to identify the slain man or say how many robbers got away.

Fred D. Phillips, the president, entered the bank before opening time and was confronted by two armed and masked men. They had gained entrance through a rear door. Mr. Phillips ran into the street and shouted an alarm.

As the robbers fled through the rear door, seven or eight citizens gave chase, one killing one of the fugitives. The other immediately dropped his pistol and lifted both hands.

The gangsters disregard for laws—even Federal Laws, is emphasized again by the following newspaper reports of underworld activities with machine guns, reprinted from recent issues of the *Chicago Tribune*. Machine guns were legislated out of existence by the Federal Congress a year ago. The *Tribune* items follow:

New York, Dec. 20.—(Special)—Five armed men, one of them carrying a *submachine gun,* held up the First National bank at Fort Lee, N. J., today and escaped with between $15,000 and $18,000.

Columbiana, O., Dec. 26.—(Special.)—Blasts of lead from a *machine gun* and a riot gun endangered the lives of Columbiana residents today when four bandits covered their escape with a volley of bullets after robbing the Union Banking company of loot estimated at $3,000.

"You can have all my money, but don't harm me," said Dr. Emil Miller, Chicago dentist, as he was ordered to hand over his money by two local gunmen.

Then he reached in his pocket as if to surrender his wallet, but, instead of a wallet, his hand came out with a .38 caliber pistol. He fired once and one of the bandits named Frietag went down, wounded in the stomach.

Then up stepped Frietag's companion, Howard Calkins, 21, of 2118 N. Kilbourn Ave. Dr. Miller let him have it. The bullet caught Calkins in the back.

The two astonished bandits ran down the street, dodging bullets until Dr. Miller's pistol was emptied. They managed to reach the automobile in which a companion was waiting.

A few hours later they were arrested in the office of Dr. Henry G. Lescher at 4158 Armitage Ave. Cragin police then arrested the driver of the car, John Andody, 22, who confessed the gang had committed about fifteen robberies of merchandise and liquor trucks in the past month.

Dr. Miller identified the two wounded men at the Bridewell. He told them he was sorry he had to shoot, but . . .

"I got mad and couldn't help it. I really don't like bandits at all, and I don't like the idea of giving away money to strange men just because they point a gun at me.

"You might tell your bandit friends that it is useless to hold me up, because I haven't much money and I wouldn't give a dime of it away to any robbers."—*Chicago* (Ill.) *Tribune*.

Los Angeles, Calif., AP , Jan 31.—Two men who held up a suburban bank within a block of a police pistol range were killed by the deadly fire of expert marksmen today, a third was captured and an officer was wounded in a wild gun battle.

A girl reporter emerged as heroine of the affray, summoning eighteen members of the San Gabriel Valley pistol team who mowed down the two men as they fled from the Southern County Bank.

The dead men were identified as Clarence H. Smith, forty-three years old, of Los Angeles, and E. C. Yates, forty-two, of Beverly Hills. Smith's brother, Frank H. Smith, forty-four, of Glendale, was captured.

Policeman Joseph Fritch was shot in the right hand, losing three fingers from the blast of a sawed-off shotgun. Officers later discovered three automatic pistols, two short-barreled pistols and two automatic shotguns in possession of the trio.

San Jose, Jan. 7.—Samuel Cardinelli, 63-year-old storekeeper, last night snatched a revolver from a shelf and killed a bandit who had backed him into a back room of his shop at Saratoga avenue and Williams road. The bandit was identified from fingerprints as Victor Mariucci, 24.—(San Jose (Calif.), *Tribune*).

While the robbery was in progress, Tracy Tidd, proprietor of a store across the street from the bank, blazed away at the gang's lookout with a riot gun from his second story window.

The lookout turned a machine gun on the window. Tidd said about 40 bullets pierced the glass. A moment later the bandits leaped into their machine, fired a final burst from their gun, and fled. Some observers said a woman was in the automobile.

Walter Liggett, crusading editor of the *Midwest American,* a weekly newspaper, was assassinated by *machine gunners* in the presence of his wife and small daughter in Minneapolis on Dec. 9. Isador (Kid Cann) Blumenfeld was indicted for the murder.

MAY 1936

STEUBENVILLE, O., Jan. 26 (A.P.).—Lester Downing, 29, of Alliance, died last night, the second man in five years shot fatally in a robbery attempt on Roscoe Smith's store at Bergholz.

Sheriff Ray Long said Smith, 75, shot Downing last Tuesday when Downing and another man entered the store bent on robbery. The other man, registered as Nelson Steven, 44, is held under $2,500 bond.

Smith shot and killed Richard Johnson under similar circumstances in 1931.

WASHINGTON, D. C., Feb. 12 (U.P.).—The "Sullivan law" of New York State, which provides heavy penalties for anyone possessing or carrying a gun without a permit, will be examined in detail by the Senate Munitions Committee.

The committee, it was understood, will undertake to trace armament from the gangster through retailer, wholesaler, and to its source. An effort also will be made to show that state laws designed to prevent illegal possession of guns are ineffective and easily evaded.

Investigators would not reveal a complete list of witnesses, but it was understood that Acting Sergeant Henry F. Butts, ballistics expert of the New York City Police Department, would be asked to tell how criminals obtain weapons despite the drastic state law.

The committee planned to begin an inquiry on Monday into the source of weapons found in possession of revolutionists.

Police today sought to identify a bandit slain last night in an attempted robbery of a grocery at 6204 Irving Park Boulevard by the owner, August Maurin, 40 years old.

The killing of the bandit broke up a partnership of two gunmen who have committed more than fifty robberies on the northwest side in the last two months, according to the Irving Park police. The second bandit escaped last night.—(Chicago Daily News.)

A bounty on the lives of stickup men is the idea of Harry Hibbe, gun-toting druggist of 3658 North Pulaski Road, Chicago.

Mr. Hibbe, a slim man of 50 years, is still batting a thousand, with a record of having been held up eleven times in seven years. Several bullets have crashed through his modest shop during that time, netting two dead bandits and two wounded.

"That's one that missed me," remarked Mr. Hibbe today, pointing to a hole in the wall. "I have been lucky, but I do know how to handle a gun. Always have."

Recalling the last holdup in the place, only a month ago, Mr. Hibbe adjusted his glasses and said:

"He got away with a little money. But at least I have one to my credit. I killed him outright when he came in here seven years ago. Another one died on a hospital table.

"I received several threatening letters at the time, but I don't pay much attention to that kind of thing."

The druggist mixed himself a glass of soda water and resumed.

"I don't have any sympathy for people who will come into a man's place and take by force what he has earned. I never go to showups. Only if they (the stickup men) are being shown up on slabs. Easy money guys, that's what they are."

The homespun vigilante, who has spent all of his fifty years in Chicago, offered this advice to storekeepers who are bothered by the same type of customer:

"Keep a cool head. That's it. Brainwork and a cool head, a gun, and, well—nerve, and you have nothing to fear."

Mr. Hibbe added that when he owned a drug store at 3201 North Kedzie Avenue before 1915, "None of this stuff happened in those days."—(Chicago Daily News.)

Veteran of two previous shooting affrays with bandits, A. R. Collins, cashier of the Washington-Vineyard Street branch of the Bank of America, shot from the hip yesterday to wound and capture a gunman apparently intent on locking Collins and a coworker in a vault.

A bullet from the banker's pistol cut the bandit down as he sprinted for an exit as a patron interrupted the robbery which already had netted the man upward of $1,000.

It was reported that Merritt has a police record dating from 1927 and that he has served terms in the reformatories at Preston and Ione, being on parole from the latter institution at this time.

Banker Collins was instrumental in the capture of two bandits in 1932 when he wounded one and disabled their automobile with a rifle following a holdup. In 1933 he shot at and missed a lone bandit. And in 1923 six gunmen escaped with plunder following a robbery that included Collins as one of the victims.—(Los Angeles Times.)

Prosecutor Wachenfeld, speaking before the Newark Exchange Club January 23, blamed lack of federal legislation for the continuance of sales of firearms in New Jersey.

"There is a crying need for such legislation," Wachenfeld said. "I understand there is some strong lobbying by representatives of ammunition interests. After every crime conference the last three years resolutions were adopted and dispatched to Washington. But there was no result.

"The lack of legislation prohibiting mail order houses from sending guns here nullifies completely our efforts to check the sales of guns. If I need a gun all I have to do is sit down and write a check, mail it and Uncle Sam brings the gun to my very door."

Fortunately for Prosecutor Wachenfeld, none of his listeners arose to remind the lawyer that his "efforts" were not "completely nullified." Perhaps, like the prosecutor himself, everyone present was ignorant of the fact that there already exists a federal law forbidding shipment of pistols and revolvers thru the mails.

The career of Emmet "Three-fingered" Snyder, bandit, gunman and accused murderer of a southern Indiana deputy sheriff, was believed near an end Friday night in a Newport, Ky., hospital where Snyder was found in a corridor with a bullet hole through his body.

Detective William Holland of the Newport police, who is familiar with Snyder's record and who identified him Friday night, told The Courier-Journal he did not believe the bandit would recover.

Holland said he understood Snyder was shot during a holdup Friday morning at Dayton, Ohio, and believed he was brought to the Newport hospital by a confederate.—(Louisville (Ky.) Courier Journal.)

PEKIN, Ill. (Star) Feb. 20.—The expert marksmanship of 70-year-old George Slone, Sr., today had resulted in two bandits being wounded, one critically, after they had held up the Texaco filling station at Second Street and Broadway here last night.

Clark Tracy, 31, of Peoria, who is in the Pekin Hospital with bullet wounds in his spine and groin, and was reported to be near death, was sent to Joliet penitentiary April 26, 1930, from McLean County for burglary, police records show. He was sentenced to serve one year to life, but was paroled May 8, 1931, and later discharged as a parolee. He lived with his brother at 431 Meyer Avenue, Peoria.

HOW THE SULLIVAN LAW WORKS

Editor's Note: Here is a letter from an N. R. A. member in Brooklyn in which he wastes no words in pointing out how The Sullivan Law works. The letter:

It is with the greatest of difficulty that I restrain myself from cursing, roaring and tearing the roof off the building. I put in an application with the Police Department for a pistol permit and I have been refused. It took them two months to make up their minds to disapprove my application.

None of my references have been questioned. Nobody has been down to my office to see if I am Treasurer of a legitimate concern, they haven't tried to verify the fact that I have lived and worked in this neighborhood all my life. They just disapproved my application because I didn't smile in my pictures, I guess.

Gentlemen, I am calling for your aid. I am a legitimate business man in the finance business. I am a sportsman and have an inherent love for guns. I have won medals, been a member of the C. M. T. C. for two years, and I can handle a gun. I am treasurer of this company and it is my duty to handle large sums of money and deposit them at the end of the day. I have never been arrested in my life. I can submit an unlimited number of character witnesses as well as business references. My bank will vouch for my responsibility and personal and business integrity.

It is a ridiculous system of society which allows thieves to get all the pistols, gas bombs, machine guns, etc., with very little difficulty but stops an honest citizen from getting a pistol to protect himself and his interests from our modern highly organized crime.

You would almost think that criminal lords have such powers that they have issued instructions to the New York Police Department to refuse permits for pistols to all legitimate citizens, so that robbing will not be such a hazardous occupation. They'll soon be creating a *Society for Prevention of Cruelty to Thieves and Robbers,* here in New York.

1937

JANUARY 1937

We haven't a great many readers in South Africa but are wondering if perhaps the thief mentioned in the following article, taken from the *Washington Star,* has been reading our *Guns vs. Bandits* section of the RIFLEMAN:—

"After missing eggs from nests for several weeks, a farmer of Munro Bay, South Africa, found $2.50 in cash left in the coop by the thief."

Would-be bandits are often foiled when confronted by determined resistance. The case of Herbert Smith, a robber of Chicago, is a timely example. When confronted by a gun in the hand of Joseph Kiaud, during the process of rifling the till in Kiaud's place of business, Smith remembered the saying about a live coward and started to leave without asking permission. Kiaud opened fire putting the bandit in the hospital and saving the contents of his till.

When three bandits trussed up Michael Pascarello, after having kicked and beaten him into seeming submission, they proceeded to forget him—much to their later regret.

From his cramped position behind the counter Pascarello could see his safe being robbed of $2,000, and the bandits rummaging around for more.

He writhed furiously, finally freeing his hands, crawled from behind the counter until one hand reached his revolver. Ankles still bound he dragged himself upright and began shooting.

Wasting no time on ceremony the bandits dropped their guns and fled, one collapsing in the doorway, shot through the abdomen.

Pascarello hobbled to the street in time to obtain the license number of the bandit car and fired two more shots both of which proved ineffective.

Due to Pascarello's courage he saved $6,000.00 which the holdup artists failed to locate.

The captured bandit was identified as James Cummings, 34, whom police say has a prison record dating from 1922.

Mrs. Frances Franklin of Chicago for the second time proved that resistance to holdup men pays in her business.

A year ago her drug store at 5125 Division Street was the scene of an attempted holdup, during which Mrs. Franklin grabbed one of their guns and chased two robbers out of her store.

Last spring two gangsters entered her store again and after menacing her 19 year old clerk, started to clean out the till. Mrs. Franklin heard the commotion from behind her prescription counter, came out with her gun and again routed two would-be bandits, this time wounding one.

These Chicago bandits seem hard to convince but now perhaps they will leave Mrs. Franklin's store alone before she really hurts one of them.

As Walter Winchell would say, "an orchid" to Mrs. Margaret Toth and her husband, Police Officer Michael Toth of Chicago.

Officer Toth was shot three times when he threw himself between a bandit's gun and his fellow officer, Thomas Bourke, thereby doubtless saving a life.

Although convalescing from the recent birth of a son, Mrs. Toth gave three pints of blood to her husband in an effort to save his life.

Olaf Ohlson is waging a private war of his own against gangsters and holdup artists in Chicago. Five casualties in nine holdups are already on the books which seems to us a very creditable record for a one man army. The latest atttempt to turn Ohlson's drug store into a "stickup man's paradise" occurred a short time ago when three armed men entered the place and, after obtaining about $100, leisurely departed. Ohlson seized his gun and followed the bandits to the street where he fatally wounded one before the man could gain the getaway car.

What with having their clients sock them in the face, pull fake faints and otherwise behave in extremely unconventional fashion, bandits last night passed through a harrowing and fruitless evening.

Philip Menick, 301 K street northwest, was the first non-conformist encountered by the bandits. Four of them, two with drawn guns, invaded his store. Menick let fly a haymaker which caught one of the robbers on the jaw and caused his gun to explode. Completely unnerved, the bandits fled.

"I was so excited I forgot it was a holdup," apologetically explained Menick later.

Not a bit excited was Miss Edith M. Sandiland when a robber with drawn gun entered the cleaning store at 1426 Wisconsin avenue northwest, where she is employed.

"I just threw up my hands and pretended to faint. This scared the robber and he fled," she explained.

By this time word apparently had passed through the underworld that victims were in an unconventional mood and it was decided to sneak up on the next client. Miss Florence Cook, 23, 1445 N street northwest, was grabbed from behind by a man armed with a heavy stick. He attempted to snatch her purse. Screaming and kicking, Miss Cook refused to be robbed and the man fled.

Major Ernest W. Brown, Superintendent of Police, was only a few hundred yards from the store when Miss Sandiland was doing her bit to make life hard for a hold-up man. Had her report reached headquarters a little sooner the Major might easily have gotten in on the night's fun.—*Washington Post 11–18–36.*

James Claro of Brooklyn, New York, loses no time when he goes into action. John Messina and the customers of his bakery shop were being relieved of their cash a short time ago when Claro, who drives a truck for a flour concern, came from a back room, grasped the situation in a glance, drew his revolver and opened fire. Result—cash returned, one wounded bandit and another victory for an armed citizen.

Fred LaBelle of Saginaw, Michigan, is a man who believes in protecting his property so when three men attempted to hi-jack the LaBelle Tavern last September they found it tough going. As the men fled in their car with some of the tavern's equipment LaBelle opened fire with four shots, one of which proved fatal to Joseph Hoover, member of the gang, and a second shot wounded Herman Hollerbeck.

Two farm boys from near Allendale, Illinois, found farming poor training for bank robbers last summer when trying to turn a bit of "easy" money by robbing the local bank. Town vigilantes trapped both boys in a nearby alley and in a blaze of gunfire killed one outright and badly wounded the other. These vigilantes in the midwest are trained to shoot when necessary, as a result of which bank robbers seldom operate in that section.

THE ARMED CITIZEN

Neighbors had been complaining of a "Peeping Tom" so Officer John Hraha, of Chicago, left a revolver with his wife when going on duty one night last September. About midnight a man's face suddenly appeared in a window of the Hraha home. Mrs. Hraha opened fire and the man fled clutching his side as if wounded. The neighbors have stopped complaining.

FEBRUARY 1937

Cleveland, March 2 A P—Charles Hewett, 49, former Gloversville, N. Y., sharpshooter, finds his marksmanship effective in preventing holdups. Two armed men tried to hold up his store here yesterday. From a secret panel, Hewett produced a revolver, killed one, and said he believed he had wounded the other. Hewett has an expert rifleman's medal won when he was a member of Company G, Second Regiment, New York National Guard.—*Cleveland Plain Dealer.*

When the revolver with which Fred Wagner sought to resist four armed robbers misfired, his companion, Albert Ott, blazed away with a rifle and saved $700 which the two were taking to Wagner's tavern on North Halsted Street, Chicago. Wagner and Ott were driving from the bank when forced to the curb and stopped. As Wagner drew his gun, four armed men jumped from the other car. Wagner's gun failed and Ott, in the rear seat, picked up his rifle and opened fire on the bandits, who promptly fled.

Congratulations are in order for the plucky guard at the Campello branch of the Brockton National Bank who fought it out with bandits and successfully put them to rout. The courage of the guard is the more admirable because he is not a young man. However, when the hour for action arrived he proved himself more than a match for these swaggering bandits, and his nerve in "shooting it out" with them single-handed was splendid. A few more demonstrations of this sort will curb these bank holdups.—*Boston* (Mass.) *Post.*

A combination hard to beat in an emergency is quick thinking and quick shooting, as Mrs. Mary Wanamaker of Detroit, Michigan, proved. By speaking to her husband, as he appeared in the doorway during a holdup of her dress shop, she was able to distract attention of the armed bandit long enough to reach a .32 caliber revolver and fire several effective shots. Even though the man escaped capture, we doubt if he again bothers Mrs. Wanamaker's place of business.

For a good many years the authorities have been trying to discourage householders from keeping pistols in their homes.

The theory against promiscuous arming of the citizenry is that it leads to more accidents and more murders than anything else. Further, the authorities say, a householder who is surprised by an armed burglar hasn't a chance. Shooting it out is only a short cut to the cemetery.

All this is very good in theory, but in fact it has given a thoroughly armed underworld an enormous advantage over the rest of humanity. The affair which happened in Norwalk last night was a good example of the other side of the argument. William Clougher, chain store manager, was awakened by his wife who heard a prowler downstairs. Clougher took his pistol and went to investigate. He flashed a light down the stairs, and there stood a burglar.

The burglar aimed his gun and pulled the trigger several times. Clougher shot in return and the burglar fell. The first bullet had pierced the intruder's heart.

When the police came and examined the burglar's body this is what they found:

A .45 caliber automatic with 42 rounds of ammunition.

A six shot, .25 caliber revolver.

A five shot .32 caliber revolver.

A gold locket containing morphine.

A complete kit of burglar's tools including hack saw, jimmy, pass keys, and so forth.

Mr. Clougher deserves the hearty thanks of the community. As for the laws restricting the sale of weapons, here is a demonstration of their complete absurdity.

The burglars apparently haven't been told that it's against the law to be armed.—*Bridgeport* (Conn.) *Post*, December 16, 1936.

Peter Caudiano, a produce dealer in Gary, Indiana, was awakened one night last year by someone attempting to enter his home through a window.

Caudiano keeps a loaded revolver handy for such emergencies and so was not helpless to protect his home and family. He fired twice at the prowler who fled only to collapse after going a short ways.

The prowler later was identified as Frank Staples, whose wife told police he had been making many night trips away from home lately. From this information officers believe Staples to be responsible for a series of recent burglaries.

Tony Motzkis, night watchman of Kansas City, earned a pay increase and a new suit of clothes this summer when he shot and captured a burglar. James Fallek, owner of the store being burglarized, appreciated good work and so is increasing his "Burglary Insurance" cost this way. The burglar admitted seven prison sentences.

NOVEMBER 1937

Nation-wide publicity has recently been given a Midland, Mich., dentist, a member of a vigilante group in that place, whose marksmanship accounted for the death of one bandit and the wounding of another in an attempted holdup of the Midland Bank. This display of marksmanship on the part of a law-abiding citizen, whose right to possession of a gun fortunately had not been questioned as it might have been in some states, seems a timely illustration of the efficacy of the doctrine so long advocated by the N. R. A. Our Secretary, Mr. C. B. Lister, in congratulating Dr. Hardy on his commendable forethought and preparation for just such an emergency said: "I hope that you will accept the enclosed annual member's card in the National Rifle Association as a little token of appreciation from us for your work in proving that an honest citizen in possession of a gun and trained in its use is a valuable asset to any community."

Similar incidents of apprehension of unsuspecting criminals who are not prepared to meet the valor and confidence of a well trained citizen-gunman can be multiplied many times by a glance at most any metropolitan daily. That these incidents will become increasingly frequent is indicated in the tremendous increase in rifle and pistol marksmanship involving much practice and a familiarity with firearms. Dr. Hardy's opportunity to provide protection for his community came after years of training which was linked up with one of America's most attractive sports. Our RIFLEMAN readers, therefore, can heartily join with Mr. Lister in congratulating Dr. Hardy on his meeting of this emergency as a true rifleman. It is strangely coincident that Dr. Hardy, a Michigan man, should come along just at this time to back up Detroit Commissioner Pickard's statement "that if ninety percent of the citizens were armed and knew how to use their guns, banditry would stop."

APRIL 1938

Huntington Park's (Calif.) first soda-pop-bottle bandit met death in a fusillade from the revolver of his intended victim. Shortly after 9 p.m., M. E. Bartholomew, 55-year-old grocer, closed his store and started home. As he neared his home a man stepped into his path. "This is a holdup, come across," Bartholomew quoted the bandit as saying.

When he hesitated about giving up the store's receipts the man hit the grocer and felled him with a pop bottle. When the grocer hit the ground he reached for a revolver he carried and fired six times at the man standing over him. All shots took effect, killing the bandit instantly.

Two robbers held at the Town Hall station in Chicago were debating today whether a woman threatened isn't even more furious than a woman scorned. Their capture dated from the moment a police squad was notified to go to Belmont and Racine avenues and look for a woman carrying a revolver.

At the intersection the squad found Mrs. Lillian Tulley in full pursuit after two men. Mrs. Tulley was brandishing a gun and covering ground. So were the men. One of them even outran the squad, but the police picked up the other and took him to the station. There he identified himself as Louis McNevin who said he was paroled from the Stillwater (Minn.) prison after serving ten years for robbery.

Late in the evening the two bandits had entered the drug store operated by Mrs. Tulley and threatened her with an automatic pistol, seized the contents of the cash box and then fled.

Mrs. Tulley ordered one of her clerks to notify the police, then seized a revolver from a handy drawer and set out after the men.

1938

Sharpshooting Postmistress Kamp, of Mokomis, Ala., small wayside station southwest of Atmore, settled her two-year-old account with burglars when she riddled a bandit with her late husband's .45 revolver.

Two years ago her husband died of heart failure when he grabbed his gun and attempted to rout a burglar who had broken into the post office, located in the Kamp's general store.

About 3:30 a. m. Mrs. Kamp heard an intruder. She grabbed her gun and investigated. Before the intruder could escape the quick shooting postmistress had drilled him through the thigh. Brought to Brewton, the would-be burglar admitted he was wanted as a fugitive Atlanta jail breaker. The wounded prisoner admitted he and his wife had been arrested in Atlanta but that he recently escaped jail there.

Courage which sent him into a blazing building last December to rescue a cripple and receive the Meritorious Service Medal again sent Eugene Ferdinand Wemple, of Washington, D. C., on an heroic mission when he brought about the capture of a gunman.

For the second time within a little more than a week Wemple found himself staring into the muzzle of a revolver from behind the counter of a Sanitary Grocery Store of which he is manager. When the first holdup occurred Wemple missed his man. But this time with twelve customers and John Ownes, a clerk, cowering before the menacing revolver, Wemple waited for the intruder to scoop up the contents of the cash register and reach the door. Then he darted forward. Leaping on the running board of a cab, Wemple chased the robber until he finally cornered him when the gunman left the cab and dashed into a house. There, Wemple kept him imprisoned until police arrived. (*Washington Herald*.)

Confronted by two men while a third remained in the car, Arthur Walker, attendant at a filling station in Clifton Heights, Pa., was ordered to "Stick 'em up and give us the cash." Both pointed pistols at him.

Walker laughed: "You're too late, buddy, my brother just took the money down to the house. Look! I'll show you."

He opened the cash drawer, shoved $12.00 aside and grabbed an automatic. The bandit near the door fled while Walker cut loose at the other. One bullet plowed into his head as the second grazed his hand. The third thudded into his chest, and he fell head foremost through the door. His companions dragged him to the car and sped away.

The believed victim of Walker's daring, died of gunshot wounds later in the Fitzgerald-Mercy Hospital. With his death, police were questioning three other men, one of whom was identified by the attendant who seized a revolver instead of the cash in the register.

A youthful grocery store bandit was wounded one night and escaped only with the aid of his companion when the pair were met by a burst of gunfire from the revolver of an elderly Seattle grocer.

The grocer, Leander Benner, sixty-three, raised his revolver and fired as one of the gunmen covered him with a pistol.

One of the bandits entered Benner's store before 8 o'clock and loitered by the candy counter, buying a dime's worth of candy, the grocer said. A few moments later, the second bandit, brandishing a pistol, walked through the door, commanding: "Stick 'em up. This is a holdup."

The grocer did not look up. Instead he sidled toward the cash register where he kept his own revolver, he said.

"I grabbed it, raised it and fired. The fellow with the gun sort of staggered. I hit him in the chest, I think. He turned and the other fellow ran to him. Then they ran out of the store together," Benner related.

"I had that gun put there three years ago after another holdup. I said then nobody would ever get away with it again. If I hadn't had the gun, I don't think I'd have been much of a match for them." (Seattle (Wash.) *Post-Intelligencer.*)

MAY 1938

One bandit was shot to death and his companion was wounded in a gun battle with the owner and clerk of a liquor store at 5901 Irving Park Boulevard, Chicago.

The dead bandit was identified through finger prints as Joseph Massina, 2152 North Moody Avenue. His only police record was an arrest as a suspect in a murder case two years ago.

The owner of the store, Nicholous Schmidt, and his clerk, Karl Stutte, had pistols close at hand because of a number of bandit raids in the neighborhood.—*Chicago Tribune.*

What seems to be the classic case against the abuses of the drastic New York Sullivan Law is that of Joseph Olesky, 25, a cab driver in New York City. The New York World-Telegram in relating the story tells how Olesky found a loaded gun in the back of his cab after giving a ride to three men picked up on the lower east side. Upon the advice of his wife he turned the gun over to the police. As a result Olesky has spent sixteen days in the Tombs, has been convicted of violating the Sullivan Law, has been deprived of his hack license on the grounds that he has a "criminal record"; all because he turned over to the police a gun which accidentally came into his possession.

He finally found a judge that seemed to believe his story and who gave him a suspended sentence but when he asked for return of his hack license they told him he would have to find the man who owned the gun to clear himself of his "criminal record." So Olesky started out on a man hunt that was to take him six months, while his wife called in her mother to care for their two-year-old son, in the shabby tenement flat and got herself a job; uncomplainingly scrubbing floors from 3 to 8 in the morning, earning $9.00 a week. Olesky thought he would know the fellow if they met and he concentrated on the poolrooms, bars and other hangouts until he found his man. Now he is waiting hopefully for the return of his license so that he can go back to work.

A one-inch toy "watch fob" pistol, which has a miniature trigger and firing pin and which ejects a jet of flame when a small blank pellet is discharged, is a "dangerous weapon" and the Sullivan Law of New York has been invoked to protect against it. A clerk in Louis Tannen's novelty shop scratched her finger in demonstrating the gun to a customer and police investigating the "shooting" poured into his store to gravely confiscate the fourteen guns. Tannen was placed under $500.00 bail.

Charles Lindemeyer, 1241 West 31st Street, Chicago, Illinois, a drug store clerk, outwitted a robber and shot him to death after a holdup of the store at 7200 South Racine Avenue.

Lindemeyer told Englewood police he was alone in the store when the robber drew a gun and forced him into the basement. The clerk had a small automatic pistol in his pocket, he said, but prudently kept it there when the gunman had the drop on him. When he reached the basement, however, Lindemeyer drew his gun, ran out a back entrance, and confronted the bandit as he walked out of the front door with $8 of the store's money.

"Hands up," shouted the clerk.

The robber reached for his own revolver and Lindemeyer opened fire. Seven bullets struck the bandit and he was dead when police arrived.—*Chicago Tribune.*

Harry McCracken, 75, retired cowpuncher and range rider, lived again—for a brief interval—the days of 1870.

Hans Schmidt, 36, walked into the store owned by H. F. Albers at 3511 S. Broadway. Albers' wife, Mary Lou, stood behind the till.

"Come on, lady, hand over the cash," ordered Schmidt and at the same time he waved a gun at McCracken, who sat near the stove.

"Sit still and don't move," the holdup said to "Mac".

But Schmidt didn't reckon with the training that had been McCracken's. Men in his set never had been told to "sit still and don't move" while another man tried to rob the cash drawer.

"This might be 1934," said "Mac" to himself, "but this baby is going to learn some Western history—right now."

While Schmidt was scooping silver and currency into his pockets, McCracken dashed for the rear door. The gunman leveled his gun and pulled the trigger. There was only a click. He pulled the trigger

again. This time a bullet crashed through the door, missing the aged man's head.

In less time than it used to take Buffalo Bill to swing his leg over a saddle, "Mac" came out of the back room.

He came out shooting.

Armed with an old-fashioned revolver—older even than the community—McCracken fired once. He shot the gun from Schmidt's hand. Two fingers were seriously injured.

The holdup whirled around. "Mac" said he thought he was going to fire again.

"So I let him have another one. The bullet went clear through his shoulder."

Schmidt fled, dropping $30 as he wheeled through the door. He was soon captured.

Back in the liquor store, "Mac" was modestly explaining "it wasn't much."

"Back in the old days," he said, "we had a lot of trouble and more than once I have seen rough-necks dealt with by the gun. The law wasn't much in those days. We made it as we went along."—*Rocky Mountain* (Denver) *News.*

FEBRUARY 1939

Colonel Colt's appraisal of the revolver as the great equalizer was borne out recently in Boston, when 70 year old William J. Kennedy shot it out with three gunmen attempting to rob his grocery store. The armed trio entered Kennedy's store and announced, "This is a holdup." As one of the gunmen started toward the cash register, Kennedy suddenly whipped a gun from his pocket, and with the remark, "That's what you think," opened fire. Result: one bandit fatally wounded; no holdup.

Chicago's annual roll of hoodlums slain in the commission of crimes honors three private citizens whose bravery and quick thinking resulted in the deaths of an equal number of burglars or assailants. Stanley Slovik, bartender, after having been robbed by two men, followed them out of the tavern in which the robbery occurred, killed one of the pair. Hoyt Enox, 22 years old, was slain when he attempted to rob Luther Harper. Edgar Cary found Burdette Hancock tampering with a washing machine coin box in his basement, shot him when he resisted arrest. The total list includes twelve criminals and hoodlums slain by civilians or private watchmen.

Dr. Robert Lee Bradfield, druggist of Vienna, Virginia, was responsible for the capture of two men accused of kidnapping a Washington taxi-driver as well as attempting to rob his drug store. The Doctor shot one of the men in the leg in a rough-and-tumble with the burglars, which enabled police to nab the pair.

1939

An attempt by two young bandits to hold up Richard Henry's general store in Chestnut Level, Pennsylvania, broke up the village prayer meeting and brought out a militant citizenry, armed with everything from shotguns to clubs and pitchforks. The pair entered the store with drawn pistols. Disregarding the threats of the trio, Mr. Henry grasped his own pistol, shot one of the bandits. The other escaped both the rain of lead from Henry's pistol and the posse of villagers. When the posse returned they found Mr. Henry standing guard over the wounded man.

SEPTEMBER 1939

Two men wanted for questioning in Washington regarding recent robberies there, and in Baltimore for a pistol battle with railway officers, were captured when two Fredericksburg (Va.) policemen each fired a shot at their fleeing automobile. Both bullets took effect, one striking the rear tire, the other puncturing the gas tank. It later was found that the pair had forced a Washington driver at the point of a gun to drive them into Virginia. One was identified as having been convicted of armed highway robbery in Texas in 1935, when he had been given a five-year suspended sentence.

The accurate shooting of the local policemen was credited to recent target practice engaged in by the force.—Fredericksburg Free Lance-Star.

THE ARMED CITIZEN

Bullets fired by a straight-shooting deputy sheriff, son of a Glendale (Cal.) police officer, left a bandit suspect dead recently, another wounded, and a third in the county jail, and were credited with frustrating a cafe holdup. Deputy Manning, whose marksmanship wrote finis to another chapter of the "crime doesn't pay" story, was trained in pistol practice by his father, and often competes in pistol matches of the Glendale police department.—*Glendale News-Press.*

A Los Angeles liquor dealer, whose store had been the scene of two holdups and a double slaying, was waiting with a shotgun when a robber entered not long ago. The masked man, a .45 pistol in his hand, began looting the cash register. Proprietor Rex Sutton's shotgun roared. The robber was fatally wounded in the head. Said to resemble the thief who had once before held up Sutton's store, he may also have been the one who, several months before, shot and killed a clerk and customer during another raid on the same place.—*Glendale News-Press.*

Two Los Angeles bandits recently came to the end of criminal careers through the courage of L. T. Upton, manager of a local liquor store. The bandit pair entered the store late in the evening, and menacing the proprietor with the most feared of short-range weapons, a sawed-off shotgun, were handed the contents of the till. The two then made the fatal mistake of underrating their victim, who, as they turned to leave, seized a .38 caliber revolver and opened fire. Result: both of the men out of commission; two criminals "paying the price." A search of the room occupied by one of the bandits revealed assorted loot from several places robbed shortly before by the pair.—*Santa Monica Topics.*

NOVEMBER 1939

That a percentage of our newspapers, like some of our shortsighted, or rather, misinformed, legislators, are in favor of laws prohibiting the possession of firearms by Mr. John Citizen, has sometimes been all too painfully evident. Not all of our papers, however, subscribe to this fallacy of an unarmed citizenry being the best kind, as witness the following editorial from the Alhambra (Cal.) *Post-Advocate.*

"ONE LESS BANDIT—

"The other day a bandit in Los Angeles attempted the holdup of a man, shooting him in the process. After he opened fire, a nearby police officer did, too, with the result that there is one less bandit in the world. The intended holdup victim will recover.

"Crime statistics show that the great majority of criminals is composed of youths who lack judgment and are quick to pull the trigger. All too often there is no policeman near when they attempt their crimes.

"The result has been easy pickings for criminals, particularly in those areas whose government officials have been so misguided as to advocate laws against firearm ownership.

"Such laws—like the Sullivan law of New York—make crime safe for the criminal; for the criminal will have a gun anyhow—laws were just made to break in his opinion. Only the honest citizen is affected by such laws. The law that is needed is one requiring every head of a family to own a gun and have regular practice in its use."

Perhaps the most interesting feature of this is the fact that Alhambra is a suburb of Los Angeles, and Los Angeles, like Detroit, has succeeded in materially reducing the number of major crimes committed in the city, solely through the *reputation* of its police and civilian population. Banditry-at-large, and particularly the armed element of that gentry, *know* that the police force of that enlightened city, plus many business men, have guns and can use them to infinitely better advantage than can the bandit, though he may be as well armed.

Contrast this case history of a city prepared to deal with lawlessness effectively with an incident of another sort that occurred recently. The police of an Eastern city were setting a "trap" for a gang of service station robbers, and in the scuffle that ensued when the gang showed up a detective, formerly the chief of police of that city, was shot. This seems no more than another case of an heroic officer wounded in line of duty, until detectives had to admit that not one of the marauders was armed, and therefore, the detective undoubtedly was shot by one of his fellow cops. Even more interesting is that this former chief, during his tenure in that post, *failed to give the force under him any training in marksmanship.*

Through the unending efforts of those legislators and "just shooters" who do realize the value of an armed, prepared citizenry, and police officers whose guns are more than badges of office, public opinion is fast reaching the point that unwise anti-gun laws cannot be passed, and are in many cases influencing police forces to pay proper attention to marksmanship training for their officers as a splendid form of life insurance. But there is much to be done before *all* of our legislators will admit the value of these ideas. What we have to do is convince them—and it can be done, with such examples.

CHAPTER 5
"THE ARMED CITIZEN" IS BORN
1958 to 1977

SEPTEMBER 1958

Law enforcement officers cannot at all times be where they are needed to protect life or property in danger of serious violation. In many such instances the citizen has no choice but to defend himself with a gun. Below are accounts of recent instances digested from newspaper clippings sent in by NRA Members.

Suspicious of the 2 men who entered his store and asked for cold drinks, Frank Pattitoni of Detroit grabbed his rifle as he entered a large refrigerator. One bandit slammed the refrigerator door closed while the other struck an 85-year-old friend of Pattitoni's who tried to help. Pattitoni opened fire through a window of the big cooler, killing 1 of the 2 bandits who were looting the cash register. The other one escaped.

Four years ago, Pattitoni, now 69, received a Citizens Medal of Valor from the Detroit Police Dept., for killing 1 robber and wounding another. (June 24, AP)

When grocery-store-owner George Crawford, Stockton, Calif., was ordered by an armed bandit to 'hand over the money,' Crawford pushed the bandit's gun aside and pulled his own .38 from under his apron and fired 4 times. The bandit fell, mortally wounded.

This is Crawford's fourth encounter with armed robbers, and the second one that he has killed. (Feb. 3, UP)

Eva McMillan of Dallas, Tex., grabbed a .32 automatic when she saw a prowler in her yard. Pistol in hand, she went outside to investigate and the prowler lunged at her. Miss McMillan fired and he started to run. She fired twice more, ran inside, and called the police who found the wounded prowler cowering on a nearby porch. (May 29, AP)

Dr. P. W. Bowman of Washington, D. C. was awakened at 5 A.M. by cries for help from the home of a 91-year-old neighbor. The 69-year-old doctor leaped from his bed, grabbed his pistol, and reached the street just as an armed man was coming from the neighbor's house. He ordered the robber to drop his gun and held him at bay while his wife called police.

Upon investigation the police found the aged victim had been beaten and robbed. (Aug. 5, *Daily News*)

Mrs. Gladys Yesh of Gary, Ind., had been held up 5 times in her liquor store when she decided to get a gun. She purchased a .32 cal. revolver and then received instructions in its use from the Police Dept. On June 27 as she was about to close her store a man entered, asked for a bottle of whiskey, and instead of paying for it drew a gun and knocked Mrs. Yesh to the floor. Mrs. Yesh drew her gun and fired, killing the robber. (June 29, *Chicago Tribune*)

Walter J. Howe

OCTOBER 1958

Kenneth Dietz of Chicago operates a tavern in the first floor of an apartment building. A tenant called upon him to investigate shadowy movement in an apartment known to be rented by people who were away at the time. Dietz knocked on the apartment door and, when he received no answer, he opened the door with a pass key. As he entered, a figure swinging a tire iron lunged at Dietz who fired one shot from his .45 automatic pistol. The dead burglar was identified as an ex-convict with an arrest record. (*Chicago Tribune*)

A prowler who gained entrance to the second-floor porch of an East Side Cleveland home by using the roof of his car as a ladder, panicked when Phyllis Stewart, 14, saw him in her room and screamed. Her father, Donley Stewart, roused by the noise, grabbed his rifle and caught the fleeing intruder in the driveway. Stewart, 38, held the intruder at rifle point until the police arrived. (*Cleveland News*)

When 3 men entered his store—one of them armed with a revolver—and started coming over the counter after him, Anthony Regusa went for his gun. He came up firing and exchanged shots with the fleeing robbers. Regusa was certain that he had hit at least one of the robbers, and the police in searching found one of them dead in an alley behind the Kansas City, Mo., store where the holdup took place. (*Kansas City Star*)

After freeing himself from a washroom in which he had been locked by 2 robbers, grocer Charles DiMaggio, 54, grabbed a rifle and fired one shot at the fleeing pair. They split up, one of the robbers getting into a taxi. DiMaggio followed in another taxi and, when the robber's vehicle slowed down, the grocer leaped out of the taxi he was in, took aim, fired, and seriously wounded the robber. DiMaggio's grocery store on New York City's Lexington Avenue, was the scene of the holdup. (*New York News*)

A 57-year-old Stickney township, Ill., grandmother, Mrs. Vanda Jensen, always carries her .38 cal. pistol when she takes the day's receipts from her store to her car. On a recent evening as she walked towards her car a masked man rushed her, threw a blanket over her head, struck her several times, and knocked her to the ground. Mrs. Jensen fired once and the bandit fled. A short time later in a nearby hospital where she was being treated Mrs. Jensen saw a young man seeking treatment for a bullet wound. She told authorities who notified police. The bandit admitted the attack. (*Chicago American*)

DECEMBER 1958

Morris Pastor, a 79-year-old North Philadelphia tailor, grabbed a pistol from under the counter when a bandit menaced him with hand in pocket and demanded all his money. The would-be thug fled. (*Philadelphia Inquirer*)

A bandit entered the dry cleaning shop of Elmer Fetter of Columbus, Ohio, and said, "This is a stickup." The 71-year-old owner snatched a pistol from beside the cash register, poked it in his assailant's face, and sent him scrambling out the door. Fetter said all he owns is in the shop and the pistol by the cash register is there to protect it. (*Columbus Dispatch*)

A nighttime prowler broke into the Los Angeles home of Robert Howell and entered his daughter's bedroom. Her screams awakened the father, who rushed in with an automatic pistol. Police booked the intruder and questioned him about a series of 14 prowling and attack cases in the vicinity of the prowler's home. (*Los Angeles Times*)

Two holdup men entered Mrs. Sarah Waphen's delicatessen in Cincinnati and ordered her at gunpoint to put the money in a bag. Mrs. Waphen took a .32 automatic from her dress pocket and fired twice, sending them fleeing. The proprietress usually carries the pistol while in the store. (*Cincinnati Post-Times Star*)

When a burglar crept through a window of a bar-and-grill on Stage Gulch Rd. near Sonoma, Calif., he found a shotgun in the hands of proprietor Don Wagner pointed at his head. The burglar-conscious owner, who sleeps in his barroom to forestall such incidents, called the sheriff's office who discovered the prisoner was on bail pending trial on other criminal charges. (*Sonoma Index-Tribune*)

When Abraham Gordon, vice president of a Brooklyn check-cashing firm, arrived at 8:45 A.M. to open for business, a bandit jammed a gun in his back and demanded that the cashier's cage be opened. Gordon stalled with, "I can't open it until 9 o'clock when the boss comes." When boss Edward Kargman arrived at 8:55 A.M., he scanned the scene, dashed behind a partition, and whipped out his gun. The apprentice bandit, startled by this move, was then covered with a gun held by Gordon, whom he had not searched. (*Daily News*)

1959

JANUARY 1959

Grocer Bernard Frey of Buffalo, N. Y., thwarted his third holdup in 5 years by jerking out his own revolver when a bandit pointed a pistol and demanded money. The robber pleaded, "Don't shoot," dropped his gun, and fled the store. (*Evening News*)

For the third time in 14 months, W. M. Gibson captured burglars looting his employer's store at Acme, W. Va. Gibson shot one and held 2 others at gunpoint for the state troopers. He had previously trapped 2 burglarizing the store, and on another occasion grabbed 3 making off with goods of great value. (*Charleston Daily Mail*)

A paroled robber was shot and his 2 companions fled when Emanuel Johnson surprised them burglarizing his St. Louis cleaning shop. A single round from the owner's .45 cal. revolver felled the parolee, who later identified the co-conspirators for the police. (*Post-Dispatch*)

Arthur Hardwick, operator of a Buffalo, N. Y., liquor store, grabbed at his holster and dropped a suspected bandit with a single shoulder shot. The package store owner has a penchant for resisting robbers: in 1957 he held a thug and 2 companions at gunpoint until police arrived. (*Evening News*)

A fusillade from proprietor Albert Canton's licensed pistol greeted 2 gunmen when they attempted to rob his New York candy store. Blood spatter indicated hits on the fleeing thugs by the owner's 6 shots. (*World-Telegram*)

Joe Blonder, a Portland, Oreg., grocer, snatched his pistol from beside the cash register when a bandit menaced him with hand in pocket, demanding all the money. Police charged the would-be robber with assault and robbery by fear. (*Oregon Journal*)

A 16-year-old Dallas, Tex., schoolgirl, awakened by an intruder in her bedroom, fired a revolver and sent him flying through a closed window. The girl's mother then aimed and fired and later identified a suspect captured by the police. (*Texarkana Gazette*)

Ed Affhauser, 57, had never fired a gun in his life until a bandit entered his Longmeadow, Mass., liquor store and demanded the money. The merchant snatched a revolver from under the counter and fired, scoring twice. Police held the badly wounded gunman under hospital guard. (*Boston American*)

MARCH 1959

When 2 gunmen entered a Cleveland food store, they wheeled and fled the shop after walking into owner Sam Melluso and his pair of matched revolvers. Since suffering a $300 robbery a year ago, grocer Melluso keeps his guns handy. (*Cleveland Plain Dealer*)

Mrs. Mary Hines, running from the back room of her Wilmington, N. C., drive-in with pistol in hand after 2 men snatched the money from her cash register, held the robbers at bay until sheriff's deputies arrived.

As Shelby Friese counted the day's receipts, 2 armed bandits beat on the locked door of his father's Chicago gas station, shouting it was a stickup. The attendant grabbed his pistol and fired through the glass. One gunman dropped dead, shot through the chest; the fleeing accomplice and 2 other conspirators, the latter wanted by police for other robberies, were later rounded up. Friese said he kept his gun near him since the service station had been victimized twice before by robbers. (*Chicago Tribune*)

Kenneth E. Cottam, 21, slept in the rear of his Littlefield, Ariz., service station until awakened by a burglar in the office. The robber broke for the door when called upon to surrender and Cottam fired at the fleeing figure. Seconds later, the felon was captured at his getaway car and held for police. (*Kingman Mohave Miner*)

When the burglar alarm at the Miamitown, Ohio, Farmers State Bank sounded, Howard Gieringer and Wilbur Fagaly grabbed rifles and ran from their nearby stores in pursuit of 2 fleeing bandits. Reinforced by another citizen, Bruce Hawkins, they captured the bank-robbing pair in a getaway car on a dead-end street facing the Miami River. Police recovered $600 taken from the bank teller. The gunmen were both former felons, one of whom had recently completed a 10-year term in Ohio Penitentiary. (*Cincinnati Enquirer*)

George Crawford, a Stockton, Calif., market owner, deflected a bandit's pistol by striking his arm, then shot the gunman dead with a revolver carried under his grocer's apron. Crawford, who is never without his gun when in the store, has thwarted 3 previous robberies: in 1953 he wounded one holdup man, killed another in 1956, and sent a third fleeing in another robbery attempt the same year. (*AP*)

APRIL 1959

A convicted felon tried to hold up Chester Newton's gas station on the White Horse pike near Camden, N. J. Newton, holder of an NRA pistol classification, picked up his revolver from under papers on the counter near the cash register. The jittery bandit fired and fled the station. Newton, only slightly wounded through his heavy winter clothing, stood in the doorway and fired at the retreating gunman. Police found the bandit dead in the gutter, still clutching a cal. .32 revolver. (*Philadelphia Evening Bulletin*)

Robert Luden, who shoots with the Windsor, Ontario, Border Pistol Club, heard a prowler tinkering with the door of an upstairs apartment. Armed with one of his target pistols, he went to the stairs and called to the intruder to come out or be shot. One man emerged, to be held at gun point as 2 others scurried from the scene. (*Windsor, Ontario, Daily News*)

Ricco Bruce, proprietor of a lodge near Fowler, Calif., became suspicious when one man entered his bar and bought a drink while another waited outside in a car. Going to the rear of the lodge, Bruce loaded a shotgun he has kept since being robbed early last year and started toward the bar, only to meet the man from the car with a pistol in his hand. The bandit fired and missed. Bruce shot once and the bandit fell dead. The accomplice fled. The sheriff's office revealed the dead man was a parolee. (*The Fresno, Calif., Bee*)

John Skonoukos hooked up a homemade burglar alarm system from his Toledo, Ohio, restaurant to his home. When the alarm sounded, he grabbed a pistol and ran to his darkened restaurant where he shot a robber rifling the cash register. (*Toledo, Ohio, Blade*)

Paul Lewis, a Prichard, Ala., businessman, kept his cal. .38 pistol in his bedroom after his home had been the target of several recent burglary attempts. When Lewis awoke to hear tampering at the bedroom screen, he fired at the intruder. The burglar was struck 4 times as he climbed through the window. (*The Mobile, Ala., Press*)

Mrs. Barbara Chappo, a Gary, Ind., mother of 4 young children, was startled awake by a man pounding on the door demanding to be let in. When the stranger circled the house and tried to gain entrance from the rear, Mrs. Chappo got her husband's 12-ga. shotgun, loaded it, and fired through the floor. Reloading, she fired again toward the kicking and pounding intruder, the shot smashing through the glass pane. When police arrived, the intruder was dead. (*Chicago Daily News*)

Dale Leonard, 17, working in a Dayton, Ohio, pharmacy storeroom, saw 2 gunmen force his boss to lie on the floor while they rifled the register. By prearranged signal, Leonard alerted co-owner Mrs. Pauline Gleadell in her apartment at the rear. As the robbers emerged from the store, Mrs. Gleadell met them with her shotgun, wounded one, and held the other at bay until the police arrived. (*UPI*)

A burglar entering a Martins Ferry, Ohio, drive-in found George Connors, the night watchman, asleep on a cot and began beating him on the head with a tire iron. Though severely slashed, Connors grappled with his assailant and managed to draw his cal. .38 revolver. He fired 2 shots, killing the burglar instantly. (*Zanesville, Ohio, Signal*)

Bronx building superintendent Anthony De Oliviera fired a shotgun at a robber breaking into coin boxes of basement vending machines. Police took the felon, a known narcotics addict, to Bellevue Hospital prison ward and charged him with burglary and possession of burglar tools. (*New York Daily News*)

A robber, simulating gun in pocket, entered a Menlo Park, Calif., market and demanded "all the money in the till." When the clerk had cleaned $190 from one register, the bandit moved him over to a second machine and demanded its contents. At this point another grocery employee, Albert Franklin, Jr., who had armed himself with the company's cal. .38 revolver, attacked from the rear. Jerking the robber's hand from the gun pocket, Franklin trained his gun on him until police arrived. It was later discovered the hoodlum had a long record of arrests. (*Palo Alto, Calif., Times*)

Camden, N. J., auto dealer William G. Rohrer returned to his office in the late evening to pick up a package and saw an intruder dart from the room. Grabbing a pistol from the desk, Rohrer ran to the showroom floor and captured the burglar before he could make his escape. (*Camden, N. J., Times*)

A bandit attempting to rob a liquor store in Denver, Colo., yelled, "So you want to shoot it out!" when clerk Jack Diven reached for a gun. There was an exchange of shots and the bandit, shot in chest and wrist, staggered out the door and fell. He died 30 minutes later. Diven wounded a youth during a similar holdup attempt 2 months earlier. (*AP*)

JUNE 1959

After a series of break-ins of his gas station near Mooresville, N. C., Roy Bumgardner was sleeping in the place when 2 intruders removed an air conditioning unit to gain entrance. The station operator fired his cal. .38 revolver at the burglars, dropping one at the scene, the other fleeing with a leg wound only to be captured later by police. (*The Charlotte Observer*)

Johnny Williams was hired to stand guard in his uncle's Detroit restaurant last Christmas after the sixth break-in. Williams' nightly vigil paid off in April when he surprised 2 burglars in the restaurant and fired his shotgun over their heads. One fled; the other advanced and was killed with a single blast. (*Detroit Free Press*)

When all the customers had left the Fort Worth grocery and he had finished his soft drink, a young thug shoved proprietor W. H. Browne aside, brandished a pistol, and demanded that the store owner's wife empty the register. Browne pulled a cal. .38 pistol from under his belt and shot the gunman dead. (*The Fort Worth Press*)

Hope Crane opened fire with a cal. .22 pistol when burglars attempted to gain entry to his Atlanta store. Crane had returned to his place of business late in the evening and found evidence of theft. He fired at the burglars when they returned to come through the window for the second time. Four suspects were arrested with part of the loot, one requiring treatment for a bullet wound. (*Atlanta Journal*)

As Paul Smith was unlocking the door of his Fort Worth market, he felt a gun in his side. Smith whirled, knocked the gunman's hand askew, drew the cal. .38 revolver which he carries to and from his store and fired twice. The bandit fell and Smith turned and shot at an accomplice who came running at the sound of the firing. The wounded men fled to their car and were captured by police after a 90 m.p.h. chase. (*Fort Worth Star-Telegram*)

JULY 1959

A burglar who had spent 17 years in prisons for crimes in Ohio, Indiana, and Illinois, was killed robbing a restaurant near Lima, Ohio. Proprietor Lowell Tullis grabbed his rifle when the restaurant intercom alarm system aroused him in his nearby home. When the intruder balked at Tullis' demand for surrender, one shot ended a 25-year criminal career. (*The Lima Citizen*)

Held up 6 times in recent months and veteran of a recent gun battle with a bandit, Angelo Giangrosso again decided to shoot it out when an armed thug and a companion invaded his New Orleans liquor store. "I figured I had to," said Giangrosso. "He looked like he intended to kill me." In an exchange of shots, the gunman fell mortally wounded as his confederate fled. (*New Orleans Times-Picayune*)

Estquio Banayat, co-owner of a Sacramento, Calif., grocery, was sweeping the floor when a gunman entered and demanded the money. Partner Damaso Gumangan sensed trouble and emerged from the living quarters in the rear with a cal. .32 pistol. One shot from the bandit went wild and the grocer fired, hitting the gunman in the shoulder. Police arrested the felon. (*The Sacramento Bee*)

Albert Faller, a former Marine member of rifle and pistol teams, awoke when a burglar tampered with the bedroom door of his Pittsburgh home. Faller jumped out of bed with his cal. .32 pistol in hand and the intruder fled down the steps and out the front door. When the burglar failed to heed a call to halt, Faller leaned out the window and fired twice. Hit by both shots, the prowler staggered to the street and fell unconscious 2 blocks away. Police identified him as the "Cat Burglar" who, in 1949, pleaded guilty to 42 burglaries and was recently paroled after serving 10 years of a 20- to 40-year sentence. (*Pittsburgh Post-Gazette*)

When the customer pulled a gun after ordering a bottle of whisky, Dave Zusman drew his pistol from under the counter of his Kansas City, Kans., liquor store and fired 5 times. The critically wounded bandit fled to a getaway car with Zusman in pursuit and was captured by cruiser police after a shooting chase. (*The Kansas City Times*)

Three youths, free on bond while awaiting trial on 6 breaking and entering charges, were surprised by Sam Lovelace as they tried to burglarize his Shelby, N. C., service station. Lovelace fired one shotgun blast, killing one of the robbers. The fleeing accomplices were quickly picked up by the sheriff's office. (*Greensboro Daily News*)

A young thug who tried to rob the Grand Rapids, Mich., grocery of Albin Kuligowski fled when the proprietor pulled a cal. .38 pistol from his pocket and fired. Police took the bandit into custody at his home when he called them, confessed the crime, and pleaded for medical treatment of a gunshot wound. (*The Grand Rapids Press*)

Recently Eberhard Herz was tending his father-in-law's Los Angeles, Calif., store when 2 gunmen, armed with a Luger pistol and a sawed-off shotgun, entered. After making Herz empty the register, the bandits demanded whisky. Masking his movements as he put several bottles into a bag, Herz took a cal. .38 revolver from under the counter and shot at both bandits. One died instantly; the other fell critically wounded, shot in the forehead. Police said the bandits had staged 6 robberies in the past 36 hours and more than 100 in the past 3 months. (*Los Angeles Mirror News*)

Thwarting a holdup in Indianapolis, Ind., recently was liquor clerk Victor Sclipcea who reached under the counter for his revolver when a bandit entered brandishing a pistol. Sclipcea fired, critically wounding the gunman and bringing to 3 the number of would-be holdup men he has shot. (*The Indianapolis Times*)

A bandit pair entered Jack Swartz' San Francisco market, one pinning the proprietor's arms behind him as the other scooped money from the register. Swartz broke away and ran behind the counter for his cal. .38 revolver and fired a warning shot as the bandits fled the store. Though the confederate made his escape, Swartz' former captor stopped dead and was taken by police. (*San Francisco Examiner*)

James R. Pickett had closed his Baltimore tavern and retired to his living quarters upstairs when he heard a suspicious noise below. Pickett got his gun, found glass broken in the tavern door, and seized a burglar whom he held at gunpoint until police arrived. (*Baltimore Sun*)

In Tierra Amarilla, N. Mex., shopkeeper Albert Wheeler called on neighbor Jack Taylor to cover the front when the intercom alarm rang in the store owner's bedroom. Wheeler went to the rear office where he surprised an armed burglar who attempted to escape. Neighbor Taylor's 12-ga. shotgun dropped him near the door. (*The Santa Fe New Mexican*)

A stick-up man was shot dead when Chicago grocer Jessie Thomas wrestled him to the floor, Thomas drawing and firing his pistol in the struggle. The slain bandit's rifle-bearing accomplice fled the store. (*Chicago Daily Tribune*)

THE ARMED CITIZEN

AUGUST 1959

Josephine Morreale shouted to husband Domenick who was in the back room of their Irwindale, Calif., liquor store when 2 bandits entered and demanded the money. One gunman ran to the back, pistol-whipped the proprietor, fired one wild shot, and fled with his companion. Morreale, knocked to the floor, fired 3 times. Sheriff's men found one critically wounded bandit bleeding in a clump of bushes outside the store, arrested the accomplice near the crime scene. (*Los Angeles Herald Express*)

In Huntington Park, Calif., liquor store proprietor Ray Glass did as he was told when one of 3 bandits pointed a Luger pistol and forced him to lie on the floor. After cleaning out the register, the bandits made for their getaway car, arms filled with 6-packs of beer and bottles of whisky. As they stowed away the loot, Glass found his revolver and ran outside to fire at the bandits who rushed to get in the car. Two made it, but the gunman with the Luger ran alongside the moving car, tried frantically to get in, then slipped and fell to the street, his gun skittering along the pavement. Glass held him at gunpoint for police. Detectives soon picked up the accomplices and found Los Angeles police wanted the trio also for a previous robbery. (*Daily Signal*)

Martin Marchello was aroused from bed in the rear of his Los Angeles liquor store by the crash of a display window. Seizing a rifle, Marchello ran to the front and fired at a burglar passing bottles out to his 2 accomplices. The burglar dropped, critically wounded, as his partners fled. (*Los Angeles Examiner*)

Teddy Jett of Borger, Tex., was friendly to 2 young hitchhikers he had picked up until the one in the back seat struck him on the head with a steel rod. Jett slammed on the brakes, grabbed his pistol from under the seat, and disarmed his assailant. Then, with blood spilling down his face, he drove them at gunpoint into nearby Vega and turned them over to the sheriff. (*The Amarillo Daily News*)

When Ray Bandle drove by his Las Vegas garage, he spied a light in the closed office. Slipping quietly into the building, Bandle trapped a burglar and held him at gunpoint until police arrived. (*Las Vegas Review-Journal*)

OCTOBER 1959

Four months ago Paul R. Guenin shot a burglar in his New Orleans grocery. Again plagued by a series of break-ins, Guenin began sleeping in the back room of the place. When he awakened to the sound of stealthy intruders, he tried the connecting door, found it locked, and went out the back to surprise 2 thieves piling loot into cartons. Guenin fired through the window and shot one, the other escaping into the night. (*New Orleans States-Item*)

Leonard Conwell and son Robert had just closed their Bear Creek, Pa., restaurant when a car pulled up. Victimized by vandalism and 6 burglaries in recent months, the Conwells quietly watched 4 youths get out and go to the rear. When the burglars smashed the glass in the door, the father opened fire with a cal. .22 rifle. The trio fled to their companion in the getaway car. The Conwells gave chase in their car and captured 2 who required treatment for bullet wounds. The 2 who escaped were rounded up by police when they were identified by the wounded confederates. (*Wilkes-Barre Times-Leader*)

John Paul, who lives in a basement apartment below his St. Paul, Minn., furniture store, heard intruders' footsteps and got his cal. .38 revolver. In the dim glow of a street light, Paul saw 2 burglars and fired several shots at them. One dropped at the scene, critically wounded; the other smashed through the window but was later captured at his home. (*The Minneapolis Star*)

Dominick Litz, watchman for a Miami, Fla., sausage company, investigated with drawn pistol when he heard a noise in the plant. Litz surprised a burglar descending a stairway and fired one shot when the intruder kept coming on. Police described the dead man as a felon with a 3-page criminal record. (*The Miami News*)

An ex-convict with a fresh bullet wound from a previous robbery attempt was killed by the owner of a Portland, Oreg., drive-in as he chopped his way into the restaurant with a hatchet. Proprietor Phil Anderson, awakened in his nearby home, sped to the restaurant with gun in hand. When Anderson entered, the burglar struck him on the arm with the hatchet and fled. Anderson shot him dead just as he reached the highway. (*The Oregonian*)

NOVEMBER 1959

After his father-in-law was killed by a bandit in his Oakland, Calif., liquor store, Forrest Norman Anderson became the proprietor and bought a cal. .38 pistol for protection. When a gunman entered the store and announced a stickup, Anderson emptied the cash register's contents into the paper sack and waited until the bandit left the store. As Anderson grabbed for his pistol under the counter, the gunman glanced back, returned to the store door and raised his pistol. Anderson fired 6 times and the bandit fell dead without firing a shot. (*Oakland Tribune*)

Two youths who confessed to 6 jewelry store burglaries were captured at gunpoint by bartender James O'Brien when they switched targets by breaking into a Coram, N. Y., saloon. O'Brien slept in a room off the bar and grabbed a rifle when the burglars entered. The bartender held one at bay and the fleeing accomplice was captured by police near the getaway car. (*New York Daily News*)

When 2 armed paroled felons invaded a Shreveport, La., grocery and herded 4 employees and a customer into the cold storage box, proprietor Charles Whorton protested. One thug, who had already threatened the employees, thereupon fired a wild shot at the floor, striking Whorton in the ankle. At this point, 16-year-old Louis (Bubba) Hoffman, the store helper, struck the bandit on the head with a soda bottle, smashing him unconscious to the floor. During this struggle proprietor Whorton's brother Larry ran to a neighbor, borrowed a cal. .38 revolver and returned in time to fire at the second bandit running for the getaway car. The bandit fell, critically wounded. (*Shreveport Times*)

After the fourth robbery of their Judson, Minn., implement company, Harvey Rengsdorf and Edwin Fischer went on the alert. From his nearby home Rengsdorf noted prowlers, got his shotgun, phoned the sheriff, and ran to the store with partner Fischer. Two youths inside were preparing to rob the safe while a third sat in a nearby getaway car. When one left the store to get burglar tools and failed to heed a warning to stop, Rengsdorf fired his shotgun. Wounded by the pellets, the felon made it to the getaway car and escaped. The abandoned accomplice, though armed with a pistol, yielded to Rengsdorf's threatening shotgun and informed on his confederates. Police picked them up at their homes. (*New Ulm Daily Journal*)

When burglars stole many valuable tools from Clyde Inman's garage in San Bernardino, Calif., the proprietor began sleeping in the place. Inman was recently awakened by 2 tire thieves who turned to run when the owner flicked on the lights. Inman grabbed his rifle and fired, killing one burglar just outside the garage. The accomplice and the driver of the getaway car were caught by police near the crime scene. (*San Bernardino Daily Sun*)

J. W. Baxter, Oklahoma City grocer, reached under the counter for his gun when an armed bandit told Mrs. Baxter to hand over the money. Two shots sent the holdup man fleeing empty-handed. (*The Daily Oklahoman*)

Virgil Ruskin got out of bed and returned to his Columbus, Ohio, restaurant on a hunch that the place might be burglarized. The restaurant had been broken into 3 times in recent weeks so Ruskin, armed with a cal. .45 pistol, hid inside until an intruder broke in through a window. The proprietor fired one shot and the burglar meekly surrendered. (*The Columbus Citizen*)

Two gunmen kidnapped an Eclectic, Ala., town policeman and used the officer to gain admittance to the home of Carl Ray Barker in the early morning hours. Barker, an Eclectic banker, was taken by one gunman into town to open the bank's vault, his wife, child, and the town policeman being held hostage by the armed companion pending a safe return from the bank. When the time-vault resisted opening, the gunman returned Barker to his house and, after some debate, took the policeman away with him to get tape for binding all hostages until morning, when another attempt was to be made on the vault. Barker, now held in his home with wife and child by the second armed man, asked if he could make coffee. The robber assented and Barker put water on the stove and got it boiling. "I took the scalding water to the living room," said Barker. "When he held his cup, I just poured the water in his face and grabbed his gun." Barker pistol-whipped the robber into submission, loaded a shotgun and waited for the return of the other bandit. When the door opened, the captive policeman dived out of the way and Barker killed the would-be bank robber with 2 blasts. Barker said he feared for his family's safety and, "I didn't want my bank to get a bad name about being robbed." (*UPI*)

FEBRUARY 1960

Odell Teague was on the way to open his Cleveland cafe when he saw 2 burglars hauling cases of whisky through the smashed window of a state dispensary. When the robbers said, "Beat it; this is none of your business," Teague drew the revolver he began carrying after 2 holdups of his place and held the thieves until police arrived. (*UPI*)

In 1956 a bandit who robbed Decatur, Ill., liquor clerk James W. Miller of $1052 was captured 3 days later and sentenced to prison. Recently paroled from his 20-year term, the bandit returned to the Decatur store with drawn pistol and again announced a stickup. Miller, unrecognized by his old assailant, dropped to the floor and came up firing a cal. .32 pistol, felling the paroled felon with 4 bullet wounds. (*The Review*)

As Roman Kosinski, a Chicago jeweler whose avocation is target shooting, waited on customers he heard window glass crash and saw a masked man grab a tray of diamond rings. Kosinski snatched a cal. .45 pistol from a drawer and fired. The thief fell to the ground and his 2 companions hustled him to a getaway car. Police soon found the car and arrested a suspect with a bullet wound, the slug later established by police to have been fired from Kosinski's pistol. (*Chicago Sun-Times*)

In 18 years of operating his Chicago tavern, John Fahey has killed 3 bandits and wounded 5 others. The 70-year-old saloonkeeper thwarted a recent holdup by grabbing a 1917 Colt revolver, one of 6 guns he keeps in hidden spots behind the bar, and shooting a would-be robber who came in at closing time and said, "This is a stickup!" (*Chicago Sun-Times*)

1960

In Saraland, Ala., the berserk husband of a woman charged with possession of illegal whisky killed one police officer and wounded another but, as he tried to make his escape, was shot dead by Carlos McDonald, the proprietor of a nearby shop. (*UPI*)

After buying $2 worth of gas at a service station near Bowie, Md., the customer pointed a gun at attendant Gilbert Roy Gertz and said, "Give me what you've got in your pocket." Gertz reached in, pulled out a cal. .25 pistol, and killed the bandit with a single shot. (*The Washington Daily News*)

MAY 1960

When 2 bandits said, "It's a stickup; everybody stay put," Los Angeles jewelry clerk Kenneth Walton lunged for the cal. .38 revolver he keeps handy on top of the safe. One bandit scuffled with Walton, bit him on the arm, and Walton fired 3 times. The robber fell with a bullet in his heart and the accomplice fled during the melee. (*Los Angeles Times*)

Chicago jeweler William S. Kraicek, suspicious of the stranger who entered his shop, quietly removed his pistol from a drawer behind the counter. When the stranger pulled a cal. .32 pistol and announced a stickup, Kraicek fired 3 times. The bandit, an ex-convict, was taken to hospital and pronounced dead on arrival. (*Chicago American*)

When a robber attacked him in the darkness of his back yard, Bruce Haughey mounted lights on the garage behind his Topeka, Kans., home and secreted a cal. .38 pistol to carry on the walk to the house. Recently, home from work, Haughey put the car in the garage, got his pistol, and emerged into the yard to be met by 2 robbers. Haughey fired, wounding one of the felons with 2 bullets as the confederate fled. (*Topeka State Journal*)

Sixty-year-old George Saddic managed to reach his cal. .38 revolver and fire 2 shots at his assailants just before collapsing in his Philadelphia candy store from an assault by 3 bandits. When police responded to a report of gunfire, they found a suspect lying on the sidewalk near the candy store, a paralyzing bullet wound in his back. (*Philadelphia News*)

In St. Catharines, Ont., Mrs. J. C. R. Fitzgerald, a widow in her 80's, refused when a burglar broke into her bedroom and demanded her jewelry. Instead, Mrs. Fitzgerald reached for her cal. .38 revolver in the shoebag hanging on the door near her bed. The burglar tried to wrest the gun away, the widow fired, and the would-be jewel thief fled the house. "The last time I remember firing it was many, many, years ago," said Mrs. Fitzgerald, "but my gardener has kept it cleaned and loaded for me." (*Buffalo Courier-Express*)

Bartender Curtis H. Scott closed his East St. Louis, Ill., tavern for the night, walked past the nearby alley, and was accosted by 2 robbers who forced him at gunpoint to return to the saloon. Pushing the bartender inside, the bandits grabbed the cash box containing $823 and were about to leave when the burglar alarm went off. Scott pulled his cal. .32 revolver and fired, the panicky bandits abandoning the loot in their haste to reach the getaway car. They made good their escape but 2 surrendered to police shortly after dropping off their bullet-wounded companion at a hospital. (*St. Louis Post-Dispatch*)

Two men bought soft drinks in Cecil Saunders' York County, Va., general store, shot him in the knee with a cal. .22 pistol, then demanded all the cash. The storekeeper gave them over $400 in bills and the bandits fled to their car. Saunders grabbed his cal. .38 revolver and hobbled to the door, firing at the running felons. Police found the car and the bandits parked a few miles down the road, both occupants bleeding from lung and groin wounds. (*Newport News Daily Press*)

In New York City's theatrical district, actor Jay Scott awakened in his apartment and saw a burglar on a fire escape opening the window of a nearby flat. Scott tried to telephone police, but gave up when he heard a woman scream as the intruder entered her apartment. The man fled in panic, burst into the hall, and entered the next apartment where more female screams caused him to flee to the scene of his original entry. As he climbed back out the window, actor Scott, in his apartment window, fired one shot from a hunting rifle. Felled with a leg wound, the intruder was taken by police on the fire escape landing. (*New York Journal-American*)

In Fort Fairfield, Maine, Mrs. Otis Flannery woke her husband, grabbed a Luger pistol, and ran across the road to their store where they surprised 2 burglars. Mrs. Flannery forced the pair to lie at gunpoint on the floor and held them until a policeman arrived to take them to jail. Then Mrs. Flannery discovered 2 accomplices at the nearby getaway car. They fled at her approach but halted when she fired the Luger at them. Mrs. Flannery held the gun on her prisoners and called police again. (*Fort Fairfield Review*)

In Chattanooga, Tenn., ham radio operator George Zarzour had just retired when he heard someone tampering at the window. With the crash of glass, George, now joined by brother Abe who had been sleeping, armed himself with a cal. .38 revolver and gave another to Abe. When the burglar reached through and opened the window, George slipped through the door to the street, flicked on the outside light, and fired at the figure inching in. The would-be burglar fled into the night, collapsed 2 blocks away, and died while undergoing surgery for 3 bullet wounds. (*Chattanooga News-Free Press*)

JUNE 1960

Frank Guido was in the back of his Bronx liquor store when 2 bandits brandishing guns herded his clerk to the rear. Guido picked up his cal. .38 revolver from a shelf, tucked it in the belt under his sweater, and awaited the gunmen. "These bums told the clerk and me to lie on the floor," said Guido. "Then one of them said, 'Get up and open the register!'" Guido got up, pulled his gun, and started firing. He hit both thieves in the head. (*New York Daily News*)

As the intercom burglar alarm sounded, Wes Johnson jumped from bed, grabbed a ready cal. .45 pistol and 12-ga. shotgun, and hurried to his nearby Deeth, Nev., tavern. There Johnson found 2 women seated in a getaway car while their male companions pillaged the saloon. Johnson herded the women from the car and fired his pistol through the window at the thieves. The 2 burglars fled through the front door together, and Johnson finally brought both men down with buckshot from his shotgun. (*Elko Daily Free Press*)

Sixteen-year-old John Rubel was with his grandmother in the living quarters over her Chicago tavern when they heard glass break in a window below. John raced downstairs, grabbed the cal. .32 revolver behind the bar, and pointed it at a man climbing in the window. "You're too young to use that gun," said the burglar, and John fired, the burglar tumbling out the window and fleeing the scene. Police soon arrested a suspect with a bullet wound in his shoulder. (*Chicago Daily Tribune*)

After calling the sheriff to report 2 suspicious men sitting in a car near his Pharisburg, Ohio, grocery and gas stop, Stanley Rhoades resumed the business of putting stock in order. Moments later 2 masked gunmen entered and Rhoades dropped behind the counter and reached for his cal. .22 pistol. One gunman, crouched near the floor, inched down the aisle towards Rhoades. As he rounded a display case, the grocer shot him in the head. Rhoades then crept after the second gunman, who fired at him and ran to the door. Rhoades stood up, took careful aim, shot again, and wounded the bandit in the shoulder. After tugging frantically at the door with his remaining good arm, the felon turned and surrendered. (*The Marion Star*)

AUGUST 1960

When a bandit with a record of arrests on narcotics charges pointed a pistol and said, "Give!", Manhattan grocer Victor Comacho nodded, reached under the counter, and came up clutching his pistol. Comacho fired and the bandit fell to the floor with a bullet in his head. When police arrived, they charged grocer Comacho with homicide and violation of the Sullivan Law in having an unlicensed pistol. (*New York Journal-American*)

In Columbus, Ga., Mrs. Thelma D. Lee, a mother of 5 small children, awoke to see an intruder at her bedside. Mrs. Lee, whose husband must work at night, eased a cal. .22 revolver from under her pillow and fired. The intruder fled to another room and Mrs. Lee fired at him again. Police found his body face down nearby. (AP)

Joseph A. Marino had just left his New Orleans pharmacy and gotten in his automobile when a thug grabbed the car door, pointed a pistol at Marino, and said, "Yeah, it's me again." The pharmacist, recognizing the bandit as one who had recently held him up, seized his cal. .38 pistol resting on the seat and fired 5 times. The gunman fled into the night. When police and Marino later were called to a hospital where a bullet-wounded man sought aid, Marino identified him as his 2-time assailant and the police recognized him as a fugitive with a record of 28 arrests. (*The Times-Picayune*)

After burglars looted his Ford, Wash., store the ninth time, 83-year-old A. L. Davis slept in the place armed with a cal. .38 revolver. Recently, when Davis heard sounds of a break in, he hurried to the front and critically wounded a youthful burglar with one shot. Inside the walk-in beer cooler, Davis caught 2 others, one of whom had just been released after serving a sentence for burglarizing the same store. (*Spokane Daily Chronicle*)

Shortly before midnight 2 men roused Oscar Gruter in his Santa Clara, Calif., motel and asked for a room. Suddenly, one of them grabbed Gruter by the throat and the companion headed for the adjacent bedroom. Hearing the melee, Gruter's wife, Johanna Marie, left the bed, grabbed a cal. .38 revolver, and met the intruder. The bandit lunged at her, she fired, and he fled with a bullet through his hand and chest. Johanna Marie then came to her husband's call for help and killed the bandit with 2 shots. (*San Jose News*)

NOVEMBER 1960

In October 1958 THE RIFLEMAN reported Charles Di Maggio's wounding of a robber after a taxicab chase in New York City. Again, for his 12th success in the last 15 years, Mr. Di Maggio caught a thief. The East Side delicatessen owner foiled the latest bandit when he let the armed man rob the till and flee out the front door. Then, following the pattern of the past, Di Maggio grabbed his rifle, ran to the street, and fired 2 warning rounds over the fugitive's head. Alerted by the shots, a patrolman arrived and the frightened felon fell into his arms. (*New York Journal-American*)

James Cummins of Cincinnati heard noises in his adjacent cafe and ran from his home with shotgun in hand to investigate. When a burglar ran out, Cummins called on him to halt, then felled the escaping thief with 2 barrels. (*Cincinnati Enquirer*)

After 5 years of operating his Monahans, Tex., liquor store, Charlie Key met his first holdup man, shot him twice with a cal. .38 pistol, and held him for police. The shotgun-armed bandit had herded Key and a customer to the rear to tie them up when Charlie grabbed his pistol from under the counter and fired. (*Odessa American*)

Tormented by burglaries of his Seiling, Okla., cafe, Floyd Hansen slept in the back room, hoping to catch the thieves. When he awakened to sounds of breaking and entering, Hansen crept to the front and fired his pistol at prowlers inside the restaurant. Both burglars scrambled out a window and died nearby from the cal. .45 wounds. (*Stillwater News-Press*)

NRA instructor Herbert J. Crook, resident care-taker of a Hazel Park, Mich., out-patient clinic, awoke to spy an intruder in the hall. When the burglar jumped at him, Crook fired one shot from his cal. .38 revolver and killed him. Police revealed the felon to be a parole violator with a 20-year criminal career which started when he was only 5. (*Detroit Free Press*)

Maintaining a vigil in his Austin, Tex., grocery after a series of break-ins, Hale Hornsby surprised a burglar and shot him in the arm with a cal. .45 pistol. The wounded man, a 4-time penitentiary inmate, was taken by police. (*Austin Statesman*)

Distaff citizens recently have armed themselves and figured in arrests of felons. In Portland, Oreg., Mrs. Frankie D. Williams trained her gun on a burglar in her tavern and held him for police, and in Jasper, Tenn., Mrs. Gene Taylor shot a burglar with a cal. .32 double-barrel derringer, while in Romulus, Mich., a 14-year-old girl fired a 12-ga. shotgun at a gang of hoodlums who attempted to force their way into her home. (*Oregon Journal, AP, Detroit Times*)

Dr. Samuel M. Rosenbaum sat in his Philadelphia office when an armed man burst in and demanded money. When the doctor tried to talk him out of the holdup, the robber pistol-whipped him to the floor. Dr. Rosenbaum, who carries a revolver for protection, pulled his cal. .38 and fired. The bandit fled with a bullet in his leg and the doctor called police. An alerted patrolman picked up the wounded felon when he panicked after seeking aid from another doctor. When the holdup man was brought to trial and sentenced to a 3-to-10-year prison term, Judge Theodore L. Reimel said, ''I want to compliment you, doctor. If we had more men like you, there would be fewer crimes committed in our streets.'' (*Philadelphia Bulletin*)

Three young East St. Louis, Ill., armed men, plotting a robbery, drove to Ulles Akins' grocery ''because it looked easy.'' While one stayed near the getaway car, 2 donned masks, entered the store, and pulled a gun on the proprietor. Akins dived behind the counter and came up firing his cal. .38 revolver. Police found one man dead on the floor. (*East St. Louis Journal*)

Alarmed by a series of burglaries in the vicinity, Alfred L. Davis lay in wait for the fifth night in his Laclede, Mo., store when a plate glass crashed and 2 burglars entered. Davis fired at one figure silhouetted in the doorway, the blast killing the intruder instantly. Police arrived to take the dead man's accomplice into custody, later tracing 3 earlier burglaries to the pair. (*Brookfield News Bulletin*)

Delos Badgero, 65, a handy man for a Linden, Mich., auto agency, sleeps in the place with his double-barrel shotgun nearby. In the past, Badgero has thwarted many acts of vandalism and burglary. Recently, Badgero was again awakened by burglars. This time he critically wounded one with a single blast and held the other at bay until police arrived. (*Detroit Free Press*)

1961

MARCH 1961

After beating and kicking 61-year-old Benjamin Bailer in his Philadelphia tavern, 3 bandits cleaned out the register and sauntered to the door. Bailer crawled to a shelf where he kept his cal. .38 revolver, fired at his tormentors, then got to his feet and began a pursuit. He found one of the men dead in the street a short distance away and abandoned the chase to have his own wounds dressed. (*Philadelphia Bulletin*)

In Arjay, Ky., general store owner Curt Mills was shot in the shoulder by one of 2 masked bandits who fled when Mills grabbed for his pistol. Before they could make their getaway, however, Mills killed the one who shot him and wounded the other. (*Lexington Leader*)

An ex-convict entered a St. Louis dry goods store, struck owner Clarence E. Skala on the head with a brick-filled sack, and bound and gagged him. After looting the store, the felon left and Skala freed himself. Picking up his cal. .25 pistol Skala ran to the door where he met the bandit who had stopped his flight and returned to the store. Skala fired twice; the bandit dropped his loot and fled with a bullet in his stomach. Dogs from the canine corps soon traced the wounded man. (*St. Louis Post-Dispatch*)

After a rash of drug store holdups by armed thugs who pistol-whipped several of their victims, Montreal pharmacist Wilfred Gagnon kept his cal. .38 revolver handy. When 2 men entered, one brandishing a gun, Gagnon let them clean out the register, then shot the armed man dead as the pair fled the store. (*Toronto Daily Star*)

Pete Smith, wearied by a series of burglaries that were "picking him clean," began sleeping in his Rockingham, N. C., grill. About 3:30 A.M. Smith heard tampering at the door and, at the sound of a break-in, fired his cal. .22 rifle at the intruder. The burglar died instantly. (*Charlotte Observer*)

After 14 burglaries in 12 years, Fred Williamson set a burglar alarm in his Indianapolis restaurant and rigged it to ring in his nearby home. When the alarm recently sounded, Williamson took his 12-ga. shotgun and got to the restaurant in time to kill a fleeing burglar. (*AP*)

APRIL 1961

Two bandits menaced 25 patrons in a Denver bar when the tavern owner, James V. LaBriola, burst from the back room with his cal. .25 pistol. LaBriola felled one bandit who was looting the cash register, then shot the confederate who was holding the customers against the wall. (*Denver Post*)

After 4 burglaries in as many weeks, John T. Craig set a burglar alarm in his Munford, Tenn., restaurant and waited in his nearby home with a 12-ga. autoloading shotgun at hand. When burglars struck again and the alarm sounded, Craig dashed to the restaurant and fired at 3 burglars. One fell, too badly wounded to join his pellet-riddled companions who fled, only to be apprehended when a confederate in the getaway car abandoned them. Police completed the roundup with the arrest of the driver, the only one not shot by Craig. (*Memphis Commercial Appeal*)

When the customer at the counter in Mrs. Daisy Parker's Philadelphia luncheonette menaced her with hand in pocket and announced a stickup, Mrs. Parker edged away, grabbed her cal. .32 revolver from under the counter, and came up firing. Three shots sent the bandit lurching out the door. After picking him up, police closed a second case when another robbery victim identified him. (*Philadelphia Bulletin*)

St. Louis sundry store owner Charles Brown was bound by 3 armed bandits and thrown into a rear room. Brown freed himself in time to seize his hidden cal. .45 pistol and open fire on the fleeing trio. One dropped critically wounded, and police quickly caught the others. (*St. Louis Globe-Democrat*)

Three stocking-masked bandits herded Baltimore pharmacist Joseph Freiman to his narcotics supply, divided the drugs, and turned to clean out the till. Mr. Freiman grabbed the cal. .38 pistol he had previously secreted in case of a holdup, shot one bandit dead, critically wounded another. The third, who fled to a getaway car, was identified to police by the wounded felon. (*Baltimore Sun*)

Jerry Jackson, a 62-year-old Chicago bartender, exchanged shots with 3 gunmen who tried to hold up the saloon. Jackson, who suffered a leg wound, killed one and sent the other 2 fleeing empty-handed. (*Chicago Daily News*)

JUNE 1961

In Atherton, Calif., an armed burglar broke into the bedroom of Dr. and Mrs. William W. Tevis, snatched a wallet from the night table and, disappointed at its meager contents, ordered the physician to get his trousers from the closet. Mrs. Tevis, at the burglar's command, headed for her purse in the living room. The gun-waving burglar followed her, and Dr. Tevis, now armed with a cal. .32 pistol taken from the closet, called out. The bandit whirled and the doctor shot him 3 times. (*San Francisco News-Call Bulletin*)

When a young hoodlum clubbed 59-year-old Seeber K. Stokes to the floor and demanded money, the St. Petersburg, Fla., grocer reached behind the counter for his gun and killed his assailant. (*St. Petersburg Times*)

Beaumont, Tex., liquor store owner Earl R. Hudson ran for his pistol when a knife-wielding holdup man panicked and began stabbing Hudson's teen-age son. Hudson fired 5 shots and killed the would-be bandit-murderer as the seriously wounded boy slumped to the floor. (*Beaumont Journal*)

When Rufus Freeman caught 2 safecrackers in his store near Minter City, Miss., and one turned on him with a shotgun, Freeman killed him with his own shotgun. The pistol-armed accomplice ran through the store firing at Freeman, and the storekeeper felled him with one more blast. (*Memphis Commercial Appeal*)

Rt. Rev. Msgr. D. A. Lemieux, a skilled hunter, reached for a 12-ga. shotgun and a cal. .32 revolver after hearing glass break in his Chicago, Ill., rectory. He surprised 2 men rifling a buffet. As they advanced on him, Msgr. Lemieux warned them to stand fast. The men persisted, the priest warned them again and then felled one, a convicted felon, with a shotgun blast in the abdomen. (*AP*)

A 16-year-old boy entered Joseph LaCour's St. Louis, Mo., drugstore and asked to see some watches. As LaCour turned the youth pulled a cal. .32 revolver and said, "This is a holdup." LaCour dropped to the floor, took his own pistol, shot the lad in the hand, and held him for police. The young holdup man then admitted participating in 6 other robberies. (*St. Louis Globe-Democrat*)

THE ARMED CITIZEN

AUGUST 1961

Oklahomans recently figured in the armed citizens' fight against criminals. Walter Becker of Longdale awoke to hear a burglar in his adjoining general store and service station. Becker killed the prowler with a cal. .22 rifle. And in Pharoah, grocer Wayne Bryant got his shotgun and surprised 2 men cracking his safe. When one of the burglars scrambled for a shotgun leaning against the wall near the safe, Bryant shot him in the chest. (*Oklahoma City Oklahoman & Okmulgee Times*)

After closing their Perdido, Ala., grocery, Mr. and Mrs. John Huff, 64 and 61, left their garage and headed for their home carrying the day's receipts. Three men jumped from the darkness and wrestled with them. Mrs. Huff pulled free and whipped out her .38. Her series of shots scared off the assailants. With the help of dogs, the sheriff had the 3 in jail the next day, one with a bullet in his leg. (*AP*)

In Fort Worth a bandit strode into a liquor store, pulled open his coat to reveal a pistol under his belt, and told proprietor E. R. Alexander to give him all the money. "I was ready for him," said Alexander. "I pulled my .38 from under the counter and started firing." The bandit managed to get off one wild, bottle-smashing shot and staggered toward the door with a bullet in his chest. (*Fort Worth Star Telegram*)

A hand reached out and cut a piece from the screen door, reached in and opened the door. The noise awoke Dallas, Tex., resident Charles Louis Forgey, who loaded his cal. .38 revolver and went to investigate. He found a prowler kneeling by his mother's bed and ordered him to the kitchen. As Forgey turned to summon aid, the prowler broke for the door. Forgey killed him at the door with one shot. (*Dallas Times Herald*)

In Maplewood, N. J., gas station operator John Gardner, Sr., was knifed on the arm by one of 2 bandits who then ordered him to clean out the till. Gardner whipped out a pistol and shot his assailant in the chest. Both men took flight and escaped. When the critically wounded bandit sought aid in a Newark hospital, police took him in custody for the Gardner felony and held him as a suspect in 2 earlier robberies. (*Elizabeth Daily Journal*)

SEPTEMBER 1961

Two hoodlums rushed into Floyd E. Mock's hardware store in Kansas City, Mo., struck a customer with a gun, and began beating Mock. Mock's clerk rushed hammer in hand to his aid, struck one bandit on the head and was shot down. Even while being beaten, Mock reached under the counter for his cal. .22 pistol and opened fire. Although himself shot in the shoulder and groin, Mock managed to kill one of the thugs and wound the other. (*AP*)

A man stepped from behind a soft drink machine and stated, "I'm going to blow your head off," as Lee Phillips left his Bibb, Ga., service station with the receipts in a bag. Phillips raised the cal. .45 automatic he carried and shot the would-be thief twice. Police were able to follow a blood trail to where the wounded holdup man lay in the bushes. (*Macon News*)

Two 16-year-old boys, in a stolen pickup truck and armed with a shotgun, came to James F. Dittmore's general store and gas station and forced the Verona, Calif., proprietor to lie on the floor while they took money from his wallet and the cash register. They were unable to operate the gas pump when they tried fueling the truck, and made Dittmore help them. When an arriving car gave him the chance, Dittmore ran back to the store, grabbed a cal. .30-30 rifle, and came back shooting. He shot one dead and clubbed the other over the head with the rifle. (*Las Vegas Sun*)

A young gunman entered a Richlands, N. C., bank and forced the teller at pistol point to fill a paper sack with money. When the bandit had left, Warren Taylor, the teller, ran to the vault and returned with a 20-ga. shotgun kept there for just such emergencies. Taylor opened fire and felled the thief. (*The Fayetteville Observer*)

Mrs. Winnifred Carter, who learned to shoot on her father's Georgia farm and who still practices occasionally on the range, heard her husband's call for help from the front of their Chicago, Ill., grocery store, picked up a gun, and went forward to find her husband being attacked by a hammer-wielding would-be thief. She took another gun from under the meat counter and began shooting with both. Of 8 shots fired, the bandit was hit 7 times. (*Chicago Daily News*)

NOVEMBER 1961

A paratroop combat veteran of WW II, James Pandolfi was awakened by the sound of breaking glass as a thief hurled a piece of flagstone through the front door of his Buffalo, N. Y., appliance store. Pandolfi took a cal. .32 automatic from a nearby table, rushed to a bay window, and fired one shot at the thief who was fleeing with a stolen TV set, felling him mortally wounded. (*Buffalo Evening News*)

Noticing one man in the phone booth and another loitering inside the door of his Philadelphia, Pa., drugstore, Timothy Resnick became suspicious and picked up a cal. .38 pistol and held it out of sight under a counter. The man by the door held up an entering customer and the man in the phone booth, a paroled bank-robber, came out gun in hand and firing at Resnick. The druggist shot 4 times, killing the gunman with bullets in the mouth and side. (*The Philadelphia Inquirer*)

Two youths knocked on the door of 73-year-old George Z. Michaels' New York City basement workshop and, as he opened the door, demanded money saying they had a gun. Michaels fired one shot, felling one with a bullet in the abdomen. Police later picked up the wounded one's companion and booked both for attempted robbery. (*World-Telegram*)

Armed with a cal. .22 revolver, a thief 3 months out of prison after serving a 10-year term for armed robbery, entered John Waldrick's Albuquerque, N. Mex., store, forced Waldrick to hand over his wallet and empty the cash register. As the robber reached the door, Waldrick drew his own weapon and felled him. (*Albuquerque Tribune*)

After once having merchandise stolen from the Toledo, Ohio, carryout of which he is co-owner, Charles Jackson was armed and waiting inside after closing up when 2 burglars entered. One lunged at him when he told them to put up their hands, and Jackson fired twice, killing him. He followed the other outside and shot him in the hip as he made toward a companion in a getaway car. Police later arrested the driver on charges of burglary. All 3 men had previous police records. (*Toledo Blade*)

DECEMBER 1961

Two men awoke John Zimmerman as they pried loose the door plate on the main entrance to his Dearborn, Mich., sports shop. Zimmerman seized a 12-ga. shotgun and called for them to halt, then fired one shot as they broke for the door, killing one and critically injuring the other. The previous Thursday Zimmerman had found a 20-year-old inside his store, and fired at him twice. The wounded burglar turned himself in. (*Dearborn Press*)

JANUARY 1962

As William Harlin was leaving his Oak Park, Mich., sporting goods store, a 16-year-old escaped delinquent with a 16-ga. shotgun stepped from behind some trash cans and tried to force him back into the store. Harlin drew a cal. .32 automatic and shot the youth in the chest. Waving the shotgun the young holdup ran and tried to duck behind Harlin's car, but Harlin killed him with another shot. (*Detroit News*)

Before dawn, a holdup man in a stolen car pulled into the Linden, N. J., gas station where Robert Haut is employed, came up to Haut and announced a stickup, stabbed Haut in the cheek, and snatched a wallet. Haut pulled out his gun and shot his attacker twice in the abdomen, wounding him critically. (*N. Y. Mirror*)

A policeman once gave Mrs. Hatsuyo Yasui what turned out to be very good advice indeed. He mentioned that if ever she should have to defend herself from a gunman, to shoot often so as not to give any opportunity for him to fire back, and to shoot low. When a shotgun-wielding 17-year-old entered her husband's Los Angeles liquor store and demanded money, Mrs. Yasui ran to the rear of the store, took a cal. .32 automatic pistol, and came out firing the gun in both hands. Of six shots fired, the holdup man was hit 5 times and was dead an hour later. (*Los Angeles Mirror*)

Having wrecked a stolen car down the road, 2 young gunmen attempted to gain entrance to the Memphis, Tenn., home of Holmes Winford on the pretext of summoning a wrecker. Failing this, they shot in the glass, forced their way in, and began beating Winford. Mrs. Winford, hearing the commotion, peeked through her bedroom door and saw the youths beating her husband. She loaded an old cal. .38 pistol in the dark, and stepped out to confront the gunmen. One opened fire on her and missed, and Mrs. Winford then shot and killed one and downed the other with a bullet in the hip. (*UPI*).

A conspiracy by 4 Detroit hoodlums to rob Joseph Triglia, proprietor of a check-cashing firm, backfired when Triglia shot one and neighbor Charles Hughes captured another. Approaching the Triglia home from the rear, one of the gunmen grabbed Triglia's wife in the backyard, her screams alerting her husband who ran to the door with gun in hand. There he met the other bandit and Triglia shot him in the head. The struggling wife broke free and her assailant vaulted the fence, only to be spotted and captured by neighbor Hughes. (*Detroit News*)

1962

Alarmed by the sound of a car stopping suddenly outside his Arundel, Quebec, branch bank, manager Charles Curtis Farran looked from his office window to see armed, hooded men piling from a pickup truck outside. Farran ran up the back stairs to his apartment over the bank as the robbers fired at him. As Farran was loading his shotgun the bandits had lined up customers and tellers downstairs and demanded the safe be opened. Told that only the manager had the combination, they scooped the cash from the tellers' drawers and fled—but Farran was waiting. As the thieves climbed into their truck, he fired 3 shots. The truck then sped away. Shortly after, police found the stolen truck abandoned, with a dead hoodlum inside police identified as having been killed by Farran. (*Montreal Star*)

A man entered Walter A. Watkins' Columbus, Ga., package store, ordered a bottle of whisky, and then pulled a cal. .38 pistol and announced a holdup. Watkins took his own pistol from under the counter and fired once, killing the holdup man. (*Ledger-Enquirer*)

In the hospital awaiting removal of a bullet, a youth with an extensive police record admitted having twice previously held up the Wilmington, Del., combination grocery store-service station where he had been shot by the operator, Mrs. Thelma Lance, during his third attempt. (*Evening Journal*)

MARCH 1962

When a customer in his Indianapolis, Ind., package store drew a 9" hunting knife and held it to his throat while demanding money, manager John Sorrentino handed it over. But Sorrentino took a cal. .38 revolver from a drawer as the thief left and fired a shot as he stepped into the street, and then pursued him firing as a car tried to pick him up. The thief stumbled and fell. Sorrentino summoned police who found the knife and cash and took the man into custody. (*AP*)

While one man held a shotgun pointed at him through the screen door of his Hamilton, Ga., cafe, another herded J. H. Roberts around the counter toward the cash. As Roberts passed his wife, she handed him a cal. .38 revolver and Roberts opened fire, felling the man in the cafe with bullets below the heart and in the arm. Roberts then turned his fire on the man outside, who drove away. Already wanted by police in connection with another holdup, he was soon picked up in his bullet-holed auto. (*The Atlanta Journal*)

Tampa, Fla., night service station operator Alfonso Pierce was approached by a man with a gun and told to 'reach'. Pierce took a cal. .38 revolver from his pocket and fired 3 shots as the bandit ran. An anonymous tip led police to the man, dead in a trailer. (*AP*)

Clarence Williams was awakened and armed with a pistol by his mother, who had seen a prowler wearing heavy canvas gloves and a cap pulled low over his face forcing a window of their Houston, Tex., home. While Mrs. Williams phoned police, Clarence and his father, armed with a rifle, circled the house. As they closed in, the marauder shot the elder Williams in the foot and then wheeled to shoot Clarence, but the hammer of his pistol caught in his heavy gloves. Clarence emptied his own weapon at the exconvict and killed him. (*The Chronicle*)

From his living quarters in the rear of his Big Springs, Kans., store, W. C. Long was able to hear sounds of breaking glass. He armed himself with a 12-ga. shotgun and went to the store where he found 2 men. One shot killed one, who had a long record of convictions, and wounded the other. (*AP*)

A bandit with a revolver and a note demanding money entered Joseph Nahas' Detroit, Mich., grocery store. Nahas ducked behind a counter, grabbed a revolver, and fired 3 shots, 2 of which put the holdup man in the hospital in critical condition. (*Detroit Free Press*)

Having been robbed at gunpoint and ordered to the rear of his South Salt Lake, Utah, store by a thief wanted elsewhere for seriously wounding a clerk in another holdup, Carl A. Templin grabbed his cal. .38 automatic and rushed to the street as the gunman headed toward his car. Templin fired, the thief returned the fire and sped away in the car. The store owner jumped in his pickup truck and chased the holdup man until he stopped his car, got out, put his gun on the sidewalk, and surrendered, wounded in the arm. (*The Salt Lake Tribune*)

A customer entered the Gardena, Calif., liquor store where retired policeman Lee Burris is a clerk, drew a revolver, and demanded money or Burris' life. Burris, his spectacles knocked off by the bandit, drew his cal. .38 revolver and killed the would-be robber with bullets in the chest and side. (*Los Angeles Herald & Express*)

Jack Dickison and his son Paul have captured 7 men in recent burglary attempts in their Cincinnati, Ohio, service station. Hearing the alarm in their home, they armed themselves again with a cal. .22 rifle and a shotgun, and went to the station. As the thief fled from the front of the station. Paul fired 3 shots from his rifle, dropping the breakin. Police arrested an accomplice nearby and charged both with breaking and entering. (*The Cincinnati Enquirer*)

Brandishing a cal. .22 pistol, a thief entered James E. Ralph's Little Rock, Ark., package store and said "Give me your money and put your hands up," to the clerk on duty. As the clerk handed over the money from the cash register, Ralph fired a .30-30 rifle from the rear of the store, killing the holdup man. (*Arkansas Gazette*)

After handing over the cash from one cash register to the robber who confronted him in his Chicago, Ill., drugstore, Mitchell Novick reached behind a second cash register for a gun and shot the thief twice in the chest. (*Chicago American*)

APRIL 1962

After loitering in A. A. Dear's Anniston, Ala., market for several minutes, a man pulled a pistol and demanded that Dear give him the money in the cash register. Dear then was forced to lie behind the counter. Dear had a cal. .38 revolver on a shelf, and rose firing when he heard the thief close the front door. The holdup man fell dead on the sidewalk, hit by 3 shots. (*The Anniston Star*)

Willie L. Culpepper was seated at a desk in his Los Angeles, Calif., service station when a man walked in, brandished a gun, and announced a stickup. Culpepper reached into the desk as if for cash, but came up with a cal. .38 revolver. The gunman fell dead with bullets in the mouth and chest. (*Los Angeles Examiner*)

Two bandits, one armed with a pistol, attempted to grab 74-year-old Clark Pevehouse in his Dallas, Tex., grocery. Pevehouse knocked his attacker's gun away and grabbed his own cal. .32 pistol from under a counter. He shot the gunman 3 times. The second man attempted to grab him and Pevehouse shot him twice. One robber was dead and the other in serious condition upon arrival at hospital. Said Pevehouse, "If more people would fight, there would be fewer holdups." (*The Dallas Morning News*)

A Marine deserter came into the liquor store operated by Miss Isabel Amato in Los Angeles, Calif. He brandished a cal. .45 automatic and demanded the cash. But when he looked away for an instant, Miss Amato grabbed a cal. .32 pistol and fired 3 killing shots. (*Los Angeles Examiner*)

Eugene Jewell was worried about being held up some night as he left his Bakersfield, Calif., grocery with the receipts, so he carried a cal. .22 pistol in his right hand. When 2 men grabbed him one night, he turned and fired 2 shots, critically wounding one man. (*The Bakersfield Californian*)

Two masked men, one armed, pushed their way through the customers to pursue Jack Kapell to a storeroom in his Detroit, Mich., bar. Kapell took a gun he kept in the storeroom and wounded the 2 would-be thieves with one shot each. (*The Detroit News*)

JUNE 1962

Faced with a pair of burly strangers who demanded to see her husband's prized gun collection, Mrs. Audrey Quirk, a 100-lb. housewife of Peabody, Mass., demurred. When the pair tried to force their way in, Mrs. Quirk picked up a loaded .45, pointed it at the men and threatened to shoot. The pair promptly left. Mrs. Quirk's husband, Frank, is a Navy Chief Petty Officer, instructor on a local Naval Reserve Pistol team, and a prominent gun collector. (*Boston Herald-Traveler*)

With one hand thrust forward in his pocket and a handkerchief over his face, a man walked into a grocery store in Tulsa, Okla., operated by Charles L. Diven and told the grocer: "This is it. Give me the money." Grabbing his cal. .45 automatic, the grocer replied. "This is it alright, take your hand out of your pocket." The gunman wheeled and ran away, Diven holding his fire. (*Tulsa Sunday World*)

Intending to loot a safe in the basement of an exhibition hall in San Francisco, an armed burglar awakened 2 San Franciscans who had stayed in the hall through the night to guard their display of guns—part of a local rod and gun club show. One exhibitor, Jack Morris, picked up a shotgun and fired twice, seriously wounding the burglar. (*San Francisco Chronicle*)

Hearing noises at the side door of their service station near Albany, N. Y., Bryan and Harrison Bresett realized that 2 men were attempting to break in. One of the brothers grabbed a revolver and ordered the intruders to stop, but the pair ran away. Shooting over the heads of the fleeing hoodlums, the Bresetts managed to catch one, who had slipped and fallen. Further investigation by police led to the arrest of 7 other members of a gang allegedly responsible for 36 burglaries in the Albany area. (*Albany Times-Union*)

Investigating noises in the basement of his home in Milwaukee, Wis., Robert G. Schumaker encountered a prowler with a deer rifle and shotgun taken from Schumaker's locker. Neither gun was loaded, but Schumaker's revolver was, and he held the intruder at bay for police. (*Milwaukee Journal*)

Three youths, 2 of them armed, had just gotten $100 from the cash register in a liquor store in Yonkers, N. Y., and were attempting a getaway when one of the trio was hit in the shoulder by a shot fired by Sam Jacobs, son of the store owner. Seeking treatment from a local doctor, the youths said the wound was accidental, but the doctor refused to believe the tale and called police. Under questioning, the bandits admitted the robbery and 4 others in that area during the preceding 6 weeks. (*Yonkers Reporter Dispatch*)

When police answered a call recently in Accokeek, Md., they found 2 robbers lying face down next to their wrecked getaway car and a band of armed citizens standing guard. The two men had been seen by a telephone company employee to enter the local bank and pull a gun. The employee raced to a nearby hardware store to call police and, while doing so, the store's proprietor, Robert W. Perrygo, armed himself with a pistol and shotgun and started for the bank. Meanwhile, another telephone company worker, Richard Knowles, parked his truck in an alleyway in such a way to block the bandits' escape. When the thieves got into the escape car Knowles fired a shotgun blast through the rear window. The car smashed into the parked truck, and Perrygo and other citizens who had armed themselves converged on the pair. The bank loot, about $10,000, had been stuffed into a bag and thrown into a barrel during the melee but was later recovered by police. (*A. P.*)

Douglas Zeman, a college sophomore, was in his family's living quarters to the rear of their grocery store in Chicago, Ill., when he overhead men's voices in the store tell his parents they were being robbed. As the bandits, 3 of them, marched the couple toward the rear of the building at gunpoint, Zeman took a .38 revolver and hid in the bathroom. When the gunmen came into sight, the student killed one of them with shots at close range. The others managed to escape empty-handed. (*Chicago Tribune*)

Two men, accused of being members of a nation-wide gang which has been looting public telephone coin boxes, were captured by a tavern owner near Bear, Del. John A. Sarapulski noticed the pair tampering with the telephone outside his tavern, called state police, and held the men at gunpoint until the police arrived. Telephone company investigators said the prisoners were members of a syndicate under surveillance for more than a year in several parts of the country. Sarapulski had been alerted to the syndicate's activities by telephone company investigators after the booth outside his tavern was robbed a short time earlier. (*Wilmington Morning News*)

JULY 1962

After being aroused by a homemade burglar alarm in his grocery store next door, Clifford Carlson of Minneapolis, Minn., armed himself and surprised 2 men in the act of looting the store's cash register. Carlson downed one with a chest shot. While hunting for the second burglar, he found a car with motor running near the store. Shortly thereafter he had the second man trapped and held him for police. The incident brought Carlson's bag of burglars to 6 since 1959. (*St. Paul Dispatch*)

A youth with a stocking over his face and brandishing a .22 rifle entered a service station in Fitzgerald, Ga., and told owner W. A. Tucker to empty his cash register. As the youth attempted to escape with $900, Tucker got his 12-ga. shotgun and downed the thief with one shot. (*Savannah Morning News*)

Tudoe Stoini had closed his restaurant in Blue Ash, Ohio, and, with his wife, was walking to their auto when a man suddenly appeared and grabbed a plastic bucket carried by Mrs. Stoini. It contained $2800. Before the thief could get away, Stoini drew a revolver and brought him down with several shots in the shoulder and abdomen. (*Cincinnati Inquirer*)

At the point of a gun, David C. Warren, proprietor of a beverage store in Cleveland, Ohio, turned over $104 to 3 young bandits. As he did, however, a customer entered the store and the thief, who was armed, slipped the gun into his pocket. At this point, Warren drew his .32 from under his apron and shot the armed bandit down. The other 2 turned to flee, but Warren stopped one with a shot in the back. The third member of the trio escaped but was later apprehended. (*Cleveland Press*)

One man was hospitalized with gunshot wounds and 3 more were jailed after an abortive attempt to burglarize a feed store owned by I. V. Lynch in Hale Center, Tex. Lynch, whose home is 60 ft. from the store, said he heard the lock on the store's front door being forced. He got out his 12-ga. shotgun, turned a spotlight on the store front and fired as the burglars tried to flee. (*Amarillo Daily News*)

The owner of a market in Columbus, Ohio, Theodore Patsioures, pretended to follow the orders of 2 bandits who had entered the store and demanded money, but instead he triggered a homemade alarm system which was wired to a doorbell in the living room of his home adjoining the store. His 63-year-old wife heard the distress signal, picked up a pistol, and ran to the scene. One of the yeggs had fled when the alarm went off, but the other was still there when Mrs. Patsioures arrived. She held him at gunpoint until police took her prisoner away. (*Columbus Dispatch*)

When Henry Lee of Washington, D. C., heard noises at his front door in the middle of the night, he got his gun and went to investigate. He got to the door just as an intruder crashed through. The housebreaker was sent to a hospital with a .38 wound in his right shoulder. (*Washington Post*)

While making a routine check of his sporting goods store in Monahans, Tex., Lyle Saunders heard noises in a back room. He drew his gun, discovered a burglar at work, and held the intruder until police arrived. (*Monahans News*)

Alerted by a telephone call from a friend who said his grocery store was being burglarized, A. M. (Bill) Shook of Hale Center, Tex., armed himself and hurried to the scene. There he found the store lights on and a window pane in the front door missing. He flushed the burglar out of hiding and held him at gunpoint for police. It was the second time in a little over a week that a citizen of Hale Center, a town of less than 2000 people, had thwarted a burglary with a firearm. (*Lubbock Avalanche*)

A man acting as advance guard for a team of burglars had broken into a radio and television store in Newark, N. J., and was about to douse the store's lights when he was spotted by one of the store's owners, Clifford Lucas. Lucas downed the intruder, hitting him with one of 2 shots. The rest of the party sped away. (*Newark Evening News*)

A man entered a liquor store in Los Angeles, ran behind the counter waving a 20″ butcher knife and demanded that the clerk, Nathan Dorman, give him money. Dorman reached under the counter for a .45 and fired 6 shots at point-blank range, killing his assailant. (*Los Angeles Examiner*)

Anxious to put a stop to a wave of Thursday night robberies (4 in 5 weeks) at their tavern in Topeka, Kans., Darrell G. Johnson and Lanny Ellis armed themselves with shotguns and waited for the burglar after closing. The thief arrived, looted a vending machine and had started on the cash register when Johnson surprised him and ordered him to stand still while Ellis called for police. Meanwhile, in a car outside the tavern sat a police officer who also had hoped to catch the bandit, but who didn't know the thief had been caught until squad cars summoned by Ellis arrived. (*Topeka State Journal*)

AUGUST 1962

After spending the night on a cot in his Detroit grocery, Simpkin Green awoke to find a man coming out of a cooler. He reached under his pillow for a .32 pistol and ordered the intruder to halt. When the command was ignored, Green fired, downing the stranger with a bullet in the knee. (*Detroit Free Press*)

Arriving at his home in West Brighton, N. Y., butcher Joseph Mauro was accosted by thugs who demanded his money. Mauro drew a gun, sending the bandits fleeing. (*Staten Island Advance*)

Two burglars used a key to enter a cafe in Midland, Tex., but once inside they aroused the cafe manager, Willie Haynes, who was sleeping in the kitchen. When the intruders began to run, Haynes yelled for them to stop. They didn't and Haynes fired with a .22 rifle as they went out the door. One of the thugs was hit and his accomplice took him to a hospital where both were arrested. (*Odessa, Tex., American*)

David C. Warden, operator of a nightclub in Wichita, Kans., had moved into the club because of a rash of burglaries and and was waiting with a 12-ga. shotgun when 2 men tried to break in. He had been awakened a short time before by the ringing of a telephone, a trick used by burglars to learn if there is anyone at the scene of their intended burglary. Warden didn't answer and was prepared when the 2 men arrived. Both wound up in custody with leg wounds. (*Wichita Eagle*)

An ex-convict and his accomplice were in jail in Tucson, Ariz., after they attempted an armed robbery at a liquor store run by Joseph Kadjan. The store owner and his assistant, John Dearhammer, came up with guns when faced with the bandits and held the pair for police. The ex-convict tried to shoot it out with Kadjan and Dearhammer, but his gun wouldn't fire. (*Tucson Daily Star*)

After leaving a nightclub in New Orleans, Roger Perino and a friend were getting into Perino's car when a man approached and shoved a screwdriver into Perino's ribs. Perino reached into the auto for a concealed .32 automatic, shoved the man away, and fired, wounding his assailant in the chest. (*New Orleans Times-Picayune*)

After being knocked down and robbed by 2 men, Mrs. Frances Busenbark, proprietor of the A&A Grocery in Portland, Oreg., grabbed a .38 pistol and chased the men down the street. A service station operator, Don McKay, saw the chase, armed himself, and followed the bandits in his car. They pursued one of the thugs into a house; Mrs. Busenbark covered the front and McKay stationed himself at the rear. They forced the bandit out by threatening to come in shooting, and held him for police. (*Portland Oregonian*)

Herman Casavantes, manager of an apartment house in El Paso, Tex., awoke one night to find that a stranger had forced his way in. Casavantes told the man to leave, but the intruder ignored the order and shoved him aside. Casavantes drew a .25 automatic and shot the intruder in the chest, seriously wounding him. (*El Paso Times*)

From his home across the street from a market in Chicago, Concepcion Martinez, operator of the market, saw a man smash a window in the front door and enter the building. He found the man looting the market, cornered him behind a meat counter, and shot him to death. (*Chicago Daily News*)

One man was in police custody with bullet wounds in the right arm and another was in critical condition in a Chicago hospital after an attempted robbery at a tavern operated by Frank Drabik. Drabik shot both men after they had clubbed him to the floor with pool cues. (*Chicago Daily News*)

An armed, masked bandit entered a store in Avra Valley, Ariz., about 30 miles east of Tucson, and told the wife of the owner, Henry Clay East, to open the cash register. Unseen by the gunman, East slipped out of the store and returned with a 12-ga. shotgun. He fired through a screen door just as the gunman turned toward him. The bandit died instantly. (*Arizona Republic*)

A burglar alarm wired to the cash register in the Watch Hospital, a store in Inglewood, Calif., awakened the owner, Ray Bader, who lives on the property. Spotting a man hunched over the register, Bader fired a volley of 5 shots from his .357 magnum revolver, fatally wounding the burglar. (*Los Angeles Examiner*)

A single blast from a shotgun fired by Richard Beedle halted an attempted robbery at a gas station north of Williamsport, Ind., and wounded all 3 of the burglars. Beedle, who operates the station and lives over it, was awakened by breaking glass. When he saw the trio at the cash register, he fired. One of the robbers went down; the others fled but were arrested later on information taken from the one who didn't get away. (*Terre Haute Tribune*)

OCTOBER 1962

From the backyard at his home in Elmont, N. Y., Sidney Perlstein heard the sound of breaking glass at the home of a neighbor. He then saw a man crawl into a basement window. Remembering that the owner was away for the day, Perlstein got the revolver he uses as a member of a local gun club, went to the neighbor's house, and rang the door bell. When no one answered he ran around to the back just in time to see the burglar run away. Six warning shots and a half block later, Perlstein collared the man and held him for the police. (*Long Island Daily Press*)

Faced with a mob of about 20 youths advancing on him armed with bottles, belts, and chains, Robert Rose, a service station attendant in Detroit, fired 2 warning shots into the ground. As the gang continued to advance, Rose fired a shot into the leg of one of the assailants. The shots brought police who arrested several members of the gang. (*Detroit News*)

While spending the night in the tavern where he is employed near North Wilkesboro, N.C., Bristol McDaniel was awakened by the sound of a door being forced. He hid, waited until 2 men got inside, and turned on the lights. At the point of a .38 McDaniel ordered them to be seated while he called the police. (*Winston-Salem Journal*)

The husband of Mrs. Margaret Byars of San Mateo, Fla., was away at work when Mrs. Byars became aware that there was a prowler in her backyard. The stranger first yelled for her to open a door and then proceeded to break it down. In the meantime Mrs. Byars had gotten a rifle. As the would-be intruder smashed at the door, she fired 3 times. The prowler promptly vanished. (*San Mateo Times*)

A Tucson, Ariz., department store owner, Nick Parise, was sleeping in his store until he was awakened by the sound of a prowler. He picked up a gun, investigated, and found a man looting a gun case. He marched the would-be burglar to the front of the store and held him there until he could attract the attention of a policeman. (*Arizona Daily Star*)

Memories of 2 recent robberies plus the appearance of a suspicious-looking stranger in his store prompted Harry Smith of Flint, Mich., to duck through a rear door and take out a .22 revolver. As Smith watched, the stranger pulled a gun, told a clerk to fill a paper sack with money, and began looting customers. When he had a chance, Smith came out firing. The bandit shot back at Smith but dropped the loot and ran. Shortly thereafter, police arrested the man at a hospital where he had gone for the treatment of 2 gunshot wounds. (*Flint Journal*)

Awakened by noises in his home in Rosamond, Calif., Kenneth B. Walker got up, walked into his living room, and discovered his television set was missing. Seeing the back door open, Walker armed himself with a .22 pistol and started out. He met the burglar returning to the house and shot him twice. (*Bakersfield Californian*)

Hearing the sound of breaking glass in his grocery store in Germantown, Ohio, James Estep grabbed his shotgun and rushed into the store from his adjoining bedroom. There he saw a man climbing through a window. He told the intruder to stop. The command went unheeded and Estep fired, mortally wounding the burglar in the head. (*Dayton Daily News*)

When Mrs. Arletta Norton, wife of the operator of the Valley Drive-In in Mt. Vernon, Ky., returned to the restaurant one night after closing, she found 2 youths inside frying hamburgers and helping themselves to candy, cigarettes, chewing gum and other stock items. When police answered Mrs. Norton's call, they found her, armed with a .38 revolver, firmly in command. (*Lexington Leader*)

After noticing a youth close the door on a display case in his jewelry store in Detroit and start for the door, Fred Weinstein grabbed a revolver from behind a counter and ordered the suspected thief to halt. When police arrived, they found 8 diamond rings in the youth's possession. (*Detroit News*)

The owner of a laundromat in Venice, Calif., Mrs. Mabel Sims, was awakened one morning by the clatter of change in the store. Through a window, she saw 2 men scooping change from a coin-changing machine. She called the police and then armed herself with a shotgun and a pistol. When the 2 thieves started to leave the scene, she stopped them and told them to wait for the police. One broke and ran away but the other remained. (*The Roberts News*)

When a man approached Mrs. R. B. Rhodes in her grocery store in Savannah, Ga., and demanded money, the 58-year-old woman grabbed a pistol and sent the man fleeing from the store. With the gun in hand, Mrs. Rhodes pursued the would-be robber until he surrendered 2 blocks away. She and 2 store employees guarded the man until police arrived. (*AP*)

NOVEMBER 1962

After beating and robbing 66-year-old Fred Yeager in Los Angeles, a pair of hoodlums forced the elderly man to take them to his place of business to get more money. When they arrived, Yeager grabbed a .38 pistol and began firing as the pair fled. He stopped one of his assailants with a fatal bullet in the chest. (*Los Angeles Herald-Examiner*)

After being ordered by an armed bandit to surrender the contents of the cash register in his liquor store south of Wilmington, Del., proprietor Renato Giovannozzi opened the register drawer with one hand and, with the other, grabbed a .38 revolver from a shelf. He fired several shots, critically wounding his assailant and sending an accomplice fleeing from the scene. (*Wilmington Morning News*)

Two men walked into a Denver, Colo., liquor store, pulled a gun and ordered proprietor Frank Levine into a back room. They forced him to lie on his stomach, taped his hands behind his back, and took his wallet, but they did not notice a revolver in Levine's side pocket. As the hoodlums left the ransacked store, Levine got loose. He came up behind them on the street and held them at gunpoint for the police. (*Denver Post*)

From the kitchen in her home next to the frozen custard stand she operates in Columbus, Ohio, Miss Bess Barton saw 2 persons breaking into the stand. She telephoned police, got a gun, and accosted the pair—a man and woman—as they were leaving the scene. Miss Barton turned the pair over to police who arrived shortly thereafter. (*Columbus Dispatch*)

While moving into a new home in North Hollywood, Calif., Robert Fuller, an actor in a television western series, heard noises at a window. He grabbed a pistol, dashed out the front door, and caught a man about to crawl through a window. Fuller held the man at gunpoint while a passing motorist called police. (*AP*)

James Childs pretended to be getting money, as he had been ordered to do, while a robber was looting his appliance store in Newark, N. J. Instead, he got a shotgun from under a counter. The thief, who had been holding his hand in his pocket as if to conceal a gun, surrendered and waited at gunpoint for arresting officers. (*Newark Sunday News*)

Determined to stop a rash of burglaries in his bar in Torrance, Calif. (3 in one week), Richard Munz was waiting inside with a shotgun and a .22 auto pistol when a man forced his way in. Switching on the lights, Munz ordered the intruder to stand still. The burglar ran but got only 100 yds. before he fell dead, hit by one of Munz's bullets. (*Long Beach Press Telegram*)

Armed with a pistol, 2 youths held up a liquor store operated by Otto J. Englert in Los Angeles. As the pair emptied the cash register, Englert grabbed a pistol and shot one of the bandits 3 times. The other tried to escape, but police, drawn by Englert's gunfire, apprehended both. (*Los Angeles Herald-Examiner*)

An armed man demanded money from Carlyle J. Stroup, the manager of a Charleston, S. C., drugstore, but Marion Jervey, who had been visiting with Stroup, grabbed the barrel of the holdup man's gun and attempted to take it. As the 2 struggled, Stroup seized the weapon and, when the bandit broke away from Jervey, he fired one fatal shot into the bandit's heart. (*Charleston Evening Post*)

Al Mauk, night manager of a liquor store in Los Angeles, discovered a man looting a cash register at 3 A.M. one morning. Instead of putting his hands in the air, as Mauk ordered, the burglar reached for his pockets. Mauk shot him to death. (*AP*)

The manager of a waffle shop in Dallas, Jesse Ford, Jr., saw a man enter the store, pull a knife, and attack a woman customer. Ford grabbed a .38 pistol and, as the assailant ran out the door, fired several shots. The knife wielder fell dead in the parking lot outside the shop. (*UPI*)

After working the gas pumps at a service station in Chicago, the attendant, Jerry Harmen, entered the station office to find a man at the cash register. The intruder held his hand in his pocket to indicate he was armed and ordered Harmen to turn over the contents of the till. He then ordered Harmen into a back room. Harmen started walking, but when he reached a door, he wheeled, drew a gun, and fired, killing the bandit. (*Chicago Sun-Times*)

Responding to a woman's scream for help in a neighboring apartment, E. F. Schaaf of Willcox, Ariz., seized his .22 pistol and hurried to the scene. There he found his neighbor's apartment ransacked and a masked man hiding in the bathroom. Hoping to hold the man at gunpoint, Schaaf instructed his wife to call the police, but the intruder fled. Schaaf halted him with a fatal shot. (*Arizona Republic*)

FEBRUARY 1963

While walking her dog, Mrs. Victoria Roginski, an apartment house manager in Cleveland, Ohio, noticed 3 men working on a car in the darkness behind the house. She got her .32 pistol and returned to find the trio removing the tires and battery from a station wagon. One of the car strippers ran when Mrs. Roginski appeared, but the other 2 remained stationary while a neighbor called the police. (*Cleveland Press*)

After surprising a prowler rifling a cash register in a Los Angeles market, the store manager, Sanford Mitchell, got off one shot before the burglar got away. Police traced the man to a nearby apartment house where they found him lying in a hallway with a bullet wound. Mitchell had been sleeping in the store, armed, because of a recent wave of burglaries. (*Los Angeles Herald-Examiner*)

Claiming their auto had run out of water, 4 men gained entrance to the mountain cabin of 83-year-old Tony Lunsford, near Leicester, N. C. Before he opened the door, however, Lunsford slipped a .32 revolver into his pocket, a precaution he has followed for years. Once inside, the men, who were armed, rushed the mountaineer, and Lunsford started firing. All 4 of the attackers were apprehended by police, 3 of them with gunshot wounds. (*AP*)

Police answering a call from an automatic laundry in Freeport, La., arrived at the store to find 2 youths being held at gun point by the manager, Elmar Davison. From his quarters on the premises, Davison had heard noises in the laundry, and, through a pane of glass which is a mirror on one side but transparent on the other, saw the pair enter and go to work on a coin box with a tire iron. (*Freeport Journal-Standard*)

1963

As a result of a burglary in his combination grocery-liquor store in Worley, Idaho, Ernest Lagow was sleeping in the rear of the store when he was awakened by the sound of breaking glass. Nothing happened right away, but several hours later Lagow was again awakened—this time by sounds within the store. Taking his .30-30 rifle, he discovered a man carrying a case of whisky. He ordered the man to stop, but when the intruder made a move as if to draw a gun, Lagow fired. The thief, who died shortly thereafter, had been convicted of burglarizing the same store several months earlier. (*AP, UPI*)

After discovering and reporting the theft of automotive equipment from an auto rental firm in St. Joseph, Mo., the owner of the firm, Harold Martin, returned to the scene armed with a revolver and shotgun. He saw a man prying the lid from the gasoline tank of a truck and ordered the intruder to put up his hands. The burglar jumped into a car—which he later admitted stealing—and attempted to escape, but a blast from Martin's shotgun changed his mind and he surrendered. (*St. Joseph Gazette*)

Police responding to a burglary call at a jewelry store in Seattle, Wash., arrived on the scene to find R. W. Bartlett holding the thwarted would-be thief at gun-point. Bartlett, who holds a permit to carry a pistol, had been passing by when he saw a man break a window in the door of the jewelry shop. (*Seattle Times*)

Overhearing an order to his partner working in the next room to "Stand against the wall," Los Angeles service station owner Johnny Carpenter grabbed a pistol from his desk and turned in time to see a man—gun in hand—peering into the room. Carpenter shot him dead. Leaping over the fallen gunman into the next room Carpenter felled a second bandit with 3 more shots as the bandit fled through the station door. A third man escaped in a get-away car. (*San Fernando Valley Times*)

An Atlas, Ill., mother of 5, Mrs. Frank Rodhouse, returned home with her 4 daughters to face a shotgun-armed intruder. The man herded them to an upstairs room where he bound Mrs. Rodhouse. Slipping her bonds when the man left the room, she obtained a .38 pistol and 3 cartridges from a dresser drawer. Moving quietly downstairs she got instructions from her 15-year-old son, who had also been bound, on how to load and fire the pistol. Returning to an upstairs room she found the man preparing to attack her 13-year-old daughter. Mrs. Rodhouse pointed the gun at him and fired 3 times. As the would-be attacker turned toward her with raised shotgun, he fell at her feet mortally wounded. (*Pike County Democrat Times*)

As he was about to enter his home in Wake Forest, N. C., Henry Pearson was ambushed by 2 men. During a struggle one of the pair got Pearson's wallet while the other pistol-whipped him. Finally Pearson was able to get his .22 revolver out of his pocket, and he started shooting. One of the attackers fell dead, and the other man ran away. (*AP*)

MARCH 1963

Aroused at 2 A.M. by noises coming from the back bedroom of his Houston, Tex., home. Willie I. McDonald armed himself with a cal. .44 pistol and went to investigate. Finding a man going through bureau drawers, he held the intruder at gunpoint while he called police. As McDonald hung up the phone the intruder rushed at him with a hammer. McDonald fired 4 quick shots, 3 of which struck the bandit. (*Houston Post*)

John Jonaikis, in an attempt to end a series of burglaries which had netted robbers more than $1000 from his Chicago Heights, Ill., service station, kept an all-night vigil with a loaded shotgun that finally paid off. Jonaikis, sleeping in his car, was awakened by the sound of breaking glass and saw a man rifling his cash register. When the discovered robber was ordered to surrender he attempted to flee. Jonaikis fired and wounded him with one shot. (*Denver Post*)

In a Harbor City, Calif., liquor store, a man waited quietly for owner Robert Drake to finish talking on the phone. After Drake hung up, the man pulled a gun, scooped money from the till, and then backed towards the front door still pointing the pistol. At this point someone entered the store. Drake snatched a gun from under the counter and fired at the robber who fell seriously wounded. (*Long Beach Press Telegram*)

When Denver, Colo., cab driver Edward Dixon had a knife pressed against his neck by a passenger who ordered him to hand over his cash, the cabbie gave the bandit his change purse and wallet. When the robber ordered him to keep driving. Dixon quickly drew over to the curb, pulled a gun from under the seat, and held the bandit at bay as he radioed his dispatcher to call the police and inform them that he had arrested a robber. (*Denver Post*)

Jack Earle, 72, a Chicago, Ill., service station attendant, became suspicious when a man entered the station and pretended to be using the phone. Earle, victim of a former robbery and a vicious beating, slipped a gun out of a drawer and into his jacket pocket. When a second man entered and announced a stick-up Earle fired directly at him flooring him with one shot. As the bandit tried to rise, cocked gun in hand, Earle shot him again. The bandit was removed in serious condition by police. Two accomplices were picked up later. (*Chicago Tribune*)

Forced to lie on the floor while a gun-toting bandit rifled his cash drawer and fled, a Houston, Tex., grocery store owner, Robert Way, raised up to see the armed robber starting back towards the store. Way snatched a pistol from under the counter and went out after him. When the thug raised his gun, Way fired 3 times. The bandit was killed instantly. (*Houston Chronical*)

Clarence D. Henry was more than a match for a man who entered his St. Louis, Mo., candy store, pulled a revolver from his coat, and pointed it at him. Henry, who had previously lost $400 to an armed bandit, closed his hand on his cal. .38 revolver and brought it up from under the counter. He fired twice and the robber fell dead with 2 bullets in his chest. (*St. Louis Post Dispatch*)

When a newly installed burglar alarm went off in David Thune's Brooklyn, N. Y., apartment, he grabbed a .32 pistol and rushed to his service station next door. Surprising 2 men burglarizing the premises. Thune ordered them to come out with their hands up. Instead, both men rushed at him. Thune called on the men to stop. When they kept coming he fired once, felling one bandit with a fatal wound in the chest. The second thief tried to knock Thune down but was dropped, seriously wounded, by a second shot from Thune's gun. (*Brooklyn Eagle*)

A 72-year-old Chicago, Ill., grocer, James V. Smith, was knocked to the floor by a thug who demanded his money. Smith reached under the counter, got a .38 pistol, fired once, and his assailant fell dead. (*Near North News*)

Rev. Father O'Donnell, rector of St. Patrick's Roman Catholic Church, in Chicago, Ill., was awakened by the screams of his housekeeper and cook. Obtaining a .45 automatic, O'Donnell and another priest rushed downstairs to find an intruder, armed with 2 knives, ransacking the living room. O'Donnell fired once hitting the burglar in the leg. He held the man until police arrived. It was then that the priest learned that his housekeeper had been fatally stabbed and that his cook was seriously wounded. (*Chicago Daily News*)

APRIL 1963

Kansas City, Mo., taxi driver Austin Whitfield picked up a fare who turned out to be armed with a pistol. When the 'passenger' ordered Whitfield to keep driving, the cabbie swerved to the curb, grabbed his pistol, and shot and wounded the robber. (*The Kansas City Star*)

Awakened in his Goldsboro, N. C., home by the barking of his dog, Air Force Sgt. Edsel G. Sutherland loaded his shotgun and went to the kitchen. When Sutherland entered, a man grabbed the end of his shotgun. Edsel pulled the trigger and the intruder fell to the floor mortally wounded. (*Goldsboro New Argus*)

Peter Davitto, Chicago, Ill., food shop manager, who had previously been robbed of $425, became suspicious of a man who sat in his shop drinking coffee. When the man left and returned later brandishing a .22 pistol and demanding money. Davitto grabbed his own pistol and fired 4 shots at the thug who fell mortally wounded. (*Chicago Daily Tribune*)

Two men entered Clarence Page's Little Rock, Ark., liquor store and demanded money. Reaching one hand toward the cash register as if to get the money, Page used the other hand to scoop a .38 pistol from under the counter. One bandit got off one shot. Page got off 2. One armed thug fell dead with a bullet through the heart, and the other robber took a bullet in the shoulder. (*Ft. Smith Times*)

A knife-toting bandit was no match for Malone, N. Y., storekeeper Miles Mallette. When the would-be bandit entered, nodded towards the cash drawer, and said, "Hand me what's in there," Mallette obliged by reaching under the counter and whipping out a pistol instead. He held the thug at bay until the police arrived. (*Malone Evening News*)

A St. Louis, Mo., grocer ran into a new type of robber when a man entered his store, brandished a jagged piece of broken bottle, and demanded money from the cash register. Grocer Gleason Franklin opened the register and withdrew a .25 pistol instead. The grocer made the would-be bandit lie on the floor until police arrived. (*St. Louis Globe Democrat*)

MAY 1963

When Mrs. Darlene Cucchiara was awakened by noises, this Pleasant Hill, Calif., mother of 4 small children loaded her .22 revolver and went downstairs to investigate. She found a man waiting just inside the kitchen door. When the intruder attempted to grab her. Mrs. Cucchiara fired 6 shots at her assailant at close range. He screamed and jumped through the open kitchen window. He was found in critical condition in the driveway by police. (*Oakland Tribune*)

Awakened by noises in his Tucson, Ariz., cycle shop, owner D. E. Musselman, armed himself with a revolver and went to investigate. As Musselman crept towards the back of his shop he observed a man break a window and crawl inside. Waiting until the intruder was inside the shop, the store owner ordered him to stand where he was. Musselman held the prowler at gun point until police arrived. (*The Arizona Daily Star*)

Caretaker Reed Pitchford, of Chicago, Ill., Grant Memorial AME Church, had been sleeping in the church office when awakened by the sound of someone breaking in. When the intruder kept coming at him, Pitchford drew his pistol and fired twice. The intruder fell dead at his feet. (*Chicago Sun Times*)

Houston, Tex., liquor store owner, Sidney Scalise, found himself looking down the barrel of a .22 pistol as he was ordered by one of 2 men to hand over the money. Scalise gave the armed bandit $60 from the register, and $25 from his own wallet. As the men ran from the store, Scalise picked up a .45 he kept under a cover on the counter. As the thugs reached the corner 100 ft. away, Scalise leaned out of the shop door and took aim. One of the bandits brought his gun up and Scalise fired at him 4 times, dropping the man with a critical wound in the temple. Both were escaped convicts. (*Houston Press*)

Floored by the fists of a would-be robber, San Francisco bar owner, Ralph Chiappetta, was ordered by the thug to hand over his money. As the bandit rifled the cash register, Chiapetta got his .32 automatic and started firing. The robber staggered out and fell dead with 4 bullets in him. (*Oakland Tribune*)

JUNE 1963

When Cleveland, Ohio, housewife, Mrs. Patricia Harmon, home alone with her 8-year-old daughter, heard the noise of breaking glass in the basement, she grabbed her husband's cal. .32 pistol and went downstairs to investigate. As she entered the kitchen she was confronted by a masked intruder. Mrs. Harmon fired 4 shots at him and the man fell dead at her feet. (*Akron Beacon Journal*)

A father and son teamed up to attempt an armed robbery of Arthur Domzyk's tavern in Chicago, Ill. As the pair entered, the son fired 3 shots and ordered everyone to lie on the floor. Instead, owner Domzyk grabbed a .38 pistol and started firing. Both the father and son were hit as they fled the tavern. Apprehended by police when they applied for medical treatment, the son was found to have been seriously wounded. (*Chicago Sun Times*)

A St. Louis, Mo., woman, Mrs. Helen Lowery, awakened at 2:15 A.M. to find a man armed with a butcher knife standing beside her bed. She grabbed her revolver and fired several shots at the intruder as he fled. A short time later a man called police from a phone booth and was picked up badly wounded in chest and hip. He readily admitted being the man who had broken into Mrs. Lowery's home. (*St. Louis Post Dispatch*)

Pedestrian Jean Gorman, walking 2 blocks from her Minneapolis, Minn., home, was accosted by a man who attempted to snatch her purse. She pulled a pistol from the purse and shot the footpad in the left side. The assailant fled the scene and turned up a short time later at a hospital, where he was placed on the critical list. (*St. Paul Pioneer Press*)

As Mark Levins, owner of a Chicago, Ill., sporting goods store, was preparing to close for the night, he was confronted by an armed bandit who ordered him to stand in the rear of the shop. As the bandit started scooping money out of the cash register, Levins slipped a pistol out of a filing cabinet. He ordered the bandit to surrender, but instead the intruder turned his gun on Levins. Each man fired his weapon twice—and the bandit fell dead with a bullet in his heart. (*Chicago Sun Times*)

AUGUST 1963

Two robbers entered Anthony Anello's Kansas City, Kans., food store and held up Anello, a clerk, and a customer. After relieving the victims of $350, the bandits ordered them into a back room and made them lie on the floor. Cautioning them to stay there for 5 minutes, the bandits fled. Anello rose and went to the front of the store, where he kept a loaded shotgun. Grabbing the gun, the storekeeper raced out of the front door and saw the men running up the street. He yelled for them to stop and when one of the bandits swung around with a pistol in his hand Anello fired. One bandit fell dead and the other escaped. (*Kansas City Times*)

When Wheatfield, N. Y., gas station operator George Houck, who lives above the station, was awakened by a noise, he got his gun and went downstairs to investigate. He arrived just in time to apprehend a robber leaving by the front door. Calling the man to halt, Houck held the robber at gun point until the police arrived. (*Buffalo Courier-Express*)

William Modesitt was awakened after midnight by noises in his Brazil, Ind., home. Modesitt saw an intruder in the living room. Obtaining his shotgun he quietly surprised the intruder and held him at bay until police arrived. When the man was in custody, it was learned he was on probation for second-degree burglary. (*The Brazil Daily Times*)

Miami, Fla., liquor store attendant, Robert Washbish, was robbed at gun point by 3 men, 2 of whom were armed. As one of the bandits took $250 from the cash drawer another thug grabbed several bottles of whisky. At this point Washbish came up with a cal. .38 pistol. One of the bandits fell wounded while the other bandits fled in a hail of bullets, only to be picked up a short time later by the police. (*The Miami News*)

Los Angeles, Calif., jewelry store operator Edward Kovacs was alone in his store when 3 men walked in and demanded his money. When one of the robbers drew his gun, Kovacs pulled out a .25 auto and fired. One of the bandits fell wounded and the others fled. (*Los Angeles Times*)

NOVEMBER 1963

When Ferrill LaRue, husband of the operator of a Los Angeles, Calif., rest home, heard the screams of one of the aged lady guests, he got his .30-30 rifle and rushed downstairs in time to see a prowler coming out of her room. The intruder struggled with LaRue for the rifle. Mrs. LaRue, hearing the commotion, grabbed her cal. .32 pistol and came on the scene as her husband struggled with the intruder. She called on the man to stop, and when he didn't Mrs. LaRue fired once, the bullet piercing both the man's cheeks. When police arrived, one of the aged residents was found to have been beaten severely and her room ransacked. (*Los Angeles Times*)

After Plymouth, Fla., homeowner, Ray Horne, had been robbed twice he started sleeping with a 12-ga. shotgun beside his bed. Awakened by noises in the early morning, he observed an armed intruder entering his bedroom door. Horne raised his gun and fired. The wounded robber fled but became entangled in a chain outside and crawled under Horne's house where he died. (*Orlando Sentinel*)

Edward Visnaw, Portland, Oreg., bakery owner, was tallying the day's receipts when he heard a knock on the door. He was confronted by a man who flashed what seemed to be a badge. The man said he was a detective and had a tip that the bakery was to be robbed. The man said he would return to the police car and radio for another car. Visnaw became suspicious because of the man's youth and slipped a revolver into his pocket. When the "detective" returned, he told Visnaw to lock the door. As Visnaw did so the man hit him several times over the head with a blackjack. Warding off the blows, the baker pulled out his revolver and shot his assailant dead. (*Oregon Journal*)

Bill Cason, a Kiowa, Okla., store owner, who had been robbed of more than $4000 in 4 different burglaries, rushed to his store when 3 bandits tripped the burglar alarm. One of the robbers turned and fired 2 shots at Cason. Cason shot the bandit dead as he tried to get to the rear of the store. One of the robbers fled and Cason held the other at gun point until police arrived. (*Wichita Falls Times*)

MARCH 1964

An armed bandit took $405 at gun point from Cleveland, Ohio, tavern owner, Edward W. Kawitt. As the thug fled, Kawitt grabbed a cal. .38 pistol and fired a shot at him. Minutes later the robber was found dead behind the store, the loot clutched in one hand and the gun in the other. (*Cleveland Plain Dealer*)

Furniture store owner Edward Poquette's wife was aroused by the sound of breaking glass behind their Gary, Ind., radio and TV shop. Poquette obtained an automatic pistol and went outside to investigate. He saw 3 burglars removing merchandise from a service station across the street. Poquette ran across the street as one intruder fled, fired one shot, and held the other 2 bandits for police. (*Gary Post-Tribune*)

Grocer Robert Brakefield surprised 3 intruders breaking into his Columbia, Miss., store. Brakefield fired 2 shots, wounding one of the would-be robbers, and held the trio until police arrived. (*The Commercial Appeal*)

Allison R. Ward was finishing chores at his Cheshire, Oreg., farm, when he was accosted by 2 thugs armed with knives. They ordered him into the house, demanded the keys to his truck, and trussed him up. Ward's wife arrived and was herded into the room with her husband. As the men left the house and started toward the truck, Ward slipped his bonds, grabbed a hidden cal. .30-30 rifle, and went to the door. He fired one shot which kicked up dirt between the fleeing intruders, who dropped their knives and were held for arrival of police. (*Eugene Register Guard*)

San Jose, Calif., grocery store owner Stephen Menzemer and his wife were approached in their store by a lone bandit wielding a butcher knife. He threatened to kill them unless they turned over the money. Menzemer gave the thug $70. When the bandit fled, Menzemer grabbed a pistol and ran outside. He fired one shot over the robber's head and held him at gun point until police arrived. (*San Jose Mercury News*)

1964

APRIL 1964

Isaac Knisley, Lantana, Fla., service-center owner, surprised a man coming out of his closed gas station carrying the cash register. Calling to the thief to halt, Knisley held a gun on the robber until police arrived. (*Palm Beach Post*)

As motel clerk Benjamin Renchenski was accosted by an armed bandit in Detroit, Mich., he purposely jammed the cash register and explained the trouble to the robber in a loud voice which attracted the attention of Charles Grisson, one of the owners. When Grisson saw the intruder holding a gun on his clerk, he fired 3 shots into the thug, who fell critically wounded. (*Detroit Free Press*)

Mrs. Anna Roscoe was tending her Gary, Ind., store as 3 armed women entered and announced a stickup. Mrs. Roscoe said in a loud voice, "So you have revolvers." Her husband, Thomas, grabbed a cal. .38 pistol and entered from a back room. When the female bandits, who were dressed as men, saw the gun they rushed to the door. Roscoe fired one shot and one robber dropped to the floor with a bullet in the shoulder. Roscoe held her at gun point until police arrived. (*The Gary Post-Tribune*)

THE ARMED CITIZEN

One-armed store owner, Winston W. Hilton, was approached by a man in his San Bernardino, Calif., store, who demanded his money at gun point. Grabbing a cal. .45 automatic from under the counter, Hilton ordered the robber to drop his gun and to lie on the floor, where he held the man until the police arrived. (*San Bernardino Daily Sun*)

East Ridge, Tenn., shop owner, T. C. Faires, had taken to sleeping in his shop because of attempted burglaries. Hearing a noise at 3:30 A.M., Faires armed himself with a shotgun and went out the front door around to the back of the store. There he found a man trying to pry open a window with a screwdriver. Faires covered the would-be burglar with his gun and took him to his nearby home where his son called police. (*Chattanooga News Press*)

JUNE 1964

An armed bandit entered Thomas Corcoran's Compton, Calif., pawn shop and ordered 2 customers to put their hands up. Corcoran seized a cal. .38 pistol and opened fire. The bandit was felled with 4 bullet wounds. Corcoran sustained a slight wound in his arm from the intruder's fire. (*Los Angeles Examiner*)

In his Long Beach, Calif., motel, Vinor Gilbertson and his wife were herded into their living quarters by a rifle-wielding bandit. After binding both of them with towels, the intruder ransacked the office. Gilbertson loosened his hands, got a cal. .38 pistol, and returned to the office. When the bandit saw Gilbertson, he made a grab for his rifle. Gilbertson killed him with a single shot. (*Los Angeles Times*)

When E. W. Corrick was accosted by an armed robber in his Galveston, Tex., grocery store, he turned over the day's receipts to the bandit, at the same time grabbing his own gun. As the intruder started to flee, Corrick ordered him to stop. The bandit turned and fired his gun at the grocer. Corrick returned the fire and the bandit fell, wounded. (*Houston Chronicle*)

A man brandishing a gun entered Leonard Mann's New London, Conn., store at closing time and demanded money. Mann recognized the gun as a toy and pulled his own gun from beneath a counter. The would-be bandit stood quietly until police arrived. (*The Hartford Times*)

Sporting goods store assistant George Elliott was awakened at 3:00 A.M. above his employer's Orillia, Ont., store by the barking of his dog. Obtaining a high power rifle, he crept down to the store and caught 2 thugs in the act of taking out a quantity of merchandise. Elliott made the burglars lie face down on the floor at gun point until police arrived. (*The Clinton Daily Packet and Times*)

AUGUST 1964

Hearing noises after she had retired, Mrs. Joan Thompson, a Chicago, Ill., expectant mother, called police on a bedroom phone. As a man entered her room holding a pistol, Mrs. Thompson reached into a bureau drawer, pulled out her husband's automatic, and shot the intruder once. The man lunged forward and struck Mrs. Thompson on the head with his gun. Mrs. Thompson fired again. The bandit staggered out a rear door and was found dead by police. (*Chicago Sun Times*)

In Independence, Kans., Harley R. Pierce was in the rear of his store when he heard a man demand money from his wife. Pierce grabbed a cal. .32 pistol and went into the store to find 2 men, one armed with a sawed-off shotgun, accosting his wife. The store owner fired one shot at the armed thug. The wounded bandit came at him and Pierce fired another shot as he struggled with the bandit. The man fell to the floor seriously wounded. Pierce held his gun on the other intruder until police arrived. (*Independence, Kans., Examiner*)

Twice in one week bandits tried to burglarize R. C. McCoy's Dallas, Tex., apartment building. The first time the bandits fled. Two nights later McCoy surprised 2 robbers trying to break into the laundry-machine coin boxes. McCoy held the thugs at gun point until police arrived. (*Dallas Times Herald*)

At San Ramon Village, Calif., tavern owner Lawrence A. Wilson returned to his restaurant to check the night's receipts. He and the bartender were ordered by the one remaining patron, at gun point, to empty the cash drawer. Wilson complied and he and the bartender were herded into a back room and told to stay there 5 minutes. When the bandit started to leave, Wilson pulled out a cal. .38 pistol and opened fire. The armed thug returned Wilson's fire, but missed and fell critically wounded. (*Oakland Tribune*)

SEPTEMBER 1964

Accosted by an armed thug in his Washington, D. C., grocery store, Allen M. Firtag grabbed a cal. .25 automatic and started shooting. Five shots later the would-be robber lay on the floor critically wounded with 2 bullets in his right side. Firtag and his wife had been beaten and robbed once before. (*Washington Post*)

Two armed thugs walked into Charles DiMaggio's New York delicatessen and demanded money. As one bandit emptied the cash register, the other herded the grocer into a back room. DiMaggio got a cal. .22 rifle which he kept there. Sighting through a hole in the door, DiMaggio fired a shot. The gunmen returned the fire and fled. A short while later a man walked into a nearby hospital with a gunshot wound in the chest. Police summoned DiMaggio who identified the man as one of the robbers. The man had a record of 9 previous arrests. (*Rochester Democrat & Chronicle*)

When Florida State Sen. Hayward Davis walked into his Lake Placid home and saw his wife and 2 small children sitting on the couch, he knew something was wrong. Just then he saw an armed intruder holding a gun on his family. Mrs. Davis was forced to tie up her husband with neckties. The gunman then pushed the Senator into one closet and the 2 children into another, and forced Mrs. Davis to drive away with him in the family car. Davis, freeing himself, ran into the garage and got a shotgun. The gunman and Mrs. Davis returned. When the intruder found that Sen. Davis was not in the closet, he grabbed Mrs. Davis and told her to tell her husband to come out. When the man started to choke Mrs. Davis, Sen. Davis fired a shot at him. The thug fired 2 shots from his pistol and Sen. Davis fired a second shot which fatally wounded the man who had terrorized his family. It was later learned that the man was an escapee from a Florida prison. (*Fort Lauderdale News*)

OCTOBER 1964

Alone in his Little Rock, Ark., beverage store, Floyd Strickland was approached by 2 thugs, one of whom was carrying a single-shot rifle with a sawed-off barrel. Without saying a word, the armed bandit fired at Strickland, wounding him in the arm. Strickland pulled out his pistol and fired 5 shots at the intruders. Both robbers were felled—one was dead and the other had 2 broken arms. (*Arkansas Gazette*)

Gunsmith Joe Doutre was working at a bench in his San Jose, Calif., shop when a man walked in and held a knife to Doutre's ribs and struck him twice over the head with a ball-peen hammer. As the gun shop owner lay dazed on the floor, the man kicked him and then bound and gagged him. Doutre managed to free himself and observed his attacker shoving revolvers and pistols into a bag. As the robber ran from the shop, Doutre grabbed a loaded pistol and felled the bandit with a single shot. (*San Jose Mercury*)

Clerk Gerald Pampuch was waiting on a customer in Kenneth D. Dugdale's Minneapolis, Minn., grocery store when a bandit entered the store and demanded money. Dugdale, who was in a back room, observed the bandit taking the money. He picked up his 12-ga. shotgun and followed the thug to the front door. As the bandit headed for a getaway car, Dugdale fired twice, seriously wounding the would-be robber. The driver of the getaway car was picked up 15 minutes later. Both admitted the robbery to police. (*Minneapolis Star*)

Clyde W. Goodner, returning with his wife to their Merit Island, Fla., home in the early evening hours, observed a man attempting to get into Goodner's pick-up truck. Goodner, who was armed with a cal. .38 pistol pulled it on the would-be thief and held him at gun point while Mrs. Goodner called the police. When police arrived Goodner learned that the man was an escaped convict serving a sentence for robbery. (*Brevard Sentinel*)

NOVEMBER 1964

When Queens, N.Y., grocer Frank Felicetti was awakened in his store by the sound of breaking glass, he went to investigate. Finding himself confronted by armed thugs who had previously robbed and beaten him, Felicetti begged them not to beat him again, and to go ahead and take the money. The robbers took the cash and 55 cartons of cigarettes and headed toward the door. Felicetti reached under the counter and grabbed a pistol and commenced firing. One bandit fell critically wounded while the second thug ran out the front door with Felicetti behind him. The grocer chased the man and fired 3 shots. The bandit fell dead. (Felicetti was later arrested for violating the Sullivan Law.) (*Long Island Press*)

When an invalid named Sullivan was robbed of $15 at the point of an ice pick in his San Antonio, Tex. apartment, he was told by his assailant not to call the police or he would come back and "cut your heart out." The invalid called the police and they patrolled the area for about 20 minutes. Later the thug returned and entered Sullivan's apartment by a rear door. As the intruder started toward him Sullivan pulled out a cal. .32 pistol and dropped the man with one shot. (*San Antonio Light*)

Mrs. Ollie K. Havner was awakened at 4 A.M. in her Charlotte, N. C., home by a flower pot falling into the sink. Mrs. Havner got a cal. .22 pistol from her dresser drawer just as a man carrying a dish towel started to enter her bedroom. Mrs. Havner fired at the intruder and he fell critically wounded. (*Charlotte Observer*)

When farmer George Greenwell of Alto Pass, Ill., saw an unidentified trespasser walking across his cornfield, he got his shotgun and held the man at gun point until police arrived. The man later confessed he was one of 2 men who had robbed a bank of more than $9000 earlier in the day. (*Chicago Tribune*)

DECEMBER 1964

In the early morning hours in Stewartstown, Pa., Harry H. Grimm heard the lock being forced on his apartment door. Grabbing a 12-ga. shotgun, Grimm shouted, "If you come in, I'll shoot." When the door burst open Grimm dropped the intruder with one fatal shot. It was later learned that the would-be burglar had broken into the same apartment 3 times previously and had served 18 months for one of the break-ins. (*Erie Times News*)

An armed bandit entered Darry Duckett's Chicago, Ill., package store and told Duckett to "give me every nickel you've got." Duckett reached under the cash register and came up firing. The bandit fell dead with a bullet in his chest. (*Chicago American*)

THE ARMED CITIZEN

When Chicago, Ill., housewife, Mrs. Tommie S. Owen, heard someone tell her husband, who had just answered the door, "This is a stickup," she got a cal. .25 automatic pistol and went to aid him. As the bandit started toward her with raised gun, Mrs. Owens fired once. The bandit, clutching his midsection, tried to fire his gun, but it misfired. He fled, but was found by police a few doors away, mortally wounded. (*Chicago Daily News*)

Frank McMinn heard noises in the kitchen of his Sacramento, Calif., home, left his bed, and picked up a shotgun. Going to the kitchen, McMinn surprised 2 men who quickly started out the back door. He fired at one, and when police arrived they found one of the intruders in the back yard suffering from shotgun wounds. (*The Sacramento Bee*)

Hearing noises in the early morning hours behind a restaurant next door, a Hamden, Conn., citizen, Salvatore Amendola, got his 12-ga. shotgun and went to investigate while his wife called the police. When Amendola saw 2 men trying to break in the restaurant's back door, he ordered them not to move. Both the thugs tried to run and Amendola fired one shot in the air. One intruder kept running, but the other stood meekly until police arrived. (*New Haven Register*)

1965

JANUARY 1965

Statesville, N. C., service station owner, Larry O. Shives, was accosted by a man at closing time who ordered Shives to turn over all his money or he would be shot by a man across the street who was covering him with a shotgun. Instead of complying, Shives pulled a pistol from his pocket and held the man in custody while his wife called the police. (*Statesville Record*)

Mr. and Mrs. Francis Lindsay returned to their home in Spokane, Wash., to find that the glass in their back door had been broken. Mr. Lindsay rushed into the house and saw a man going out of the front door. Mr. Lindsay got a gun, ran out the front door, and held the man at gun point until police arrived. It was discovered that the house had been ransacked—and the man was an escapee from a mental hospital. (*Spokesman Review*)

An 18-year-old Stockton, Calif., youth, John G. Burnett, returned to his home for lunch. When he heard noises coming from a bedroom Burnett got a cal. .22 rifle and surprised an intruder in the act of burglarizing the home. Burnett kept the gun on the robber and called police. The man's truck was found parked a block away, and contained cameras and other items which the man reportedly admitted taking from another home. (*Stockton Record*)

Baltimore, Md., cleaning establishment owner, Rufus Owens, was sleeping on a cot in his place of business. He was awakened by the sound of a window being forced. Grabbing his shotgun Owens went to investigate and surprised a would-be burglar coming through the window. Not having a phone, Owens, holding his prisoner at bay, unlocked the front door. A short time later a policeman making his round noticed the unlocked door, came in and took the intruder into custody. (*The Evening Sun*)

MARCH 1965

As Donald Carter of Rapid City, S. Dak., passed a service station in the early morning hours, he noticed a man entering the station through a window. Carter hurried to his home, told his wife to call police, and then returned to the station with his rifle. Carter held the burglar at gun point until police arrived. (*Rapid City Daily Journal*)

Alerted by a noise from the direction of their dining room, Mr. and Mrs. C. G. (Chuck) Wylie of El Paso, Tex., both armed themselves and went to investigate. In the dining room they confronted an armed robber who had broken in by cutting open a screen door. The man lunged at Mr. Wylie and the homeowner hit him on the head with his gun. Then while Mr. Wylie covered the robber, Mrs. Wylie called police. (*El Paso Herald-Post*)

From his residence in the rear of his store in Duncan Mills, Calif., Silvio DeCarly heard noises and saw a light flashing inside the store. DeCarly called the sheriff's office and then, armed with his rifle, moved around to the front of the store. Two thugs inside the store came out with their hands up when they saw DeCarley with the rifle. He held the 2 at gun point until a deputy sheriff arrived. (*Santa Rosa, Calif., Press Democrat*)

J. L. Campbell, operator of Silver Falls Lodge near Silverton, Oreg., was awakened by his wife who had heard noises in the main part of the lodge. Campbell, armed with a .22 pistol, surprised 2 burglars. He held them at gun point and had his wife call Harry Luckett, Supt. of Silver Falls Park. At this time Campbell was aware that confederates of the 2 he had captured were outside somewhere. Shortly after Luckett arrived, one of the 2 burglars jumped him in an attempted escape. Campbell wounded one and recaptured both. Police took the burglars into custody and later picked up 3 persons who had waited outside the lodge during the events inside. (*Silverton Appeal Tribune*)

APRIL 1965

When Columbus, Ohio, bar owner Mrs. Helen McCoy found 2 men ransacking her place of business, she fired twice at the thugs, and then held them at gun point until police arrived. It was later learned that the 2 had been responsible for more than a dozen break-ins in the area. (*Toledo Blade*)

Taylorsville, Ky., farmer Roscoe Poe was alone in his home watching television when 2 men armed with a pistol and a shotgun broke into his house. Hearing the noise, Poe grabbed a double-barrel shotgun and felled one of the intruders. When the other barrel misfired, Poe ran to a bedroom, got a revolver, and shot the second intruder dead. (*The Courier-Journal*)

Two men entered a Chattanooga, Tenn., service station and asked attendant Lawrence Witt for cigarettes. As the men started out the door, one turned around, pointed a cal. .22 pistol at Witt, and demanded "Give me all you got." Witt drew a pistol from his pocket and fired 3 shots, fatally wounding both robbers. (*Chattanooga News-Free Press*)

When 3 men attempted to hold up Rilus Graham's Phoenix, Ariz., package goods store, the proprietor grabbed a pistol and fired 7 shots at the thugs, one of whom fell seriously wounded. The other 2 fled. (*The Arizona Republic*)

Woodrow Smith was awakened in the early morning hours by a noise from his Palm Beach, Fla., general store next door. Armed with a cal. .38 pistol, Smith went to investigate. As he entered the store, a man attempted to flee with a quantity of pistols and ammunition. Smith held the robber at gun point until police arrived. (*Palm Beach Post*)

Attracted by the scream of a guest in his Tulare, Calif., home, A. C. Nicholson armed himself with a shotgun and confronted a man attempting to steal Mrs. Nicholson's purse. The burglar grabbed for Nicholson's gun and the householder shot him dead. (*Santa Barbara News Press*)

JUNE 1965

In his New Haven, Conn., package goods store, Walter Pashkowsky was approached by 2 men who demanded money. After handing over $100, and as the pair started to leave, Pashkowsky took out a gun and held one man for police. The other fled. (*New Haven Register*)

As Raymond A. Nielsen, a druggist in Denver, Colo., watched 2 gunmen herd serveral customers into the back of his store, one of the bandits fired a shot at him. Nielsen dropped to the floor and picked up a secreted automatic pistol. He came up firing and one of the bandits fell dead. (*Drug Topics*)

Awakened by a noise in her Coatesville, Pa., home, Mrs. Rose McCullough took a pistol and went to investigate. When she opened her bedroom door, she was grabbed by an assailant. Mrs. McCullough fired several shots and then ran to a neighbor's house for help. Police found the intruder wounded on the kitchen floor. Later it was learned he had recently been released from prison. (*Philadelphia Inquirer*)

When a robber placed a gun at the head of Washington, D. C., storekeeper Arthur D'Appolito's wife and said "Shut up", the D'Appolito's German shepherd dog lunged at the gunman throwing him off balance. He fired 2 shots at the dog but missed. D'Appolito grabbed a rifle and fired one shot, hitting the robber as he ran out the door. A confederate dragged the wounded man to an adjacent parking lot. D'Appolito followed and held both captive until police arrived. (*Washington Post*)

Three would-be bandits, one armed, entered Henry Aldama's, Chicago, Ill., grocery store and demanded money. Aldama handed over the cash register receipts and told them there wasn't any more money. The armed bandit fired a shot past the grocer's ear and then pistol whipped him. Aldama showed them a cigar box of change, then grabbed a revolver and fired, killing one bandit and wounding the other two. (*Chicago Tribune*)

JULY 1965

Jaime Montalvo was in the back room of his Brooklyn, N. Y., grocery store when he heard someone tell his clerk, "This is a stick up". Montalvo grabbed a cal. .38 revolver, for which he had obtained a permit only the day before, and rushed into the store. He fired once at the armed thug. The wounded bandit fired 3 shots which missed Montalvo, and ran from the store. He collapsed and died on the pavement 100 ft. away. (*New York Herald Tribune*)

El Monte, Calif., package goods store clerk William A. Love was held at bay by 2 armed thugs. Love put $400 on the counter. As one of the bandits started to scoop up the money, Love drew a cal. .45 pistol from under the counter and fired. The pair fled, leaving the money on the floor. Later, police found the dead body of one of the bandits. (*San Gabriel Valley Daily Tribune*)

Two men, acting strangely, entered the North Nashville, Tenn., grocery store of Wayne C. Garner and ordered cigarettes. Garner placed the cigarettes on the counter with one hand and grasped a cal. .38 revolver under the counter with the other. When one of the thugs drew a cal. .45 automatic out of his pocket, Garner quickly raised his gun and fired. The gun-wielding bandit fell dead and his companion fled. (*The Nashville Tennessean*)

THE ARMED CITIZEN

When Jacksonville, Fla., storekeeper Homer Thomas was confronted by an armed man who said, "Give me what you've got under the counter", Thomas whipped out a cal. 25 pistol and fired. The bandit fled but was later found dead under a nearby porch. His cal. .38 pistol was found on the floor of Thomas' store. (*Jacksonville Journal*)

Three bandits entered the Chicago, Ill., grocery store of Mrs. Alberta Lathon and demanded money. When she produced the cash one of the thugs slugged her. As the robbers turned to flee, Mrs. Lathon grabbed a pistol and fired one shot, critically wounding one of the bandits. (*Chicago Sun Times*)

AUGUST 1965

Aroused from the back of his Detroit, Mich., area store by early morning noises, Novatus Johnson got his 12-ga. shotgun and surprised an intruder prying open a window-screen with an iron bar. As the would-be burglar lunged at him with the iron bar, Johnson fired. The man fell dead. (*The Detroit News*)

Two men entered the Phoenix, Ariz., store of Lynn D. Loui and purchased some groceries. As Loui made change, one of the men pointed a pistol at him and forced him to empty the cash register into a paper bag. When the bandit demanded more, Loui grabbed a cal. .22 pistol from under the counter and started firing. The bandit fell wounded. (*The Phoenix Gazette*)

William Brown was approached in his Newark, N. J., shop by a man and woman. The man, with his hand jammed in his pocket as if he were carrying a gun, demanded the contents of the safe. Brown, who is 80, opened the safe, withdrew a cal. .38 revolver, and fired 2 shots wounding the man. The bandit fled and was picked up later by police. (*New York Sunday News*)

When Mr. & Mrs. Robert Zamie were confronted by a pistol-wielding bandit demanding money from their Phoenix, Ariz., tavern, Mr. Zamie complied. However, as the robber turned to leave, Mrs. Zaime reached under the counter and passed Mr. Zamie a loaded revolver. He fired one shot at the intruder, who fell seriously wounded. (*The Arizona Republic*)

Mrs. Dee Brookshire entered her Dayton, Ohio confectionary store at 1:30 A.M. to check equipment in the basement. Hearing a noise, she quietly picked up a shotgun. Finding an intruder standing behind the counter, Mrs. Brookshire clicked off the safety and the thug whirled around and cried "Don't shoot me". The store owner ordered the intruder to put up his hands and sit down. Mrs. Brookshire called the police and held the bandit at gun point until they arrived. (*Dayton Daily News*)

OCTOBER 1965

In Miami, Fla., Paul Baker, Jr. pulled into the driveway of his home in the early morning hours. He took his pistol from the glove compartment of his car and started toward his front door. A belt was thrown around Baker's neck from behind. Baker resisted and he and his unknown assailant fell to the ground. Baker fired 4 times at the would-be mugger, killing him instantly. It was later learned the man had a long police record. (*Miami Herald*)

Dr. Buford Whitt and his family were in their semi-darkened Huntsville, Ala., home when they heard the sound of someone breaking through a rear door. Dr. Whitt got his gun and surprised the man inside his home—he fired once at the intruder—who staggered outside and collapsed seriously wounded. (*Huntsville Times*)

Sleeping in his Possum Grape, Ark., cafe because of recent robberies, William Marlin Willis, the owner, surprised 2 men attempting to rifle the restaurant cash register. One of the intruders shot at Willis, who fired back, killing the would-be bandit. The other fled. (*Memphis Commercial Appeal*)

When Christine Coghlan, a 14-year-old girl who had been trained in the use and handling of the shotgun by her brother, observed 2 men climbing through the window of her Crystal Lake, Ill., home, she loaded and cocked a shotgun and waited until they entered. She forced one of the intruders to call her mother who was at work. Christine's mother then called police who arrived and took the 2 intruders into custody. (*Rockford Morning Star*)

Two men walked behind the counter of clerk John Robert Kromer's Pico Rivera, Calif., liquor store towards the cash register. Kromer quickly drew a revolver from under the counter and held the 2 thugs until police arrived. One had a pellet gun tucked into the waistband of his trousers. The other had a concealed 9″ dagger. (*Daily News*)

NOVEMBER 1965

Howard R. Chisim, who lives behind his Battle Creek, Mich., grocery store was awakened in the early morning hours by noises coming from the store. Grabbing a pistol, he went to investigate. Encountering 2 men, Chisim ordered them back into the store, made them deposit their loot on the counter, and then marched them into the walk-in cooler to await the arrival of the police. (*Battle Creek Enquirer And News*)

In bed in his Anchorage, Alaska home, Dr. Robert W. Miller was stabbed in the chest by a knife-wielding intruder. Mrs. Miller coaxed the intruder into the living room. While they were gone Dr. Miller located his pistol and went after the armed thug. He fired several shots at the intruder, killing him instantly. It was later learned that the man was wanted by the FBI for assaulting a woman and then threatening her with a gun. (*Anchorage Daily News*)

As Charles Di Maggio was closing his New York City, N. Y., grocery store 3 thugs entered and forced Di Maggio into a washroom in the rear of the store. One of the bandits pointed a pistol at Di Maggio and warned: "I would rather shoot you than look at you. We always wanted to get you, Di Maggio, and we're taking no chances this time." The stick-up men took $300, a wallet, keys, and wrist watch from the grocer and then returned, single file, to the front of the store, pausing at the cash register. This gave Di Maggio time to get out his rifle which was hidden in the washroom; he inserted one cartridge and fired. The single bullet went through the upper chest of the last bandit and into the body of the second. The last thug staggered out the door and fell dead into the gutter. The second bandit made it to about a block away and collapsed at the feet of a policeman, he was taken to the hospital in critical condition. The third bandit escaped with the money. During the past 10 years, Di Maggio has had 26 attempted robberies, 11 of which were successful. He has captured 15 thugs, and killed 3. (*New York Daily News*)

FEBRUARY 1966

In St. Marys County, Md., Earl R. Compton was awakened by screams and the sound of a car horn. Getting into his trousers and grabbing his gun Compton ran outside. He found a man attempting to attack a woman in a car. Compton ordered the man out of the car and the attacker jumped him. Compton fired one shot and the man staggered toward his own car and got in. He was dead when police arrived. The woman stated that the man had been following her, blinking his lights. She mistook him for a police car. (*Washington Evening Star*)

In Santaquin, Utah, restaurant owner Russell Jarvis, who was staying in an apartment behind the restaurant, heard noises. Jarvis picked up a gun and went to investigate. He found a pane of glass removed from a window. Suddenly a man dove out of the window and started to run. Jarvis halted the man and held him at gun point until police arrived. The burglar admitted to police several other robberies in the area. (*Utah County Daily Herald*)

Mrs. David Arceneaux was working in the yard of her Lafayette, La., farm when 3 men, one armed with a shotgun, appeared. Mrs. Arceneaux screamed and one of the men grabbed her and held her down. The other 2 men went into the house. Mr. Arceneaux, who had been sleeping, was awakened by the screams of his wife. Picking up his pistol, he turned just as the man with the shotgun entered the room. Arceneaux shot him dead. The other 2 intruders fled. One of the men was picked up by police a short distance from the house. (*The Denver Post*)

When a suspicious looking man entered James Fitzsimmons' store in West Los Angeles, Calif., the store owner secreted a pistol in a money bag under the counter. The man suddenly turned to Fitzsimmons, pulled a revolver, and said, "This is a holdup. Put the money in the bag and hand it over." Fitzsimmons grabbed the gun inside the bag, held out the money sack and fired at the armed thug who fell fatally wounded. (*Los Angeles Herald Examiner*)

MARCH 1966

When Girdwood, Alaska, tavern owner, Joe Dannich, discovered 2 men attempting a getaway after having burglarized his tavern, he grabbed his shotgun and fired into the air. The thugs, who had just entered their car, halted. Dannich's wife then called the police. (*Anchorage Daily Times*)

After 12 thefts in 5 years, druggist Royce P. Christiansen became suspicious when 2 men entered his Houston, Tex., store. As one of the men started towards him, Christiansen grabbed a gun. He then noticed that the other thug, who was approaching him from a side aisle, was pulling a gun from his pocket. The druggist fired 3 times at the man with the gun who fell seriously wounded. The other would-be bandit fled. (*The Houston Post*)

In San Francisco, pharmacist Tom Merigan was approached in his drug store by a thug who placed a gun against the druggist's head and demanded narcotics. Merigan complied. When the would-be bandit turned to flee, the druggist reached under the counter, grabbed a pistol, and fired 3 shots at the thug who fell seriously wounded. (*San Francisco Chronicle*)

Sleeping in the rear of his Beaufort, S. C., appliance store as a result of a series of burglaries, D. L. Koth heard his cash register bell sound. Arming himself with a shotgun, Koth went into the store and found a man rifling the cash register. As the thug started towards him, Koth ordered him to lie on the floor and held him there until police arrived. (*Charleston News and Courier*)

Dallas, Tex., grocery store owner, B. J. Potts, was awakened by the barking of his dog outside his store. Potts went to investigate and found a broken window. He took a revolver from under the counter and routed an intruder from the back of a storeroom. The thug picked up a piece of lumber and turned towards the grocer. The store owner fired 2 warning shots but the man kept coming and Potts fired again. When police arrived, the would-be burglar was dead. (*Dallas Morning News*)

1966

THE ARMED CITIZEN

APRIL 1966

Answering a knock on the door of his Millville, N. J., home in the early evening, Russel Burcham was confronted by 2 thugs, one with a pistol, the other with a piece of lead pipe. They demanded money. Burcham wrestled one of the men to a closet door and managed to get a rifle. He fired once, wounding one bandit, who fled. The other thug was held at gun point until police arrived. (*Philadelphia Daily News*)

Sleeping in a room at the rear of his Kansas City, Kans., television repair shop, Charles Riley was awakened by the sounds of scuffling. He went into the store in time to see a shotgun-armed intruder hit his wife in the head with the shotgun barrel. As the would-be bandit swung the gun towards him, Riley grabbed the gun barrel. Mrs. Riley got a pistol from a shelf and fired, killing the robber. It was later learned that the dead bandit had a long police record. (*Kansas City Star*)

As Mrs. Jaetta Hensley was preparing to retire in her Des Moines, Iowa, home, she was startled by the sound of breaking glass. Arming herself with a pistol, Mrs. Hensley waited. When she heard the thug nearing her bedroom, Mrs. Hensley kicked open the door and ordered the startled man to halt. A neighbor who heard the break-in called police who took the intruder into custody. (*Des Moines Tribune*)

As Vernice Benny Baynum returned to his South Whittier, Calif., home, he saw a strange car in front of his house, and noted his garage door was ajar. When he entered his home, he heard noises coming from his bedroom. Baynum grabbed a shotgun and started for the bedroom when a man started running towards the front door. "Stop," ordered Baynum. The thug complied and was held at gun point until police arrived. (*The Santa Ana Register*)

When Pensacola, Fla., tavern owner, Earl Childress, surprised an armed thug in the store after closing hours, he drew a pistol and ordered him to halt. The intruder lunged and Childress fired. When the bandit lunged a second time, the tavern owner mortally wounded the man. (*The Pensacola Journal*)

MAY 1966

Mrs. Bertha Simmons was awakened in the middle of the night by screams for help outside her Columbus, Ohio, home. She heard a man pleading, "Don't hit me again. I gave you all I got." Mrs. Simmons, 81, got out of bed, grabbed a pistol from her dresser drawer, and ran out onto her front porch. She observed 3 men with lead pipes beating a cab driver over the head. Mrs. Simmons started firing and the thugs fled. When police arrived at the scene they credited Mrs. Simmons' action with saving the cab driver's life. Later she received a citation for bravery. (*National Enquirer*)

Joseph Bausone, manager of a Dallas, Tex., package goods store, was approached by a man who ordered a bottle of whiskey. As Bausone turned to fill the order, the intruder drew a pistol and demanded that the shopkeeper open the register. At that moment a passerby looked into the store and saw the holdup in progress. The thug fired one shot at Bausone, who dove under the counter and came up with his own gun and got off 4 quick shots. The would-be bandit staggered out of the store and fell dead. (*Dallas Times Herald*)

In Pontiac, Mich., Robert Clark was working in his service station when he heard noises at the rear door of his building. Clark called his assistant, Larry Seaton, and then phoned police. Seaton arrived on the scene armed with a rifle and spotted 2 men running from the station. One fled into a nearby field, and the other jumped into a car where he was held at gun point by Seaton until police arrived. (*Pontiac Press*)

A Norton Township, Mich., pool hall owner, Eddie Morgan, sleeping in quarters at the rear of his establishment, was awakened in the early morning hours by pounding noises. Arming himself with a shotgun, he went to investigate and surprised 2 men who had knocked a lock off the front door. One of the intruders fled and Morgan held the other thug at gun point until police arrived. (*Muskegon Chronicle*)

JUNE 1966

Illie Dave, owner of a Houston, Tex., grocery store, was surprised by an armed thug who walked into his store and drew a pistol. Dave retreated and when an opportunity presented itself he picked up his own gun and fired at the intruder. The would-be robber fell mortally wounded. It was later learned that the man had recently been released from jail after serving a term for burglary and theft. (*Houston Post*)

In Tulsa, Okla, druggist Edwin R. Curry, who had been the victim of several holdups, was accosted by a gun-toting bandit. Curry grabbed a gun from under the counter and fired 4 shots at the bandit. The would-be robber fired 3 shots at Curry before falling dead on the floor. It was later learned that the robber had a record in several states. (*Tulsa Tribune*)

Robert K. Ashburn and his wife were alone in their Norfolk, Va., grocery store, when a pistol-wielding bandit walked in and demanded money. As Ashburn gave the man money, the thug pointed the gun at Ashburn's wife and demanded more. At that moment Ashburn grabbed his own pistol and fired. The thug staggered out of the store and collapsed, mortally wounded, a block away. (*Virginia Pilot*)

When Denver, Colo., tavern owner Gerry Jones returned to his closed establishment in the early morning hours to pick up the receipts, he was joined by an employee. While they were conversing, Jones heard a noise at the back door. As the employee went to phone police, Jones hid behind the bar and waited until 2 intruders entered the tavern. Jones then fired a warning shot and held the men at bay until the police arrived. (*Denver Post*)

Bronx, N.Y., apartment tenant Joseph Mac-Hatton, hearing noises on his fire escape, grabbed a rifle and went to investigate. Finding a masked man in his kitchen, MacHatton opened fire. The would-be burglar fell mortally wounded. (*New York Daily News*)

AUGUST 1966

A prospective customer at the coin shop of James A. Berkel, Belleville, Ill., suddenly drew a gun and said: "All right, let's go." Berkel, who was standing behind the counter, grabbed his revolver and fired twice. The would-be bandit got off one shot but fell mortally wounded. (*Belleville News Democrat*)

In his Las Vegas, Nev., apartment, John J. Miller was preparing to go to work. Alerted by the growling of his dog, Miller obtained a revolver from his bedside table, and went into the living room to investigate. He confronted an armed intruder. Miller fired and the would-be bandit fell mortally wounded. (*Las Vegas Review Journal*)

Absecon, N. J., motel keeper, Harold Becker, was approached by 3 men who asked for a room. Becker assigned them a room and then quickly closed the main lobby door and ran for the second floor. The 3 men broke down the lobby door and started after Becker, who meanwhile had obtained a rifle. When the would-be bandits closed in, Becker fired at them and one of the thugs fell wounded. One of the remaining men fled and the other was held until police arrived. (*Bridgeton Evening News*)

In Portland, Oreg., Lee E. Stewart, was returning to a closed service station to pick up his car. On approaching the building he noticed someone inside. When he went to investigate, the intruder brandished a gun. Stewart retreated to his car and obtained his own pistol. He returned and ordered the would-be bandit out at gun point. Stewart held the man at gun point while he called police on his citizen's band 2-way radio. (*Portland Oregonian*)

When Charles Bombeck prepared to wait on a customer in his Kansas City, Mo., package goods store, he was suddenly facing a drawn gun. The 'customer' made Bombeck empty the cash register. As the thug turned, Bombeck grabbed a gun from under the counter and fired. The intruder staggered out into the street and fell wounded. (*Kansas City Times*)

NOVEMBER 1966

Grocer Salem Totah and his son were in their San Francisco, Calif., store when 2 men walked in and robbed him at gun point. One robber fled with the loot while the other armed bandit walked around the counter and knocked the grocer down. Totah reached under the counter and got his pistol. The bandit fired at the shopkeeper and missed. Totah fired 3 shots at the bandit. The armed robber was dead on arrival at the hospital. (*San Francisco Examiner*)

North Hollywood, Calif., liquor store owner Brooks Burton faced the same gunman who had robbed him 3 times previously. The bandit ordered Burton to the rear of his shop where he took money from the safe and Burton's wallet. As the bandit turned to leave, Burton moved to the cash register and got his own gun. The armed thug fired one shot at the storekeeper who followed him out, shooting at the robber. The bandit returned the fire and then suddenly cried, "I'm hit!" He threw his gun in front of him and collapsed in the street. He was dead on arrival at the hospital. (*Los Angeles Herald Examiner*)

Cary, Ill. tavern owner Kenneth Stroner, who was sleeping in his tavern, was awakened by a disturbance behind the bar. He obtained a pistol and surprised 2 men in the process of burglarizing the tavern. One of the robbers jumped through a plate glass window and escaped, but Stroner shot the other burglar. When police arrived, they discovered the wounded man had $250 on him. It was also learned that the man was on probation. (*McHenry, Ill. Citizen Newspapers*)

Wayne McWilliams, who was sleeping in the office of his Visalia, Calif., automotive center, was awakened by the sound of someone prying the lock off the front door. As he went to investigate there was the sound of breaking glass and an intruder came through a window—only to be held by McWilliams until police arrived. (*Visalia Times-Delta*)

MARCH 1967

In Portsmouth, Va., two men walked into Robert H. Oliver's jewelry store and asked to see a watch and a bracelet. Oliver became suspicious and went to a back room to obtain a pistol. As he returned to the store, one man pointed a gun at him and said, "This is a holdup." Oliver ducked behind a partition and fired 2 shots at the fleeing bandits. Moments later one man was picked up by police, wounded by a bullet from the jeweler's pistol. (*The Norfolk Virginian-Pilot*)

1967

A prisoner who escaped from the Federal Reformatory at Chillicothe, Ohio, while serving a stolen car sentence, was recaptured without firing a shot because, Deputy Sheriff Dwight Beery reports, farmer Wendell Bryant, who lives near Frankfort, Ohio, got his shotgun out and backed up the lone deputy who answered Bryant's call and helped to trace the prisoner. Deputy Earl Kuhn reported to Deputy Sheriff Dwight Beery, that the prisoner appeared ready to make a break at one point but did not do so "because of Mr. Bryant standing in an advantageous position. I couldn't have asked for better assistance." The Ross County Law Enforcement Officers Association honored Bryant at a special meeting. (*Chillicothe, Ohio Gazette*)

Frank E. Pahler and friends were in a parked car across the street from a Mountaintop, Pa., service station. Pahler suddenly noticed someone walking around inside the closed station. Going to his home and obtaining his shotgun, Pahler returned to the service station and apprehended an intruder whom he held at gunpoint until police arrived. (*Hazleton, Pa. Standard-Speaker*)

Pearl Ferguson, a Sacramento, Calif., veteran of 4 previous holdups in her little grocery store, was accosted by an armed thug who said, "This is a stickup." "Go ahead and shoot," she replied. As the gunman edged towards her, Mrs. Ferguson reached for a hidden pistol, cocked it, and pointed it at the startled bandit. He fled into the street shouting, "Don't shoot, I give up, I give up." (*Ukiah, Calif. Daily Journal*)

APRIL 1967

Awakened by suspicious noises, Mrs. Catherine Drains, who lives behind her Los Angeles, Calif., record shop, got her .38 caliber revolver just as two shadowy figures broke open her front door. She wounded one in the upper arm, the other in the stomach. Police arrested both. (*Los Angeles Herald-Examiner*)

Milton (Bud) Hunter, a Raleigh, N.C., music store employee, saw through a window 2 men holding up a liquor store next door. He got a revolver and started across the alley just as the holdup men, one armed with a sawed-off shotgun, ran out. One threatened to kill Hunter. He pulled his pistol and shot one of them in the leg. Police later arrested the pair and found $586, taken in the robbery, on one of them. Raleigh Police Chief Tom Davis' letter of commendation said, "We appreciate this splendid example of good citizenship and initiative." (*The News and Observer, Raleigh, N.C.*)

In West Haven, Conn., apartment dweller Theodore Zembrowski heard noises in the hall as if someone was trying to break in. With his .45 caliber pistol, he went out and halted 2 men. One fled. The other, arrested, allegedly admitted he was involved in 2 break-ins. (*The New Haven, Conn., Register*)

Ex-Marine William C. Kelley has won his third personal battle with holdup men at his Los Angeles, Calif., service station. When two men demanded the cash, Kelley gave them $32.63 from the cash box. One man went after him for more. Kelley shot the holdup man 3 times with a .25 automatic, then went inside for his .38 caliber revolver. Both men drove off meanwhile. Kelley said he shot another bandit through both legs in 1965 and, later that year, killed a holdup man who shoved a shotgun at him saying, "You're going to die." Pushing aside the shotgun, Kelley, a pistol expert, shot first. He remarked, "I don't doubt anything a man says when he's pointing a gun at you." (*Los Angeles Herald-Examiner*)

Store-owner Robert Grimm, of Phoenix, Ariz., was inspecting his store property in the early morning hours when he noticed some of his possessions stacked up outside. Grimm got his gun and stationed himself on the roof. Shortly after 4 a.m., a man drove up and started to load the material in his car. Grimm told him to halt. When the bandit refused, Grimm fired 2 shots into the ground. The man was halted by a shot in the leg. (*Phoenix Gazette*)

Noticing an attempted attack on a 71-year-old woman in an empty garage near his home, an unnamed Dayton, Ohio, citizen grabbed his pistol and ran outside in time to prevent a rape and hold a 25-year-old man at gunpoint until the arrival of police. Police declined to name the rescuer, fearing reprisals from underworld friends of the prisoner, a criminal. A detective did say, however, "They don't make many citizens like that anymore." (*Dayton Daily News*)

In Del City, Okla., 2 armed thugs relieved supermarket manager Raymond E. Patterson of $3,000 and backed him into his office at gunpoint. The beleaguered store manager grabbed a hidden pistol and shot one of the bandits dead. A quick-thinking customer scooped up the fallen robber's pistol and fired several shots at the dead man's fleeing partner, breaking the rear window of his auto. The suspect's car was later stopped by police, who found a loaded sawed-off rifle in it, and booked the man on a charge of armed robbery. He had a prior conviction. (*The Daily Oklahoman*)

North Hollywood, Calif., college professor Michael I. Silverman and his wife were awakened in their bedroom at 4 a.m., by a noise in their living room. Silverman called the police from his bedroom phone, grabbed a pistol, and went to investigate. When he saw a man run from the house, Silverman fired a shot over his head. The suspect ran back into Silverman's house, raised his hands in surrender, and quietly waited for the police to arrive. (*Los Angeles Times*)

Store owner Claude (Bud) Willsey won his seventh gun battle with bandits when an armed robber walked into his Berkeley, Calif., liquor shop and demanded money. The thug took $70 from the cash register and started to leave. Willsey's wife grabbed a shotgun, fired at the bandit, but missed. Willsey picked up his pistol and wounded the bandit, who was then apprehended by police. (*Oakland, Calif. Tribune*)

JUNE 1967

As Joseph Lobue was closing his Sacramento, Calif., tavern for the night, two hooded robbers armed with pistols jumped him. Lobue pulled his own gun and pointed it at them. "It looks like a standoff," said one robber. Both fled empty-handed. (*San Francisco, Calif., Examiner-Chronicle*)

A gang of 5 cornered Louis Rivezo, a Brooklyn, N. Y., undertaker, as he left his home. Slamming him against a fence, they robbed him of $150 and mauled him. Rivezo fired 3 shots from a revolver, for which he had a permit. One fell dead and the gang scattered. (*Poughkeepsie, N. Y., Journal*)

Service station attendant Edward Stambaugh, Provo, Utah, was counting the day's receipts when a car drew up on the drive and a man came around the car, gun in his hand. With no lost motion, Stambaugh scooped up a .38 caliber revolver and took one shot at the surprised "customer." The man fled. Station owner Al Nielson commented, "We always have the gun here just in case." (*Salt Lake City, Utah, Deseret News*)

Walter Pahuta became suspicious when three men walked into his Elba, N. Y., grocery store at closing time. He secured his .25 caliber pistol. When one of the intruders pulled a gun, Pahuta ducked behind the counter and fired one shot. The trio fled. All were rounded up later, one with a bullet wound in the shoulder. (*Batavia, N.Y., Daily News*)

While Nick Perciballi was transferring money to the cash drawer of his Akron, Ohio, grocery, an armed thug held him up. Perciballi warned: "I have the same thing you have." The gunman fired and missed. Perciballi shot him in the stomach and again in the back as he turned to flee. Police arrested him at a hospital, together with two other men. (*Akron, Ohio, Beacon-Journal*)

Two Sacramento, Calif., brothers, Daniel and Michael Valverde, were alerted in the early morning hours by noises at the rear of their home. Arming themselves with a shotgun they found three men loading a truck with property from a neighbor's garage. Daniel held the men at gunpoint while his brother summoned the police. Sheriff John Misterly commented: "We could use more good work such as this by citizens. I compliment them." (*Sacramento, Calif., Bee*)

Receiving a sheriff's alert to watch out for an escaped convict, Max Brugh, 71, a retired mail carrier living near Nace, Va., searched outbuildings on his farm, pistol in hand. He surprised the convict there and held him at gunpoint while Mrs. Brugh called police. (*Fincastle, Va., Herald*)

Burglars plagued the Veterans of Foreign Wars Club in Winter Garden, Fla., to the point where Manager James Cothern stayed after hours on guard. When two men broke in, Cothern wounded one critically and downed the other with a pistol bullet in the arm. (*Orlando, Fla., Sentinel*)

Mrs. Donald Coughlin observed two men breaking into the coin box of an outside telephone near her home in Portland, Oreg. Alerting her husband to call police, she went outside with a shotgun and held the pair at bay until the police arrived. (*Salem, Oreg., Capital Journal*)

When David Varady of Inglewood, Calif., was awakened by the sound of shattering glass, he glanced out his window and saw two men burglarizing a store across the street. Grabbing a gun, Varady halted the pair as they emerged from the store with $120 in loot. He held them at gunpoint until police arrived. (*Los Angeles, Calif., Herald*)

"Give me all the money you have here," demanded a man armed with a big knife of Cleveland, Ohio, van lines clerk, Mrs. Patricia Cawthon. Mrs. Cawthon walked calmly to a nearby closet, picked up a snub nosed automatic pistol, turned to the knife-wielding bandit and said: "Where do you want it?" The thief ran out the door. (*Cleveland, Ohio, Plain Dealer*)

The Russell Hagermans, an elderly East St. Louis, Ill., couple, were awakened by a knock at their door at 1:15 a.m. When Mrs. Hagerman answered, an intruder grappled with her. Hagerman, hearing his wife's screams, grabbed a .25 cal. automatic and fired one shot. The intruder collapsed, fatally wounded. (*St. Louis, Mo., Post-Dispatch*)

AUGUST 1967

A lone gunman held up Arch Jinkins' Long Beach, Calif., store, forcing Jinkins and a clerk to lie on the floor while he emptied the cash register. When a customer entered, the gunman robbed him and ordered him to the floor. When a second customer entered and distracted the gunman, Jinkins snatched up his cal. .25 pistol and dropped the gunman with 2 bullets. (*Los Angeles Herald Examiner*)

Because of recent burglaries, Dennis Dunning was sleeping in the rear of his father's Tacoma, Wash., sporting goods store. Awakened by the sound of breaking glass, he saw a man coming toward him with a crowbar. One blast from his shotgun dropped the intruder with mortal wounds. (*Spokane Daily Chronicle*)

The day after Harvey Schreibman, 34, partner in a New York City printing firm, got his pistol permit, two gunmen held him up for the $1,100 payroll he was carrying. One hit him on the head from behind. The other kicked him and snatched the payroll satchel. Schreibman drew his cal. .38 revolver and fired 5 shots. One holdup man fell dead. Police captured the other a block away. (*New Brunswick, N. J., Sunday Home News*)

Mr. and Mrs. Charles E. Millican were alone in their Fort Worth, Tex., grocery when a man walked in, bought a pack of cigarettes, then threatened them with a length of pipe and demanded their money. Millican, 67, fired one shot from a .22 pistol kept under the counter. The holdup man fell, mortally wounded. (*The Dallas Morning News*)

George Peterson, a Californian visiting Boise, Idaho, went for a little target practice in the hills near the Idaho State Prison with his cal. .45 pistol. Just then, 2 convicts broke prison under a hail of bullets and ran along the highway. Peterson halted them with his .45. Guards said one convict was serving 75 years for murder, the other 14 years for rape. Peterson said, "I was just trying to do what any citizen would do." (*Idaho Daily Statesman*)

Badly beaten after the third holdup of his little Washington, D. C., secondhand shop. Eddie Eisenstein, 39, survived the critical list and vowed "never again." When 3 armed men took his money and tied him up in a fourth holdup, Eisenstein slipped his bonds and fired 6 shots. Four bullets hit one robber, killing him. Police said the slain man was a paroled felon already under indictment in another case. (*Washington Star*)

Mitchell Nashar, ordered by an armed thug to hand over his money, tripped over a box trying to get to the cash register of his Detroit grocery. Angered, the thug hit him over the head with his gun. Nashar grabbed his own pistol. The thug's gun misfired 3 times and a fourth shot went wild. Nashar returned the fire, seriously wounding him. (*Detroit News*)

Hearing noises, Mrs. Nellie Peterson investigated and found 3 men cutting a basement window screen of her Oak Park, Ill., home. She phoned police and got a pistol which her late husband "had had around the house for 40 years" but which she never had handled. The intruders came up from the basement, saw the pistol, and dived downstairs again. Police arrived before they could get away. (*Chicago Tribune*)

An intruder will remember the night he invaded the basement of St. Mary's Catholic School in Covington, Ky. He found himself looking down the barrel of a .38 revolver held by pistol-packing Rev. Edwin B. Heile, who surprised him and took him into custody until police arrived. (*Columbus, Ga. Ledger*)

As Nicholas Makris was locking his place of business in Detroit, Mich., for the night, he was attacked by two men. One, wielding a tire iron, knocked him to the ground and began to kick him. Makris drew a pistol and seriously wounded both attackers. (*Detroit News*)

When a runaway teen-ager from Michigan attempted to hold up John Brown's pharmacy in Phoenix, Ariz., with a .22 pistol at closing time, Brown took his .38 revolver from a shelf near the cash register and fired twice. The holdup man was hit in the left arm and chest. (*The Phoenix Gazette*)

OCTOBER 1967

After 3 burglaries of his Newark, N. J., home this year, Robert Brennan heard prowlers on the second floor. Investigating, he found 2 intruders. Brennan wounded one with his .22 revolver. The other fled through a window. (*Newark News*)

Rudy Valentino, a suburban Philadelphia, Pa., auto dealer, happened to pass his closed showroom late at night and noticed a light in the office. Throwing open the office door, he knocked down one of 2 young prowlers. Then he grabbed his loaded .45 automatic from his desk and held both until police arrived. (*Philadelphia Daily News*)

When 2 Seattle taxicab passengers suddenly attacked driver H. P. Altman, Jr., one choking and the other beating him, Altman fired a tear-gas pencil. One robber leaped out with eyes streaming. The cab hit a building, trapping the second robber inside. Altman stood over him with a tire jack until police came. (*Seattle Times*)

Lemuel Earl and his wife were awakened by suspicious noises in their store, in front of their home at Mendon, Utah. Armed with a .45 automatic, Earl investigated. In front of the store, he confronted a youth who claimed to be alone. Just then, Earl saw a rifle barrel emerge from the shattered window of his store. He fired a shot which wounded one bandit and caused another to dart from the store with his hands up. Police arrested the 3, and said they found a stolen car with 4 rifles in it. (*Ogden Standard Examiner*)

Approached by a man carrying a pistol, Mel Wildermuth, a Sidney, Ohio, farmer, swung at the intruder with the handiest thing in his yard—a mop. Then he ran into his house under a hail of bullets, got his shotgun, and drove the gunman away with a blast. (*Dayton Journal herald*)

Herbert Armstrong, 36, drove up to his Chicago filling station to find 2 gunmen holding up the 2 attendants on duty. Snatching up a revolver kept at the station, Armstrong dodged behind a wall as the gunmen turned on him. He wounded one fatally. The other fled with about $100. (*Chicago Sun-Times*)

When a man walked into Andrew Pursley's Salt Lake City, Utah, grocery and asked for chewing gum, Pursley turned to get it—and turned back to find himself staring at a pistol. He pulled his own pistol, shot the gunman, and routed him with a possible stomach wound. (*Salt Lake City Tribune*)

To protect his father's Tacoma, Wash., sporting goods store after burglars stole $2500 in goods the 2 previous weekends, Dennis Dunning, 21, spent the night inside. He heard a front window crash. A burglar with a 2½ ft. steel bar approached him. Dunning killed the man with one shot from a 12-ga. shotgun. Two alleged accomplices were arrested later. (*Seattle Post-Intelligencer*)

A bandit leaped over the counter of Clarence Taylor's Oakland, Calif., store and ordered Taylor and wife to lie on the floor. As Mrs. Taylor, a deaf mute, could not hear the command, Taylor relayed it in sign language. When the bandit menaced him with a revolver, Taylor, thinking he was going to be shot, pulled a .38 and fired point-blank. Then he loosed 5 more shots. The bandit, fleeing, fell dead outside the store. (*Oakland Tribune*)

At 4 A.M., John Stannard, owner of a used-car business at New Milford, Ill., heard noises in the office adjoining his home. With a .22 rifle in hand, he cornered a prowler in the office until deputies arrived. (*Rockford Labor News*)

Simon Sakowitz, 71, was hit on the head with a hammer by one of 2 intruders who broke into his Chicago home. He shot and wounded one of them, and held him for police. (*Chicago Sun Times*)

In the late evening hours, George Allen David was alerted in his Ft. Collins, Colo., home by an unusual sound. Going to a locked file cabinet he took a gun and went outside to investigate. He found a man draining gasoline from a parked truck into a can. David ordered the man not to move and held him at gunpoint until police arrived. (*Ft. Collins Coloradoan*)

NOVEMBER 1967

Violence was averted in northwest Washington, D. C., because Mrs. Ellen Von Nardroff, an attractive brunette, took a detective's advice and armed herself with a 20 ga. shotgun. Detective L. E. Simmons gave her the advice after an intruder broke into her home, attempted to attack her and stole $50. The same man, a husky 6-footer, got halfway upstairs to Mrs. Von Nardroff's bedroom on a noisy second attempt—only to be met by her with the shotgun and a visiting girl friend with a pistol. The intruder was arrested and held.

Mrs. Von Nardroff said she had practiced considerably with her 20 ga. after the Washington detective recommended a shotgun, properly handled, as the most effective defensive arm for ''a lady who lives alone.'' (*Washington Star*)

Ever since a young man with a black glove on his right hand robbed her of $150 at knife point, Mrs. Sue Ball, 59, a Hollenbeck, Calif., cafe proprietor, carried an 8 mm. pistol. Six months after the robbery, she said, the same man came to her rear door and grabbed at her. Her one shot killed him instantly. (*Los Angeles Herald Examiner*)

At Inglewood, Calif., John Bitters saw 2 men take a television set from a parked pickup truck and slip it into the rear seat of their car. When he confronted them, they ran. Bitters fired one shot into the ground and ordered them to halt. Police then arrested the pair. (*The Citizen, Inglewood, Calif.*)

Gerald Boyum, a farmer of Farmington Twp., Minn., returned from a weekend fishing trip to find 2 rifles, a shotgun and car accessories missing from his home. While he was calling the sheriff, a strange car with 2 youths drove up. Boyum held the 2 at shotgun point. Deputies arrived, searched their car, and found the missing firearms in the trunk. (*Rochester, Minn., Post-Bulletin*)

Restaurant owner Emilio F. Quintana waited quietly while two burglars knocked a hole in a rear wall of his Phoenix, Ariz., cafe. When the thugs finally crawled through, Quintana held both of them at gunpoint until police arrived. (*Tucson, Ariz., Daily Citizen*)

When a shaggy-haired young tough led 4 others in an attempt to break into a house occupied by a 14-year-old girl baby sitter, the girl's 12-year-old brother, Roy Bourgault, drove them off by firing a .22 pistol into the ground at their feet, the Palm Beach County (Fla.) Sheriff's Office reported. Returning later, the gang smashed windows with beer bottles and the leader began climbing into a bedroom. Again the boy drove him off with warning shots from the .22. Police arrested the tough, his fourth arrest in 14 months. They said he had been twice fined $25 and once reprimanded for driving 100 mph. in a 45-mph. zone. They identified him as John M. Whitman, 19, youngest brother of the slain University of Texas killer. (*Associated Press*)

Because of a burglary, Les Harris, Chicago (Ill.) homeowner, brought a .38 caliber pistol and taught his wife Auriel to use it. A few nights later, finding an intruder climbing through her window, she shot him in both hands. When a man with bullet wounds in both hands sought hospital treatment, police were notified and Mrs. Harris identified him. He was charged with attempted robbery. (*Chicago Tribune*)

Charles Bradbury, of Miami, Fla., visiting in New Orleans, was thrown to the sidewalk by a man who leaped on him from behind a parked car and placed a knife at his throat. Taxicab driver Joseph Hirstius, passing just then, stopped his cab and with his personal pistol held the attacker until police arrived. (*New Orleans Times-Picayune*)

THE ARMED CITIZEN

When he was robbed of $125, Carl B. Peters, Long Beach, Calif., store clerk, shot and wounded two holdup men with a .38 revolver before police answered the store's silent alarm. (*Pomona, Calif., Progress-Bulletin*)

Donald Wayne Roach, investigating a noise in his suburban Portland (Oreg.) backyard, fired one shot over a fleeing intruder's head. While a neighbor phoned police, Roach searched and disarmed the man. Police said he was wanted as a suspect in a $12,000 bank robbery. They arrested 2 other suspects nearby. (*Oregon Journal*)

DECEMBER 1967

Police summoned to Ernest Carter's Middletown, Ohio, grocery found Carter and clerk Junior Langworthy sitting on a suspected robber. They said the suspect entered the store and pointed a pistol at Carter. Langworthy picked up a shotgun and covered him. The 2 then disarmed him and sat on him. (*Cincinnati Enquirer*)

Ed Osborne heard a shot in his Ukiah, Calif., tavern and rushed in to find a holdup man with a sawed-off shotgun standing over his bartender. Osborne, believing the bartender dead, shot the bandit fatally. Later it developed that the bandit had merely clubbed the bartender with his sawed-off gun, causing it to fire accidentally. A coroner's jury ruled the bandit-shooting justifiable homicide.—*Sacramento Bee.*

Baby-sitter Julia Roman, 18, got a .357 Magnum revolver from the next room when she heard someone breaking through a window at 3 a.m. in a Chicago home where she was minding 2 small children. When the intruder advanced, she fired. He staggered out, mortally wounded. The death was termed justifiable homicide.—*Chicago Sun-Times.*

Alone in her Phoenix, Ariz. home, Ethel Juniel heard someone trying to break in. On his second attempt, the intruder smashed a rear window with a bumper jack. When he reached in to undo a door latch, Miss Juniel shot him dead with a .22 pistol. (*Arizona Republic*)

Drake University coed Becky Moore, 20, knew the rifle wasn't loaded. But the man and woman who were prowling her parents' farm house in Polk County, Iowa didn't. They fled when Becky, alone in the house, emerged from her pantry hiding place, rifle in hand. (*Sioux City, Iowa, Journal*)

Charles Smith, owner of Smith Motor Sales, Carbondale, Ill. and his son surprised a burglar trying to blow torch his way into their office safe. Smith pulled a pistol and fired when the man reached into his pocket, apparently for a weapon. Police arrested the wounded man and 2 others on a burglary charge. (*Evansville, Indiana, Courier*)

An Illinois State Penitentiary parolee who couldn't kick the crime habit paid with his life when he and 2 other men broke into the Sleepy Hollow, Ill. home of Dr. Roland Russell. As the gunmen were occupied tying Russell's wife and son to a bed, the doctor edged back to a table where he kept a loaded revolver. He fired 4 times, mortally wounding the parolee. The dying man's companions fled. (*Chicago Daily News*)

A length of clothesline slung from a tree down through a skylight let a young burglar into Sipos Bakery in Perth Amboy, N. J. A pistol in the hand of owner George Sipos, 30, routed him out from behind a showcase and held him for arrest. Police Chief Paul Jankovich plans to commend Sipos for apprehending the burglar. (*The Evening News, Perth Amboy*)

Shot 6 times, a Washington, D. C. part-time gas station attendant routed 2 hold up men and held a third at bay until police arrived. Jumped by the armed trio in front of the station, Edward O. King, 24, drew a .32 revolver and traded shot for shot with the thugs. Two fled. Though badly wounded, King kept the third man cowering in a phone booth with an occasional shot in his direction. The latter was charged with assault with intent to kill. (*Washington Evening Star*)

Neumann's Gun Shop in Detroit had already had 500 shotguns, rifles and pistols stolen. So part-time watchman and gunsmith Terukazu Miyamoto, 29, was ready with a rifle when a brick crashed through a show window barely a month later. The intruder ignored Miyamoto's warning shot and turned as if to aim a gun. Miyamoto shot him. The burglar died. (*Detroit Free Press*)

National Rifle Association Safety Instructor Richard G'Nosa proved more than a match for the 2 bandits who tried to hold up his Cassady Pharmacy in Columbus, Ohio. Alerted by the pair's "furtive" behavior, he had the .38 revolver he keeps in the store at the ready when one of the men shoved a pistol in his face. "I came up with the gun and fired," G'Nosa said. His assailant fell wounded, the second fled. (*Columbus Ohio Evening Dispatch*)

1968

JANUARY 1968

One robber was dead, another probably wounded, after the pair held up Miami, Fla., grocer Ben Branham. Gun in hand, one took $35 from the cash register, ordered Branham to lie down behind the counter. Branham slipped a .38 revolver from beneath a nearby blanket and fired twice at the men. One fell, mortally wounded. The other snatched the $35 from his hand and ran, limping. The dead man had served 13 years in prison for burglary and robbery. (*Los Angeles Times*)

Mrs. Frances Albrecht was grinding meat in her Pittsburgh, Pa. grocery store when 2 young bandits marched in and demanded money from her son who was minding the cash register. When one drew a gun, Mrs. Albrecht pulled a pistol from a cigar box and warned, "You'd better get out or I'll shoot!" The bandit fired once. Mrs. Albrecht fired back, killing him with a single shot. The second bandit fled, empty handed. The dead bandit's gun was a starter pistol which fired only blanks. No charges were filed. (*Danville, Va., Bee*)

When 3 armed bandits robbed his Philadelphia sandwich shop, owner Albert Proetto grabbed a gun from under the counter and gave chase. He wounded one man. A suspect was promptly arrested by police when he was brought by his parents to a hospital for treatment. (*Philadelphia Inquirer*)

Hearing glass shatter in his Tampa, Fla. store, Fernando Carreras picked up a pistol and dashed from his apartment in the rear to investigate. Coming upon a prowler removing glass from the front door, Carreras fired one shot. The man fled but was found dead a few blocks away. (*Tampa Tribune*)

Seattle, Wash. grocer Paul S. Edwards wounded an unarmed 16-year-old who, pretending to have a gun in his pocket, bluffed Edwards' wife into giving him a bag of money from the store cash register. "Stay back or I'll kill you," the boy cried when Edwards entered. Edwards dropped the youth with one shot from the revolver he always carries. (*Seattle Times*)

A stocking-masked robber bent on robbing Cohen Beverage Stores, Inc., in Rochester, N.Y. thought better of it when clerk Earl Vogt, 70, reached under the counter and drew a pistol. Though armed with a revolver, the crook backed out of the liquor store when he found himself looking into somebody else's gun. (*Rochester, N.Y., Democrat & Chronicle*)

When 77-year-old Mrs. C. C. Talbot, of Shreveport, La., heard someone forcing her screen door at 1:40 a.m. and calling out threats at her, she fired one shot from a .22 caliber rifle. Police later arrested a prowler with a bullet wound in his left arm. (*Shreveport Times*)

Armed with 2 pistols, a holdup man slipped into a closed San Francisco tavern as a bartender was leaving and forced owner Herman Warren to give him $350 from the till. He then ordered Warren and his wife, Norma, another bartender and a janitor to lie on the floor. The bartender tackled the man as he fled and was shot in the leg. Thinking his wife had been shot, Warren got a .38 revolver from his office and brought down the bandit. Police charged the man with suspicion of robbery and assault with intent to kill. (*Oakland Tribune*)

Carrying $300 from her husband's Seattle, Wash. tavern, Mrs. Robert E. Lee climbed into her car at 3:19 a.m. to find a stranger inside. He lunged at her and she screamed. Lee ran up and shot the man with his .22 pistol. (*Seattle Times*)

Randy Carter was lunching with the vice-president of the Bank of Caneyville, Ky., when a teller dashed into the restaurant yelling that the bank had been robbed. Carter and the bank officer obtained a gun, ran to the bank and found the robber outside in his car with $849 in a pillow case. Carter fired, and the robber jumped out and ran. Carter stopped him with a second shot. (*Lexington, Ky., Herald*)

MARCH 1968

A small businessman who shot straight killed a holdup man who didn't in a Pineville, La., gun battle. Fruit stand owner Ralph Nugent and his wife were alone in the stand when a man entered, pulled a pistol, and ordered Nugent to fill a paper bag with money. When a customer came in, the gunman pocketed his pistol and ordered Nugent to lower the bag behind the counter. As Nugent did so, he drew a .38 from under the counter and ordered the thug to drop his gun. The gunman fired a shot through Nugent's sleeve and ran for the door, still firing wildly. Nugent fired 4 shots. Each found its mark. (*Monroe, La., News-Star*)

Four hoodlums beat and robbed a Cleveland, Ohio, woman, then scattered. One dashed into an apartment building at E. 55th St., only to be confronted by the revolver-armed manageress, Mrs. Victoria Roginski. Police dog at her side, Mrs. Roginski held the hoodlum until police arrived. (*Cleveland Press*)

An intruder smashed a glass front door panel in Nathaniel Davis' Stockton, Calif., home and threatened to kill Davis unless admitted. Davis, a 69-year-old recluse, killed the man with a .22 rifle. (*San Jose, Calif., Mercury*)

A youthful gunman made the mistake of announcing his intention to hold up Fowler's Pharmacy in Greenville, S. C. while his pistol was still in his pocket. Before he could draw, pharmacist Eugene Estes grabbed a .38 revolver from beneath the counter and shot him. (*The Greenville, S.C., News*)

ARMED CITIZEN, NEW YORK VERSION

When an intruder whom police later identified as a criminal with 16 arrests, including for burglary and rape, confronted stockbroker Robert E. Scharf and his wife one Saturday evening in the Scharfs' fifth-floor New York City apartment, Scharf demanded, "What are you doing here?" The intruder lunged at him, Scharf said, with a 5-inch-blade knife. Scharf fired twice with a .38 pistol. The second bullet wounded the intruder severely. Police arrested Scharf and took him to the station house on a charge of illegal possession of a pistol. (*N. Y. Daily News*)

When the "patient" stepped into Dr. Ramon Bandillo's office, the Bronx, N. Y., physician remembered him in a flash and jerked a .38 revolver from his desk. "You're not getting anything this time!" he yelled, "Hands up!" Two years earlier, the same "patient" had robbed the doctor at knife point of $126. When police arrested him, they found a steak knife in his pocket. (*New York Times*)

Three men ambling aimlessly around the Huntsville Grocery in Brighton, Ala., were so very obviously "casing" the store that owner Robert Steel tucked a pistol in his belt. The trio departed and returned, brandishing pistols. When 2 began beating him, Steel fatally wounded one. The others fled. (*The Huntsville, Ala., Times*)

A masked bandit pointed a pellet gun at Vancouver, B. C., grocer Elzear Lavoie and inquired, "How would you like to be held up?" Drawing a .22 revolver, Lavoie countered with "How would you like this one?" Crying, "No! No! No!" the bandit and 2 masked companions fled. (*New York Times*)

A man entered Gregory Fontana's store in San Diego, Calif. and drew a gun. Fontana reached under the counter and pulled out his own pistol. Tense silence reigned for several seconds. It was broken by the intruder. "I have nothing else to say," he said. Putting his gun on the counter, he fled. (*Evening Tribune, San Diego, Calif.*)

Mrs. Evelyn Jones, 58, of Los Angeles, was sitting on her porch when, shortly after 1 A.M., 2 strangers approached across her lawn. When she asked what they wanted, one raised a sawed-off .22 rifle in a paper bag and snarled, "Don't move or I'll shoot!" Mrs. Jones' dog lunged at the man, who fired one wild shot. Mrs. Jones drew the .38 revolver she carries "for protection" and killed the armed intruder. His companion fled. (*Los Angeles Times*)

JUNE 1968

When Jack R. Herring heard 2 burglars forcing a window of his Shelby, Ohio, parts company, he got his gun, waited until they were inside, then caught one. The other, trapped indoors, hid in the basement but gave himself up before police arrived. (*Shelby, Ohio, Daily Globe*)

Three bank robbers made only one mistake when they held up the Valley National Bank in Carefree, Ariz., and got away with $52,050. They took an escape route past a target range at North Mountain, Ariz.

Practicing on the range was the Maricopa County Sheriff's pistol team, rated one of the best in the West in combat pistol shooting. Hearing of the bank robbery, the deputies climbed into 2 cars just as the getaway car sped past. The deputies caught up and were met with gunfire.

Riddling the robbers' car, they brought it skidding to a halt. The driver was dead behind the wheel. A second robber cowered in the back, begging for mercy. A third fled. He was brought down with 6 bullet wounds. The stolen money was recovered intact.

An armed bandit entered the Merrillville, Ind., drugstore of Michael Hamang with a cocked revolver. Michael, Jr., 14, slipped from a nearby drawer the .25 caliber automatic that his father had bought after a recent holdup. The boy fired just as the bandit shot at Mrs. Hamang. Mrs. Hamang escaped with powder burns on her thumb. The bandit died of a stomach wound. Lake County (Ind.) police declined to file charges against the boy. "Obviously self-defense," they said. (*Drug Topics Magazine*)

Freddy Earnest, a Memphis, Tenn., service station attendant, was getting ready to go off duty when a man walked in and asked for change for $10. He then said, "Never mind the $10. I'll take it all." Earnest pulled a pistol from a desk drawer and fired 6 shots. The intruder stumbled out of the service station door. He was found dead 30 yds. from the station. (*Memphis Commercial Appeal*)

Elmon Pulley, a Stewart County, Tenn., grocer, was in the back of his store when 2 men walked in and pulled a pistol on Mrs. Pulley. She grabbed a shotgun and blasted the pistol from the hand of the intruder. The 2 men ran from the store. The body of one of the men was found the next day in a roadside ditch. (*WSM-TV Nashville*)

An armed robber confronted Louis J. Carby in his Houston, Tex., store, apparently thinking Carby was alone. When a woman clerk emerged from a back room, the flustered bandit shot at her and missed. Carby meanwhile grabbed a .22 cal. pistol and shot the bandit twice, killing him on the spot. (*Houston, Tex., Chronicle*)

A Breckenridge, Tex., grocer, hearing his store burglar alarm go off, caught a looter inside. When the man tried to flee, the grocer fired a shotgun blast. Surrendering, the burglar explained: "I gave up burglary when those shotgun pellets started falling around me." Police said he admitted to 11 previous burglaries. (*Wichita Falls, Tex., Times & Record News*)

Mrs. Verda Byrd, 44, of Claremont, Okla., got out of her car in Tulsa to make an early morning phone call and found herself trapped in the phone booth by a youth who thrust what she thought was a pistol into her back. The youth forced her back into her car and clutched her. Snatching her .22 caliber pistol from the seat, she shot him and ran back to the phone booth to summon police. The wounded youth started the car and rammed the booth, but fell dead. Mrs. Byrd escaped uninjured. (*Tulsa, Okla., World*)

Three robbers cornered Ben Hankin, 68, a retired interior decorator, in his Jacksonville, Fla., apartment. Forcing him to sit down, they demanded his money. Hankin faked a dizzy spell, slumped over, and pulled his .38 caliber handgun from its hiding place. In the exchange of shots that followed Hankin escaped unhurt. Police arrested the 3 robbers, one of them wounded in the head, in a nearby parking lot. (*Greenville, S.C., News*)

OCTOBER 1968

Using a cal. .32 pistol he bought last year after being stabbed in the head by a holdup man, Leon Beach, 53, a Newark, N.J., grocer, routed 3 gunmen who tried to rob him and his partner, Joseph Opatowski. Beach drew his holstered pistol and fired a shot which sent 2 of the gunmen running. The third, holding a pistol to Opatowski's head, stood his ground. Beach dropped him with a bullet that wounded him critically. (*The New York Sunday News*)

Reaching for his handgun instead of his stethoscope, Dr. Wally White of Burlington, Vt., frightened off a carload of hoods who approached him as he made a night deposit at his bank. At the bank, several men got out of a car and headed for White, apparently bent on robbing him. When White reached into his jacket for his gun, one of the men shouted, "He's armed. Let's get out of here." The men cursed and fled. (*Burlington, Vt., Free Press*)

Handicapped by a glass eye, San Antonio, Tex., service station operator Mario Girela had never fired a pistol in his life until 2 bandits, one of them armed, held up his Sunglo Fina service station. Nevertheless, Girela grabbed the station's pistol and felled one of the escaping pair with a shot in the dark from 150 ft. Police picked up the wounded youth and recovered $5 of the $60 stolen. The youth's confederate escaped. (*San Antonio, Tex., Evening News*)

Two armed youths robbed Cumminsville, Ohio, shopkeeper Nicholas Mueller, then shot and wounded him in the arm and shoulder as they made a break for a getaway car driven by a third youth. Mueller returned their fire, seriously wounding one of his assailants. Two teenage suspects were later picked up by police. (*The Cincinnati Enquirer*)

As a burglary suspect was being booked in the San Patricio County, Tex., jail, he grabbed an officer's pistol and fled. At a nearby filling station he forced 2 Dallas boys, Larry Trujillo, 17, and his brother Timothy, 10, to drive him away in their car. When the car spun out of control shortly afterward, the boys scuffled with the man. Though Larry was shot in the leg, the boys managed to wrest the pistol from the fugitive and flee on foot. When the man pursued them, Larry turned and fired, wounding the man in the jaw. Police then recaptured him. (*Houston, Tex., Chronicle*)

Awakened at 3:30 a.m. by someone pounding on his back door, Tucson, Ariz. rancher Ben H. Schermerhorn blasted a would-be intruder with a .410 shotgun after the man announced he had cut Schermerhorn's telephone wires and then threw a garbage can through a window. Under police guard, the garbage can thrower was treated at a local hospital. (*The Arizona Daily Star*)

When a robber barged into Dell's Liquors in Phoenix, Ariz. and demanded cash at gun point, it was old hat to clerk Nelson Brewer, the victim of 6 previous robberies. Ordered by the gunman to pick up a bill he had dropped, Brewer bent down, grabbed a .357 Magnum revolver from under the counter and dropped the thug with one shot to the head. (*The Arizona Republic*)

Three gunmen met a deadly fusillade from a .38 revolver when they attempted to hold up Andrew Snyder, proprietor of the Serve-U Market in Union Gap, Wash. When one of the trio barked, "This is a holdup," Snyder whipped a revolver from his belt, killed 2 of the men and critically wounded the third. (*Seattle, Wash., Post Intelligencer*)

Hearing someone kicking at the front door of her Shelbyville, Ind. home, then enter, Mrs. Gertrude Miller, 74, grabbed her .22 revolver. When she found the intruder rummaging through bureau drawers in her bedroom, she fired. Police found a dazed man with 2 bullet wounds wandering in Mrs. Miller's yard and charged him with burglary. (*The Shelbyville, Ind., News*)

NOVEMBER 1968

The *Milwaukee Journal* objected to the "Armed Citizen" editorially on Aug. 19 with the assertion that it is "dangerously irresponsible" to publish such items. All such items, we must point out, come from newspapers. Are they being "dangerously irresponsible?"

Two men entered Burton Sussman's Trenton, N.J., taproom just as Sussman was preparing to close. He turned to find himself staring down the barrel of a gun. The gunman's pal held a knife. When Sussman pulled his .38 from his pocket and shot the knife-wielder, the other man dropped his gun and fled. Police took the wounded thug into custody. (*Newark (N.J.) Evening News*)

Thirty-five years of NRA membership served Clark W. Fishel well when he discovered an intruder in his Allen, Tex. home. Armed with a .38 Special Smith & Wesson, he stalked the man from room to room in his darkened home and finally subdued him. The intruder had a long criminal record and was out on probation from a previous burglary conviction. (*Dallas (Tex.) Times Herald*)

Returning to their Brightwaters, N.Y. home after a morning cup of coffee, Howard and Augusta Newins heard male voices upstairs. Newins grabbed a .22 rifle, yelled up to the uninvited guests that he had a gun. The latter departed from the Newins home by an upstairs window. Newins fired several shots after them as they escaped with part of his coin collection. (*Islip (N.Y.) Bulletin*)

Twice in the last 2 years, Houston, Tex., storekeeper Ronald A. Yeates has routed trios of burglars from his auto salvage shop. In Nov., 1966, he wounded all 3. A few weeks ago, Yeates surprised another burglary-bent threesome in his shop when they ignored his order to halt, he wounded one with his shotgun, as the others fled. Minutes later, police captured the other 2 not far away. (*Houston (Tex.) Chronicle*)

Tipped off at 3 A.M. that his Mount Carmel, Tenn. grocery was being burgled, manager Otis Muncie notified police, then armed himself with a 12-ga. shotgun and went to see for himself. At the store, Muncie found crowbars lying beside the door, which had been forced. Entering, he surprised a burglar and shot him in the hip when the man refused to halt at Muncie's command. (*Kingsport (Tenn.) Times*)

Houston, Tex. pharmacist Charles Stewart and an assistant were working into the small hours at Stewart's Varsity Drug Store, taking inventory after a burglary a few days earlier. At 3:30 A.M., they heard someone break in the front door. As the intruder approached, brandishing a tire iron, Stewart grabbed a pistol and shot him dead. The victim was a man who had previously served a prison term for burglary. (*Houston (Tex.) Chronicle*)

Armed with an empty shotgun, a Pennsylvania housewife drove 5 escapees from the Northumberland County Prison into the hands of police. The 5 had turned up at the Eugene Troxell home in rural Sunbury, Pa. and asked for water. When Troxell complied, 2 of them threatened him with knives and demanded his car keys. Ostensibly going for the keys, Mrs. Troxell came back with a shotgun and bluffed the men into releasing her husband. The fugitives were picked up later near the Troxell home. (*Williamsport (Pa.) Sun-Gazette*)

Two elderly sisters and a loaded rifle proved more than a match for a pair of prowlers who tried to enter the sisters' home in Cross Cut, Tex. Hearing the prowlers outside, Mrs. Jennie Stone confronted the intruders as they entered the kitchen. Though one threatened to "shoot her head off", the sight of Mrs. Stone's gun changed his mind. Both men fled. (*Cross Plains (Tex.) Review*)

Store owner Kim Coffin foiled a robbery attempt in his Agoura, Calif. shop when a man entered and attempted to make a grab from the store's cash register. Coffin drew a gun and held the man until police arrived. (*The Van Nuys (Calif.) Valley News*)

1969

MARCH 1969

After a St. Louis, Mo., householder stopped 4 youths from beating up a passerby, the youths returned half an hour later for revenge. Charles Roy looked out the window of his McPherson Ave. home just in time to see one of the 4 raise a shotgun and fire 2 blasts at his house. Roy returned fire with a pistol, wounding one and driving the others away. (*St. Louis, Mo., Post-Dispatch*)

Robbed repeatedly in recent years, Chicago cab driver Charles Nichols carries a .25 pistol in his cab. When a fare asked Nichols to drive him home, then pulled a gun and demanded money, Nichols wounded the would-be robber 3 times. (*The Chicago Tribune*)

When Mrs. Paul Jaksich heard glass breaking at 4:45 A.M. at the service station next to her Omaha, Neb., home she roused her husband and 18-year-old son. The men armed themselves and held at gunpoint 2 thieves they caught coming out of the station. One of the intruders was armed with a starter pistol. (*Omaha, Neb., World-Herald*)

Hearing his clerk cry for help, Hartford, Conn., grocer Reginald A. Leslie peered out from a back room to see 3 robbers, one armed with a gun, beating his employee with a table leg. Leslie ducked back, grabbed a .32 automatic and fired several shots at the bandits, killing one of them. The other 2 fled. (*Hartford, Conn., Times*)

Robbed of $25 by 2 bandits while she was minding her father's Los Angeles record store, 14-year-old Karen Young grabbed a pistol and followed the men out of the store. As they stood on a center divider in the middle of the street, she fired 3 times. The robbers fled down an alley. (*Huntington Beach, Calif., Evening News*)

When Buskirk, N.Y., Postmaster Paul Dreher surprised 2 men trying to open the post office safe, he called State Police, then got a revolver from his home nearby and confronted the pair. They started to flee by car but stopped when Dreher fired a warning shot into the air. He held them at gunpoint until police arrived. (*The Knickerbocker, Albany, News*)

Seventy-year-old Herman B. Mathis was taking a stroll in Los Angeles when 2 men dragged him into a vacant doorway. There, one held him in a strangle hold while the other went through his pockets. Suddenly, Mathis broke loose, grabbed a 7.65 mm. automatic from his waistband and killed one of his assailants, sending a second shot after the dead man's accomplice. (*Los Angeles Herald Examiner*)

Seeing a night club robbery in progress, Ken Faulkner of Emeryville, Calif., stopped his car, got a pistol from a card room next door and returned in time to fire a warning shot at a man running out of the club. The man pulled a dagger with a 6″ blade but was disarmed by a night club customer. Police recovered $132 taken from the club's bartender and held the man on charges of armed robbery, carrying a concealed arm and violation of probation. (*Oakland, Calif., Tribune*)

A Chicago spinster, Josephine Pierce, shot and killed an intruder who broke into her apartment as she was watching television. When the man demanded money, she pretended to faint and was carried to her bed. As he threatened to rape her, Miss Pierce took a pistol from beneath her pillow and shot him 3 times. Police said the dead man was wanted on charges of aggravated assault and robbery. (*The Chicago Tribune*)

Six convicts in the Camden, N.J., County Prison Annex overcame 2 guards, handcuffed them, and fled from the medium security prison on foot. Hunters, aware of the break, found 3 of the convicts hiding in a sanitary landfill area 2 miles from the prison. They held them until police arrived. (*The New Brunswick, N.J., Daily Home News*)

When a pair of prowlers attempted to loot the Pennsylvania Rifle, Indian and Dutch Museum, a private institution at Intercourse, Pa., at 3 A.M., owner Clarence Haushover, an NRA Member, awakened and routed them with a 16-ga. shotgun. Haushover fired 3 blasts to halt the pair, 2 well over their heads. Pellets from the third shot wounded one. Shotgun empty, Haushover bluffed the other into surrendering. (*Lancaster, Pa., Intelligencer Journal*)

A 5-yr. analysis recently revealed that mere presence of a firearm, without firing a shot, prevented crime in more than a third of the cases reported in "The Armed Citizen." Shooting usually can be justified only where crime constitutes an immediate, imminent threat to life or limb or, in some circumstances, property.

The above accounts are from clippings sent in by NRA members.

JUNE 1969

Richard A. Kaiser, an NRA member and competitive pistol shooter, saw a man break into a garage across from his home at Edgington, Ill., at 2:45 A.M. So he loaded a .357 Magnum revolver and went across while his father, David, called police. Richard caught the man with the contents of the garage cash register and some tools and covered him until police arrived. The police meanwhile arrested an alleged accomplice in a car nearby. Sheriff William R. Boyle praised Kaiser "for having the courage to make an apprehension of this kind by himself." (*Rock Island, Ill., Argus*)

As Mrs. Sarah Edmondson, 55, was walking to work at a bakery in Baltimore, Md., at 5:30 A.M., a young thug punched her in the face and stomach and knocked her to the street. "You know what I want!" he said. What he got was a cal. .32 pistol bullet in the neck from a handgun that Mrs. Edmondson yanked out of her handbag. Police followed a trail of blood and arrested a 26-year-old suspect. (*Baltimore, Md., News-American*)

Raleigh Parker, 17, heard noises at the family service station behind the Parker home in Gervais, Oreg., and investigated gun in hand. He apprehended 2 youths attempting to burglarize the station and held them until police arrived. (*Salem, Oreg., Statesman*)

Two men, one armed with a cal. .22 starter pistol, walked into Robert Spector's auto parts store in Detroit, Mich., and demanded his money. Spector replied by pulling out a semi-automatic pistol. The man with the .22 meekly handed it over and waited to be arrested. The other ran off. (*Detroit, Mich., Free Press*)

Noting 2 suspicious-looking men in his Bridgeport, Ohio, appliance store before closing time, Clarence Harris returned that night with his shotgun just in time to halt the theft of several portable TV sets. His warning shots drove off the 2 burglars. (*Wheeling, W. Va., News Register*)

Due to recent break-ins, Guy Eugene Tillery, owner of a Dallas, Tex., boat shop, was on guard inside his building when 2 men cut through a back fence and pried open a rear door at 9:30 P.M. Ordered not to move, one of the men fired at Tillery. He returned the fire, wounding both men, one seriously. A third man, stationed outside as a lookout, was arrested by police. (*Dallas, Tex., Times Herald*)

When Philip D. Hawks, a restaurant employee, requested a customer to cease swearing before women in the restaurant at Rockford, Ill., the customer whipped out a knife and waved it in Hawks' face. Hawks drew a pistol from under the counter and held the knife wielder until police arrived. (*Rockford, Ill., Morning Star*)

Sam Totah, 56, who operates a small grocery in San Francisco, Calif., is listed in police records as wounding a bandit in 1964 and killing another who fired 3 shots at him in 1966. The gunman who entered Totah's store and stuck a cal. .25 semi-automatic at him evidently didn't know he was picking on the wrong victim. Totah killed him with one shot. A police check revealed that the dead bandit's pistol was stolen in 1966. (*San Francisco, Calif., Examiner & Chronicle*)

Willie Stone, sitting in his country store in Florence County, S.C., was suddenly confronted by a man with a drawn pistol and a stocking concealing his face. "Don't move," the holdup man ordered. Stone reached his pistol from under the counter and fired one shot. It hit the holdup man in the shoulder. Police later arrested a suspect at a hospital where he had gone for treatment of a gunshot wound. (*The State, Columbia, S.C.*)

After being robbed 4 times in 3 months, Sam Liebowitz, a Brooklyn, N.Y., tavern owner, bought a cal. .22 rifle. Awakened in his upstairs apartment at 4 A.M. by noises in his tavern, he went down gun in hand—and, he said, was jumped by a prowler. In the tussle, the prowler was fatally shot through the head. New York City police charged Liebowitz with illegal possession of a firearm. (*New York Daily News*)

Seven burglaries in 6 months prompted Ernest Toland, Sweetwater, Tex., cafe proprietor, to keep an all-night watch after closing time. About 2 A.M. one night, 5 youths broke into the cafe. Toland ordered them to halt. When they refused, he fired one shot from his 16 ga. shotgun, wounding one youth slightly and causing another to surrender. The rest fled. (*Abilene, Tex., Reporter-News*)

AUGUST 1969

"This is a holdup" announced 2 men who got into Chicago taxicab driver Robert Harper's car. Taking $40, they beat Harper when he denied having more money. Harper lost control of his cab, but in the confusion, he drew his cal. .38 revolver and fired 5 shots, killing one holdup man and wounding the other. Although the revolver was registered, Harper was charged with unlawful use of it, police said, on recommendation of the State Attorney's office. (*Chicago, Ill., Tribune*)

Two men entered the grocery of E. T. Hunter, 77, Ormond Beach, Fla. One asked for cigarettes. As Hunter turned around, the other pointed a pistol at his head and demanded cash. When Hunter grabbed for the pistol, the bandit hit him over the head with it. Mrs. Hunter meanwhile grabbed a gun from under the counter, fired, and missed. The shots forced the bandits to flee on foot. Neighbor Charles Hines spotted them and covered one with a gun until police arrived. The other was arrested later. (*Daytona Beach, Fla., Journal*)

After 2 milk deliverymen were killed in separate holdups in Miami, Fla., last year, Lewis Wilhite, Sr., armed his wholesale candy and tobacco truck with a carbine. Recently an ex-convict, pistol in hand, tried to break into the truck. Lewis, Jr., warned him off. When he persisted, Lewis, Jr., fired 4 shots from the carbine and wounded the ex-convict. (*Clearwater, Fla., Sun*)

A month after they were charged with 13 burglaries and released, 2 teenagers tried the front door of Mrs. Carl Corino's home in Burlingame, Calif., then began to break in the back door when she did not answer. Mrs. Corino fired one shot through the door from her husband's .32 revolver. One of the youths was found about a block away, police said, with a fatal bullet wound in the chest. (*Los Angeles, Calif., Times*)

Because of recent burglaries, Clinton Funk, Philadelphia shipper and warehouseman, was guarding his warehouse with a cal. .45 automatic when he saw a prowler. As Funk approached, the man slammed a warehouse door on him, knocking him down. Funk fired through the door, inflicting a fatal wound. The prowler proved to be a narcotics addict with a record of 20 arrests. (*Philadelphia, Pa., Evening Bulletin*)

A gunman demanded patron Gus Lombardo's money as he left Earl McCrary's St. Louis restaurant, and fired a shot that wounded Lombardo in the elbow. McCrary quickly fired a shot through the screen door at the fleeing bandit. A suspect, identified by McCrary, was arrested shortly afterward. (*St. Louis, Mo., Globe-Democrat*)

Suddenly awakened, Mrs. Margaret King, Godfrey, Ill., found an intruder standing in her bedroom. She fired 2 shots from a cal. .22 pistol. The intruder fled. Police later detained a man who sought treatment for gunshot wounds in the chest at a nearby hospital. (*Belleville, Ill., News-Democrat*)

A courageous girl of 17, Gail Baldwin, was aroused by a noise at a window of her Los Angeles, Calif., home in a burglar-ridden neighborhood. Getting a 12-ga. shotgun from a closet, she fired a blast through the window. It hit a prowler in the head. Police held the man as a suspect in 3 previous burglary attempts just prior to the shooting. (*Los Angeles, Calif., Herald-Examiner*)

As Mrs. Ken Haynes, owner of an Anchorage, Alaska, drive-in, parked at a bank with her husband to deposit $1,000 in cash, 2 bandits grabbed her money bag and sped off. Haynes drew a pistol and fired at the bandits' car. It collided with another car, whose occupants took the number of the bandit vehicle. Within an hour, police located the getaway car, arrested 2 men, and recovered the stolen money. (*Anchorage, Alaska, Daily Times*)

A pounding noise at 2:45 A.M. awakened apartment owner Philip T. Gambacurta, of Rochester, N.Y. Getting his cal. .38 revolver, he investigated and found a man prying the hinges from an inside stairwell door. Gambacurta ordered the man to halt, and shouted to his wife to call police. At that, the man ran. Gambacurta fired one shot after him. Police later arrested as a suspect a man with a gunshot wound in the arm who claimed he accidentally shot himself while cleaning a pistol. (*Rochester, N.Y., Times Union*)

NOVEMBER 1969

Among 22 New Yorkers who received Civilian Commendations from Mayor John V. Lindsay Sept. 9 for fighting crime were Vincent J. Mauro, Jr., and Bennett Cohen, both pistol permit holders. Mauro, owner of a dry cleanery, joined police in arresting a gunman, his second assist of the kind. Cohen, a Manhattan realtor, saw three men punching an elderly man in a hallway on E. 92nd St. He drew his revolver, ordered them to stop, and fired a warning shot into the air when they fled. Two surrendered. It was the third crime halted by Cohen in three years. (*New York City Police Department press release.*)

Mrs. Hilda Katz, owner of a small Baltimore, Md., grocery store, handed over $68 from her cash register to a bandit brandishing a .22 pistol. She then grabbed her own pistol from beneath the counter, fired once, and hit the bandit in the chest. His return fire wounded her in the left hip, not seriously. Police found him face down half a block away, dead. (*Baltimore, Md., Sun*)

When a passenger in John Obert's cab in Seattle, Wash., pulled a knife on him and demanded money, Obert drew his pistol, took the would-be robber's knife and radioed for police. (*Seattle, Wash., Times*)

Service station operator Frank Labato of Denver, Colo., came into his station to find three men rifling his cash register. He quickly drew his .32 revolver from a desk drawer, and gave chase, wounding one man and recovering the stolen money. (*Rocky Mountain News, Denver, Colo.*)

A. Viereck, 54, a Houston, Tex., store manager, tried to foil a holdup man by spraying a chemical preparation at him but an electric fan blew the chemical away. The gunman shot Viereck four times and took $50 to $75. Viereck is expected to recover. (*Houston, Tex., Chronicle*)

A teenager who had reportedly twice raped a neighborhood woman at knife point was seriously wounded when he returned to the same Phoenix, Ariz. area and invaded the bedroom of another intended victim, Bessie Clark, 21. As he fumbled in the darkness, she shot him with a .22 revolver. (*Phoenix, Ariz., Republic*)

Mountain View, Ga., service station night manager Donald Grant wounded and captured a careless robber who put profit before more immediate matters. The slipshod heist artist put down his pistol and used both hands to stuff money taken from Grant into his pockets. This gave Grant a chance to grab his own gun and fire. (*Atlanta, Ga., Constitution*)

Hearing a scream for help in his apartment building, Gary Collins of Dallas, Tex., rushed into the hallway with a gun to investigate. He found a man attempting to assault a woman in the doorway of her apartment, and held the assailant at gunpoint while the woman summoned police. (*Dallas, Tex., Morning News*)

Mrs. Kathrine Lawrence, 72, of Atlanta, Ga., went to her bedroom and obtained a pistol when a man kept beating on her front door and demanding a drink of water. When the intruder kicked in a window and threatened to kill her, Mrs. Lawrence fatally wounded him. (*Atlanta, Ga., Constitution*)

Mr. and Mrs. Theodore R. Burch, Maryland Heights, Mo., were awakened at three A.M. by two men standing in their bedroom door wearing women's hats and veils. Although one held a pistol, Burch jumped out of bed and slammed the door in their faces. When they broke down the door, he drove them away by firing a shotgun. (*St. Louis, Mo., Globe-Democrat*)

Attacked by a knife-brandishing thug who demanded money, John Leeds, night manager of a Hamilton, Ohio, motel, refused to comply, ducked as the hoodlum lunged, and grabbed a revolver from beneath the counter. Two shots sent the would-be robber fleeing headlong, empty handed. (*Cincinnati, Ohio, Enquirer*)

After three men took $600 from his cashier at gunpoint, Los Angeles restaurant manager Sam Lacatus, 47, opened fire with a .45 pistol he got from under the counter. As one robber ran through the restaurant's plate glass door, Lacatus hit him. The other two escaped with the money. (*Los Angeles, Calif., Times*)

1970

"THE ARMED CITIZEN"—AND NOT A SCRATCH

Some advocates of handgun confiscation have asserted repeatedly that the possession of firearms by private citizens endangers the owners more than criminals who attack them. Like most persons familiar with firearms, we doubt this. Yet this mistaken statement appears in a staff report of the National Commission on Causes and Prevention of Violence, in which personal protection by firearms is termed "largely an illusion" and "rarely effective" in urban homes.

Here, on the contrary, are many instances, taken at random from the news, where a firearms in private hands averted or halted a crime without anyone being shot. Many more such instances could be given in which the mere sight of an armed, determined citizen ended a crime attempt on the spot. In such cases, it often proves unnecessary to fire a shot.

FEBRUARY 1970

Robert Keller had just left his Washington, D.C., apartment when a hoodlum held a knife to his ribs and took a ring and fur overcoat. Before he could take anything else Keller's young son, Bernard, opened the apartment door and began firing his air gun. The robber fled down the steps. (*Washington, D. C., Post*)

Centerville, Ill., farmer Frank Betz saved 3,000 lbs. of stolen mail when he found a mail truck parked in his field about 8:30 p.m. Three blasts from his shotgun frightened away the two robbers who were going through the mail in the truck they had stolen at gunpoint from its driver. Authorities said 98% of the mail was untouched. (*St. Louis, Mo., Globe-Democrat*)

Hearing prowlers in her back yard, Georgia A. Edwards of San Antonio, Tex., hid in a closet with a pistol. When two men broke into the house and turned on the bedroom light, she shot one man in the jaw. Both fled. The wounded man was later apprehended. (*San Antonio, Tex., Light*)

Two men with robbery on their minds were dissuaded when they discovered that their target, Columbus, Ohio, gunshop owner Charles R. Braun, was armed. The men entered the shop and one drew a knife, but when they saw that Braun was wearing a gun in a belt holster, they turned and fled. (*Columbus, Ohio, Dispatch*)

After cleaning out a Detroit, Mich., dry cleaner's cash register at gunpoint, a thief tried to run out the front door. But he accidentally locked himself in. Mrs. Leamon Gainer, the clerk, drew a .38 revolver from her purse and shot the thief in the shoulder. He dropped his gun and the money. (*Detroit, Mich., Free Press*)

Two burglars breaking into Don Hash's service station near Vista, Mo., didn't expect a reception. But Hash, who was sleeping in the station, held a pistol on the pair and called the sheriff. (*St. Clair County, Mo., Courier*)

Jethro Brown of Houston, Tex., closed his Washateria for the night and pocketed the day's receipts. As he started for home, he noticed a man following him. The man walked ahead, then wheeled and pointed a sawed-off .22 rifle at him and said, "Hold it." Brown jerked his .38 revolver from his belt and fired, killing the robber. (*Houston, Tex., Post*)

James Freeman of Florence, Oreg., awoke from a nap one afternoon to hear banging on his house. He rushed to the door, pistol in hand, just as an intruder came through the door. He held him at gunpoint until an officer arrived. The officer had already picked up the robber's confederate on his way to answer the call. More than $1,500 in goods stolen earlier was recovered. (*Eugene, Oreg., Register Guard*)

Things didn't work out as planned when two would-be robbers, armed with a pistol and rifle, strolled into a Philadelphia, Pa. check cashing agency and told cashier Sadie Goldman, "This is a stick up." Miss Goldman wasn't easily intimidated—she pulled out a pistol and fired at the men, who fled empty-handed. (*Germantown Courier, Philadelphia, Pa.*)

Three men tried to sell Stacie B. Hunt of Flint, Mich., a TV and a woman's coat, but Hunt recognized the coat as one stolen from an acquaintance three days earlier. He held the men with a shotgun until police arrived. The men later admitted to 172 burglaries and 67 thefts from autos in Flint. (*Flint, Mich., Daily Journal*)

A teenage boy tried to hold up Monta Lee Savage of Uniontown, Pa., and threatened her with a four-foot section of rubber hose. She promptly drew her .25 automatic, disarmed the youth, and held him for police, who arrived to find her with pistol in one hand and permit for it in the other. (*Uniontown, Pa., Evening Standard*)

When a man drew a .32 revolver and demanded money from Los Angeles store clerk Sam Villa, he got $80 from the cash register. But Villa triggered a silent alarm, drew a .38 revolver, and exchanged shots with the robber. The robber staggered outside and died. Villa was wounded in the chest and hand. The incident was photographed by a hidden movie camera. (*Los Angeles, Calif., Times*)

APRIL 1970

Returning to his Holden, Mass., home for lunch, Leslie Spofford surprised two men forcing open his rear door. The pair fled. Spofford pursued and caught them, covering them with a pistol until police arrived. Police said both men were wanted nearby for housebreaking and in Washington State for armed assault.—*Massachusetts State Police by Capt. Stanley W. Wisnioski.*

An intruder had forced open a window and had one leg inside Myron Klimaszewski's apartment in Baltimore, Md., when Kilmaszewski awoke about 4:00 a.m. He pointed a pistol at the man, ordered him to freeze, and called the police, forcing the man to stay in his position straddling the window sill until officers arrived. (*Baltimore, Md., Evening Sun*)

Two youths entered Frank Zielski's store in Buffalo, N.Y., and demanded money. One held his hand in his pocket as if he had a gun. Zielski backed away from the cash register, pulled his pistol from his belt, and fired one shot into the air. The youths ran empty-handed from the store. (*Buffalo, N.Y., Courier-Express*)

After being plagued by repeated break-ins at his service station, P. R. Miller of Richmond, Calif., hid in the back of the station at midnight with a shotgun. When a burglar broke into the station a half-hour later, Miller fired a warning blast and made the burglar lie on the floor until police arrived. (*Richmond, Calif., Independent*)

Three men from Montrose, Colo., were on their way home from a hunting trip when they surprised four youths beating a State patrolman with rocks. The patrolman had stopped the youths for a traffic violation and the four boys had jumped him. The hunters stopped the scuffle and held three of the youths at gunpoint; the other young man and a juvenile girl who was in the car escaped but were captured shortly afterward. (*Denver, Colo., Post*)

Huntsville, Ala., merchant Floyd Maddox saw someone trying to remove the burglar bars from the window of his store late at night and called police. Investigating officers arrived to find Maddox, armed with a shotgun, holding the would-be burglar captive on the roof of the firm. (*Huntsville, Ala., Times*)

Mrs. Guytrelle Pruitt didn't answer the late-night knock on the door of her home near Hartwell, Ga., but saw a pickup truck parked in front of the house and heard someone climb through a window at the rear of the home. She and her daughter held the intruder at gunpoint until officers could arrive. (*Anderson, S.C., Independent*)

A would-be robber wielding a pistol approached William E. Baize of Bakersfield, Calif., in a self-service laundry and demanded money. He was so surprised when Baize pulled a pistol of his own that all he could do was stare openmouthed until police arrived to apprehend him. (*Bakersfield, Calif., News Bulletin*)

Mrs. Anita Osterman was prepared when a man came into the Wichita, Kans., store where she was a clerk, pulled out a knife and said, "Give me all the money." She reached under the counter for a .38 revolver, pointed it at the man, and said, "No." He fled. (*Wichita, Kans., Eagle*)

Two men came into a coin-operated laundry where Ocella S. Willard of Rockford, Ill., was sitting, grabbed her purse and ran. She shouted that she was armed, then fired a shot from her pistol into the ground. The pair dropped the purse and ran faster. (*Rockford, Ill., Morning Star*)

A young man who knocked on William Cohoon's door in San Jose, Calif., and demanded money, had a gun butt protruding from his waistband. Cohoon left the door, saying he would get some money, but come back with a pistol instead. He fired a warning shot as the stranger fled. (*San Jose, Calif., Mercury*)

MAY 1970

We are now demonstrating through The Armed Citizen one of the most important and most overlooked facts about firearms—that their mere presence often deters crime without the firing of a shot. To emphasize this, The Armed Citizen hereafter will consist only of cases in which crimes were halted without casualties. NRA members are asked to send instances of this kind from newspapers or official police reports, giving the name, place, and date of publication or report and name of sender. Address Armed Citizen, NRA, 1600 Rhode Island Ave., N.W., Washington D.C. 20036.

Awakened by a loud crash just after midnight, Mrs. Leona B. Ciechanowski, alone with her three children in her Camden, N.J., home, saw a man entering downstairs. She called police, then waited. When the man came upstairs, Mrs. Ciechanowski held him at bay with a pistol until police arrived. (*Camden, N.J., Courier-Post*)

Returning home, George King, Jr., of Macon, Ga., heard noises upstairs. He got his pistol, went upstairs and cornered three intruders. Police charged the three, plus a fourth man, with 46 counts of burglary. After further investigation, they were also charged with the rape of a Macon housewife. (*Macon, Ga., Telegraph*)

Twelve-year-old Gail Burdine, alone in her parents' home near Eufala, Okla., watched while a man knocked on the doors, then broke through a glass patio door. She meanwhile loaded and cocked a .410 ga. shotgun. When the intruder stepped through the smashed door, she pointed the gun at him and said, "That's far enough." The man turned and ran. She reported his auto tag number and description to police, who arrested a suspect. (*Muskogee, Okla., Phoenix*)

One robber held a .22 pistol on service station attendant Buddy Richards of Columbia, S.C., while his partner smashed the station's cash register with a pickaxe. The two then left the station, but Richards pulled a revolver and ordered them to halt. He made them lie down on the pavement outside the station and flagged a passing police cruiser. (*Columbia, S.C., State*)

Seeing two men get out of a car at 3 A.M. and break into the closed Flat Rock, Ind., service station where he was a part-time employee, Ray McClure alerted William Porter, who lived nearby. The pair called police and four more neighbors. The latter took shotguns to the station and captured the two burglars. Two men and two women drove up to collect the buglars and the armed citizens captured the foursome, too. They held all six for police. (*Indianapolis, Ind., Star*)

Mr. and Mrs. Jessie Jones of Clearview, Wash., drove into their driveway just in time to see a pickup truck, loaded with what looked like their television set, leaving the other end of the driveway. Jones chased the truck. Finally catching it, he held the driver at gunpoint while a passerby called police, who arrested the driver. Jones recovered his TV set. (*Everett, Wash., Herald*)

Insurance premium collector Samuel F. Barnes of Richmond, Va., was approached by three youths, one wielding a stick, after leaving a house where he had made a collection. He backed off, drew his pistol and fired a warning shot into the ground. The youths quickly fled. (*Richmond, Va., Times Dispatch*)

When a holdup man wearing a ski mask and brandishing a pistol entered Lester B. Johantgen's jewelry store in Minneapolis, Minn., Johantgen, who said he was "sick and tired of being held up," grabbed a shotgun and pointed it at the man. As the surprised gunman fled, Johantgen's son knocked him down, disarmed him, and held him for police. (*Minneapolis, Minn., Star*)

Service station attendant Luke Button of Akron, Ohio, filled a car with gas, only to have the driver demand money at gunpoint. When Button reached into his pocket and drew a .32 revolver, the driver drove away—fast—hastened by two warning shots from Button's gun. (*Akron, Ohio, Beacon Journal*)

Two men came into Mrs. D. C. Wood's grocery store near Fayetteville, N.C., armed with a pistol and said they were going to rob her. She picked up a shotgun and threatened to fill them full of buckshot if they didn't leave. The men fled to their car and drove away. (*Fayetteville, N.C., Observer*)

JUNE 1970

Stopping at a small grocery on his way to hunt coyotes, Leon Parkman, of Beeville, Tex., walked into a robbery. Getting his .30-30 rifle, Parkman pursued and captured the robber. The money was recovered. (*Beeville, Tex., Bee-Picayune*)

At a Chillicothe, Ohio, service station, a young man bent on robbery produced a blackjack and told station manager Ray A. Kimbler, Jr., "Don't move." Kimbler grabbed a pistol and detained the man until police arrived. (*Chillicothe, Ohio, Gazette*)

When Mrs. Bertha Todd's daughter-in-law found an intruder pawing through dresser drawers in a bedroom of their Baltimore apartment, she shouted. Mrs. Todd grabbed a shotgun and held the intruder at bay while her daughter-in-law called police. (*Baltimore, Md., Sun*)

When Robert Mauk, sales manager of a Louisville, Ky., used car lot, saw two men trying to start a car on the lot at 2 A.M., he got a revolver and ordered them to stop. One man started to drive the car away but stopped when Mauk fired a warning shot. The other ran, but was apprehended by police as he was getting into another stolen car down the street. (*Louisville, Ky., Times*)

As a gun-wielding youth was in the process of holding up Ernest Duncan's grocery store in Kansas City, Kans., Duncan's wife entered the store. The youth's attention was distracted momentarily—just long enough for Duncan to reach under the counter and produce his pistol. He disarmed the gunman and held him for police. (*Kansas City, Mo., Times*)

El Paso, Tex., service station attendant Kevin Murray was accosted by a man holding his right hand under his shirt as if he had a pistol. The man ordered Murray into the service station office. Murray reached into his car, pulled out his .38 automatic, and held the thug at gunpoint while a customer called police. (*El Paso, Tex., Times*)

When grocer Bonnie Lee Meeks, of Anderson, Calif., told four teenagers to leave his store at closing time, one drew a 9 mm. pistol. Meeks covered the youth with his own .38 revolver and disarmed him. The other three fled, but were arrested soon afterward. (*Redding, Calif., Record-Searchlight*)

A man walked into Donald Hoberman's jewelry store in Omaha, Nebr., and asked to see some rings. When Hoberman opened a display case, the man grabbed a rack containing several rings and run out the door. Hoberman got into his car and chased the man, stopping and holding him at gunpoint until officers arrived. (*Omaha, Nebr., World-Herald*)

Joseph A. Panaro was alone in his Wilmington, Del., liquor store when a gunman entered and demanded money. Panaro said he didn't have any, and the man ordered him to empty his pockets. Panaro pulled a .22 pistol from his pocket, and the gunman turned and fled. (*Wilmington, Del., Evening Journal*)

Dale Oakes of Watsontown, Pa., arrived at his coin-operated car wash near Milton, Pa., just in time to see two young men pry open a coin box and take money from it. The pair attempted to flee, but stopped when Owens fired two warning shots from his .30-06 rifle. He then held them at gunpoint until police arrived. (*The Daily Item, Sunbury, Pa.*)

Returning home from a skeet-shooting tournament, Gary K. Loyd and his son Keith, 15, of Boise, Idaho, encountered two burglars in their storage room. They covered the pair with their skeet guns until police arrived. (*Boise, Idaho, Statesman*)

Two young gunmen pulled up to the Mission Hotel in Houston, Tex., and demanded that hotel employee Mrs. Genevieve Touchstone give them money. She snatched a pistol from the desk and warned them she would shoot if they didn't go away. The gunmen fled. (*Houston, Tex., Chronicle*)

Four Canoga Park, Calif., young men heard glass breaking at a business next door to their house and found a man loading a typewriter onto a pickup truck. Michael Iler, armed with a 12-ga. shotgun, stopped the man and held him at bay while Scott Conley called police. (*Van Nuys, Calif., News*)

AUGUST 1970

Hearing sounds at his door, Gennie Conner of Avondale, Tenn., picked up his gun and went to investigate. When he returned to his bedroom, he found a burglar rummaging through a jewelry box. He captured the burglar, who was later accused by police of three other break-ins. (*Chattanooga, Tenn., Times*)

When two men attempted to rob a Rockford, Ill., motel, clerk Hubert Hagwood picked up a small revolver from behind the cash register. As he cocked it, the men fled. (*Rockford, Ill., Morning Star*)

Summoned by his wife's screams, Norman E. Ramey of Los Alamitos, Calif., ran downstairs to find a knife-wielding intruder in his home. He disarmed the man at gunpoint, and held him for police. (*Santa Ana, Calif., Register*)

A Whittier, Calif., woman was alone in her home when she heard someone breaking in a side door. She located a pistol and called out that she would fire through the door if the burglar did not leave. He ran away. (*Whittier, Calif., Daily News*)

When a man broke in the rear door of the Salem, N.H., home of Karlis Dums, he found Dums waiting for him, revolver in hand. The burglar turned and fled empty-handed, and was picked up shortly thereafter by police. (*Lawrence, Mass., Eagle-Tribune*)

Awakened by a baby crying, Scott Emerson of Dallas, Tex., went to investigate and surprised a burglar padding down the hall in stocking feet. Emerson drew his pistol and held the man, who later admitted to several burglaries and rapes. (*Dallas, Tex., Morning News*)

Seeing a strange car near a neighbor's house while the residents were away, Edward E. Jacobs of Atlanta, Ga., found two men in the house. He went next door and called police, borrowed a shotgun, and returned to hold one of the men for officers. The other escaped but was captured later. (*Atlanta, Ga., Constitution*)

Restaurant operator Bill Hamrick of Memphis, Tenn., was inside his closed cafe when he heard someone smashing the lock on the front door. He got his pistol and held the surprised intruder for police, who also arrested two accomplices in a car parked nearby. (*Memphis, Tenn., Press-Scimitar*)

Larry Thompson's San Jose, Calif., apartment had been burglarized recently, so when he heard two men pounding on his door he armed himself with a pistol. When the pair kicked in the door Thompson fired two warning shots. One man ran but his partner stood frozen in his tracks. Thompson kept his gun trained on the man until officers arrived. (*San Jose, Calif., Mercury*)

Joseph Hueftlein, 80, was in a rear room of his Cincinnati, Ohio, food store when he heard a man ordering his wife to hand over money. Heuftlein grabbed his gun and covered the man until police arrived. (*Cincinnati, Ohio, Enquirer*)

Mr. and Mrs. Clifton Fryman thought they heard burglars in their Dallas, Tex., pharmacy, so they called police and entered the store with the officers. When a burglar suddenly appeared and pointed a pistol at Mrs. Fryman, her husband stepped from behind with a rifle and disarmed the man. (*Dallas, Tex., Times Herald*)

Thomas A. Ciccone returned to his Wilmington, Del., home one evening to find the first floor ransacked. Hearing a noise on the third floor, he got his revolver, quietly climbed the stairs, and captured the burglar. (*Wilmington, Del., Morning News*)

Dublin, Calif., rancher Francis Croak was tired of prowlers on his property, so he and his son kept watch from a barn one night. When a trio arrived and began tampering with the barn lock, Croak told them to halt. They fled. Croak shot out a tire on their truck with a shotgun, fired several warning shots, captured the three, and held them for sheriff's deputies. (*Dublin, Calif., Herald News*)

Ozell Von Stephens returned to his Sarasota, Fla., home and found it ransacked. Noticing someone behind the shower curtain in his bathroom, he armed himself with a pistol and ordered the intruders—two armed teenagers—to come out, then called police. (*Sarasota, Fla., Herald Tribune*)

SEPTEMBER 1970

Atlanta Ga., police answering a call found Mrs. James F. Brown, wife of the night superintendent of police, calmly holding a burglary suspect at gunpoint. Seeing two men drive up to a neighboring house while the owners were away, she had grabbed a pistol and captured one. The second fled. (*Atlanta, Ga., Constitution*)

After a burglary attempt was made on Ralph Niese's tavern in Hamler, Ohio, Niese decided to sleep there for a few nights. Awakened at 5 A.M. one day by a car stopping at the rear of the tavern, he saw two men approaching the rear door with sacks in hand. He met them with a shotgun and marched them to the town jail. (*Farmland News, Archbold, Ohio*)

Aroused from bed by noises at the front door of his Oakley, Calif., tavern, Melvin Pereira took a .22 rifle and surprised two teenagers trying to break in. He held one of them; the other ran, but was apprehended later. (*Contra Costa Times, Walnut Creek, Calif.*)

A gunman entered Mrs. Sommie Biller's restaurant in Detroit, Mich., leaped over the counter and demanded money. Confronted by Mrs. Biller's .38 revolver, the startled bandit leaped back over the counter and dashed out the door. (*Detroit, Mich., News*)

When Mrs. June Chastain of Hamlin, N.Y., entered her home, a stranger grabbed her from behind and forced her up the stairs. As she neared the top of the stairs, she kicked back, knocking him down the stairs. She then rushed to the bedroom, grabbed a hunting rifle, and chased the man from the house. (*Rochester, N.Y., Times-Union*)

A would-be robber walked into a grocery in Scottsdale, Ga., and pointed a cal. .25 pistol at the operator. When he found himself facing the operator's .45, he pocketed his gun, grinned, said "I was just kidding," and walked out. Then he went around the corner and robbed a supermarket. (*Atlanta, Ga., Constitution*)

Hearing noises late at night in his Cheswold, Del., gunshop, Gerald Lewis rushed down from his apartment above in time to see a man flee with two handguns. Lewis grabbed his shotgun, ran into the street and fired a warning shot. The man dropped the handguns and was arrested. (*Wilmington, Del., Morning News.*)

Returning to her apartment from shopping, Ann Pinkerton of Trenton, N. J., found a man helping himself to her food. Her screams were heard by Mario D'Antonio and his son John, who rushed to her rescue and cornered the intruder with shotguns. The man was accused of breaking into two other homes in the neighborhood. (*Trenton, N. J., Times*)

A teenaged boy stepped up to Roy L. Dorsey's car in a Kansas City, Mo., parking lot, and pointed a pistol at him. As Dorsey, 81, talked to the youth, he brought a pistol from beneath his car seat. The youth ran, but Dorsey gave chase and held him for police. (*Kansas City, Mo., Star*)

Willie F. Brown awoke about 2 A.M. to discover an intruder standing in a darkened room of his San Antonio, Tex., home. Brown held the man at rifle point while his wife called police. (*San Antonio, Tex., News*)

Seventeen-year-old Clifford Keith of Kansas City, Kans., encountered a stranger with a gun when he was leaving for work. He ran into his house for a shotgun and returned to disarm and hold the man at gunpoint while his mother called police. The man had been fleeing State highway patrolmen. (*Kansas City, Mo., Star*)

When a Seattle, Wash., grocery store manager refused to cash a check, the "customer" produced a pistol and told the manager to go to the back room. The manager pulled his own pistol from a hip holster, and the man turned and fled. (*Seattle, Wash., Times*)

Mrs. Rosland Albury of Key Largo, Fla., was awakened from a nap by a young intruder pulling at her kitchen screen. When he got inside he found himself staring into the barrel of her .32 pistol. She called police; then when the youth said he was hungry, she fixed him a peanut butter sandwich. (*Jacksonville, Fla., Times-Union*)

OCTOBER 1970

Seeing two men breaking into his car in Seattle, Clifford W. Barks, 29, of San Diego, Calif., fired his pistol into the air. The men fled. Barks was then charged with discharging a firearm and was convicted in Municipal Court. On appeal, however, Judge F. A. Walterskirchen dismissed the case because a prosecution witness failed to appear. The judge rendered an informal opinion that the Seattle city ordinance is unconstitutional because it makes no exception for firing guns in defense of self or property. (*Seattle, Wash., Times*)

The Denver Post has named service station manager Dave Vigil of Denver to its "Gallery of Fame" for stopping a robbery at his station. A man pulled a gun on Vigil and took $156. As he was leaving, Vigil took a .22 revolver from a drawer, stopped the robber, disarmed him, and held him for police. (*Denver, Colo., Post*)

Receiving a tip from a neighbor at 4 a.m. that someone was trying to steal his pickup truck, Joe Goodnight of Concord, N.C., grabbed his gun and ran to investigate. He chased and caught two men and a woman who were stealing the truck. (*Concord, N.C., Tribune*)

Hearing the owner of a clothing store next door yell for help, Charles W. Parker, a Jackson Heights, N.Y., realtor, grabbed his .38 revolver and responded. He found the store owner struggling with a robber, whom he ordered to "put your hands on top of your head and stand back against the wall," keeping him there until police arrived. (*Long Island, N.Y., Press*)

Dennis Wagner of Pasadena, Calif., looked out his window near midnight and saw two youths break into the yard of an auto center nearby. While his wife called police, Wagner cornered the youths and held them at gunpoint until officers arrived. (*Pasadena, Calif., Star-News*)

A man walked into James Cole's bar in El Paso, Tex., picked up a beer bottle, smashed it against the bar, thrust it near Cole's face, and demanded money. Instead of money, Cole took a .38 revolver from the till, whereupon the man dropped the bottle and ran out. (*El Paso, Tex., Times*)

Hearing a noise late at night in his Tallahassee, Fla., store, Mel Gidden left his apartment in the rear to investigate, armed with a .22 rifle. He was jumped by the intruder and disarmed, but Mrs. Gidden picked up the fallen rifle and hit the burglar on the head. Gidden held him at gunpoint until a deputy sheriff arrived. (*Tallahassee, Fla., Democrat*)

Two youths armed with a pistol attempted to rob a Des Moines, Iowa, delicatessen, but turned and fled when owner David Fishel pointed a revolver at them. The restaurateur foiled a similar attempt less than two years ago. (*Des Moines, Iowa, Tribune*)

Michael Korecki, owner of an Elmira, N.Y., liquor store, didn't scare easily when three men attempted to rob his store. He picked up a pistol kept nearby and told them, "Get out or I'll blast you." The three fled. (*Elmira, N.Y., Sunday Telegram*)

A 15-year-old boy described by police as being "very wild and under the influence of drugs," was captured and held at gun point by Clifford Morningstar whose Middletown, Ohio, home he attempted to enter illegally. Morningstar turned the youth over to the police who charged him with being under the influence of drugs and damaging property. (*Middletown, Ohio, Journal*)

Mrs. Wesley Heinrich of Redding, Calif., returned home to find two men burglarizing her house. Seeing the culprits run into the brush surrounding her home, Mrs. Heinrich ducked inside the house and came out with a .22 rifle. She flushed the pair and held them until police arrived. (*Red Bluff, Calif., Daily News*)

Matthew Meyers, proprietor of Matty's Hideaway in Cornwall, N.Y., heard someone breaking into his establishment late at night and armed himself. He apprehended the intruder, holding him at gunpoint until police arrived. (*Newburgh, N.Y., Evening News*)

An Anchorage, Alaska, man heard someone breaking into a school next door at 3 a.m. While his wife called police, the man got a gun and stopped the burglar. (*Anchorage, Alaska, Daily News*)

NOVEMBER 1970

Henry O. Coldani, Jr., a Stockton, Calif., bar owner, heard breaking glass at a wig shop next door, picked up his pistol and went to investigate. He found a burglar leaving the shop and held him until officers arrived. (*Stockton, Calif., Record*)

Four youths, one carrying a gun, entered a San Jose, Calif., market and ordered the clerk, Lawrence Ruiz, to empty the cash register. Ruiz turned on one of the robbers only to be hit on the head with a hammer. During the melee a second clerk, Steven Scott, grabbed a rifle under the counter and stopped the attackers. Only one of the hoodlums managed to escape. (*San Jose, Calif., Mercury-News*)

Opening his front door at 11:00 p.m., Robert Epstein of Brattleboro, Vt., discovered two men with stockings drawn over their faces, one of them carrying a knife. Epstein quickly slammed the door and yelled out that he had a gun, whereupon the strangers fled. (*Brattleboro, Vt., Daily Reformer*)

A man entered an Oklahoma City, Okla., dry cleaner's shop where Clarence Mays, 62, was working, and ordered Mays to open the cash register. Believing the man had a concealed firearm, Mays ducked behind the counter to get a gun. The crook ducked on the opposite side. Peering over the counter he looked straight into Mays' gun barrel. A moment later he crawled to the door and ran down the street. (*Oklahoma City, Okla., Daily Oklahoman*)

Late one evening W. A. Hendrix became suspicious of two men busily loading a station wagon in front of a Birmingham, Ala., construction site. Taking a shotgun from his home, Hendrix went across the street to investigate. The pair attempted to escape in the car, and when they refused to stop, Hendrix fired. The car crashed into a tree; one man fled and was captured later; Hendrix held the other until sheriff's deputies arrived. (*Birmingham, Ala., Birmingham News*)

When White Plains, N.Y., service station attendant Wallace Rouse, 60, found a man taking money from the station's cash register, he grabbed a gun and fired at the thief. The latter dropped the money and ran. (*New Rochelle, N.Y., Standard-Star*)

Harold K. Holt was parked at a Waynesville, Mo., drive-in when he saw a boy breaking into a nearby service station. Holt drove over to the building and ordered the youth out at the point of a shotgun. State troopers were notified and took charge of the suspect. (Springfield, Mo., *Leader-Press*)

Mrs. Colleen Remey of Santa Ana, Calif., woke up one morning and saw an intruder advancing toward her with a raised knife. When she screamed, he fled the room. Her husband armed himself, pursued the intruder, and captured him before he could unlock the patio door and escape. (Santa Ana, Calif., *Register*)

After his Milwaukee, Wis., home had been burglarized, Henry Renner, who works nights, purchased revolvers for his wife and 16-year-old daughter. Some time later, Mrs. Renner was awakened by a suspicious early-morning noise downstairs. She and her daughter armed themselves, and confronted a hooded intruder. The daughter fired three times and chased the man out of the house into an alley where he disappeared. (Milwaukee, Wis., *Journal*)

N. D. Stanford grabbed a shotgun when awakened by suspicious noises coming from his Cobb County, Ga., country store. He exchanged shots with an armed intruder who fled, leaving his shoes behind. (Atlanta, Ga., *Constitution*)

Four would-be robbers of a Point of Rocks, Md., liquor store were thwarted by a 40-year-old woman clerk, Mrs. Amelia Young, who produced a .38 revolver from beneath the counter and trained it on them. The four fled by car. (Frederick, Md., *News*)

When a robber pulled a knife and demanded money from St. Louis, Mo., food store owner William Heidemann, Mrs. Heidemann quickly passed her husband a pistol. The thug hurled the knife at Heidemann, missed, and fled amid a hail of pistol shots. He was later arrested. (St. Louis, Mo., *Post-Dispatch*)

DECEMBER 1970

An electronic alarm sounding at Neill Doane's home one night alerted him that his Londonderry, Vt., sporting goods store had been illegally entered. After notifying the police, he called several friends, then went armed to the shop. They captured three burglars emerging from the store laden with guns and ammunition, and held them at gun point until police arrived. (Brattleboro, Vt., *Daily Reformer*)

Frank Messineo of Downey, Calif., ignored his door bell when it rang at 3:00 a.m. But a few minutes later, he heard someone entering his apartment through a side window. Messineo took a .25 automatic and captured the burglar. (Huntington, Calif., *Daily Signal*)

Springfield, Mo., jewelry store owner Robert Lockmiller purchased a revolver after robbers stole several thousand dollars in merchandise. One month later, when two armed hoodlums entered his store, Lockmiller immediately grabbed his revolver and concealed himself in the store office. After one of the bandits fired, Lockmiller fired twice, scaring the two out of his store. (*Springfield, Mo., Daily News*)

During Washington, D.C., civil disturbances in September, a crowd of youths slipped past police lines and attempted to break into the Monarch Novelty Co. Greeted by the owner's son, who was armed with a shotgun, the crowd retreated, moved down the street, and looted another store instead. (*Washington, D.C., Star*)

David Kline, a night-clerk in a Phoenix, Ariz., market, thwarted a robbery attempt by two youths during early morning hours. One grabbed Kline around the neck and held a knife to his stomach, while the other cleaned out the cash register. When two customers entered, the pair ran into the back of the store. That gave Kline an opportunity to grab a shot gun and apprehend the youths at the back door. (*Phoenix, Ariz., Gazette*)

Noticing someone breaking into a neighbor's apartment, Gary Messersmith, of Santa Ana, Calif., phoned police and went to the rear of the apartment with his shotgun. He arrived in time to intercept a man climbing out of the rear window with a typewriter. Messersmith covered him until police arrived. (*Los Angeles, Calif., Times*)

Albert Gottfried and Norbert Melczak, officers of a Toledo, Ohio, Federal Credit Union, were transporting a $70,000 payroll when the driver of another car and a gunman attempted to rob them. The driver tried to force Gottfried's car off the road. That maneuver failing, the armed man stepped out into the street and shouted, "Hold it!" Gottfried pointed his revolver at the man. He dropped to the ground and the payroll car sped safely past. (*Toledo, Ohio, Times*)

Two men entered Joseph Albion's Niagara Falls, N.Y., jewelry store and asked to see the "big, expensive stuff". After Albion showed them a ring, one of the men drew a pistol, and ordered the store owner to wrap up some of the jewelry. Pretending he did not hear, Albion grabbed a pistol and aimed it at the two. The gun wielder fired once, barely missing Albion, before both would-be bandits fled to a car. (*Niagara Falls, N.Y., Gazette*)

When Ernest N. White of Seattle, Wash., observed two suspicious men leaving a local dry cleaning establishment, he called police and followed with a rifle. One of the men dropped a bag of money when White confronted them. At gunpoint White held the two until police arrived. (*Seattle, Wash., Outlook*)

Joseph Ragone of Mamaroneck, N.Y., routed a man who produced a revolver in Ragone's liquor store and demanded money. The store owner grabbed a gun and fired two shots over the man's head, before the robber fled down the street. (*Mamaroneck, N.Y., The Daily Times*)

A man wearing a paper-bag mask drew a pistol on Leon Matthews, intending to rob the Augusta, Ga., store, in which Matthews works. Pulling out his own gun, Matthews scared the man out of the store. (*Augusta, Ga., Chronicle-Herald*)

A 250-lb. lioness that escaped near Boring, Oreg., killed a horse, wounded one dog, and was about to mutilate another, when children's screams alerted Dan D. Tanory. He grabbed his big-game rifle and shot the lioness in time to save the dog. (*Portland, Oreg., Oregon Journal*)

Mere presence of a firearm, without a shot being fired, prevents crime in many instances, as shown by news reports sent to The Armed Citizen. Shooting usually can be justified only where crime constitutes an immediate, imminent threat to life or limb or, in some circumstances, property. These accounts are from clippings sent in by NRA Members. Anyone is free to quote or reproduce them.

JANUARY 1971

Ivory D. Prewett of Avondale, Penn., surprised two men who were attempting to burglarize his garage. Arming himself with a shotgun, he ordered the intruders to stop. Instead the two ran for the back door. Prewett fired twice, but the two escaped. (*West Chester-Paoli, Penn., Daily Local News*)

In holding up a Miami, Fla., restaurant, two armed robbers covered employee Patricia Hepburn, 19, so closely that her co-worker, Otis Shabazz, 40, could not use his pistol. Vaulting over the counter, Shabazz forced one robber to flee and held the other for police. (*Miami, Fla., Herald*)

After closing the Seattle, Wash., gasoline station where he is employed, auto mechanic Edward Wagner was driving home when a car carrying four masked men forced his car off the road. They then ordered him to toss out a money bag containing change from the station. When one of the robbers attempted to retrieve the money, Wagner pointed a gun at him. The four sped away after firing a shot that missed Wagner. (*Seattle, Wash., Post Intelligencer*)

Investigating a noise in his garage, Glenn A. Finley of Danville, Ill., surprised a youth who ran, shouting, "If you shoot me you'll be in hot water." The boy stopped after Finley fired a warning shot from his pistol. He was later taken to the police station, and released to his mother. (*Danville, Ill., The Commercial-News*)

A burglar alarm connected to Brooks Mundy's Huntsville, Ala., grocery store sounded at his home late one night. Taking a shotgun, Mundy went to investigate. He discovered a man hiding outside the store and another climbing through a broken window. The merchant held both suspects until police arrived. (*Huntsville, Ala., The Huntsville Times*)

At 3 a.m., James Perry Knott of Big Spring, Tex., observed three suspicious-looking youths entering the office of a local motel. Following them with a shotgun, Knott saw one force the manager toward a back room at knife point, as the other two bagged money from the cash box. When Knott entered with his gun, the youths fled. (*Big Spring, Tex., The Big Spring Daily Herald*)

1971

Mrs. Deloris Ehle of Ft. Wayne, Ind., was suspicious of two men who parked in her driveway. Consequently, she did not respond when they knocked first on her front door, then on her back door. But when they took a ladder from her garage and removed one of her window screens, she grabbed a shotgun. Seeing the armed homeowner, the two men fled. (*Ft. Wayne, Ind., The News Sentinel*)

When two armed men attempted to rob Dale Meadows' Tulsa, Okla., drug store of cash and narcotics, Meadows gave them what they wanted. But as they were leaving he got a pistol and fired at them. One man shouted, "Don't shoot." The other dropped a pillowcase in which they had placed the drugs and cash. Both fled out the door. (*Tulsa, Okla., The Tulsa Tribune*)

Mr. and Mrs. Michael McWilliams of Palmetto, Fla., pulled off the road to rest at a closed gas station near Titusville, Fla. at 2 a.m. About an hour later, they were awakened by noises made by two prowlers who had entered the station. McWilliams grabbed a .22 pistol and held the suspects until a passing Deputy Sheriff came along. (*Miami, Fla., The Miami Herald*)

An Oakland, Calif., restaurant owner and handgun expert, Leroy Taylor, was working alone when an armed youth entered, demanded money, and ordered Taylor to face the wall. Instead, Taylor grabbed a revolver under his apron and fired three shots into the wall, deliberately missing the youth by several inches. The robber fainted, dropped the money, then recovered and ran. Taylor has trained policemen, movie cowboys, and has given shooting demonstrations at Disneyland. (*Oakland, Calif., Oakland Tribune*)

THE ARMED CITIZEN

Edward Esper was about to close his Worcester, Mass., grocery store when two holdup men entered and one produced a gun. Pretending to get money from the cash register, Esper drew a .22 pistol and exchanged shots with the bandits, who fled empty handed. (*Worcester, Mass., Metropolitan News*)

MARCH 1971

Reporter Luther Mowery was in a *Chattanooga* (Tenn.) *Times* staff car when a robbery bulletin and suspect description sounded on the car's police radio. The suspect was thought to have fled on a city bus, so when Mowery spotted a bus pulling out near the crime scene, he stopped it. Boarding with a pistol from the staff car, Mowery seized a man sitting in the front seat who shouted, "Okay, okay, you got me." (*New York, N.Y., Editor & Publisher*)

Howard J. Matlock of Charleston, Tenn., was walking early one morning, when he noticed two men attempting a break-in at a local store. After telephoning the police, Matlock returned to the store with his shotgun and held the suspects until the officers arrived. (*Chattanooga, Tenn., The Chattanooga News-Free Press*)

An intruder cut through a screen door and entered the home of Mrs. Dale Larsen of Pleasant Grove, Utah. Discovering Mrs. Larsen inside, he lunged at her with his knife. Mrs. Larsen picked up a rifle and fired, causing the man to run out of her house. (*Salt Lake City, Utah, Salt Lake City Deseret News-Salt Lake Telegram*)

Drew Turner of Springfield, Mo., awoke early one morning to see two men take a bicycle from a neighbor's yard and load it into a truck. After phoning the police, Turner and his son followed in their car, stopping the truck a few blocks away. The son held a .22 rifle on the suspects until police arrived. (*Springfield, Mo., The Springfield Daily News*)

A youth entered the San Gabriel, Calif., market where Mrs. Marjorie Wooley was working. Producing a pistol, he demanded money and was about to leave the store with $49 when Mrs. Wooley's husband, Charles, came out of the back room with a gun. Mr. Wooley fired twice at the suspect, who dropped his gun and surrendered. (*San Gabriel, Calif., The San Gabriel Valley Tribune*)

Shortly after Washington, D.C., jeweler Charles E. Clarkson's home had been burglarized, two men entered his shop and asked him to appraise several pieces of jewelry. The articles, particularly a wristwatch, looked familiar. They were. They were his! Clarkson grabbed a revolver and held the two suspects for police. (*Washington, D.C., The Washington Post*)

Hands thrust into his pockets to suggest a concealed pistol, a man entered a Waukegan, Ill., tavern and demanded the cash box. When bartender Emil Ladewig picked up a pistol and aimed it at the suspect, the intruder immediately bolted out the front door. (*Waukegan, Ill., The Waukegan News-Sun*)

Robert Dent of Seattle, Wash., heard noises and upon investigation, discovered two youths attempting to break into the home of a neighbor. After getting his gun, Dent held the pair for police. (*Seattle, Wash., The Seattle Times*)

Robert Stilley of Delafield, Wis., began spending the night in his service station after the soda machine had been plundered several times. Early one morning, Stilley watched as two men approached the station; then, when one attempted to break into the soft-drink machine, Stilley grabbed his shotgun and captured the man. (*Waukesha, Wis., The Waukesha Freeman*)

J. R. File, who lives near Salisbury, N.C., was awakened early one morning by an intruder who had forced open the back door of his home. Grabbing a shotgun, File chased the thief out of the house, then fired five times as the man ran down the driveway. (*Salisbury, N.C., The Salisbury Evening Post*)

Arthur Miller was asleep in his St. Paul, Minn., bar, when he was awakened by the sound of breaking glass. Taking his gun to investigate, he discovered a man crawling through one of the tavern's windows. Miller held the man at gunpoint until police arrived. (*St. Paul, Minn., The St. Paul Dispatch*)

Mrs. E. F. Saltsman of Little Rock, Ark., was working in her grocery store when a young man came in, drew a pistol, and demanded money. When she produced her own gun from under the cash register, the man fled. (*Little Rock, Ark., The Little Rock Arkansas Gazette*)

APRIL 1971

Rabbi Jacob Bergman of South Bend, Ind., was awakened by his wife, who heard noises and saw furniture being removed from a house across the street. He went over with a shotgun, captured a husband and wife burglary team, then held them for police. (*South Bend, Ind., The South Bend Tribune*)

Taking inventory inside his garage early one morning, Nicholas Salis, of Nashua, N.H., heard someone try the doors leading to the service area. Salis reached for a .45 pistol, then hid while two men broke a window and entered. He yelled, "Freeze," then held the two suspects for police. (*Nashua, N.H., Nashua Telegraph*)

Mrs. L. E. Lewter, 78, of Vivian, La., heard a strange noise about 2 a.m., so she took a .38 pistol to investigate. As she entered the kitchen of her home, a young man sprang through a window he had just forced open, struck her in the head with pipe, and then began choking her. Mrs. Lewter shot the man in the head, killing him instantly. (*Shreveport-Bossier City, La., The Shreveport Journal*)

Store owner Jack M. Campbell, 65, of Fort Worth, Tex., sat in the back of his store with his wife shortly before closing time. When two youths entered and announced, "This is a holdup," Campbell reached behind a counter and produced a shotgun. He disarmed one youth, then held both until police arrived. A third suspect was later arrested. (*Fort Worth, Tex., Fort Worth Star-Telegram*)

Grady Sims, 67, of Cleveland, Ohio, who was robbed twice during the last year and had not fired a gun in 50 years, pulled a .38 revolver and began shooting after he was robbed a third time. The three robbers escaped by car, but police later arrested two of them when they went to local hospitals with gunshot wounds. (*Cleveland, Ohio, The Plain Dealer*)

Donald H. Miller, 34, a Reading, Pa., service station operator was working alone one afternoon when two youths with a small pistol held him up. Miller pulled a .38 revolver as the two went outside with his cash. Seeing the gun, they shouted, "Don't shoot; forget it." They handed Miller his money before running off. (*Reading, Pa., Reading Eagle*)

Leland Bellot, 34, of Placentia, Calif., heard a disturbance in a room of his home where his wife and four women guests had gathered. Grabbing a .45 pistol to investigate, he discovered an intruder holding the women at gunpoint. When the man pointed his shotgun at him, Bellot fired, grazing the man's head and knocking him down. Police later charged the suspect with the armed robbery of a local service station. (*North Orange Co., Calif., Daily News Tribune*)

Former Kansas Bureau of Investigation Agent Harry Neal, 70, of Wichita, grabbed a pistol in his bedroom when he heard a disturbance at his front door. He found a man standing in the doorway, holding a gun at his wife's chest. Neal aimed his gun at the intruder, who stepped backward and lost his balance. Then Mrs. Neal closed the door, shutting the intruder out. (*Wichita, Kans., Wichita Eagle*)

David Breedlove, 13, of Richmond, Va., hurried home to inform his parents that a local store was being held up. While his father and older brother rushed to the scene, his mother called police. David's brother removed the keys from the suspects' truck. While the robbers fumbled for a spare key, David arrived with a rifle to hold the men for police. (*Bluefield, Va., Bluefield Daily Telegraph*)

When Virgil Oliver heard someone break a window in his grocery store in Morehouse, Mo., he grabbed a gun and went to investigate. He caught a man going through the cash drawer and detained him for police. (*Sikeston, Mo., The Daily Standard*)

Mrs. Barbara Floyd and her two sons were in their living quarters behind the family's Hawthorne, Calif., pawn shop when they heard a knock at the front door. Because the shop was closed, they ignored it. Moments later, a man broke into the shop through a side entrance. Armed with a revolver, Mrs. Floyd held the intruder until sheriff's deputies arrived. (*Hawthorne, Calif., The Hawthorne Citizen*)

JUNE 1971

Mrs. Keith Boyce and her nine-month-old baby were alone in their secluded home near Tulsa, Okla., one night when a stranger pulled his car into the back yard. Twice burglarized in the preceding 12 months, Mrs. Boyce didn't open the door at his knock. Instead, she waited quietly inside, holding her baby with one hand and a .22 pistol with the other. When the man kicked in another door and entered the home, the young mother fired several times, wounding the intruder fatally. (*The Tulsa Daily World, Tulsa, Okla.*)

The sound of breaking glass in his home one night woke James Siciliano, 80, of Neptune, N.J. Going to the kitchen to investigate, Siciliano discovered two men attempting to force open his backdoor. When Siciliano got a shotgun and the two burglars saw it, they fled. (*Asbury Park, N.J., The Asbury Park Evening Press*)

Philip Finazzo, a Detroit, Mich., bar owner, rushed behind the counter and grabbed a .32 revolver after an armed bandit took money from his bartender and customers. Firing several times, Finazzo fatally wounded the man and recovered the stolen cash. (*The Detroit Free Press, Detroit, Mich.*)

When his wife discovered two youths attempting to burglarize a storage area in their apartment, Judge Robert V. Wood of Cincinnati, Ohio, armed himself with a shotgun and held the housebreakers for police. They later confessed to committing a series of burglaries in the neighborhood and showed police where they had cached the loot. (*The Plain Dealer, Cleveland, Ohio*)

Daniel Booth, 61, manager of a motel in San Francisco, Calif., was working late in his locked office when a man approached, saying he had car trouble. When Booth came out to help, the man pulled a gun, forced Booth back inside, and pushed him to the floor. Booth grabbed a pistol and fired three times, wounding the holdup man. (*The San Francisco Sunday Examiner & Chronicle, San Francisco, Calif.*)

Making a routine check of his Lansing, Mich., linen service one night, Joe Sohn surprised two burglars in an inner office. Pulling a pistol, Sohn ordered one of the men to drop a shotgun and knife he carried. Instead, the man struck Sohn with the gun. Sohn shot and killed him and held his accomplice for police. (Lansing, Mich., *The State Journal*)

Mrs. Henrietta Dillon, 62, pulled a .22 pistol after two youths, one armed, entered her Roanoke, Va., grocery store and demanded money. Both fled. (*The World-News, Roanoke, Va.*)

The A. J. Cope family of Columbia, S.C., returned home one night and found evidences of looting. The daughter heard a noise in her closet. Opening the door, Mrs. Cope saw a man hiding behind some clothing. She closed it without alarming the man and got her husband, who came with a pistol and held the intruder. (*The State, Columbia, S.C.*)

When a holdup man entered a Lexington, Ky., grocery store and demanded to look into the cash register, Junior Mattingly, a clerk, pulled a gun and scared him out of the store. The would-be robber was identified and later arrested. (*The Lexington Leader, Lexington, Ky.*)

After foiling two robbery attempts in one month with his .38 revolver, Richard Petersen, a Brooklyn, N.Y., pharmacist, was unable to stop a third when he was caught unarmed. Police had impounded his revolver for laboratory tests because Petersen, who nicked a bandit in the first holdup, killed the lone gunman who confronted him in the second attempt. The third holdup succeeded when a gunman locked the unarmed pharmacist in a rest room and escaped with drugs. Released by a customer, Petersen said: "If only I'd had my gun." (*The New York Times,* New York, N.Y.)

On learning that two suspicious men were prowling around a neighbor's home, Elgin Lester of Roseburg, Oreg., grabbed a pistol and went to investigate. He knew the neighbor was out of town at the time, yet there was a light burning in one window. Hiding outside, Lester waited until one of the prowlers came out. When Lester yelled, "Halt," the man fled. Both suspects were soon apprehended by police. (*The News-Review, Roseburg, Oreg.*)

JULY 1971

Awakened by the ringing of a burglar alarm connected to his supermarket, Brooks Mundy of Huntsville, Ala., took a shotgun and waited outside his store. When two men came out carrying boxes of merchandise, Mundy yelled for them to stop, then fired when they ran. One man was hospitalized with buckshot wounds; the other was jailed. (*The Huntsville Times, Huntsville, Ala.*)

Two men, one brandishing a knife, demanded money early one morning from Thomas C. DeBarr, 23, a clerk at a Kalamazoo, Mich., restaurant. DeBarr told them the money was in a back office and led them to the office, where he picked up a shotgun. When he aimed it at the two men, they fled. (*The Kalamazoo Gazette,* Kalamazoo, Mich.)

Philip S. Summerhays, 27, noticed activity in a nearby parking lot when he arrived home late one night. Thinking somebody might be breaking into a car, he went to investigate and found a youth attempting to rape a 46-year-old woman. Summerhays drew a gun and held the youth for police. (*The Salt Lake Deseret News,* Salt Lake City, Utah)

William T. Bower, 44, of Pittsburgh, Pa., was delivering milk one morning when a man held a knife to his throat and seized cash and food stamps. As the thug ran, Bower pulled a gun and fired into the air, alerting nearby police who chased the man into a house and captured him hiding under a bed. (*The Pittsburgh Press,* Pittsburgh, Pa.)

George Pierce, an apartment manager in Palo Alto, Calif., was notified one midnight that someone was attempting to break into the ground-floor apartment of a young co-ed. Pierce and his son armed themselves, went downstairs, and apprehended a knife-wielding intruder who had already entered the building. (*Palo Alto Times,* Palo Alto, Calif.)

When Frank Carter, a Carnegie, Okla., farmer, saw three men beating a town marshal who had stopped them for drunk driving, Carter grabbed a rifle from his truck and ordered them to back off. The thugs fled, but were later captured in a state-patrol roadblock. (*The Daily Oklahoman,* Oklahoma City, Okla.)

LaVerne K. Berry of Battle Ground, Wash., saw two youths loosening the lug nuts on the wheels of his car. Grabbing a gun, he went out, apprehended the youths, and held them for police. (*The Columbian,* Vancouver, Wash.)

Jim Hinerman, 27, a pizzeria owner in Columbus, Ohio, grabbed a pistol when the owner of another shop came in and shouted he had been robbed. Running out of his store, Hinerman chased the robber, firing several shots before the man dropped his loot and escaped in a car. (*The Columbus Evening Dispatch,* Columbus, Ohio.)

Andrew Piscatelli, 56, a crippled motel manager in South Amboy, N. J., was in a back room when he heard a robbery in progress at the front desk. Grabbing a gun, Piscatelli, who has two artificial legs, wheeled his wheelchair into the room and ordered the armed bandit to drop his gun. The two struggled briefly, then Piscatelli shot the robber in the leg. Piscatelli got the robber's auto tag number as he fled, and police later apprehended him. (*The South Amboy Evening News,* South Amboy, N. J.)

Larry DeHas, 33, grabbed a revolver from his service station in St. Louis, Mo., when he heard shouts from a nearby bank. It had just been robbed. Going behind his station, DeHas found the suspect and held him for police. They recovered $3,359 and seized a wine bottle the suspect claimed was full of nitroglycerin. (*St. Louis Globe-Democrat*, St. Louis, Mo.)

Edward J. Hoin, 57, reached for his snub-nosed revolver when three youths entered the Palo Alto, Calif., liquor store where he worked, pulled a gun, and demanded cash. Firing once, Hoin wounded one of the robbers and held the others for police. (*The San Jose News*, San Jose, Calif.)

Mrs. Merle Underwood, 64, a nurse in Cincinnati, Ohio, was on her way home from work one night when she was grabbed by one of two men who had been following her. She pulled a pistol out of her coat pocket and shot the man in the neck. Police later arrested the other suspect. (*The Post & Times-Star*, Cincinnati, Ohio.)

AUGUST 1971

Norman Call, 47, a motel clerk in Apollo Beach, Fla., was alone late one night when two men entered and attempted to rob him. One demanded money, then viciously pistol whipped Call. Call managed to grab a .38 pistol and hit one robber in the back, wounding him critically, before the other shot him in the arm and fled. (*The Tampa Tribune*, Tampa, Fla.)

A thug who tried to hold up a food market belonging to Isam Asker of Detroit, Mich., fumbled his gun in an attempted fancy fast-draw. The store owner picked up the gun from the floor, and shot the robber in the stomach, killing him. Acker, who has been held up 10 times in the past three years, then captured the holdup man's accomplices. (*The Detroit News*, Detroit, Mich.)

When two men attempted to rob his grocery store, W. J. Wilkinson of Beaumont, Tex., got his gun and fired. He wounded one. The other fled. (*Beaumont Journal*, Beaumont, Tex.)

When two ex-convicts forced their way into the home of Roy Ambrosen of Pacifica, Calif., the home owner tried to shove them out, but one of the men drew a knife and cut Ambrosen on the hand. Ambrosen's wife got a gun and gave it to him, whereupon the two men fled. The two were later arrested by police. (*Pacifica Tribune*, Pacifica, Calif.)

Two gunmen who robbed Ed LaGory's liquor store in Cincinnati, Ohio, dropped their loot and ran when LaGory pulled a gun and fired five times. They escaped with only four cans of beer. (*The Plain Dealer*, Cleveland, Ohio.)

Gregory Putman, a Portland, Oreg., cab driver, became suspicious of two men he picked up late one night. Stopping his cab, Putman pulled a gun and ordered them out. As one moved to get out, a pistol fell from his pocket. The two were charged later with attempted armed robbery and receiving stolen property. (*The Oregonian*, Portland, Oreg.)

Jack Allen, an Anaheim, Calif., gunshop owner, pulled a .38 revolver when one of two would-be robbers reached into his waistband for a small pistol. Firing five times, Allen scared the pair out of his store. Police later arrested them and an accomplice. (*Santa Ana Register*, Santa Ana, Calif.)

Hearing several shots from his son's store in Detroit, Mich., Anthony Radovic, 81, grabbed a gun, ran into the store, and found his son wrestling with an armed robber. The elder Radovic fired several shots, critically wounding the holdup man. (*Detroit Free Press*, Detroit, Mich.)

Two men, one armed with a machine gun, broke into a ski resort and tied up six employees in a daring holdup attempt at Soda Springs, Calif. Their plan failed, however, when they went next door to the home of Donald Schwartz, the manager. Schwartz got a shotgun and sent them fleeing with one blast. The two robbers were later jailed. (*San Francisco Examiner*, San Francisco, Calif.)

Samuel S. Cameron, associate principal of the Garfield High School in Garfield, Wash., spotted a youth who had caused a disturbance on the campus. When Cameron asked the youth to leave, the latter pulled what appeared to be a gun. Grabbing his own pistol, Cameron fired into the ground, causing the troublemaker to flee. (*Seattle Post Intelligencer*, Seattle, Wash.)

When a robber grabbed his wife and held a knife to her throat in an elevator in New York City, off-duty New York detective Stephen Hladek, 26, shoved his wife out of the way, drew his revolver, and shot the man in the heart. (*New York Daily News*, New York, N.Y.)

OUTCOME: A young mother who killed a 37-year-old felon after he forced his way into her home was cleared of manslaughter charges by District Court Judge Robert Simms in Tulsa, Okla. Mrs. Keith Boyce, alone with her nine-month-old baby in a home that had been burglarized twice before, shot the intruder with a .22 pistol while holding her baby in her other arm. (*The American Rifleman*, June, 1971, p. 12.) Judge Simms approved. "If more people did this," he said, "we would have less of the problem we have in this country." The slain man had a 20-year record of major crime, and was free on bond on a burglary charge when shot.

THE ARMED CITIZEN

OCTOBER 1971

The Reverend Frank Knight, 35, of New York City was awakened one night by a noise, and saw his tape recorder, TV set, and other personal property on the sidewalk below. When a man climbing down a ladder outside his rectory refused to halt, Knight got a .22 rifle and shot him once, wounding him. (*The Washington Daily News,* Washington, D.C.)

Bruce Hamilton, Oldham (Ky.) County Attorney, was working in his office about noon one day when a man rushed in and stabbed him in the stomach. Pulling a gun from his desk, Hamilton held off his attacker until the sheriff arrived. Hamilton was not injured seriously. (*The Louisville Times,* Louisville, Ky.)

After Mrs. Pat Clark's tavern was burglarized 10 times in the preceding nine months, she began patrolling the area around it in East St. Louis, Ill. One night, she caught two men in the tavern and held them at gunpoint for nearly 20 minutes until police arrived. (*Metro East Journal,* E. St. Louis, Ill.)

Joe Miller of Leicester N.C., surprised two burglars who were stealing several cartons of cigarettes. Firing several times with a cal. .25 pistol, Miller scared them away. As they ran, they dropped the stolen merchandise. (*The Asheville Citizen,* Asheville, N.C.)

Mrs. Dana Greco, wife of the mayor of Tampa, Fla., caught two men entering her home one night. She got a loaded handgun from the bedroom, then held the two suspects for police. "I'm really better with a shotgun," she said later, "my husband is a skeet shooter." (*The Tampa Times,* Tampa, Fla.)

Cliff Hoffman left his service station in Richfield, Minn., late one night with the day's cash receipts. As he neared his home, two men shouted for him to stop; then they aimed pistols at him and demanded money. Pulling his own gun, Hoffman fired once to scare them, but they fired back. After an exchange of gunfire, one robber lay wounded with a bullet in the hip and Hoffman had slight wounds in both legs. The other gunman and an accomplice were arrested. (*Richfield Sun,* Richfield, Minn.)

OUTCOME: Gas station attendants in Philadelphia, Pa., who armed themselves recently against holdup men reported comparatively few robberies after they began carrying guns. At one station, where 14 attendants work around the clock, one man on each shift is armed with a pistol. "We haven't had a holdup since the guns have been carried in full view," reported Dominick Caputo, an attendant. Prior to this Caputo said his station had been help up three times a month. (*The Sunday Bulletin,* Philadelphia, Pa.)

After a rash of vending machine burglaries in Fayetteville, Ark., James J. Marshall hid in a restaurant to guard his company's machines. Later, when an intruder had broken into nine of the machines, Marshall pulled a gun and held the man for the police. (*The Northwest Arkansas Times,* Fayetteville, Ark.)

Frankie Stephens and her mother were awakened early one morning by the ringing of a burglar alarm connected to their rural grocery store near Greenville, S.C. The women saw two men outside attempting to pry open the door of the store. Miss Stephens fired one shot over their heads, then held the two for the sheriff. (*The Greenville News,* Greenville, S.C.)

Two men entered Mrs. Sybil Turner's grocery store in Detroit, Mich., announced a holdup, then began emptying the cash register. When one of the robbers fired at Mrs. Turner and missed, and the other said, "I'll get her," she pulled a gun from under the counter and wounded one robber critically. The other fled. (*The Detroit Free Press,* Detroit, Mich.)

Tony Charvat and his family returned from church one Sunday to find a car with its engine running parked in the driveway of their home near Wichita, Kans. Their front door had been forced, so Charvat got a shotgun and made a search. He caught a burglar in one bedroom and held the man for the police. (*The Wichita Eagle,* Wichita, Kans.)

Wilma Becraft, owner of a market in Eugene, Oreg., pulled a gun after a bandit handed her a note saying, "Hand over your cash." She held the man for police. (*The Statesman,* Salem, Oreg.)

NOVEMBER 1971

Just as Walter Nettles, 75, closed his store at Tucson, Ariz., at 11 p.m., two armed and hooded men stepped up and demanded money. Seeing them, Mrs. Nettles ran from her car with a drawn pistol and shouted for them to leave her husband alone. One of the gunmen fired at her and missed. When she returned the fire and Nettles grabbed a .38 revolver from the car to join in the battle, the pair fled. (*The Arizona Daily Star,* Tucson, Ariz.)

Helen Friedlien, a store clerk in Cincinnati, Ohio, grabbed a gun when two men attempted to rob her one night. Although one holdup man was armed, both fled immediately. (*The Cincinnati Post and Times Star,* Cincinnati, Ohio)

Earl Presswood, manager of a diner in Shreveport, La., pulled a .380 pistol when a man armed with a .22 handgun entered his diner one day and attempted to rob him. The man fled, but was later captured by police. (*The Shreveport Journal,* Shreveport, La.)

112

Mrs. Mary F. Richardson of Kansas City, Kans., pulled a .32 automatic pistol after a young man snatched her purse while she was going to work one day. She fired once. The purse snatcher was arrested later at a local hospital with a minor wound. (*The Kansas City Kansan,* Kansas City, Kans.)

Lumpkin Loggins, a store owner in Orlando, Fla., drew a .38 revolver when two men armed with a shotgun attempted to rob him as he was closing one night. The pair jumped into a ditch and fired at Loggins but fled when the storeowner fired back. They were apprehended later. (*The Orlando Sentinel,* Orlando, Fla.)

After two convicts escaped from the county jail, Roy Bell of West Plains, Mo., got a .30-30 rifle when he saw a man running through his yard. At gunpoint, the man confessed he was one of the escapees and said he wanted to surrender. Bell held the man for the sheriff. (*Daily Quill,* West Plains, Mo.)

When a man followed her home one night, Eleanor Sanders, 34, of Westminster, Calif., got a gun, went out into her yard, and found the man peeking into her bedroom window. She fired one shot into the air and another at the prowler, causing him to run away. He was later apprehended by police. (*The Register,* Downey, Calif.)

Arcides Obregon, manager of a grocery store in Miami, Fla., got his shotgun after two men robbed the store, one knifing him in the stomach in a scuffle. Firing once, Obregon wounded one of the robbers, who later died. The other escaped. (*The Miami Herald,* Miami, Fla.)

JUDGE DRAWS GUN IN COURT—When two Soledad State Prison inmates charged with assaulting a guard scuffled with bailiffs during a hearing in Salinas, Calif., Superior Court Judge Stanley Lawson, 57, drew a pistol and placed it on his lap. It was necessary "for the protection of my staff and myself," he later said. (*The New York Times,* New York, N.Y.)

When James McCollum, an employee of an apartment building in Indianapolis, Ind., caught three men carrying furniture from the building, he got a .38 revolver and held them for police. (*The Indianapolis Star,* Indianapolis, Ind.)

Five youths armed with a sawed-off shotgun seized $1,100 from a Houston, Tex., motorcycle shop and tied up proprietor John E. Jones and his employees. As they were about to make a getaway on bikes stolen from the store, Jones worked his way loose and fired several shotgun blasts at the fleeing hoodlums. One youth, wounded slightly, was arrested on the spot, and two of his accomplices were apprehended the next day. (*The Houston Post,* Houston, Tex.)

When a burglar alarm sounded in a neighbor's home, Alfred Kaelin, a lawyer in South Land Park, Calif., went to investigate and saw a man carrying a TV leave the neighbor's house. The lawyer yelled for the man to stop. Instead the burglar tried to hit him with a crowbar. Kaelin fought with the man until Mrs. Kaelin arrived with a shotgun and held the burglar for police. (*Sacramento Union,* Sacramento, Calif.)

FEBRUARY 1972

Wounded in a gun battle with a robber, a Texas policeman lay in the street attempting to reload his revolver. As the robber prepared to fire at him again, L. B. Jackson, Oak Cliff, Tex., covered the robber with a shotgun and forced him to surrender. (*The Dallas Morning News,* Dallas, Tex.)

Anthony Pecho, owner of a Chicago grocery store, managed to reach a gun while a hold-up man threatened his elderly mother with a hammer. The robber said he would kill the woman if Pecho did not hand over the store's cash. Pecho wounded the man, causing him to release his hostage. (*The Chicago Daily News,* Chicago, Ill.)

Mrs. Willie Mae Porter, owner of a grocery store in Little Rock, Ark., was working alone when a man entered her store, shoved a shotgun in her face and demanded money. As he scooped cash from the register, she pulled a pistol from under her apron and shot him. He died later. (*The Arkansas Gazette,* Little Rock, Ark.)

Mrs. P. F. Truskey of Edmond, Okla., was sick in bed when she heard yelling and windows breaking in the front of her home. She got a .22 rifle and wounded one of three youths who were trying to break in. All three housebreakers fled. (*The Daily Oklahoman,* Oklahoma City, Okla.)

When a holdup man pulled a shotgun and demanded cash from George Dillon, a Ventura, Calif., service station operator, Dillon knocked the gun from his hands. Then Dillon pulled a pistol and ordered the robber against a wall. In an ensuing struggle, the service station operator shot and killed the robber. (*The Ventura County Star Free Press,* Ventura, Calif.)

A holdup man in Francisco Collazo's Chicago, Ill., grocery store aimed his gun at Collazo's wife and pulled the trigger twice because his demands for cash were not met. The revolver misfired both times. Collazo pulled his own revolver and killed the robber. (*The Chicago Daily News,* Chicago, Ill.)

1972

After an intruder grabbed Douglas Tackett's mother at their rural home near Richlands, Va., the 17-year-old boy got his father's .22 pistol and shot the housebreaker. The wounded man and an accomplice fled, but were later captured by police. (*The Richlands News-Press,* Richlands, Va.)

As John Michael Souter, his wife and two friends, were leaving the Souter's tavern in Kansas City, Mo., two men armed with pistols ordered them back inside. In the darkness of the tavern, Souter managed to get a .38 revolver and empty it at the bandits, killing one and wounding the other. (*The Kansas City Times,* Kansas City, Mo.)

John Mitchell, 68, of Baton Rouge, La., was driving his car one day, when three youths forced him to stop. When one of the youths pulled a pistol, Mitchell grabbed his own gun. Frightened, the youth dropped the pistol and fled with his accomplices. Examining the pistol, Mitchell discovered it was a toy. (*The Baton Rouge State Times,* Baton Rouge, La.)

Kim White, 14, of San Antonio, Tex., was lying in bed listening to her radio one night when a man pulled the screen loose on her window and started to crawl through. The young girl got a .30-30 rifle and fired one shot into a wall. The intruder fled. (*The San Antonio Light,* San Antonio, Tex.)

Held up 19 times and wounded once in the last three years, Ben Shaffer, a Cleveland, Ohio, bar owner, foiled the latest attempt. He pulled a .25 automatic and killed one of two hoodlums. The second fled. (*The Florida Times-Union,* Jacksonville, Fla.)

Z. A. Booth, a bank president in Riesel, Tex., spotted two men concealing shotguns under their coats outside his bank. As the men approached the bank, Booth ordered all customers and tellers into the bank vault. Then he waited behind a teller's cage with a .45 automatic. When one of the robbers shoved a shotgun into his face, the bank president fired and wounded the robber. Booth then shot at the second man. The robbers and an accomplice were later arrested. (*The San Francisco Chronicle,* San Francisco, Calif.)

MARCH 1972

Walter Marley, 64, of Philadelphia, Pa., heard strange noises in a neighbor's unoccupied apartment and went, gun in hand, to investigate. He arrived as three burglars were leaving. When one resisted, Marley wounded two of them. (*The Philadelphia Inquirer,* Philadelphia, Pa.)

When one of two young robbers pulled a gun in Miss Lydia Mei's liquor store in New London, Conn., Miss Mei grabbed a .38 and yelled: "Get out of here or I'll kill you." The bandits fled. (*The New London Day,* New London, Conn.)

Awakened by a strange noise in his home, Ralph Wichel of Chestnut Hill, Pa., saw a shadow in his living room. He called, "Who's there?" But he got no reply. When Wichel got a .38 revolver and fired one shot, the "shadow" ran. (*The Evening Bulletin,* Philadelphia, Pa.)

Jerome Abbott of Brooklyn, N.Y., a product distributor, was making deliveries when a knife-wielding bandit grabbed him and demanded money. Abbott pulled a licensed .25 pistol from his pocket, put it to the robber's chest, and fired. The wounded robber fled. (*Long Island Press,* New York, N.Y.)

Mike Palmieri stuck a .25 automatic into his waistband while three armed hoodlums were robbing his supermarket in Philadelphia, Pa. When they backed Palmieri and several employees into a frozen food locker, the store owner waited a short time, then rushed out shooting. He killed one robber. The other two escaped. (*The Philadelphia Inquirer,* Philadelphia, Pa.)

C. D. Maggard, 72, of Turlock, Calif., was walking home one night from his family's restaurant when three youths came up and demanded money. Although one held a bayonet in his back, Maggard managed to break away. He outran the hoodlums to his home. When he yelled for his wife to get a gun, the youths fled. (*The Modesto Bee,* Modesto, Calif.)

Three quick shots late one night broke the silence around Mrs. Ruth Geiger's isolated farmhouse near Russell Springs, Ky. A fourth shattered a lightbulb outside. Alone, Mrs. Geiger instinctively pulled out a shotgun when someone tried to force her front door. But the gun was unloaded so she grabbed a pistol and fired, scaring the housebreaker off. (*The Times Journal,* Russell Springs, Ky.)

Allen Pooley, Jr., of New Orleans, La., was at home alone one morning when two men broke into his house. He locked himself in a bedroom and armed himself with a revolver. When one of the burglars attempted to force his way in, Pooley fired two shots through the door. He heard one man yell, "I'm hit," before both burglars fled. (*The Times-Picayune,* New Orleans, La.)

Harold Gist, 15, and Robert Stone, 13, spotted a suspicious man running from car to car in the parking lot outside the Stone family's apartment in San Bernardino, Calif., early one morning. The boys got a BB gun, went outside and cornered the prowler, holding him for police. (*The San Bernardino Telegram,* San Bernardino, Calif.)

Mrs. Eugenia Valentini, 69, of Stockton, Calif., screamed for her daughter when awakened early one morning by a burglar. Snatching up a .22 pistol, Miss Anna Valentini rushed to her mother's room, shot the intruder once and held him for police. (*The Stockton Record,* Stockton, Calif.)

Lewis Maciocia, a gas station attendant in Jersey City, N.J., was working alone early one morning when three youths entered, drew knives, and robbed him. As one of the holdup men was tying Maciocia, a police car pulled up outside. While the robbers were distracted, Maciocia, not yet securely tied, drew a 7.63 mm Mauser pistol and wounded two of the bandits. (*The Jersey Journal*, Jersey City, N.J.)

Hearing screams in the woods one day, Tom O'Dell and Mike Hinsley, hunters from Oklahoma City, Okla., came upon a man armed with a knife forcing two 10-year-old girls to disrobe. The hunters ordered him to drop the knife. When he refused, one fired a shotgun blast into the air. The man fled. (*The Daily Oklahoman*, Oklahoma City, Okla.)

APRIL 1972

After six holdups, Martin Wolfe, 40, a Philadelphia dry cleaner, decided to carry a .25 automatic. In a seventh holdup, Wolfe gave the bandit the money from his cash drawer. But when the bandit ordered him to empty his pockets, he drew his .25 and wounded the man in the mouth. Police then confiscated his pistol. "I can't work without one," Wolfe said. (*The Philadelphia Inquirer*, Philadelphia, Pa.)

In climbing a tree to trim its branches, Robert Bork of Newark, N.J., caught himself on a 7,600-volt high-tension line amid the branches. Hearing his screams, a neighbor, Police Sgt. Howard Struck, snatched up a 12-ga. riot gun and shot out an insulator. The high-tension line dropped several feet, freeing Bork. He was hospitalized for burns. (*The Evening News*, Newark, N.J.)

Stanley Zawoyski, 53, was inside a phone booth when three armed robbers held up his Camden, N.J., cafe. Zawoyski pulled a pistol, came out of the booth, and fired a warning shot into the ceiling. One of the robbers fired both barrels simultaneously from a sawed-off shotgun, shattering the phone booth and narrowly missing Zawoyski. When the cafe owner fired several more shots, the robbers fled. (*The Courier-Post*, Camden, N.J.)

George Esposito of Orlando, Fla., got a pistol early one morning when his daughter told him there was a housebreaker in their home. When the intruder saw Esposito, he lunged and Esposito fired. A man was later found dead on the lawn. (*The Orlando Sentinel*, Orlando, Fla.)

Meredith E. Johnson, 42, Des Moines, Iowa, was working in his office one morning when he heard noises from another part of the building. Taking a pistol to investigate, Johnson discovered two intruders, one rifling a desk drawer. He then held the suspects for police. (*The Des Moines Tribune*, Des Moines, Iowa)

Westley F. Gill, a reporter for the Newburgh (N.Y.) *Evening News*, was covering a riot in that city when suddenly a band of enraged youths turned on him. Chasing him into a nearby home, the crowd broke down the door and was about to enter, until the home owner dissuaded them with a shotgun. (*The Times Herald Record*, Middleton, N.Y.)

Robert E. McInturff of Marshall, Mich., was asleep in his service station late one night when he was awakened by an intruder. McInturff pointed a shotgun at the man who then pulled a small pistol. After an exchange of gunfire, the robber fled. (*The Battle Creek Enquirer*, Battle Creek, Mich.)

When Morris Greene, 72, of New York City, answered his apartment door one night, a man and a woman forced their way inside, hit Greene with a wine bottle, and robbed him of $25. The man, screaming for more money, beat Greene down upon his bed. Greene managed to get a pistol from under the mattress and shot his attacker between the eyes. The woman fled. Police charged Greene with murder. (*The New York Daily News*, N.Y., N.Y.)

When two youths wearing stocking masks attempted to force their way into John Choy's New York City apartment to hold him up, Choy fired four shots from a handgun and killed one of them. The other escaped. One of the bandit guns proved to be a toy pistol. Police held Choy, 22, on charges of homicide and possession of an unlicensed firearm. (*The New York Times*, New York, N.Y.)

Doc Matthews, a farmer from Greer County, Okla., grabbed a .45 early one morning after his wife heard their truck door being opened. When the farmer ran out, a prowler jumped into a car and sped off. As he fled, Matthews shot out two of the tires and the back window, and put several shots into the car body. Police later found the bullet-riddled car abandoned. (*Wichita Falls Herald*, Wichita Falls, Tex.)

Elmer E. Nissen of Tacoma, Wash., got a shotgun when three suspicious strangers rang his doorbell one morning. When they started twisting the knob off his front door with a pipe wrench, Nissen opened the door and held the trio for police. (*The News Tribune*, Tacoma, Wash.)

MAY 1972

Mrs. Velma Priddle was alone in her home in Palo Alto, Calif., one morning when she heard a car drive up outside. A man with a screwdriver then approached her screen door. When Mrs. Priddle asked him what he wanted, he raised the screwdriver as if to strike her. She reached for a .22 rifle and wounded the man. Police later said the man had a long record of burglary arrests. (*The Palo Alto Times*, Palo Alto, Calif.)

Robert Lee Russell, a Wilmington, N.C., taxi driver, handed over his cash when one of three passengers held a box-cutting knife to his throat and demanded money. Then he drew a .38 revolver from under his seat and killed the armed bandit. When one of the man's accomplices grabbed for his revolver, he wounded the accomplice. (*The Daily News,* Jacksonville, N.C.)

James E. Baker of Monterey, Calif., grabbed a .44 Magnum revolver when someone pounded on his front door one evening. As Baker opened the door slightly, a youth shoved past the homeowner and entered. Although Baker ordered the intruder to leave, the youth threatened to kill Baker and his wife. Baker shot him in the leg. (*The Monterey Peninsula Herald,* Monterey, Calif.)

Mrs. Willie Green, 65, was clerking in a Chicago store when one of two "customers" pulled a gun and rushed to the cash register. Mrs. Green grabbed the robber's gun and screamed. The store manager, Benjamin Johnson, 82, then shot the bandit in the chest with a .38 and the other man fled. (*The Chicago Tribune,* Chicago, Ill.)

David Dwell decided to spend the night in his Fresno, Calif., stereo shop after it had been burglarized. Awakened by the sound of breaking glass, he grabbed a shotgun and yelled for two intruders to halt. When they did not obey his command, Dwell fired, scaring them out of the store. (*The Fresno Bee,* Fresno, Calif.)

When an armed holdup man in Cherry Grove, Ohio, rested his gun hand beside Albert Brautigan's cash register, the tropical fish dealer grabbed his hand and forced his revolver open. The robber shoved Brautigan backward. By the time Brautigan got his own gun, the robber had fled. (*The Cincinnati Enquirer,* Cincinnati, Ohio)

When Mrs. Thomas Gigliotti of Shrewsbury, Mass., responded to her door bell one night, three men forced their way into the home. One held Mrs. Gigliotti while the others went into the basement where her husband and two children were sitting. Gigliotti heard the intruders coming, got a gun and fired five shots, scaring the trio out of the house. (*The Evening Gazette,* Worcester, Mass.)

When an armed youth wearing a ski mask attempted to rob Anthony Knable's grocery store in Lebanon, Pa., the store owner pulled out a revolver and held the youth for police. A female accomplice was arrested later. (*The Lebanon Daily News,* Lebanon, Pa.)

When a holdup man stabbed Leslie Garner, a clerk in a grocery store in San José, Calif., Garner wrestled the knife away, pulled out a gun and wounded the man when he attempted to escape. Police later arrested the robber. (*The San José Mercury-News,* San José, Calif.)

Glyn Mealer was working in a storeroom of his Dallas, Tex., store when he heard robbers demand money from his wife. When one of the thugs opened the storeroom door, Mealer confronted him with a revolver. Astonished, the bandit tried to slam the door on Mealer, who fired, hitting the bandit in the chest. An accomplice jumped through a plate-glass window and escaped. (*The Dallas Morning News,* Dallas, Tex.)

When a passenger pulled a gun and forced Shreveport, La., cab driver Alan W. Martin to stop his car, Martin pulled out his own pistol and held the man for police. (*The Shreveport Times,* Shreveport, La.)

Herbert and Robert Huson of Cornelius, Oreg., got shotguns after two suspicious men had been seen prowling near a relative's home. Finding that a screen door had been cut, the Husons waited outside. When the burglars came out carrying furniture, the Husons held the men at gunpoint for police. (*The Argus,* Hillsboro, Oreg.)

Mrs. Maggie Feil returned to her White Swan, Wash., home with her children, Debra, 13, Mark, 11, and nephew Paul Kynell, 14, to find a man crawling out a broken window. Debra grabbed his coat and Mark began hitting him with a stick. The intruder shook loose only to find Paul had removed his ignition key. Paul covered him with a .410 while Debra called the police. (*The Herald-Republic,* Yakima, Wash.)

JUNE 1972

When two would-be robbers entered Charles Valinis' New Haven, Conn., grocery store, one immediately drew a pistol and placed it at the owner's head. Valinis managed to reach his own .22 pistol and wound one intruder. The other fled. (*Bridgeport Post,* Bridgeport, Conn.)

The Houle family of Hayward, Calif., were awakened one night by their dog as three prowlers left their yard. Timothy Houle, 18, and his brother Thomas, 20, picked up a bowie knife and a shotgun and followed the men to a second burglary. There they held one at gunpoint until police arrived. A second suspect was arrested later. (*The Daily Review,* Hayward, Calif.)

Plagued by repeated burglaries, John Farris decided to spend the night in his Memphis, Tenn., restaurant armed with a 16-ga. shotgun. About 1:30 a.m., a man broke the glass in the rear door and entered. Farris yelled at him to stop. When the intruder came at him with a tire iron instead, Farris shot and killed him. (*The Commercial Appeal,* Memphis, Tenn.)

Two men approached Myer Wallk, 64, of St. Louis, Mo., as he was walking his dog late at night and threatened to kill him if he didn't halt. Wallk drew a cal. .32 pistol and mortally wounded one assailant. The other fled. Police identified the dead man as a former convict who had been arrested 56 times since 1964. (*St. Louis Post Dispatch*, St. Louis, Mo.)

A man entered Maggie Dilworth's Greensboro, N.C., grocery, asked for cigarettes, and pulled out a .38 pistol. Mrs. Dilworth, 69, grabbed a .22 pistol. When the robber wrenched it away she dragged him over the counter. He dropped his gun and outran the irate grocer. (*The Greensboro Record*, Greensboro, N.C.)

Charles Harward's Floris, Iowa, store was burglarized so often he installed an alarm system connected to his home. Awakened one night, he and his son took shotguns and went to investigate. They caught and disarmed one man when another started shooting from inside the store, then fled by car. He and the girl driver later surrendered to police. (*Davis County Republican, Bloomfield*, Davis County, Iowa)

Three days and two nights Christopher Barry hid in his Greenriver, Vt., antique shop trying to catch whoever was responsible for a series of break-ins. Ready to give up the stakeout, he heard someone enter the store. Barry produced a gun and held the suspect until a State trooper arrived and arrested the man. (*Brattleboro Reformer*, Brattleboro, Vt.)

Luis Ponce, a New York City grocer, pulled a .38 revolver when four bandits attempted to rob him. Firing five shots, Poncc killed one of the robbers and scared the rest out of his store. Police later charged the storeowner with possession of a dangerous weapon. (*The New York Times*, N.Y., N.Y.)

Hearing his wife's screams, Albert Backofen grabbed a 12-ga. shotgun from the rear of his Springfield, Mass., grocery and ran to the front. A masked gunman took one look at the shotgun, pocketed his handgun, and begged "Don't shoot," then ran off before police arrived. (*Springfield Union*, Springfield, Mass.)

After being robbed four times, shot once, and then denied a handgun permit on grounds that his business was too small, Vidal Nunez, a New York City grocer, killed a robber with three shots from an unlicensed cal. .25 pistol. He was convicted of manslaughter. State Supreme Court Justice Joseph R. Corso gave him a suspended sentence and five years' probation with this comment: "A life was taken. But what is a decent law-abiding merchant to do—allow stealing or try to protect himself and his property?" (*The New York Times*, New York, N.Y.)

AUGUST 1972

After two windows were broken simultaneously in her Elyria, Ohio, home, Mrs. Mary Farkas got a .22 revolver, entered the kitchen, and found a man peering in. Meanwhile an accomplice climbed in a front window. Mrs. Farkas fired a shot that sent both men fleeing, one leaving behind a machete. Police apprehended three men later and charged two with malicious entry. (*The Chronicle-Telegram*, Elyria, Ohio)

When one of two armed bandits grabbed Harry Dillion's wife and pressed a gun to her temple, the Philadelphia shoe store owner pulled a .38 pistol, killed one robber and wounded the other. (*The Philadelphia Inquirer*, Philadelphia, Pa.)

Dr. Barney Benedictson of Yakima, Wash., awakened by barking dogs early one morning, observed two youths loading a pickup truck in front of a neighbor's home. While his wife phoned the sheriff, Benedictson blocked the suspect's truck with his car, then pulled a gun and held the burglars. (*The Yakima Herald Republic*, Yakima, Wash.)

A Florissant, Mo., housewife, Mrs. Beverly Barrett, investigating noises at the rear of her house, saw two youths removing a porch screen. She got a shotgun and, when one of the intruders stepped onto the porch, she ordered him to lie down. The other youth fled. (*St. Louis Globe-Democrat*, St. Louis, Mo.)

A young man made a purchase in Robert Hindman's Waukegan, Ill., service station, then grabbed a fistful of money from the startled manager and bolted out the door. Hindman got a pistol, ordered the thief to stop, and held him for the police. An alleged accomplice waiting in a car was arrested also. (*The News-Sun*, Waukegan, Ill.)

Porterville, Calif., storeowner William Baker attempted to hide when an armed masked man came into his shop. When the man began firing, Baker returned the fire, wounding his assailant. Baker eluded a second masked robber and went for help. The body of the wounded bandit was later found in a driveway, apparently dumped there by his companion. (*The Fresno Bee*, Fresno, Calif.)

Acting on a phone call reporting a prowler at his Dolphin, Va., general store, Keith Hargrave got a gun and went with his son to investigate. They found a man inside the store who immediately surrendered when he saw the Hargraves were armed. (*Richmond Times-Dispatch*, Richmond, Va.)

A man with a stocking over his head walked into Bert Curtis' Thousand Oaks, Calif., store and, wielding a gun, demanded money. Curtis reached for a gun under the counter and fired two shots that sent the bandit fleeing. (*The Press-Courier*, Oxnard, Calif.)

117

Ralph Kelley, manager of a restaurant in Detroit, Mich., grabbed a .38 revolver after a robber pulled a .22 pistol and announced a hold-up. The bandit fired twice, missing Kelley both times. Kelley then shot and wounded him. (*The Detroit Free Press*, Detroit, Mich.)

Arriving at her Fairview, Alaska, home, Fay Purnell found a man inside. He chased her around to the rear of the house where she produced a pistol and fired. The suspect, wounded, jumped into a car and drove off. He soon was apprehended by police. (*Anchorage Daily News*, Anchorage, Alaska)

Surprised by four armed men in the backyard of his Montclair, N.J., home, Dr. William L. Cassio pulled his own gun and fired three times. The men, one believed to have been wounded, fled the scene of the thwarted hold-up. (*The Star-Ledger*, Newark, N.J.)

Roy's Speed Shop in Shamokin Dam, Pa., had been the object of multiple break-ins, so owner Roy Cressinger decided to spend the night on the premises. When three youths broke in, Cressinger was ready. He held a 12-ga. shotgun on them and called the police. (*The Daily Item*, Sunbury, Pa.)

A man armed with a meat cleaver entered the Spirit House liquor store in Meriden, Conn., and ordered manager Stanley Zajac to "give me all the money." Instead Zajac pulled a pistol from under the counter and shot the would-be robber in the leg. (*The Morning Record*, Meriden, Conn.)

NOVEMBER 1972

Two youths quickly learned the error of their ways when they tried to rob Mrs. Eva Hill's St. Louis, Mo., cleaning store. The 60-year-old Mrs. Hill grabbed a shotgun from one of the robbers and began clubbing both men as she chased them out of the store and down the street. (*The Sedalia Democrat*, Sedalia, Mo.)

New York City jeweler Arnold Gessner gaped as a familiar nightmare unfolded for the 18th time. A "customer" drew a pistol and demanded money. When the thief turned to flee, Gessner pulled out his own gun and ordered the man to stop. Instead, the robber reached for his gun and Gessner fired, killing him. It was the second robber he has killed in three years. (*The New York Daily News*, New York, N.Y.)

Irvin W. Tellup of Hollywood, Fla., awakened by his wife who heard someone at the front door, got a shotgun. When the burglar attempted to open the bedroom door, Tellup released the safety, making a loud click. The intruder retreated outside the house where a partner was waiting. Tellup followed and held the men for police. A third man sitting in the getaway car was also arrested. (*Fort Lauderdale News*, Fort Lauderdale, Fla.)

Grocer Gordon Probert and his wife stayed in their Strong, Maine, store the night after a break-in attempt. The vigil resulted in Probert's apprehension of a would-be robber whom he held at shotgun point until police arrived. (*Franklin Journal and Farmington Chronicle*, Farmington, Maine)

George Barker of Bakersfield, Calif., out for an evening walk, was approached by two men who said they had a gun and demanded money. Barker whipped out a pistol and forced the men to lie on the ground until deputies arrived. (*The Bakersfield Californian*, Bakersfield, Calif.)

Hearing loud noises at the front door of her Centerville, Ind., home, Mrs. Lucy Shook got her .22 pistol just as the door flew open from a violent kick. Two shots from the homeowner's gun sent a would-be thief fleeing to join companions in a waiting pickup truck. (*The Palladium-Item and Sun Telegram*, Richmond, Ind.)

Rev. John D. B. Williams had gotten up at 3 a.m. to tend his baby when he heard strange noises coming from his Riverton, R.I., church next door. Two men on the church roof were sawing off the brass weathervane. Rev. Williams called the police, then held the men at gunpoint. (*Yankee Magazine*, Dublin, N.H.)

Hearing screams outside his roadside camper, Orland Hughes of Stillwater, Okla., stepped out to see a man dragging a woman from a telephone booth to a parked car. Hughes grabbed his .45-70 "buffalo gun" and fired a warning shot as the car drove past. The vehicle veered into a ditch and the woman scrambled free. Hughes held the kidnapper until officers arrived. (*Enid Morning News*, Enid, Okla.)

Milk truck driver Alfonso Cooper was parked on a Birmingham, Ala., street when three youths approached, two of them brandishing knives. Cooper gave them all his money, then produced a gun and ordered them to halt. Instead, the youths ran and Cooper fired, possibly wounding one. Police later arrested two suspects. (*The Birmingham News*, Birmingham, Ala.)

An unidentified Chattanooga Tenn., woman awoke to find a nude man leaning over her bed. As she was being choked, she managed to reach a pistol under her mattress and fire a shot. The man fled, leaving behind clothes and identification papers that eventually led to his arrest. (*The Chattanooga Times*, Chattanooga, Tenn.)

Tacoma, Wash., janitor Guy Shanks was taking out some trash when he was grabbed by a man who tied him up and locked him in a restroom. Shanks freed himself and when the robber returned with two accomplices the 79-year-old janitor began firing. He wounded one man as the three fled empty-handed. (*The Seattle Times*, Seattle, Wash.)

Off-duty New York City policeman David Durk was carrying home a pizza when two muggers, one armed with a knife, attacked him. Durk threw his dinner at the men and drew his pistol. He wounded one assailant and subdued the other. (*Philadelphia Daily News,* Philadelphia, Pa.)

1973

FEBRUARY 1973

When a gunman tried to push his way into the South Salt Lake, Utah, home of Mrs. Ray Sanchez, Mrs. Sanchez grabbed him, causing him to drop the gun. Her daughter picked it up, fired two shots into the floor and one at the intruder, wounding him. Police took the man to a nearby hospital. (*Ogden Standard,* Ogden, Utah)

Richard Hackbarth, an employee of a Wauwatosa, Wis., car agency, heard the sound of drilling coming from the car showroom late at night. He got a pistol and surprised two youths who were breaking into a safe. Threatened with a hammer, Hackbarth fired a shot that sent one burglar fleeing. The hammer-wielding youth was caught and arrested by police. (*Milwaukee Journal,* Milwaukee, Wis.)

When store manager Raymond Pence witnessed a stickup in progress in his Denver, Colo., market, he got a revolver from his rear office and fired a shot into a rack of pop bottles next to the two gunmen. The would-be robbers fled with only a package of cupcakes for their efforts. (*Rocky Mountain News,* Denver, Colo.)

Confronted by two armed men at the front door of his Keansburg, N.J., house, coin dealer Joseph Romeo drew a .38 automatic. When the robbers entered the house, he fired and wounded both of them. Police arrived and arrested the pair. (*Asbury Park Sunday Press,* Asbury Park, N.J.)

Pharmacist Don Dearth was working in a Long Beach, Calif., drugstore when a man came in, ordered a denture adhesive, and drew a gun. Dearth produced his own gun from a lower counter. It misfired, but the thwarted bandit didn't stay for another squeeze of the trigger. (*Independent, Press-Telegram,* Long Beach, Calif.)

Roy Danpier, Jr., 14, was alone in his parents' Chicago, Ill., home when two thieves broke in and demanded money. After one pointed a gun at him and pulled the trigger three times on empty chambers, Roy led the men to a money cache. As they left, the boy fired four shots from his father's .22, wounding one robber. (*Chicago Tribune,* Chicago, Ill.)

Carl Mayhue, a Ft. Lauderdale, Fla., liquor store owner was forced to close one of his stores due to repeated robberies. When a man carrying a sawed-off shotgun tried to rob a remaining store, Mayhue grabbed a rifle and gave chase. The thief refused orders to stop and raised his shotgun. The store owner shot and killed him. (*Sun-Sentinel and Fort Lauderdale News,* Ft. Lauderdale, Fla.)

One of two convicts who escaped from a prison work detail near Forsyth, N.C. made his way to the home of a local resident only to be faced by a shotgun-carrying homeowner. The unidentified armed citizen held the fugitive for sheriff's deputies. (*Twin City Sentinel,* Winston-Salem, N.C.)

Spotting two suspicious men wandering around his Albuquerque, N. Mex., drugstore, owner Carl De Alderete kept a close watch on the pair. When one man reached for a gun, De Alderete drew his own first. One suspect escaped, but the storeowner held the second for police who took the would-be robber's gun in evidence. (*Albuquerque Journal,* Albuquerque, N. Mex.)

While watching TV in her Las Vegas, Nev., home, 80-year-old Gladys Cunningham heard the glass in her back door shatter. Two men, one masked, were trying to force entry. Getting a gun, she fired a single shot that started the men running. (*Las Vegas Review-Journal,* Las Vegas, Nev.)

Seattle, Wash., store owner E. J. Jahoda confronted by an armed robber, grabbed the man's shotgun and turned it on him. As the would-be thief fled, Jahoda pulled the trigger only to find the safety on. "I don't know too much about shotguns," he said, "Guess I'll have to learn." (*The Seattle Times,* Seattle, Wash.)

Spotting two bandits inside a San Antonio, Tex., laundry, Gilbert Dominguez ran to his car and got a pistol. He returned to the store to find the bandits beating the 70-year-old woman attendant. Dominguez knocked down one man, shot the other in the leg, and held both at gunpoint for police. (*San Antonio Express,* San Antonio, Tex.)

MARCH 1973

Raymond Weiss was awakened about 5:30 a.m. by a knock on the front door of his Washington, D.C., home. Armed with a pistol, he opened the door and was struck by one of two men who tried to force their way into the house. Weiss fired five shots, wounding one assailant. The other escaped. (*The Evening Star and Daily News,* Washington, D.C.)

As he lives alone, Rodney Davis was surprised to find the TV going when he entered his Sacramento, Calif., home. He was even more surprised to find a parachute in the living room and a stranger asleep in his favorite chair. The man, later identified as an amateur sky-diver, had eaten half the food in the refrigerator. Davis got a shotgun and held the trespasser for the police. (*San Francisco Chronicle,* San Francisco, Calif.)

Spotting two men trying to break into a car parked at a Sarasota, Fla., motel, John Small told his wife to call the police, then got his pistol. Confronted by Small, one man fled. Small held the other until officers arrived. (*Sarasota Herald-Tribune*, Sarasota, Fla.)

Forrest Keith Butler returned to his Columbus, Ohio, apartment, unlocked the door, and found a man staring him in the face. The man struck Butler with a .25 automatic, sending him sprawling to the floor unconscious. When Butler came to, his assailant was in another room. Butler grabbed his .22 pistol and in an exchange of shots killed the intruder. (*Columbus Dispatch*, Columbus, Ohio)

Oscar Dailey was visiting his mother-in-law in her El Paso, Tex., apartment when a prowler entered. Upon being discovered the intruder began yelling. Dailey grabbed a .22 pistol from a kitchen drawer and shot the man in the leg. Police arrested the prowler, who was charged with burglary. (*El Paso Herald-Post*, El Paso, Tex.)

A man walked into the Chestnut Hill Pharmacy in Everett, Mass., brandished a magnum pistol, and demanded money and drugs from a clerk. Steven Helman, manager of the store, seized a revolver, ran around to the front of the counter, and, when the robber aimed his pistol at him, fired one shot that killed the holdup man. (*Boston Evening Globe*, Boston, Mass.)

Dale Couch was locking up his Wilson, Kans., gas station for the night when he saw two men in a closed station across the street. He ran to his nearby trailer, got a shotgun, and fired a warning shot as he approached the building. Couch stopped and held a man sitting in an apparent getaway car, but the two men inside fled out a rear door. Police arrested the driver and after an eight-hour manhunt caught his two accomplices. (*Salina Journal*, Salina, Kans.)

As Carl Petrusa walked through a New York City parking lot, two youths, one waving a pistol, jumped out from behind a car and demanded his wallet. Petrusa, a court officer, pretended to reach for his wallet, but instead came up with a gun and wrested the youth's pistol from his hand. Both would-be robbers surrendered without a struggle. (*Daily News*, New York, N.Y.)

Mike Zenzel awoke in his Berwick, Pa., home after hearing loud noises coming from his store next door. Grabbing a 12-ga. shotgun, Zenzel sneaked up to the store front where he saw cartons of cigarettes being thrown out a broken window. When a man crawled through the window, Zenzel stuck the shotgun in his back, ordering him to "Stay right where you are." Police arrived and arrested the man. (*Berwick Enterprise*, Berwick, Pa.)

Two bandits entered Tom Wong's Augusta, Ga., store and demanded money at gunpoint. When they grabbed his 11-year-old daughter, Wong ran to a back room and got his gun. The thieves fired at Wong and missed, then fled. (*The Augusta Chronicle-Herald*, Augusta, Ga.)

Three youths came into Charles Collins' Kansas City, Mo., gas station and told him they wanted his money. One youth opened his jacket and revealed a sawed-off rifle in his belt. Collins pulled out a revolver, ordered the thief to throw away the rifle, and held the three for police. (*The Kansas City Star*, Kansas City, Mo.)

APRIL 1973

Edgar Sims apprehended four youths breaking into a building next door to his Atlantic City, N. J., motel, and held them at gunpoint for the police. As a result, Sims was indicted by a grand jury and now faces prosecution for carrying an unlicensed gun. The youths, two of whom had been in reform school, were judged as juvenile delinquents, given suspended sentences, and placed on probation by a New Jersey judge. (*The Press*, Atlantic City, N.J.)

Four youths forced open the front door of Joseph Kierzek's Crestwood, Ill., home, confronted Kierzek's 14-year-old son, and told him, "Don't move or you'll get hurt." The elder Kierzek came out of his bedroom armed with a cal. .22 pistol and ordered the four to put up their hands. Instead they ran, one carrying a TV. Kierzek fired three shots, killing one intruder who was found clutching a revolver in his hand. Police arrested two other youths and began a search for the fourth. (*Chicago Sun-Times*, Chicago, Ill.)

Two men, one waving a gun, walked into Wayne Preston's Cobb County, Ga., pharmacy and came face to face with the pistol-wielding owner. Preston began firing and chased the would-be robbers out of the store. He wounded and held one man, but the other robber fled in a car driven by a third accomplice. The two were caught minutes later by the police. (*The Atlanta Constitution*, Atlanta, Ga.)

A man broke into Ruby Mae Cantrell's Knoxville, Tenn., apartment and awakened her by beating her in the face with a small blackjack. Mrs. Cantrell managed to reach the pistol she keeps under her bed and fire two shots that killed her attacker. (*Knoxville News Sentinel*, Knoxville, Tenn.)

An armed bandit entered Orr Stewart's Cleveland, Ohio, dime store and ordered Stewart to empty the cash register. Suddenly the thief was flanked by two pistol-wielding female clerks. When he turned toward one clerk with his gun, both women opened fire. The bandit fell to the floor wounded. Police removed him to a hospital. (*The Cleveland Plain Dealer*, Cleveland, Ohio)

Jack Lake drove up to the house on his Livingston, Mont., ranch and saw 15 rifles and revolvers he owned piled in his pickup truck. Grabbing a rifle, he went inside the house and surprised two men who were holding his wife captive. Lake fired two shots, wounding one man. Both intruders fled, but soon were caught and charged with robbery and grand larceny. (*The Billings Gazette*, Billings, Mont.)

Two men wearing nylon stockings over their heads attempted to enter the Arjay, Ky., home of Dr. R. R. Evans. Mistakenly believing they were hidden by darkness, the pair feigned illness to get the doctor to open the door. They left only after Evans told them he would shoot. They would have been "fools to think I wasn't armed," the doctor told police later. (*Daily News,* Middlesboro, Ky.)

One of two burglary suspects being chased by the police hid in the front yard of Nelda Jean Walters' West Covina, Calif., home. Mrs. Walters, the wife of an FBI agent, got her husband's service revolver and confronted the fugitive at the front door. When the man started to run, Mrs. Walters fired a warning shot and then held the suspect at gunpoint. Officers captured the other man moments later and confiscated capsules alleged to be dangerous drugs. (*San Gabriel Valley Tribune,* Covina, Calif.)

A young man walked into Thomas Salemi's Buffalo, N. Y., store, handed him a note demanding money, and pulled a long-bladed knife. Salemi drew a revolver from his waist holster and told the thief: "Don't move or I'll blow your head off." The man turned and fled empty-handed. (*Buffalo Evening News,* Buffalo, N. Y.)

JUNE 1973

Mary Hilton, a 70-year-old widow, heard glass shatter in her East Liberty, Pa., home, went to a window, and saw three men trying to break in. She shouted at them and then fired two shots from a revolver she keeps in her bedroom. Two of the men fled, but the third broke in, armed with a 12" knife. When she saw the knife, Mrs. Hilton fired, mortally wounding the intruder. (*Pittsburgh Post-Gazette,* Pittsburgh, Pa.)

Sammy Maddox was managing his father's Post, Tex., service station when two armed men walked in and demanded money. Maddox grabbed a shotgun and leveled it at the two who turned and fled. (*The Post Dispatch,* Post, Tex.)

Russell Merrill, alerted that someone was in his Hampton Falls, N.H., store after closing hours, picked up his hunting rifle, and headed to the store. Directed by his brother-in-law who lives across the street from the store, Merrill was able to apprehend two men and deliver them to police for arrest. (*Manchester Union Leader,* Manchester, N.H.)

Hearing noises at a bedroom window of his Ontario, Calif., home, Ronald Morris got a shotgun, went outside, and found two youths trying to pry open the window. He held the shotgun on the pair until police arrived. (*Pomona Progress-Bulletin,* Pomona, Calif.)

A man wearing a ski mask walked into a Gordon, Ga., bank pulled a gun, and ordered a teller to fill a paper bag with money. The robber then tried to escape in bank president Frank Gibbs' new car. Gibbs got a pistol from his desk, rushed outside, fired, and wounded the thief before he could escape. (*The Macon Telegraph,* Macon, Ga.)

Hearing a racket outside his Felton, Calif., home, Timothy Halpin, handicapped by a broken leg, hobbled to the front door to see a man tearing shingles off the side of the house. The man then ran around to the front porch, breaking down a fence as he came. Halpin phoned the police and returned to the porch with a rifle. The intruder attacked him and forced him back inside the house. Halpin fired two shots and killed the man. (*Santa Cruz, Sentinel,* Santa Cruz, Calif.)

Addie Whitesides, a church cleaning woman in Charlotte, N.C., was at work before dawn when she came face to face with a prowler. Screaming, Mrs. Whitesides ran for the door, followed by the man. Once outside she drew a pistol and held it on the intruder until police arrived. She has carried the gun since the church was broken into recently. (*Greensboro Daily News,* Greensboro, N.C.)

A man entered William McKno's Buffalo, N.Y., delicatessen, asked for some cigarettes, and yanked out a gun. McKno's son, William Jr., grabbed a revolver and wounded the would-be robber. (*Buffalo Courier-Express,* Buffalo, N.Y.)

When two men came into Arne Nelson's Seattle, Wash., drugstore and pointed a pistol at his son, Nelson grabbed a gun and began shooting. One bandit fired five shots and fled. The other was captured by the druggist and held for the police. (*The Seattle Times,* Seattle, Wash.)

Esther Long of Toledo, Ohio, was awakened by a man walking out of her bedroom. She took a pistol from under her pillow, fired, and wounded the intruder. The man fled but was arrested three hours later and charged with felonious breaking and entering. (*The Blade,* Toledo, Ohio)

A man began pounding on the front door of Evelyn Burkey's Hobbs, N. Mex., home and refused to identify himself or say what he wanted. When he started pounding on the back door, Mrs. Burkey got a small revolver and threatened to "blow his head off." At this the prowler dove over a back fence and disappeared. (*Hobbs Daily News-Sun,* Hobbs, N. Mex.)

THE ARMED CITIZEN

Two men, one armed with a sawed-off shotgun, entered Mario DiCenzo's Jamaica Plain, Mass., market and demanded money. DiCenzo ordered his dog lying nearby to attack, drew a pistol, fired, and wounded the man with the shotgun. The robbers fled and escaped in a car driven by an accomplice. The trio, suspects in a series of holdups in the area, soon were apprehended by police. (*Boston Herald American*, Boston, Mass.)

AUGUST 1973

A man walked into Don Lannoye's Seattle, Wash., 7-11 Store, flashed a gun and said, "I want your money!" Lannoye, who has been held up five times, pulled out a revolver and shot the robber in the chest. Police took the wounded man to a hospital. (*The Seattle Times*, Seattle, Wash.)

Jimmy Jones, a Wilmington, N.C., grocer, was in the rear office of his store when two men waving revolvers came in the front door and demanded money from a clerk. Jones ran out of the office with a pistol and in an exchange of gunfire killed one robber and wounded the other. (*Times-News*, Hendersonville, N.C.)

A gunman walked into a food store in Westwego, La., and told the cashier, "This is a holdup—give it to me quick!" The cashier picked up a gun, fired twice and mortally wounded the thief. Police found the man's body a short distance from the store and arrested a woman suspected of driving a getaway car. (*The Times-Picayune*, New Orleans, La.)

When two men, one armed with a pistol, entered James Shelton's Washington, D.C., market, the gunman snarled, "All right, old man, don't move. Let's have the money." Shelton dropped to the floor, drew his own gun and fired at the gunman, who fled. The second man confronted Shelton, who told him to leave. "I'm buying," the man replied, reaching into his back pocket. Shelton fired and fatally wounded the holdup man. (*The Washington Post*, Washington, D.C.)

A man entered Vincent Hick's Phoenix, Ariz., market, aimed a revolver at a clerk and demanded money and cigarettes. Hicks, armed with a .22 revolver, ran from the rear of the store and so startled the thief that he dropped his gun and ran. Hicks gave chase. Police joined the pursuit. The suspect jumped a fence, landing in a yard that contained a very large dog. Police found the man cowering on his hands and knees. (*Phoenix Arizona Republic*, Phoenix, Ariz.)

Hearing noises over the intercom that connects the hallways of his Middletown, R.I., motel, Fred Armbrust got his pistol and investigated. Armbrust found a prowler in a darkened room and fired once. The man ran from the motel. Police picked him up when he sought aid for a gunshot wound in his shoulder. (*The Newport Daily News*, Newport, R.I.)

A man broke into the Bartow, Fla., home of Mrs. Emily Johnson and proceeded to attack her with a knife. Though stabbed several times, Mrs. Johnson managed to reach a .22 revolver and kill her assailant. (*Orlando Sentinel*, Orlando, Fla.)

A man knocked on the door of Arthur Mulch's Wichita, Kans., home, got no response and left. He returned, parked his car in the driveway and then broke into the house, where he came face to face with Mulch and a 12-ga. shotgun. Mulch chased the prowler out of the house and blasted his car's radiator. The would-be burglar fled on foot. (*The Wichita Eagle*, Wichita, Kans.)

Robert Staring and his wife returned to their Garden Grove, Calif., home to find a nude man in the living room. The prowler immediately attacked Staring, who yelled to his wife to get a gun. Mrs. Staring handed her husband a .22 revolver, and he mortally wounded his attacker. (*The Register*, Orange County, Calif.)

After two men made an 11¢ purchase of candy in C. C. Trevino's East San Antonio, Tex., market, one pulled a gun when Trevino opened the cash register and the other grabbed the money. When the pair turned away, the 77-year-old store owner reached for a gun under the counter and fired twice, wounding one of the thieves. (*San Antonio Express*, San Antonio, Tex.)

Two men waited until all customers had left John Lamb's Currinsville, Oreg., market, then told Lamb to hand over his cash or be shot. Lamb diverted their attention by saying, "Don't you see people coming into the store?" One man went to the door, and the other turned long enough for Lamb to knock him down and run for a gun at the back of the store. Both would-be robbers fled. (*Clackamas County News*, Estacada, Oreg.)

SEPTEMBER 1973

After gaining entrance to R. H. Olds' Marietta, Ga., home, a knife-wielding intruder tied up the owner and his family. When the man went outside, Olds managed to work himself free, get a pistol and shoot the assailant when he returned. When police arrived they found in the assailant's car plans to rob five other families and a shotgun rigged to be fired by remote control. (*The Daily Sun*, Warner Robins, Ga.)

A man claiming to be a police officer forced his way into the home of a Baltimore, Md., housewife, raped her in the presence of her two children, ages one and two, then threatened the older child if the mother called the police. At that, the woman pulled a revolver and fired three times, killing the rapist. (*The Star-News*, Washington, D.C.)

Two men entered John Gennaro's St. Louis, Mo., market, looked around and left. They returned and shoved a gun in Gennaro's face. Mrs. Gennaro, who had been watching the pair, grabbed a pistol and began shooting. She wounded one of the pair. (*St. Louis Globe-Democrat*, St. Louis, Mo.)

A man walked into Roy Laos' Tucson, Ariz., pharmacy, pointed a pistol at the owner and demanded money. Instead of handing over his cash, Laos grabbed a revolver and fired two shots that sent the would-be holdup man fleeing. (*Tucson Daily Citizen*, Tucson, Ariz.)

An unidentified Dallas housewife became scared when two men who had fixed a flat tire on her car moved toward her. When one of them grabbed her and pulled her from the car she pointed a pistol in his face. The two men jumped into their car and fled. (*Dallas Times Herald*, Dallas, Tex.)

Hearing glass breaking in his Everett, Wash., market long after he had closed for the night, Arthur Burnett got a revolver and went to investigate. He found a man inside the store and announced that he was armed. When the man charged at him, Burnett fired two shots and mortally wounded the prowler. (*Seattle Times*, Seattle, Wash.)

Joe Tholt, a Highland Park, Calif., jeweler, has been robbed or burglarized 36 times in 26 years. Recently an armed bandit forced Tholt to lie on the floor and carried out cash and merchandise to a nearby car. When the man returned for more loot, the jeweler drew a gun and wounded the thief, who then ran to his car and drove away. (*Los Angeles Times*, Los Angeles, Calif.)

Two armed men entered Gerald Wetherell's Flint, Mich., market and one announced, "This is a stick-up." They forced Wetherell, an employee and a customer into a meat cooler, then returned with another customer. Wetherell took a gun from his belt and shot both robbers. (*Flint Journal*, Flint, Mich.)

Convinced that no one was home, two burglars broke down the back door of Heil DeHaven's Buckingham, Pa., home. The 79-year-old DeHaven leveled his 12-ga. shotgun at the smashed door and fired. The bandits fled and were arrested when they sought medical aid. (*The Daily Intelligencer*, Doylestown, Pa.)

Guns drawn, three men sauntered into Lloyd House's Apopka, Fla., market and demanded money. When one intruder threatened a 13-year-old cashier, House swept up a pistol from a drawer and shot him twice. House then wounded the other two thieves who returned gunfire as they fled. Both were later arrested along with two other men who were waiting in a getaway car. (*Sentinel Star*, Orlando, Fla.)

Redding, Calif., liquor store clerk William Work asked a customer to leave the store so he could close for the night, but instead the man pulled a knife. Work drew a revolver, forced the man to drop his knife and lie on the floor, and called police. (*Record-Searchlight*, Redding, Calif.)

Two men approached Luther Smith as he sat in his grocery truck on a Pittsburgh, Pa., street, and one, brandishing a gun, yelled, "Give it up Smitty." Smith yanked out a pistol and fired. The holdup men jumped into a car and sped away. (*Pittsburgh Press*, Pittsburgh, Pa.)

OCTOBER 1973

Mrs. Bob McKorell, Jr. looked out the window of her Hartsville, S.C., home and saw several people tampering with her son's pickup truck. Her husband ran outside with a pistol, fired twice in the air, and the thieves jumped in their car and sped off down a dead-end street. McKorell and his son held the four cornered thieves at pistol point until police arrived. (*The Florence Morning News*, Florence, S.C.)

Vaughn Elliott picked up his muzzle-loading rifle and hurried from his Highgrove, Calif., apartment to aid his brother, who was being attacked by burglars next door. Elliott shot one of the attackers in the chest, killing him. The second suspect and two other accomplices were caught by police. (*The Evening Telegram*, San Bernardino, Calif.)

Bartender Billie Snyder was alone in a St. Louis, Mo., tavern when three men came in. After one of them pulled out a pistol and announced a holdup, Snyder quickly reached for his handgun and fired four shots, wounding the armed man in the arm. The assailants were held at gunpoint until police arrived. (*The St. Louis Post-Dispatch*, St. Louis, Mo.)

Three men arrived for an appointment at the Winchester, Ind., coin shop of Leon Hendrickson carrying pistols in an apparent robbery attempt. But in the scuffle which followed, Hendrickson's wife shot one of the intruders fatally with a pistol and her husband held another suspect at bay with a shotgun. The third would-be bandit escaped by car and eluded police. (*The Muncie Star*, Muncie, Ind.)

A pistol hidden in a stereo saved the day when three men tried to rob former West Virginia Secretary of State Robert D. Bailey and his wife Jean. Two of the intruders, one armed with a gun, forced their way into the Bailey's Pineville, W. Va., home and demanded money. On the way to the vault, Mrs. Bailey lagged behind because "I knew I was going to pass the stereo" where a cal. 38 pistol was hidden. She grabbed the pistol and got the drop on the two robbers. Her husband at gunpoint then made a third accomplice release their son, who was being held hostage in a nearby mobile home. (*The Charleston Gazette*, Charleston, W. Va.)

Two men entered a Staten Island, N.Y., store and demanded money from owner Leonard Rose. Rose gave them $70 but as the gunmen fled, Rose grabbed a revolver hidden nearby and fired several times, hitting both men. One of the men collapsed after entering a car parked in front of the store and died of head wounds. The other man was treated for gunshot wounds in the left side and left leg. (*The New York Post,* New York City, N.Y.)

The first time 77-year-old Virginia Shoop's apartment was robbed, she lost a television set. When the same robbers returned a second time, they escaped with cash. But when one of the same hoodlums returned a third time, the Wichita, Kans., woman walked to a bureau, took out a pistol and wounded the man in the abdomen. (*The Wichita Eagle and Beacon,* Wichita, Kans.)

Police warned Jack Spivey, Jr. that burglars he had frightened away from his Oklahoma City, Okla., home might return. Later Spivey heard noises and stepped into the hallway with a cal. .22 rifle. When he spotted a man climbing through a bedroom window, Spivey fired once and killed the intruder. (*The Daily Oklahoman,* Oklahoma City, Okla.)

Store owner Joseph Hillis was suspicious when a customer warned him that two men were "casing" his Palms, Calif., business. Two armed men wearing stocking masks later entered the store and told the clerk to "get that guy (Hillis) out of the back room." The owner, from a peep-hole in his office, shouted a warning and then opened fire with a 12-ga. shotgun. One suspect died; the other was charged with murder on grounds that he had taken part in a crime in which a person was killed. (*The Santa Monica Evening Outlook,* Santa Monica, Calif.)

NOVEMBER 1973

Alerted to a burglary taking place on a lower level of his Reno, Nev., apartment house, Douglas Stewart got a gun and confronted a thief removing stereo equipment. Stewart commanded the burglar to stop and turned him over to police. (*The Nevada State Journal,* Reno, Nev.)

After Arturo Rodriguez was robbed and shot in his New York City, N.Y., grocery store six years ago, he obtained a handgun and had no further trouble—until two men robbed his grocery of $500 recently. Rodriguez fired several shots at them with his licensed gun as they fled. Apparently to "teach him a lesson," the two gunmen returned, followed Rodriguez home and killed him with an automatic rifle from about 100 yds. as he got out of his car. The killers escaped but were identified by Rodriguez's sons and brother as the same men who robbed the store. (*The New York Daily News,* New York City, N.Y.)

Sixty-year-old service station attendant Floyd Hanna was directed to lie on the floor while a gunman stole the Phoenix, Ariz., station's cash receipts. When the hold-up man left, Hanna grabbed a revolver and fired two shots into the getaway car. The robber stopped the car and jumped out yelling, "Don't shoot." Police booked the 20-year-old suspect on charges of robbery and possession of marijuana. (*The Mesa Tribune,* Mesa, Ariz.)

Hearing a cry for help, Ernest Martin spotted a bandit fleeing on foot from a Buffalo, N.Y., bank. Martin got in his car and followed the robber. "When I was about 25 feet ahead of him, I jumped out, drew my gun and said, 'Stand where you are.' " The robber did so and was subsequently turned over to the Federal Bureau of Investigation. (*The Buffalo Courier-Express,* Buffalo, N.Y.)

A young man and woman entered Boyd Robeson's Wichita, Kan., store and asked to see three expensive pistols. The male "customer" then pulled out a .22 handgun and demanded the pistols. Instead, Robeson confronted him with a 12-ga. shotgun. After an exchange of gunfire, the critically wounded armed robber fled, only to be discovered later at a hospital by police. His companion was caught by Robeson's son. (*The Wichita Beacon,* Wichita, Kans.)

Awakened by his dog barking in the backyard of his Los Angeles, Calif., home, John Cottle stepped outside and fired a .22 rifle shot in the air to scare off a possible prowler. While Cottle telephoned police, the suspect entered the house. Cottle fired a single shot in the dark and hit the burglar in the chest, killing him instantly. (*The Los Angeles Herald-Examiner,* Los Angeles, Calif.)

When a burglar began beating Martha McNeil in her Baltimore, Md., home, her son, Ernest Jr., 18, got his mother's cal. .22 pistol and fired several shots, killing the suspect. The police ruled the shooting justifiable homicide. (*The Baltimore Sun,* Baltimore, Md.)

During a robbery in her Pataskala, Ohio, store, Mrs. William Stewart placed her eyeglasses on a shelf near a cal. .22 revolver. Ordered to open the cash register, she pleaded the need for her glasses, grabbed her revolver instead and shot the man once in the rib cage. The robber gasped, "Don't do that," staggered through the door and escaped in a van with an accomplice. (*The Newark Advocate,* Newark, Ohio.)

A shot rang out in the night from John Link's New Orleans motel office. His wife grabbed her husband's .38 revolver and dashed into the office where she discovered her husband scuffling with an armed robber, whose handgun had just discharged. She shot the assailant fatally. (*The Times-Picayune,* New Orleans, La.)

Two men, one armed with a 12-ga. shotgun, tried to rob Walter Dalton, night manager of a Lynchburg, Va., motel. When Dalton resisted, one robber clubbed him to the floor with the shotgun. Dalton drew his .32 pistol and fired, wounding one of the fleeing bandits in the back. Both robbers and an accomplice were captured by police. (*The Roanoke Times*, Roanoke, Va.)

DECEMBER 1973

A carload of men pulled into the Monument, Colo., gas station of Morgan Porter and became abusive when Porter told them he could sell them no gas. One of the frustrated men "Jerked his door open and started toward me," Porter said. "I just turned so he could see my gun (in a holster on his hip), and he backed off." Porter, who said about 10% of the tourists he deals with now are "hostile and suspicious," wears the gun all the time instead of just when he works at night. (*The Colorado Springs Sun*, Colorado Springs, Colo.)

Because of recent break-ins at his Tampa, Fla., home, Raymond Hattaway was concerned when a strange car pulled into his driveway. Moments later, as the rear door of Hattaway's home was being forced open by three burglars, Hattaway fired his pistol at the suspects. One of the men was treated for a neck wound and charged by police with breaking and entering. The other intruders escaped. (*The Tampa Tribune*, Tampa, Fla.)

Dr. Grant Giles returned to his San Antonio, Tex., office one evening to find a burglar breaking into his files. When the intruder pulled a knife, Giles drew an automatic pistol and fired. The wounded assailant was treated and booked for burglary and assault. (*The San Antonio Express*, San Antonio, Tex.)

Spying three burglars carting appliances from Flem Cooley's Joelton, Tenn., home, a neighbor telephoned Cooley and service station manager Carl Tinsley. Tinsley, armed with a handgun, sped to the scene in a wrecking truck with which he blocked the thieves' car as it backed out of Cooley's driveway. The men bolted from the getaway car only to be confronted by a swarm of neighbors armed with pistols and shotguns who held them until police arrived. (*The Tennessean*, Nashville, Tenn.)

JANUARY 1974

Rev. Ellis Parker, a retired minister, heard someone open a window and enter his Gainesville, Fla., home one morning. Armed with his cal. .38 pistol, he fired once when the door to his bedroom opened, wounding an intruder in the stomach. A second prowler leaped through a window and escaped into nearby woods. (*The Sentinel Star*, Orlando, Fla.)

Sebastian Ninfo, 73, didn't panic when an armed youth entered his Reading, Pa., luncheonette and demanded money. After inviting the 18-year-old bandit behind the counter to get to the cash register, Ninfo walked to the rear of his business and returned with a cal. .32 revolver. The elderly man fired twice at the robber, wounding him in the neck. The youth escaped but was found by police at his apartment. (*The Reading Times*, Reading, Pa.)

Upon returning to her Snohomish, Wash., home, Mrs. William Newburg discovered two burglars. She held one of the men with a .22 pistol and fired three shots at the second man as he escaped. Sheriff's deputies later captured the second suspect. (*The Everett Herald*, Everett, Wash.)

One of two holdup men began savagely beating Baltimore, Md., grocer Bernard Eisen over the head with a lead pipe. Eisen snatched a cal. .38 revolver from under the counter and fired four times. One bullet hit his attacker in the forehead, killing him. The other holdup man ran. Police said the 60-year-old Eisen, "beaten up pretty bad," was hospitalized. (*The Baltimore Sun*, Baltimore, Md.)

In 1971, three robbers threw ammonia in jeweler Phil West's face and pistol-whipped him. Bound and gagged in his Cincinnati, Ohio, shop during a more recent robbery, West broke loose and struck back. While two gunmen looted the store, West emerged from the back room with his gun and began firing. One assailant fell, mortally wounded. The other robber was also shot but escaped. West suffered only cuts and bruises. (*The Cincinnati Enquirer*, Cincinnati, Ohio.)

Mrs. Betty Fagan, alone in her Taft, Calif., home, armed herself with a .357 magnum revolver when she heard noises in the garage, and went out. She found three men stealing the magnesium wheels from her son's car. One, ignoring a warning to halt, approached her. She fired a shot into a wall. "All three were out the door in a hurry," she told police. (*The Daily Midway Driller*, Taft, Calif.)

In the course of a liquor store stickup, a thief aimed a cal. .32 revolver at Newark, N.J., store owner Michael Lambusta's head and pulled the trigger. The gun misfired, and before the robber could fire again, Lambusta quickly seized his own pistol from a shelf and fired once, fatally wounding his assailant. (*The Star-Ledger*, Newark, N.J.)

Alton Nailing, 60, whose left leg was amputated in 1972, heard someone breaking through a bedroom window of his Chicago, Ill., home. He hobbled to a chair, pulled a cal. .32 revolver from under a cushion, and opened fire. An intruder fell, fatally wounded in the head and chest. Authorities ruled the shooting justified, as Nailing was protecting himself, his wife, and seven children. (*The Chicago Daily News*, Chicago, Ill.)

1974

THE ARMED CITIZEN

Peering through a window while at home alone, Mrs. Naomi Northern, of Milwaukee, Wis., saw a prowler slash her front door screen and start to pick the lock of the inner door. The 40-year-old house-wife drove him off with a shot from her cal. .22 "protection" pistol. "He looked like a madman," she said. "If I hadn't fired, he could have broken in and cut my throat." (*The Milwaukee Sentinel*, Milwaukee, Wis.)

After robbing an Atlanta, Ga., restaurant, the armed bandit ordered customers and employees to lie on the floor. As the gunman stuck his cal. .38 pistol inside his belt, customer Robert E. Speir drew his own gun. In an exchange of gunfire the suspect, whose pistol jammed after firing four shots, received eight bullet wounds in his chest, arms, legs and hip section. No one else was injured. (*The Atlanta Constitution*, Atlanta, Ga.)

A man wielding a rifle and a female companion with a knife burst into an Oakland, Calif., store and demanded money from owner George Hester. When Hester fired a cal. .22 derringer at the pair, the holdup man fled but was later found by police lying in a gutter with a neck wound. The woman was arrested at the store. (*The Oakland Tribune*, Oakland, Calif.)

Alerted by a barking dog and glimpses of prow-lers, Charles Linder, of Lafayette, Ind., got his pistol before going to the front door. There a masked man brandishing a two-foot club confronted him and shouted: "This is a stickup!" Linder raised his pistol and the thug, along with an accomplice, ran off into the night. (*The Journal & Courier*, Lafay-ette, Ind.)

When an armed bandit tried to rob a Detroit, Mich., dry cleaner, a customer, Kenneth Rice, wrested away the thief's revolver and shot at him five times. The bandit was arrested with serious wounds in the stomach and both arms. (*The Detroit Free Press*, Detroit, Mich.)

The 45th robbery of Albert Ekstrom's Bridgeport, Conn., grocery was too much for him. Ekstrom, 72, grabbed his pistol and chased the would-be holdup man out of his store. Soon afterward, police arrested a 17-year-old suspect. (*The Connecticut Sunday Herald*, Bridgeport, Conn.)

Instead of paying for a can of beer, a would-be robber sprayed tear gas in the face of Nashville, Tenn., market clerk Frances Crutcher. Reacting quickly, Mrs. Crutcher whirled, grabbed a shotgun from the corner and pulled the unloaded gun's trigger as she aimed in the direction of the thief. The terrified criminal, having fallen flat on the floor, crawled out the door and escaped but was later caught by police. "I think I did a pretty good job," Mrs. Crutcher said. "But next time the gun will be loaded." (*The Nashville Banner*, Nashville, Tenn.)

Store clerk Thomas O'Keefe sensed trouble when a "weird-looking man" with a ski cap pulled over his eyes entered a Rochester, N.Y., market. When the man whipped out a knife, O'Keefe "decided I wasn't going to the morgue" and pulled a gun. While O'Keefe telephoned police, the thwarted invader futilely hurled his knife at the clerk, then dashed out the door. O'Keefe did not fire his gun. (*The Rochester Times-Union*, Rochester, N.Y.)

MARCH 1974

When three hunters stopped east of Little Rock, Ark., to check their pickup truck's oil, a car pulled up and two of its three occupants got out. One of the two men pointed a cal. .22 pistol at hunter Lloyd Taylor and demanded his wallet, whereupon Taylor slammed the door against the robber, knock-ing the pistol away. Hunter John Rhodes then grabbed a shotgun, jumped from the truck and blasted the second robber in the leg. The other two thugs managed to get away. (*The Arknasas Gazette*, Little Rock, Ark.)

Informed by Berkeley, Calif. coin dealer Ed McConnell that a 1922 silver dollar was worth only $2, a customer drew a cal. .25 automatic pistol. The 73-year-old McConnell, whose shop had been robbed and burglarized often, coolly picked up his cal. .38 pistol and shot the intruder three times. McConnell, who learned shooting by "picking off rabbits" as a youth in South Dakota, described his action as "just a matter of self-defense." (*The San Francisco Chronicle*, San Francisco, Calif.)

As a young thief was busily rifling through mail boxes in a Cleveland, Ohio, apartment foyer, Mrs. Laura Hagans, 67 and a great-grandmother, hap-pened on the scene and drew her pistol. The trembling thief, encouraged by the determined woman to keep his hands away from his pockets, was marched to Mrs. Hagans' apartment and held until police arrived. Mrs. Hagans said she began carrying a gun after her purse was snatched for the second time. (*The Cleveland Press*, Cleveland, Ohio)

While store clerk Freida Mei was waiting on some customers in Norwich, Conn., two men scooped money from the cash register and ran. Mrs. Mei, 67-year-old mother of the store owner, picked up a gun and shot at the men as they fled. Two suspects were soon arrested, one of them suffering from a gunshot wound, police said. (*The Norwich Bulletin*, Norwich, Conn.)

In 1962, St. Louis, Mo., television repair shop owner Glenn Arrowsmith fired two shots at a burglar but missed. More recently Arrowsmith responded to a burglar alarm and spotted a thief fleeing into the night from his shop. When the criminal refused an order to halt, Arrowsmith fired one shot from his small-caliber automatic pistol, seriously wound-ing the intruder in the head. (*The St. Louis Globe-Democrat*, St. Louis, Mo.)

126

Rather than call police on a possible false burglar alarm which sounded from his nearby marina to his Lindenjurst, N.Y., home, Howard Rutherig, Jr. got his licensed cal. .38 pistol and rushed to investigate. Finding the marina's back door open, Rutherig entered and began firing when two men jumped him. One assailant fell, wounded in the stomach, and the second intruder, shot twice in the chest, escaped but was found dead near the boatyard a few hours later. (*Newsday*, Long Island, N.Y.)

Early one morning Marcella Ligneel awoke in her Brainerd, Minn., home and discovered two men trying to steal her four-wheel-drive Scout. Mrs. Ligneel, whose husband was out of town, got a gun and fired twice over the startled thieves' heads. The thwarted bandits left. (*The Brainerd Daily Dispatch*, Brainerd, Minn.)

Undaunted by what looked like a "toy" gun being held by one of three teenaged boys holding up her Decatur, Ala., store, Opal Vaughn pulled a cal. .25 pistol from her coat pocket. As the culprits fled, one of them grabbed Mrs. Vaughn's pistol. Immediately she whipped out a cal. .22 handgun from underneath the counter and fired eight shots at the getaway car. Three suspects were later arrested by police. (*The Huntsville Times*, Huntsville, Ala.)

Cries of an 85-year-old man being beaten by two men in the basement washroom of a Detroit department store were heard by Henry LaHousse, a retired police sergeant. When LaHousse entered the washroom, the victim cried out, "He's got a gun," pointing to one of the attackers. LaHousse immediately puled his cal. .38 revolver and ordered the two men outside. The assailants were charged with attempted armed robbery. (*The Detroit Free Press*, Detroit, Mich.)

APRIL 1974

Three armed men invaded the home of Mr. and Mrs. Robert Howard, Boston, Mass. One beat Mrs. Howard. All three then concentrated on subduing and tying up Howard. Mrs. Howard meanwhile got a .38 revolver from a closet and shot one of the intruders twice. All three fled, but the wounded man fell outside the house and died. (*The Boston Globe*, Boston, Mass.)**
**(Editorial note: The Boston Globe *has published 23 articles against handguns in the past several months. It is campaigning to deny them to private citizens such as the Howards.*)

Having shot two thugs in previous holdup attempts in her Modesto, Calif., store, Mrs. Virginia Clark was ready when two holdup men, one armed with a revolver, tried to make off with $140 from her cash register. Mrs. Clark unhesitatingly grabbed her cal. .38 from under the counter and opened fire. A suspect, found writhing in a nearby parking lot by police, was hospitalized but died while undergoing surgery. (*The Modesto Bee*, Modesto, Calif.)

Chicago restaurateur Larry Schwamb, 70, confronted by a knife-armed robber who grabbed $2100 in receipts, chased the robber from his Loop restaurant with his .25 automatic, fired a shot in the air, and forced the man to halt and drop his loot. Police marched both robber and Schwamb to jail. There both were fingerprinted and mugged. Schwamb was charged with having a gun not registered under Chicago law (although registered under State law) and with firing it illegally. (*Chicago Today*, Chicago, Ill.)

A would-be burglar broke a plate glass window in a West Plains, Mo., gas station early one morning, prompting owner Leon Keller to open fire with his 12-ga. shotgun. The prowler fled, apparently untouched by the single buckshot blast. (*The Daily Quill*, West Plains, Mo.)

Following a request to use his telephone, 66-year-old James Cory, a slaughterhouse operator, let a man enter his Tiverton, R.I., home. But when three other men, masked and armed with rifles or shotguns, barged in, Cory picked up a gun near the phone and said, "I'll blow your brains out." The interlopers fled to their car and drove off. Police arrested a suspect the next morning. (*The Providence Evening Bulletin*, Providence, R.I.)

When a holdup man entered the Ellis Hotel in Pittsburgh, Pa., and demanded money from the proprietor's wife, owner Frank Ellis warned him at pistol point to stand still. Instead, the robber moved and Ellis shot him in the leg. The suspect was charged with armed robbery. Ellis was slapped with an aggravated assault charge. (*The Anchorage Daily Times*, Anchorage, Alaska)

Out rabbit hunting and aware of an alert for three escaped prisoners, retired policeman George Koban, 46, of Ebensburg, Pa., spotted three suspects and ordered them to halt. They did, and proved to be the escapees. "They saw the shotgun and finally stopped when I asked them to," Koban said. "I never threatened to shoot." (*The Indiana Evening Gazette*, Indiana, Pa.)

In an attempt at purse-snatching, a mugger threw Eugenia McClellan to the ground as she was walking in Highland, Mich. The woman rolled over quickly, pulled a gun from her bag and fired three shots, hitting her assailant once in the right leg. The foiled thief was transported to a local hospital and held there as a police prisoner. (*The Detroit News*, Detroit, Mich.)

Awakened by loud noises, Mrs. Karen Baker went into her kitchen with a .22 revolver in time to see a hand reaching through the window. She fired three shots in that general direction, two hitting a wall. Two prowlers fled. (*The News-Pilot*, San Pedro, Calif.)

THE ARMED CITIZEN

When a gunman walked into a Burlington, N.C., wholesale firm and told manager Marvin Browning to fill a paper sack with money, Browning warned the thief he was going to get a shotgun from the back room. The alarmed robber ran out and was soon arrested. (*The Daily-Times-News,* Burlington, N.C.)

JUNE 1974

While a crook posing as a customer engaged a Chattanooga, Tenn., motel clerk in conversation, an accomplice armed with a sawed-off shotgun burst in and announced a holdup. The clerk, 68-year-old Lawrence Denton, yanked a pistol from a desk and fired at the man with the shotgun. The latter fired once and missed, but two of Denton's shots found their mark. The wounded intruder died. His unarmed partner fled. (*The Chattanooga News-Free Press,* Chattanooga, Tenn.)

Seeing two strangers taking two mini-bikes from the back of a Pinellas Park, Fla., motorcycle shop, Joe Kolodziej asked owner Ronald Hurn if he had just sold them. Told "no," Kolodziej halted the thieves' car at pistol point. Hurn backed him with a shotgun. Police quickly nabbed the thieves. (*The Pinellas Park Post,* Pinellas Park, Fla.)

When a robber in James Dailey's St. Louis, Mo., hamburger shop held a customer hostage with a pistol to his head, Dailey pulled a .38 snub-nose revolver from his belt and warned the gunman he would shoot both him and the hostage if necessary. A melee between Dailey, his shotgun-armed son and a total of three holdup men ensued. Dailey wounded one, his son another. (*The St. Louis Globe-Democrat,* St. Louis, Mo.)

Two armed men barged into a Grosse Point, Mich., house and struggled with owner Jeffrey Cook downstairs. A third thug rushed upstairs and held a woman there at gunpoint. Hearing the uproar, another resident, Robert Wicks, rushed from his bedroom with his Sturm, Ruger Blackhawk .44 Magnum revolver. The woman's attacker wheeled on Wicks, who shot him three times in the chest. He died. His accomplices fled. (*The Grosse Point News,* Grosse Point, Mich.)

Camping over the border in Mexico on a wedding anniversary outing, Fred Stegmann, 32, and his wife bedded their four children in a locked station wagon and crawled into a pup tent beside it. About 1 a.m., they heard noises. A prowler shoved a shotgun muzzle into the tent. Stegmann yelled but was shot in the arm. He fired "three or four" shots from a handgun, and the prowler went down. He then emptied his gun at another prowler. Wounded and bleeding, Stegmann was driven to a hospital. Mexican police found the body of a man whom San Diego, Calif., detectives identified as a known holdup man. (*The Register,* Orange Co., Calif.)

Startled in his Bend, Oreg., home one morning by the sound of breaking glass in a spare room, 81-year-old Corrie Harvey grabbed his .22 automatic pistol and confronted an intruder climbing through a window. Harvey "poured it right down on him with the flat of the gun." After slugging the culprit twice—"once for waking me and once for breaking the window"—Harvey held the suspect at gunpoint until police arrived. (*The Bulletin,* Bend, Oreg.)

Returning to his Baltimore, Md., apartment to discover two burglars climbing out a window, Randolph Fatherly took a cal. .38 revolver from behind a television set and opened fire. One suspect was shot in the back and fell dead at the bottom of the fire escape. The other burglar, wounded in the arm, surrendered. After hospital treatment, police charged the foiled thief with burglary and homicide. (Homicide charges can in some instances be placed against a suspect charged with a felony in which any person is killed.) Fatherly was not charged. (*The Baltimore Evening Sun,* Baltimore, Md.)

Sitting behind the counter in his Salt Lake City, Utah, jewelry repair shop one morning, Matthew DeSanto found himself facing a youthful gun-carrying robber. The thief fired a warning shot but scampered away in panic when DeSanto pulled a pistol and returned fire. "I shot over his head," DeSanto said. "He was a kid and had probably never done it before." Police soon cornered the culprit and made the arrest. (*The Deseret News,* Salt Lake City, Utah)

JULY 1974

Shortly after midnight two armed men burst into Rita Barron's Miami, Fla., rooming house. After the intruders robbed several roomers, Mrs. Barron's husband jumped one thief. In the confusion, Mrs. Barron got to her pistol and fired five shots. Two hit one bandit, who fell dead. The other escaped. (*The Miami News,* Miami, Fla.)

"A premonition" based on two burglaries of his shop within a week persuaded TV repairman Lester Sherrill, Boise, Idaho, to borrow a .38 revolver and spend the night in his store. About 4 a.m., two apparent ripoff artists smashed the front window and entered the store. When Sherrill yelled "Hold it," one man stopped, but the other thug lurched backward and "walked into" a warning shot by Sherrill. The wounded suspect, armed with a knife and hatchet, was arrested and treated for a back wound. His companion escaped. (*The Idaho Statesman,* Boise, Idaho.)

A youth entered Moses Hecht's variety store in Lynn, Mass., pulled a knife and announced, "This is a stickup." Hecht responded by pulling a pistol from his pocket and aiming at the would-be robber, who turned and fled. (*The Daily Evening Item,* Lynn, Mass.)

128

Attorney Michael Specchio and wife returned home in Reno, Nev., one evening and surprised three burglars inside. Specchio, who is with the Washoe County public defender's office, ordered the thieves out and fired several warning shots from his .22 revolver. One suspect was quickly arrested by police. (*The Reno Evening Gazette*, Reno, Nev.)

Peering out the backdoor window of his Charleston, S.C., home one morning, Ernest Pinckney saw two young males prowling in his front yard. Pinckney, sensing a break-in, got his gun and hid behind a kitchen counter. The two youths broke a window and came through the kitchen door, and once they were inside Pinckney got the drop on them. One escaped by pushing his companion against Pinckney. The other was turned over to juvenile authorities. (*The News and Courier*, Charleston, S.C.)

Ordered into a restroom during a robbery, Denver package store clerk Clifton Hardin pulled a gun from under his shirt and shouted at the armed bandit. When the man answered, Hardin fired one shot through the bathroom door in the direction of the robber's voice. Police followed a trail of blood to a car where the suspect lay dying. (*The Denver Post*, Denver, Colo.)

Two burglars had bound the wrists and ankles of Mrs. Faye Webb in her Chicago apartment when her husband arrived and grappled with one of the men. During the commotion Mrs. Webb managed to grab a cal. .38 revolver from a drawer. Still bound, she shot both intruders. One burglar ran screaming from the apartment and collapsed in the street, dead. The other thief, found by police under a bed, was hospitalized but died a short time later. (*The New York Daily News*, New York City, N.Y.)

As Memphis, Tenn., shoemaker E.L. King put new heels on a man's shoes, the stocking-footed patron drew a gun and demanded money. King promptly pulled a pistol and ordered the gunman to leave. Two accomplices vanished, but the "customer" lingered briefly to ask for the return of his shoes. King opened fire and the man raced away barefoot. (*The Memphis Press-Scimitar*, Memphis, Tenn.)

After handing over drugs demanded by a hooded gunman, Oklahoma City pharmacist Bill Duff grabbed his cal. .38 pistol and followed the holdup man. The suspect and his getaway-car driver disregarded Duff's command to stop, so the druggist fired several shots into the vehicle, causing it to swerve over a curb. The stickup man fell from the car, was run over by a rear wheel and suffered a dislocated hip and pavement burns. The driver escaped. (*The Daily Oklahoman*, Oklahoma City, Okla.)

AUGUST 1974

Returning home from a fishing trip, James Merchant, Cleveland, Ohio, learned that three gunmen, demanding narcotics, were inside holding his wife and daughter captive. Quickly he dashed in the back door, grabbed his 12-ga. shotgun, and wounded one gunman with a single blast. The others fired and fled. Merchant told police the trio must have mistaken his home for a dope peddler's. (*The Cleveland Press*, Cleveland, Ohio.)

After William McGrivey caught a young thief in the San Jose, Calif., market where he clerked and ordered him out, the youth and three others, one flashing a gun, entered and snatched up beer and a pistol from behind the counter. Beating McGrievy severely, they fired a shot at him and left him for dead. Later they returned for more loot. McGrievy, waiting for them with a .38, fired twice, killing one and wounding another. The survivors were arrested. (*The San Jose News*, San Jose, Calif.)

Hearing a commotion in her chicken house, Carrie Fishburn figured that local "college kids" were again raiding her farm to get chickens for a university group initiation. She immediately got her rifle and a board, and confronted five inebriated young men stumbling around the chicken pen. After she "mauled them with the two-by-four," the culprits ran when she raised her .30-'06. (*The Chicago Tribune*, Chicago, Ill.)

Ohio State Rep. Harry C. (Bud) Malott was awakened in his Williamsburg, Ohio, home by the sound of glass in his front door shattering. Snatching up the .38 revolver he keeps next to his bed, Malott confronted two would-be burglars at the front door. The armed duo responded by firing three shots, all misses. When Malott's wife yelled, "Shoot, Bud, shoot," Malott began firing. The pair escaped, one of them possibly wounded. (*The Cincinnati Enquirer*, Cincinnati, Ohio.)

Not content with snatching 71-year-old Anna Mae Motley's pocketbook, a thug barged into the victim's Washington, D.C., home the next day and demanded more money. "I told him I didn't have any money and he started to get rough," she said. "I figured I'd better change that." So she pointed her .22 revolver at the intruder and fired a blank. This didn't faze the attacker. The second shot did: He fell, fatally wounded with a bullet in the heart. (*The Washington Star-News*, Washington, D.C.)

Facing a young hold-up man brandishing a knife, 82-year-old coin shop owner Addison Smith drew his cal. .38 Special from a drawer. During a brief scuffle between the two, Smith fired one shot. The bandit then dashed out of the Pittsburgh, Pa., shop and was last seen running furiously. Smith said that none of the thieves in six prior robbery attempts at his establishment had ever managed to steal anything. (*The Pittsburgh Press*, Pittsburgh, Pa.)

Alone in his Anaheim, Calif., package store late one night, owner Dennis Ricotta was confronted by a masked hold-up man armed with a cal. .22 rifle. When the robber aimed the rifle in the store-owner's direction, Ricotta, whose store had already been robbed twice in the past year, picked up a 9 mm. pistol and fired once, fatally wounding the intruder. (*The Register*, Orange County, Calif.)

Two men, one carrying a rifle, entered a Tucson, Ariz., market and demanded cash receipts. Manager Gary Orcutt answered by grabbing a .45 automatic pistol and telling them to leave. The frightened toughs did just that. They drove off in a car which had earlier been reported stolen, police said. (*The Tucson Daily Citizen*, Tucson, Ariz.)

While cleaning her Benton Harbor, Mich., home one afternoon, Mrs. Patty Weimer was surprised by two burglars who demanded money. Struggling with her assailants, she managed to break free and yank a revolver from a drawer. The men fled. No shots were fired, according to police. (*The News-Palladium*, Benton Harbor, Mich.)

SEPTEMBER 1974

Hearing a noise in his Tustin, Wis., food store during the early morning, grocer Kiel Oesterrich investigated and found two men—one standing at the cash register, the other holding the entrance door open. He called to them to stop. When they did not, he fired two shots into the air. The burglars fled, leaving the store undamaged and the register's contents intact. (*The Oshkosh Daily Northwestern*, Oshkosh, Wis.)

To break up a scuffle between a female employee and an irate, screwdriver-waving boy friend, Joseph Kass, a Columbus, Ohio, store-owner, fired a warning shot with his .38 revolver. The woman's attacker then turned on Kass, who shot and wounded the man in the chest and arm. The man was listed in satisfactory condition. The girl was treated for a cut arm. (*The Columbus Dispatch*, Columbus, Ohio.)

Seeing a man forcing his way through the storm door screening of her Worcester, Mass., cottage, Mary Wheeler took aim with her handgun and ordered the intruder to stop. When he approached her instead, Miss Wheeler, a U.S. Law Enforcement Assistance Administration senior planner, shot and seriously wounded the thug. (*The Worcester Telegram*, Worcester, Mass.)

Awakened by sounds of a prowler in her Alamogordo, N. Mex., home, Mrs. Teresa Middlestead got her husband's shotgun from the bedroom closet and shouted down the hallway, "I've got a gun." Although Mrs. Middlestead didn't see the intruder, she heard him dash through the kitchen and out the front door. Nothing was stolen. (*The Alamogordo Daily News*, Alamogordo, N. Mex.)

After climbing through a window of the Birmingham, Ala., apartment of Mr. and Mrs. Oscar Kent, a wild-eyed intruder held the couple's two-year-old son hostage until Kent grabbed his 7.65 Mauser rifle and killed the intruder with a single-shot. The child was treated for a cut on the neck. (*The Birmingham News*, Birmingham, Ala.)

Members of the "Sons of Satan" motorcycle club demanded that Ray Frye, Mount Joy, Pa., bar and grill owner, serve them free drinks. When he refused, they grew threatening. Frye drew his gun. "You don't have the guts to shoot," the ringleader sneered and threw an ashtray at him. Frye then shot the man in the shoulder.
A jury acquitted Frye of an aggravated assault charge. Judge Anthony Appel, in congratulating the jury, termed Frye's acquittal "quite proper" and upheld a man's right to defend himself and his business. (*The Intelligencer-Journal*, Lancaster, Pa.)

After Richard Goodwin was fatally gunned down in a holdup of his St. Louis, Mo., tavern May 13, his widow Marian, 33, took over the business and armed herself with a shotgun and pistol. A month later, spotting a man lurking suspiciously outside, she got ready. When the man rushed in with a drawn gun and cried "Holdup!" Mrs. Goodwin pushed his gun aside and shot him twice with her pistol, killing him. "They didn't scare me out when they killed my husband," she said, "and they aren't going to scare me out now." (*The St. Louis Post-Dispatch*, St. Louis, Mo.)

Three youths, one armed with a knife, walked into Mike Seargent's Albuquerque, N. Mex., store intent on robbery. Seargent noticed that the knife was apparently their only weapon, so he took his gun from beside the cash register and held the thieves at bay until police arrived. (*The Albuquerque Journal*, Albuquerque, N. Mex.)

As 77-year-old Ernest Rexford Paul, his wife and granddaughter were watching television in his San Diego, Calif., home, two armed robbers broke a sliding glass door and began to enter. Paul got a cal. .45 automatic from another room and quickly squeezed off one round, fatally wounding one invader in the chest. The other man fled. (*The Los Angeles Times*, Los Angeles, Calif.)

OCTOBER 1974

Hiram Porter, 79, a retired airline employee, was warming over a chicken dinner in his Miami home at 5 p.m. when an 18-year-old with a rifle broke in and hit him in the face with the rifle butt. Porter twisted away the rifle but the youth threw him to the floor. Neighbors gathered—and watched from afar. Then Mrs. Porter grabbed a .22 revolver that they bought in February for $41.55 and shot the intruder in the chest. He died an hour later. (*The Miami Herald*, Miami, Fla.)

An armed holdup man and an accomplice forced several employees and customers in a Minneapolis, Minn., drug store to lie on the floor while the holdup men gathered up cash receipts. As they were leaving with their loot, pharmacist Charles Beecroft shot and fatally wounded one of them. Two men were arrested later and charged in connection with the robbery. (*The Minneapolis Tribune*, Minneapolis, Minn.)

Upon witnessing a murder near his Darrington, Wash., campsite, Robert Duggan of Mountain Terrace, Wash., immediately sent his family into their trailer, grabbed a .38 pistol and went to investigate. Duggan found the killer dragging the elderly victim into some bushes, and he got the drop on the criminal by firing a warning shot in the air. Both the suspect and an accomplice surrendered and were turned over to authorities. (*The Everett Herald*, Everett, Wash.)

Two men grabbed Pensacola, Fla., store clerk Edith Brown and strongarmed her out of cash register receipts. When the man with the stolen money ran, she calmly got a pistol from under the counter and chased him out of the store. Returning to the store, she found the second man still there and held him at gunpoint for police. "I was not too scared," she mused. "I knew what I had here (the gun) and I did what I thought I needed to do." (*The Pensacola Journal*, Pensacola, Fla.)

A candidate for sheriff in Arkansas who had complained that the incumbent sheriff didn't give good "service" made a strong election pitch recently by getting the drop on three burglars. Donald Ray Bougher surprised the intruders early one morning inside his North Little Rock washateria and held them at gunpoint until sheriff's deputies arrived. One of the robbers "tried every way in the world to make a deal," Bougher said. But he told them, "I'm running for sheriff and I don't make deals." (*The Arkansas Gazette*, Little Rock, Ark.)

The wife of NRA Life Member G. Bryan Leach was alone one night in her Bethalto, Ill., home when she was awakened by an intruder armed with an 8" butcher knife. The man fled when he encountered Mrs. Leach with a .357 magnum pistol in hand, but was soon captured by police. He was charged with burglary, unlawful use of weapons, possession of marijuana and possession of burglary tools. (*The Alton Telegraph*, Alton, Ill.)

A gunman charged into a Los Angeles store, told owner Johnny Chicos to hand over money, then shot and slightly wounded a bystander who dashed to the door. By the time the criminal turned back toward Chicos, the owner had picked up a pistol. Chicos fired at point-blank range, killing the assailant. Two accomplices were quickly collared by police. (*The Los Angeles Herald Examiner*, Los Angeles, Calif.)

After buying some beer at a Knoxville, Tenn., convenience food store, a "customer" pulled a gun and ordered clerk Mary Finger to stuff money into a bag. In his office, manager Charles Costner overheard the demand, got a cal. .38 handgun and seriously wounded the robber when the latter tried to shoot him. (*The Knoxville Journal*, Knoxville, Tenn.)

When a prowler broke into the Detroit, Mich. home of Mrs. Lucy Jackson late one night, she grabbed a handgun and fired five shots. The intruder fled and collapsed outside the house, wounded in the mouth and side. (*The Detroit Free Press*, Detroit, Mich.)

NOVEMBER 1974

One of the four men who entered the Bronx grocery of George Ramirez shortly after midnight levelled a shotgun in a holdup attempt. Ramirez pulled his own revolver. In a panic, the gunman fired and wounded Ramirez in the right arm, then ran. Ramirez held the other three men at gunpoint, despite his wound, until police arrived. (*The New York Daily News*, New York, N.Y.)

Fortunately for Reuben Flotz, he could see his home near Howe, Ind., while fishing in the Pigeon River. He watched as a stranger drove up, knocked without getting an answer, and entered by slitting a screen door. Flotz hurried over through a back door. He grabbed his rifle and covered the thief, who was about to steal a radio, binoculars and other valuables. Then he tried to phone police but the phone did not work. So Flotz marched the intruder 200 yds. at gunpoint to a neighbor's. (*The Goshen News*, Goshen, Ind.)

Three men surrounded Arthur Gardner outside his Seattle, Wash., apartment at 2 a.m., ostensibly to "ask directions," but one quickly pulled a gun. Gardner, a 57-year-old mortician, said, "You guys are going to be dead." He drew his own pistol and fired a shot in the air. All three men raced away. (*The Seattle Times*, Seattle, Wash.)

Pharmacy owner N. R. Baldwin, Gainesville, Fla., responded to a gunman's demand for cash by opening fire with his own .38 from behind a counter. The gunman got off two shots which hit the counter without harming Baldwin, then fled. (*The Gainesville Sun*, Gainesville, Fla.)

When a group of some 50 howling men armed with tire irons, jacks and baseball bats erupted into the street at 1 a.m., smashed the car windshield of Michael Colaianni, 22, Rochester, N.Y., and, Colaianni said, dragged him and his friends from the car, he fired three shots into the air from a shotgun. The assailants fled. Rochester police, making no other arrests, charged Colaianni with discharging a firearm in the city limits. (*The Democrat & Chronicle*, Rochester, N.Y.)

Firing 29 shots from an M1 carbine, Mike Williams riddled a white Cadillac in which two young robbers were attempting to escape with $260 taken in a holdup of his father-in-law's Oklahoma City food market. Both men, slightly wounded, were captured. Williams, 38, a city policeman for six years, said that rather than shooting to kill "all I tried to do was mark up the car to make it real noticeable" for pursuers. (*The Oklahoma City Times*, Oklahoma City, Okla.)

Hearing breaking glass early in the morning, Charles Robinson awakened to find five youths forcing the kitchen door of his Fort Wayne, Ind., home. Armed with a cal. .38 revolver and cal. .25 automatic pistol, he entered the kitchen just as a hand reached thorugh a smashed pane to unlock the door. Robinson fired two shots and sent the gang fleeing. (*The Journal-Gazette*, Fort Wayne, Ind.)

Donald Stone, returning to his Seattle, Wash., home after a short absence, caught two women burglarizing the place. He covered them with a small-caliber pistol until police arrived. The women, ages 18 and 19, who said they were employed by a youth corps, were held in county jail. (*The Seattle Times*, Seattle, Wash.)

Because he was carrying $100 in cash and intended to make a $300 bank withdrawal, Wilbur E. Carter, Dayton, Ohio, heeded an impulse to take along his .25 automatic. Sure enough, two men followed him later and cornered him in his apartment house garage. One poked forward his jacket pocket as if the pocket held a gun and announced: "This is a stickup," Carter drew his own gun. Both men ran to their car and sped off. Carter gave police their tag number. The pair was caught and charged with two previous robberies that day. (*The Dayton Daily News*, Dayton, Ohio)

1975

FEBRUARY 1975

A husky ex-convict, wanted for three murders, a rape attempt and an abduction in the six months since his parole, crashed a stolen car through a Georgia police roadblock near Atlanta and fled into the woods under police gunfire—only to be halted and captured by a lone hunter. The hunter, David I. Clark, 27, McDonough, Ga., levelled his shotgun at the convict, who was armed with a revolver and was bleeding from a head wound. The arrest ended a four-day chase that began in Florida. (AP in *The San Francisco Chronicle*, San Francisco, Calif.)

Freelance news photographer Abel Guy was driving to a market in Westminister, Calif., when he heard over his car radio that a robbery was in process at the market. As he drove up to the market, a youth carrying a .30-30 rifle and a paper bag dashed past him. Grasping a .38 revolver, Guy jumped out of his car and ordered the youth to halt and drop the rifle and the bag. The robber dropped the bag but swung around and pointed the rifle at Guy. Eventually he obeyed Guy's repeated orders to drop the rifle and surrendered. (*The Register*, Orange County, Calif.)

Hearing screams from a store near his office, real estate broker Charles W. Parker, an NRA Member of Jackson Heights, N.Y., grabbed his cal. .38 snub-nosed revolver, dashed next door and captured a would-be robber. The local police department awarded him a Legion of Honor plaque for "exceptional bravery." An NRA certified pistol, rifle and shotgun instructor, Parker has won over 40 trophies for marksmanship. The Greater New York Pistol League recognized his action with an "outstanding citizen award" inscribed "Someone Who Cared to Get Involved." (*The Sunday News*, New York, N.Y.)

Suspicious of two men claiming to be electric company representatives come to check wiring in her Joliet, Ill., home, Mrs. Velma Nelson refused to let them enter. The men then tried to barge through the door, but Mrs. Nelson snatched up a rifle and threatened to shoot if they didn't leave. The assailants hesitated briefly, then fled. (*The Herald-News*, Joliet, Ill.)

An early morning burglar alarm ringing in William Parsons' Sells, Ariz., trailer home alerted him that something was amiss in his Quijotoa Trading Post store next door. Armed with a rifle, Parsons charged into the store and found two men stuffing Indian jewelry into a sack. When one hood yelled, "Get him," Parsons shot and killed one of them. The second intruder lunged through a plate glass window and got away. (*The Tucson Daily Citizen*, Tucson, Ariz.)

With his crippled arm and leg, grocery store owner Martin Lindert of Canton, Ohio, looks like a pushover to unwary holdup artists. He isn't. Four holdup attempts on his store in five years have netted thugs not one penny. In a recent attempt by two masked men, one gun-toting hood jumped the counter and started to grapple with Lindert. But Lindert grabbed a .22 pistol from a back room and shot one man dead. The other thug fled. (*The Canton Repository*, Canton, Ohio.)

Rudely awakened one night by burglars cutting through a screen door in his Alexandria, Va., parsonage, Rev. Tom Lovern got his cal. .22 target pistol and fired several warning shots at the culprits, who fled. "I had no intention of killing them, just frighten them away," Rev. Lovern said. "I've learned that a man has to sometimes protect his family." Rev. Lovern said he obtained the pistol after his home was burglarized twice several years ago. (*The Page News and Courier*, Luray, Va.)

Having been robbed just the night before, Mrs. Carol Williams, manager of a San Antonio, Tex., convenience store, responded to another demand for money by reaching under the counter "for the money bag." Instead, she came up shooting with a .22 pistol. The frightened robber fell to the floor, crawled to the door, and ran outside with an accomplice. (*The San Antonio News*, San Antonio, Tex.)

MARCH 1975

While Dan Cassin was stacking shelves in his Atlanta, Ga., store, two robbers rushed in, fired at least one shot, and then started thrashing the store cleanup man. Cassin immediately pulled out his cal. .38 pistol and shot one intruder to death. "They came in like storm troopers, shooting and beating people," Cassin said. "I just couldn't stand and watch." (*The South Middlesex News*, Framingham, Mass.)

Thrice held up and plundered by gunmen, Peter Wallace, Central Islip, N.Y., store owner, was prepared the fourth time. When an armed bandit demanded his receipts, he ducked behind the counter and came up shooting. The bandit exchanged shots harmlessly and fled. Wallace, who was pistol-whipped in a 1973 holdup, said, "After they rob you, they shoot you or beat you up so you can't identify them. I'm just sorry I missed." (*Newsday*, Long Island, N.Y.)

When Cecil and Edna Doggett, aged 67, and 66, opened the door of their Oakland, Calif., home to what they thought were Halloween trick or treaters, four young men rushed in and began attacking them with billy clubs. During the struggle, one of the intruders dropped a .22 revolver, giving Doggett time to get his own .357 Magnum revolver from a living room drawer. The youths fled as Doggett fired twice. Two suspects, each wounded in the left leg, were taken into custody by the police. (*The Oakland Tribune*, Oakland, Calif.)

Confronted by an ice pick-waving robber in her San Antonio, Tex., tavern, Maria Villegas grappled with the intruder. An employee smashed the man in the head with a chair, allowing Miss Villegas to get a cal. .38 pistol from her purse. When the assailant ignored her warning to drop his weapon, Miss Villegas shot the advancing thug, who staggered to the door and fell outside, dead. (*The San Antonio Light*, San Antonio, Tex.)

When two intruders advanced menacingly toward Dr. Harold E. Marks in his office one night, the 72-year-old Somerville, Mass., physician pulled a cal. .38 pistol from his jacket and fired two warning shots. When they kept coming, he shot one in the leg. Police later arrested two suspects. It was the third time that Dr. Marks had repelled would-be robbers with his handgun. (*The Boston Evening Globe*, Boston, Mass.)

In response to his courteous "Can I help you, sir?" Racine, Wis., grocery clerk Tom Miottel got a bandit's handgun jammed in his face. Miottel brushed the firearm aside, thinking it a toy, but the "toy" put a bullet through the clerk's hand. When the robber turned to Miottel's mother, who owns the store, and demanded cash, the clerk seized a 20-ga. shotgun and shot him. Authorities followed the fugitive's bloody trail to a nearby apartment and nabbed him. Records showed that the robber's gun was stolen from Battle Creek, Mich. (*The Journal Times*, Racine, Wis.)

A superior court judge in Hartford, Conn., said he was "happy to see that some storekeepers protect their property against these marauders" as he sentenced two thugs who were shot and wounded by a store employee during a holdup.

Judge William L. Tierney conceded that "this court cannot advocate this type of retaliation" (by storekeepers), but he bluntly rejected defense pleas to send the men to a reformatory instead of prison. (*The Hartford Courant*, Hartford, Conn.)

Aroused at 5 a.m., Mrs. Estelle Beavan, 61, a Seattle widow, found a young man "tearing up the whole front of my house." She telephoned police. But when the man, after ripping off a storm door, bashed through a thick double-locked door, Mrs. Beavan fired one shot at about 10 ft. with a small .22 handgun that she had bought on the advice of a "relative in law enforcement." A bullet in the chest halted the intruder. Police said he was crazed by drugs. (*The Seattle Times*, Seattle, Wash.)

APRIL 1975

When a man walked behind the drug counter of William Deeg's Evansville, Ill., pharmacy, pulled a butcher knife and demanded codeine, Deeg drew his .38 pistol and ordered him to stop. Knife in hand the would-be thief continued to advance, and Deeg shot twice, killing him instantly. Local police records showed the holdup man had 41 previous arrests. (*The Evansville Press*, Evansville, Ill.)

Bennie Dixon, 79, of Chicago, Ill., was carrying a bag of garbage into the alley behind his house when he was accosted by a man who demanded his money. Dixon handed over the bag, then pulled a revolver from his pocket and shot the robber in the chest. The shooting later was ruled justifiable, but Dixon was charged with having an unregistered gun. (*The Chicago Tribune*, Chicago, Ill.)

Mrs. Sandra Jays, 25, telephoning in her Buffalo, N.Y. home, heard glass breaking. She told her caller to call police, and picked up a cal. .22 rifle. When she heard footsteps coming up the basement stairs, she fired a shot through the basement door. The shaken intruder tumbled down the stairs. Mrs. Jays ran to the cellar and ordered him to lie on the floor. The police arrived moments later. (*The Courier-Express*, Buffalo, N.Y.)

133

Two escaped convicts pistol-whipped Elmer Carlson in a Ft. Morgan, Colo., parking lot and took the keys to the farmer's pickup. Moments later Carlson's son Pete arrived at the lot, and the Carlsons pursued the thieves in the son's truck. When they forced the escapees off the road, the driver opened fire. Pete grabbed a rifle from the rear of his truck and fired back, wounding the gunman. The Carlsons held the convicts until police arrived. (*The Daily Sentinel*, Grand Junction, Colo.)

NRA Members Errol Galloway and Ralph Tolbert, both of West Grove, Pa., returning to their car after fox hunting, found another car parked nearby and heard the sound of glass breaking. When they got closer, they saw a broken window and several items piled up outside the second car and two youths inside. They held the suspects at gunpoint until police arrived. The youths later were charged with theft and three other counts. (*Chester County Press*, Oxford, Pa.)

Returning to his El Rio, Calif., home one evening, James Harper found his TV and other property on the floor next to the front door. Harper rushed into the bedroom, picked up his rifle and was inserting a cartridge when a man walked out of the adjoining bathroom, yelling: "Don't shoot." Harper turned the man over to deputies. (*The Press-Courier*, Oxnard, Calif.)

Two armed robbers in their 30's cut the alarm wires of Roy Tuggle's Coral Ridge, Fla., home and broke in. Tuggle, 56, awakened and critically wounded one with three shots from a handgun kept in his bedroom because of previous robberies. When he found the other robber holding a revolver at Mrs. Tuggle's head, he fired two shots, killing the robber. "Justifiable homicide," said Assistant State Attorney Tom Kern. (*The Sun-Sentinel*, Fort Lauderdale, Fla.)

When a young man asked for a room and then brandished a gun at Denver, Co., motel owner W. Culver Davison, 57, Davison opened the cash box and retreated, as ordered, into an adjacent room. While the robber rifled the cash box, Davison picked up a revolver and fired twice through the half-opened door, wounding him. The robber was later identified as an ex-felon, twice jailed on manslaughter and murder charges. (*The Denver Post*, Denver, Colo.)

An armed bandit entered a Minneapolis, Minn., jewelry store, demanded money from jeweler Gordon Benson and then ordered Benson to get a bag to carry some jewels from a safe. While reaching for the bag, Benson pulled out a gun, shot the robber in the shoulder and then kicked the gun out of his hand. (*The Minneapolis Tribune*, Minneapolis, Minn.

MAY 1975

A gunman entered Robert E. Merryman's drugstore in Clayton, Mo., demanded cash and narcotics, then ordered Robert Jr., 16, to drive him away in the Merryman car. "My son began to cry," Merryman said. "I saw it as another execution killing." Merryman followed outside to the car with his shotgun. Young Robert stepped aside. Merryman blasted the gunman in the head at 10 ft., wounding him seriously. (*The Tribune*, Tampa, Fla.)

When someone pounded on Donald Curry's kitchen door in Napanoch, N.Y., after midnight, Curry unlocked the door with his Colt revolver in his hand. A gunman rushed in with such force that the door knocked Curry flat. His revolver skidded away. The gunman demanded that Curry and his wife and son accompany him in Curry's car as hostages. Then he paused to get a beer out of the refrigerator. Curry retrieved his revolver and shot the gunman six times, killing him. Police said the gunman was a suspect in a previous shooting who had escaped in a commandeered car. (*The Tribune*, Tampa, Fla.)

New Haven, Conn., merchant Bruce McClenning was locking the rear door of his store when a man jumped from behind a parked car and pointed a sawed-off shotgun at him. McClenning whipped a snub-nose revolver from his back pocket and shot the robber. The man dropped the shotgun and lunged at McClenning and was hit again as both men fell to the ground. McClenning's calls for help were answered by an off-duty policeman who finally subdued the assailant. (*The Hartford Courant*, Hartford, Conn.)

Mike Eid was willing to compromise when two robbers, one holding a handgun, walked into his San Francisco, Calif., liquor store and demanded money. "I'll give you $5," Eid said. "We want it all," came the reply, whereupon Eid reached under the counter and hauled out a pistol. The robbers stood frozen for an instant and then bolted out of the store. (*The San Francisco Chronicle*, San Francisco, Calif.)

Grocer Ralph Miller handed $315 to the knife-wielding robber who confronted him in his Glen Burnie, Md., store. But when the man turned to leave, Miller pulled out a revolver and fired two shots that wounded the thief. The suspect fled but was arrested a short time later. (*The Baltimore Sun*, Baltimore, Md.)

Larry Clark was awakened in his North St. Louis, Mo., home by a noise at the front door. Finding no one there, he returned to the bedroom and heard a noise at the window. He called police, got a shotgun from a closet and found a man climbing in the bedroom window. Failing to heed Clark's call to halt, the intruder lunged at him and was slain by a blast from the shotgun. (*The St. Louis Globe-Democrat*, St. Louis, Mo.)

Seeing two youths jump from the front window of a Lynn, Mass., store, attorney Daniel Horgan followed in his car, captured the burglars and held them at gunpoint. Horgan also captured three other youths who allegedly were waiting for the others in a parked car. (*The Daily Evening Item*, Lynn, Mass.)

When Mrs. Annette Walker, 22, boarded a Chicago subway-elevated train with two small children, a loud-talking man become abusive. Two uniformed policemen ignored him and got off. The man slapped Mrs. Walker, grabbed her coat collar, and dragged her down the aisle, she said, while the conductor and five other passengers watched. After enduring this at length, Mrs. Walker drew a .22 "Saturday Night Special" from her purse and wounded her persecutor in the shoulder. Police arrested him but not her. (The Santa Monica, Calif., *Evening Outlook* and *The Chicago Tribune*)

Seeing a stranger leave her neighbor's house with a satchel of goods over his shoulder, Mrs. Lee Muir of Colorado Springs, Colo., snatched up her cal. .22 rifle. She rushed outside and held the suspect until police took him into custody. (*The Sun*, Colorado Springs, Colo.)

JUNE 1975

NRA Life Member Robert Marcotte, awakened by his daughter's screams in their Omaha, Nebr., home, grabbed an automatic pistol and ran from his bedroom to find a man at the top of the stairs. When the intruder ran, Marcotte gave chase and caught and held him at gunpoint. The man escaped when Marcotte's attention was diverted but was arrested moments later. (*The Omaha World-Herald*, Omaha, Nebr.)

James Counts closed his Phoenix, Ariz., laundry for the night and started home when a man appeared from the darkness, leveled a gun at him and demanded money. After handing over his cash, Counts pulled out a pistol and fired at the robber. The startled thief fled, dropping his revolver, which broke apart, losing his black wig, and literally running out of his shoes. (*The Arizona Republic*, Phoenix, Ariz.)

Attorney Frank Farris was awakened about 5 a.m. by his wife, who thought she heard someone inside their Nashville, Tenn., home. Farris loaded his shotgun and started down the hallway where he confronted a prowler. Farris held the man at gunpoint while his wife phoned police. (*The Nashville Banner*, Nashville, Tenn.)

Convinced the house was empty, several teenage burglars broke into the Virginia Beach, Va., home of Bruce Van Deuson. Alerted by their noise, Van Deuson got his shotgun and walked into a hallway where he apprehended and held one of the youths. The young burglar's confederates fled out a rear door. (*The Virginian-Pilot*, Norfolk, Va.)

John Stinson of Detroit, Mich., driving up a freeway ramp, was struck from behind by another car occupied by three men. Both cars stopped, and the three men, all carrying rifles, advanced toward Stinson. He pulled out a pistol and fatally shot one of the trio in an exchange of gunfire. The remaining pair were apprehended later at a hospital; police said the car they were driving had been reported stolen. (*The Detroit News*, Detroit, Mich.)

When the man at the checkout counter drew a gun and ordered Phoenix, Ariz., market owner Phil Younis to fill a bag with money, he did as he was told. Grabbing the bag, the robber put his gun in his belt, giving Younis a chance to get a pistol from under the counter. Younis ordered the thief to lie on the floor until police arrived. (*The Phoenix Gazette*, Phoenix, Ariz.)

A pair of robbers bound Scott Walker with wire and then began looting Walker's Oak Cliff, Tex., pawnshop. While lying on the floor, Walker managed to free his hands and reach a cal. .38 pistol kept beneath the counter. He came up shooting and mortally wounded both bandits. (*The Amarillo Daily News*, Amarillo, Tex.)

After locking Graham Cottingham and his wife and grandson in closets, two men tried to open the safe in Cottingham's Dillon, S. C., home. Cottingham, however, was able to free himself and get a pistol he kept under his bed. In the ensuing gunfight, one of the intruders was slain and the other wounded. (*The News and Courier and Charleston Evening Post*, Charleston, S.C.)

Driving into Huntsville, Tex., after sighting-in a deer rifle in the country, Tony Taylor and Jack Dwenger saw a police car swerve into a ditch. They parked and ran over to the vehicle where they subdued a man who was being transported to prison by a deputy sheriff. The deputy, who had been stabbed twice, credited the pair with saving his life. (*The Huntsville Item*, Huntsville, Tex.)

A stocking-masked bandit entered Billy DePoyster's Corinth, Miss., grocery and announced a holdup. DePoyster, a former policeman, pulled a pistol from his pocket and told the man to leave. The would-be robber made a dash for the door, then turned and shot at DePoyster. The store owner returned the fire as the man escaped into the darkness. (*The Daily Corinthian*, Corinth, Miss.)

AUGUST 1975

High school rifle team captain Vicki Van Male was at her after-school job in a Denver, Colo., doughnut shop when an armed man entered the store, emptied the register and ordered her to follow him outside. She did as told, but while walking managed to grab the robber's gun and wound him. (*The Arizona Republic*, Phoenix, Ariz.)

When a church secretary screamed as an intruder advanced toward her, Rev. Walter Hudson got his pistol and rushed into the office of his Anderson, S.C., church. The intruder "Looked into the gun and kinda melted away," the pastor said. He kept the man covered until the sheriff arrived. (*The Anderson, S.C., Independent.*)

Awakened about 4 a.m. when he heard noises at an unoccupied new house next to his Tucson, Ariz., home, Air Force Lt. Col. Robert Baird seized a gun and ran outside. He found three men loading a pickup truck. When they fled in the truck, Baird followed in his car and forced them off the road. In the ensuing fight, Baird wounded one burglar. Two escaped. (*The Arizona Daily Star,* Tucson, Ariz.)

Two men, one wielding a hunting knife, walked into John Capone's Roslindale, Mass., pharmacy and demanded drugs. The pair followed Capone to the rear of the store. There the druggist pulled a revolver from a hiding place, began firing and wounded both would-be thieves. It was the third attempted holdup Capone has thwarted in recent years. (*The Boston Herald American,* Boston, Mass.)

One of 16 prisoners being transported from the Detroit, Mich., Hall of Justice building to the county jail escaped from deputies, but when he tried to enter the chambers of Judge James Del Rio, he found himself staring down the barrel of the judge's cal. .38 pistol. Judge Del Rio held the fugitive until deputies arrived. (*The Detroit Free Press,* Detroit, Mich.)

An armed man approached the window of Henry Hilliard's Savannah, Ga., take-out restaurant and told the owner to give him money or he would be shot. Hilliard turned around and told an employee to get the cash. At the same time, he pulled his gun, then turned back and shot at the robber, who fled. (*The Savannah News-Press,* Savannah, Ga.)

Jeffrey Wallis, who lives above a Johnsonburg, Pa., hardware store, was awakened one night by thumping sounds from below. Creeping downstairs he spied two men apparently scraping ammunition into a bucket. Wallis returned upstairs, grabbed his .22 rifle, told his wife to call the police and then captured the crooks as they attempted to leave the store. They were apprehended with two buckets of ammo and 16 handguns. (*The Daily Press,* St. Marys, Pa.)

Three would-be Wisconsin bank robbers compounded their problems when they chose a bank located next to the Fond du Lac Gun Club. The trio, armed with a revolver and an automatic pistol, were captured by two policemen as they exited from a rear door. Any thoughts they had about escaping dissolved when they saw the three shotguns pointed their way by trapshooters Thomas Slater, Tom Towne and Edwin Steffes. (*The Fond du Lac Reporter,* Fond du Lac, Wis.)

After his Anchorage, Alaska, home had been burglarized repeatedly, former State Senator C. R. Lewis began to stake out the house. The third night six youths showed up, and when one kicked in the door, Lewis jumped out of hiding and at gunpoint forced all six to lie face down on the floor while he phoned the troopers. Lewis said he intends to "take all measures possible" to prevent future break-ins. Those measures will include "the citizen's right to bear arms," he stated. (*The Anchorage Daily Times,* Anchorage, Alaska)

SEPTEMBER 1975

"Go away and leave me alone," called out 84-year-old Emma Tate when a burglar broke open the door to her Oakland, Calif., apartment. The intruder failed to heed the warning, and Mrs. Tate, armed with a pistol, fired twice, critically wounding him. (*The San Francisco Chronicle,* San Francisco, Calif.)

Discovering a prowler in her Rapid City, S. Dak., home, Mrs. Larry Reishus called her husband who confronted the culprit. The man pulled out a knife and began slashing and stabbing Reishus, who despite the attack was able to grab a revolver from a nearby drawer, fire and slay his assailant. (*The Rapid City Journal,* Rapid City, S. Dak.)

Carl Bear was the lone customer in an Abington, Pa., doughnut shop when a man entered the store, handed the cashier a note saying he was armed and then helped himself to the cash. When the thief turned to flee, he found himself staring into Bear's pistol and surrendered with hands held high. Bear, who has a pistol permit, turned over the crook to the police. (*The Evening Bulletin,* Philadelphia, Pa.)

Three men, two of them armed, entered William Colquitt's Chicago, Ill., store and announced a holdup. After the owner handed over $75, the trio began to back out, but when they turned, Colquitt snatched a revolver from under the counter, shot three times and wounded one thief. The wounded man soon was apprehended by police. (*The Chicago Tribune,* Chicago, Ill.)

Andreas Guralas was behind the counter of his San Francisco, Calif., store when a man brandishing an automatic pistol walked in and demanded money. The robber ran to a waiting car and sped away, but Guralas grabbed a pistol, gave chase in his pickup and caught the car at a red light. When the man with the automatic appeared as if he were going to shoot, Guralas fired first and mortally wounded him. (*The San Francisco Examiner,* San Francisco, Calif.)

The attempted robbery of a Columbus, Ga., drug store was foiled when the would-be robber, armed with a sawed-off shotgun, apparently failed to see employee R. T. Daniels, Daniels took a pistol from behind the counter, fired and wounded the culprit, who was arrested minutes later outside the store. (*The Columbus Ledger,* Columbus, Ga.)

Concerned about two men outside her Jackson, Mich., home at 3:30 a.m., Gladys Durfey got the family's .22 pistol. When one of the pair entered the rear porch, Mrs. Durfey yelled, "Get out of here," firing a shot to make her point. She then phoned neighbor Robert Burgett to tell him of the prowlers. Prewarned, a shotgun-toting Burgett met the men and scared them right into the arms of two policemen. (*The Jackson Citizen Patriot,* Jackson, Mich.)

Retired school teacher Marjorie DeGarmo awoke to find a man with a rifle in the bedroom of her Wadestown, W. Va., house. She scuffled with the stranger and managed to get her pistol from the night stand. The pistol discharged, killing the man. The shooting was later ruled "justifiable homicide by reason of self-defense" by the local prosecuting attorney. (*The Dominion Post,* Morgantown, W. Va.)

An unidentified man had just pried the padlock from a garage door at the Mechanicsburg, Ohio, home of John Williams when he was confronted by Mrs. Williams, who was accompanied by her German shepherd and a shotgun. The man hastily fled the scene. (*The Urbana Citizen,* Urbana, Ohio)

A young hoodlum, carrying what turned out to be a toy handgun, entered Leon Hall's Tampa, Fla., drug store and threatened to kill Hall and his employees if they did not fill a sack he had brought with drugs. As the thief was leaving with his loot, he again threatened the employees, whereupon Hall fired three shots from the revolver he keeps in the store and killed the robber. (*The Tampa Tribune-Times,* Tampa, Fla.)

NOVEMBER 1975

Driving down a California highway, William Ketterman of Mar Vista witnessed a speeding pickup truck strike and kill a young female pedestrian. As the driver failed to stop, Ketterman pursued and forced the truck off the road. He then held a shotgun on the driver until highway patrolmen arrived. (*The Los Angeles Herald-Examiner,* Los Angeles, Calif.)

When a burglar tried to crawl through the rear window of her Amarillo, Tex., hardware store, Olive Wallace immediately phoned the police. She then got a handgun and fired one shot that sent the would-be thief fleeing. (*The Amarillo Globe-News,* Amarillo, Tex.)

When a deputy sheriff and a former police chief held up a Caddo Mills, Tex., bank and fled with a hostage, Mayor Bobby Chapman shot out a tire on their getaway car, then led a pickup truck posse of armed townspeople in pursuit. The irate citizens ran down the crooks in their trucks and held them at gunpoint on the ground until the local sheriff arrived. (*The Dallas Morning News,* Dallas, Tex.)

A man walked into A. K. Bentley's Ashdown, Ark., automotive supply store, shoved a pistol in Bentley's face and yelled, "Give me your money." Instead, Bentley ducked behind the counter, grabbed a .38 revolver and came up shooting. The stunned robber threw his gun away and ran from the store. (*The Little River News,* Ashdown, Ark.)

Two ski-masked bandits carrying shotguns abducted Hallandale, Fla., pharmacist Marshall Mounger in a parking lot and forced him to take them into his store. While the gunmen were ransacking the drug locker and the cash register, Mounger grabbed a shotgun he kept on the premises. After an exchange of gunfire, the crooks ran from the store. (*The Fort Lauderdale News,* Fort Lauderdale, Fla.)

Wielding a .22 rifle, Anna Beard, 71, confronted a startled intruder who had broken into her Dover, Ind., house. The man tried to escape by crashing through a storm door, but Mrs. Beard fired, hitting him in the arm. He was arrested later at a nearby hospital. (*The Dearborn Country Register,* Lawrenceburg, Ind.)

A Missouri state trooper had been shot three times by two armed robbery suspects when armed citizen Robert Riley of Tiptonville, Tenn., rushed to his aid. Riley fired a small caliber pistol at the assailants until they surrendered. The law officer was then rushed to a hospital. (*The Memphis Press-Scimitar,* Memphis, Tenn.)

After being shot in the hand by one of four youths bent on robbing his Milwaukee, Wis., grocery, Jose Herrera returned fire with a cal. .25 automatic he kept under a counter, mortally wounding his attacker. The other youths panicked and fled. (*The Milwaukee Sentinel,* Milwaukee, Wis.)

James Thompson, a Homewood, Pa., tailor, recognized three men who came into his shop as the trio which robbed him two weeks earlier. This time the thugs, one armed with a razor, forced Thompson into a back room. There he grabbed a revolver and managed to wound two of his assailants. The third escaped. (*The Pittsburgh Post-Gazette,* Pittsburgh, Pa.)

From the porch of his Oklahoma City, Okla., house, Eugene Barnes saw two suspicious men following a woman down a dark street. He got his .22 rifle, trailed the men and interrupted an attempted mugging. One of the men aimed a pistol at Barnes, but the gun misfired. Just then, a second armed citizen, Andrew Hall, arrived with a .38 revolver. Hall fired twice and the muggers fled into the darkness. Police Chief I. G. Purser commended the actions of Barnes and Hall as "just what we need to stop this type of hoodlumism." (*The Oklahoma Journal,* Oklahoma City, Okla.)

1976

MARCH 1976

Daniel Webb, 89 and crippled, was locking the back door of his North Nashville, Tenn., home when a man broke in and attacked him. Webb begged the intruder to let him sit down, then grabbed a hidden pistol, fired and killed his assailant. Police ruled the killing justifiable homicide but confiscated the pistol. (*The Nashville Banner*, Nashville, Tenn.)

Truck driver Dudley Jones, making a delivery in Hartford, Conn., saw three young thugs knock down a woman and steal her purse. He fired several pistol shots into the air. Two of the thugs halted and were arrested by police. (*The Courant*, Hartford, Conn.)

Ensil Malone arrived at his St. Marys, W. Va., tavern about 3 a.m. to find two burglars preparing to cart away liquor and stereo equipment. Shots from his .22 rifle sent the looters running off empty-handed. (*The Oracle*, St. Marys, W. Va.)

Three hours after a Seattle, Wash., druggist was murdered in a robbery, a man entered Richard Isaksen's Seattle pharmacy and began reading magazines until all the other customers left the store. Isaksen became suspicious and drew a pistol just as the man whirled around and pointed a gun. Seeing the druggist was armed, the would-be robber dropped to the floor, fired several wild shots, then crawled out the door. (*The Seattle Times*, Seattle, Wash.)

A gunman entered an Oklahoma City, Okla., liquor store and told owner Timothy Dryden to hand over his cash. Instead, Dryden snatched a revolver from underneath the counter and shot the robber twice. The wounded thug soon was apprehended by police on the sidewalk outside the store. (*The Daily Oklahoman*, Oklahoma City, Okla.)

Answering the doorbell and finding no one there, Richard Harry retired to the bedroom of his Anderson, Ind., home. Minutes later an intruder entered the room, and when Harry reached for a gun, the man threw a framed picture at him and fled. (*The Anderson Herald*, Anderson, Ind.)

Two holdup men confronted Dr. Arthur Gorney and his wife in a Brookline, Mass., restaurant parking lot. One held a knife to Mrs. Gorney's throat while the other took Dr. Gorney's wallet. As they fled, Dr. Gorney drew and fired his licensed handgun. One fell mortally wounded. Police arrested another man as a suspect. (*The Herald American*, Boston, Mass.)

Awakened about 5 a.m. by the sounds of someone trying to break down the front door of his Virginia Beach, Va., home, Daniel Hitt grabbed his .22 rifle. Hitt confronted a burglar inside the house and fired one shot when the man advanced toward him, disregarding orders to halt. The burglar then ran from the house. (*The Ledger-Star*, Norfolk, Va.)

Three young employees of a Barkeyville, Pa., truck stop had planned to go deer hunting after work but hadn't planned on being held up by a masked gunman. After emptying the truck stop's cash register, the robber fled into nearby woods, but was soon captured by his trio of victims who by then were all armed with deer rifles. (*The Allied News*, Grove City, Pa.)

Hearing strange noises in the kitchen of his Covina, Calif., home, Robert Griffin got a pistol, entered the room and found an intruder hiding behind a table. Griffin forced the man to lie face-down on the floor while his wife phoned the police. (*The El Monte Herald*, El Monte, Calif.)

When the alarm in his New York City apartment signaled a break-in at his nearby liquor store, Wilbert Gilliard got his .38 revolver and went to investigate. At the store he found a thief carting off a box of liquor bottles and held the man at gunpoint until police arrived. How the thief had reached the bottles through an iron grill that covered the storefront was revealed when a small monkey popped from his coat. The monkey had slipped through the grating and passed the liquor out to his human accomplice. (*The New York Daily News*, New York, N.Y.)

APRIL 1976

NRA Life Member Russell Simpson, at work in his Virginia Beach, Va., pharmacy, was startled when a "customer" pulled a semi-automatic rifle from beneath his coat and aimed at him. The two were struggling over the gun when James Merkle, also an NRA Member, intervened. When the robber swung toward him with the rifle, Merkle drew his revolver, fired once and killed the robber. (*The Virginia-Pilot*, Norfolk, Va.)

Dominico Caimi, 80, a tourist from Philadelphia, had just gotten off the elevator in an Ormond Beach, Fla., motel when a gunman came up behind him and threatened to shoot and rob him. Caimi jumped behind a pillar as the gunman fired, then pulled out his own gun and shot his attacker. Police soon arrested the wounded gunman and two suspected accomplices. (*The Daytona Beach Morning Journal*, Daytona Beach, Fla.)

When he heard a break-in in progress at his bar adjoining his Wilmington, Del., home, Charles Joyner told his wife to phone the police, grabbed a .22 rifle and went outside to find two men smashing in a bar window. After the pair failed to heed his commands to stop, Joyner fired several shots into the ground. Then both men whirled around to face him, one holding aloft an ax and the other a jagged piece of glass. Joyner opened fire, killing one crook and critically wounding the other. (*The Morning News*, Wilmington, Del.)

138

Catherine Watson was alone in her Chicago, Ill., apartment when a man broke in and threatened her with a hatchet. When her assailant turned and began ransacking a dresser drawer, however, she grabbed a shotgun she kept under the bed, fired, and mortally wounded him. (*The Chicago Tribune*, Chicago, Ill.)

After asking for cigarettes in a Minneapolis, Minn., grocery, a man opened his coat to reveal a knife and then demanded money from store clerk Margaret Clark. Instead, she pulled out a revolver and in the scuffle that ensued, fired and wounded the robber. He ran from the store but was arrested. (*The Minneapolis Tribune*, Minneapolis, Minn.)

Roused from a nap by his dog barking, Gary Hansen, a Santa Clara, Calif., city councilman, opened his front door to see two men stripping a neighbor's car. He ducked back inside and got a pistol. Thus armed, he confronted the pair and made a citizen's arrest. (*The San Jose Mercury*, San Jose, Calif.)

Buffalo, N.Y., tavern owner James Ruffin became suspicious when one of two customers asking for change kept his hand in his coat pocket. Ruffin drew his licensed handgun and ordered the man to empty his pocket out on the bar. Out came a sawed-off .22 rifle. Ruffin held the pair at gunpoint until police arrived. (*The Buffalo Evening News*, Buffalo, N.Y.)

Hearing a loud noise in her basement, Addie Mae Browning, Clarksville, Tenn., got her pistol and confronted a young man there. When he advanced and laughed at her demands to halt, she fired one shot, wounding him. He fled. (*The Clarksville Leaf-Chronicle*, Clarksville, Tenn.)

During the evening meeting at the Mystic Valley Gun Club in Malden, Mass., two men began rifling cars in the club's parking lot. Spotting the culprits, club members Frederick Leuchter and William Rosmarinofski gave chase and detained one suspect at gun point. (*The Malden Evening News*, Malden, Mass.)

Clay Jackson, 82, grabbed his shotgun when he heard intruders entering his Delaware County, Ind., house. Seeing that the homeowner was armed, the men fled, but not before Jackson managed to bash one of them over the head with the butt of his shotgun. (*The Muncie Evening Press*, Muncie, Ind.)

Asleep in an upstairs room at the rear of his Wilmington, N.C., gun shop, Charlie Todd was awakened by the sounds of roofing being ripped away. When a man eventually kicked away a boarded-up skylight and dropped to the floor, Todd was waiting for him with a pistol. He forced the intruder to lie face down until police arrived. (*The News and Observer*, Raleigh, N.C.)

JUNE 1976

A would-be rapist grabbed Barbara Sherwood at a Carson, Calif., phone booth, knocked her to the ground and began assaulting her. Sherwood, a sheriff's deputy and member of her department's shooting team, pulled a revolver from her purse and shot her assailant twice, wounding him. (*The Daily Breeze*, Torrance, Calif.)

Chicago, Ill., postal worker Randall Gordon relied on his Marine training when two gunmen threatened to harm his wife and baby unless he gave them money. While one gangster held his family hostage in a car, Gordon took the other into his house to get the money. When the gunman began ransacking the bedroom, Gordon pulled a pistol from under a pillow and shot him in the arm and leg. Gordon then got a shotgun and crawled up to the car and surprised the second thug. Disregarding orders to surrender, the man tried to draw his gun. Gordon shot him. Both wounded gunmen soon were arrested. (*The Chicago Daily News*, Chicago, Ill.)

Awakened by a noise in his Valencia, Calif., home, Ronald Barze opened his eyes to see a man with a wooden club in his hand standing in the bedroom. Barze yelled to his wife to call the sheriff as he jumped from the bed and snatched a 12-ga. shotgun from the closet. The intruder fled out the front door. (*The Newhall Signal*, Newhall, Calif.)

Two men, one carrying a pistol, entered Roy Bunch's Kingston, Tenn., market and demanded money from the store owner's wife. Bunch ran from the rear of the store armed with a pistol. After an exchange of gunfire in which no one was injured, the bandits fled from the store. (*The Roane County News*, Kingston, Tenn.)

W. A. Hanvey and his wife were closing their Anniston, Ala., store for the night when two youths walked in and one shouted, "Hold it, this is it," and raised a rifle. Hanvey picked up a revolver from beside the cash register and fired four times, killing the gunman and wounding his accomplice. (*The Anniston Star*, Anniston, Ala.)

Moments after breaking into policeman Benjamin Jaus' apartment in Honolulu, Hawaii, a burglar found himself staring down the barrel of a service revolver. Jaus turned the crook over to fellow officers, then went back to bed. (*The Honolulu Star-Bulletin*, Honolulu, Hawaii)

Bill Green and his wife returned to their Ormond Beach, Fla., home to find two armed men in the house. One intruder fired at Green who, despite a leg wound, was able to get a gun, return fire and slay his attacker. The second thug ran. Police said the slain gunman was carrying a live hand grenade in his jacket pocket. (*The Daytona Beach Morning Journal*, Daytona Beach, Fla.)

When a late night caller rang the doorbell of his East Liverpool, Ohio, home and asked to use the phone, John Eiferd became suspicious and warned his wife not to open the door until he got his revolver. When the door was opened, a masked youth entered carrying a rifle. Seeing Eiferd's revolver, however the youth turned and crashed through the door, taking the screen and wooden frame with him in haste. (*The Evening Review*, East Liverpool, Ohio)

Gaining entrance through a broken window, a man armed with a large knife appeared in the bedroom doorway of Mertie McGowan's Leake Co., Miss., home. Three shots from the homeowner's .38 revolver into the door over the intruder's head caused him to drop his weapon and run from the house. (*The Carthaginian*, Carthage, Miss.)

Houston, Tex., dentist J. Rutledge Phifer was in his examination room when he heard his mother's screams from the outer office. Grabbing a 20-ga. shotgun, he ran to the office and confronted two armed robbers. Phifer shot and wounded one man while the other escaped. At the time of the shooting, the wounded crook was being sought by police on two robbery charges. (*The Houston Post*, Houston, Tex.)

AUGUST 1976

New York State Court of Claims Judge Howard Jones was leaving his New Rochelle home on his way to court when he noticed two men apparently "casing" a neighbor's house. Judge Jones got a pistol and surprised the pair as they tried to enter the house. He made them lie spread-eagled on the ground until police arrived. (*The Daily Times*, Mamaroneck, N.Y.)

A lone gunman entered a Bellville, Ill., pharmacy and at gunpoint demanded drugs from store manager Leonard Lautz. Instead of handing over the drugs. Lautz drew a pistol and fired one shot over the would-be robber's head. The surprised crook quickly surrendered. (*The Steeleville Ledger*, Steeleville, Ill.)

After asking to see a rifle on display in Harold Von Wahlde's Anderson, Ind., gun store, a man pulled out a revolver and demanded money. Von Wahlde, 71, attempted to grab the gun and a struggle ensued. When the robber's gun misfired. Von Wahlde grabbed a cal. .38 handgun from a shelf behind him and fired one shot that mortally wounded the thug. (*The Anderson Daily Bulletin*, Anderson, Ind.)

When a man armed with a sawed-off shotgun walked into a St. Louis, Mo., carry-out restaurant and announced a holdup, manager Robert Purvis, working in the rear of the store, grabbed a revolver. Both men fired simultaneously. The robber was mortally wounded. Purvis received a hand wound. (*The St. Louis Post-Dispatch*, St. Louis, Mo.)

A ringing doorbell woke Monte Scales in his Austin, Tex., apartment. As he rose from bed, he heard what sounded like a key being inserted into the lock, then saw a man armed with a butcher knife and a screwdriver standing in the doorway. Scales threw an ashtray at the man and reached for a gun. The intruder fled. (*The Austin American-Statesman*, Austin, Tex.)

Mackroy Griffin was checking the gas pumps at the Atlanta, Ga., car rental agency where he works when a man struck him on the head with a sawed-off shotgun and snarled, "Don't move or I'll kill you." Griffin knocked the weapon aside, drew a pistol and shot his assailant, who fled. Police later questioned a suspect with a gunshot wound who entered a local hospital. (*The Atlanta Journal*, Atlanta, Ga.)

Alerted that a neighbor's home was being burglarized, Lawrence Carroll and W. C. Sneed, both of Dallas, Tex., armed themselves with a pistol and shotgun. They were waiting behind the house when four men carrying cash and jewelry appeared. One burglar escaped, but three surrendered. (*The Dallas Morning News*, Dallas, Tex.)

After waiting until all customers had left, two men, one wearing a long coat, entered a Fontana, Calif., book store and approached clerk Larry Singleton. When Singleton saw a gun being pulled from under the coat, he snatched up a pistol from beneath the counter and fired two shots. Both would-be robbers ran. (*The Sun-Telegram*, San Bernardino, Calif.)

Asleep in his Tacoma, Wash., home, Johnnie Leonard was awakened by the sound of breaking glass. While arming himself with a .357 Magnum revolver, Leonard heard two men whispering and investigated the noise. When one of the pair began climbing through a bedroom window, Leonard shot and mortally wounded him. Police, who began a search for the second man, said the slain burglar was a paroled robber. (*The News Tribune*, Tacoma, Wash.)

When two late-night prowlers threw a rock against Floyd Jones' Greenville, Pa. house, Jones sent the pair fleeing by firing two shotgun blasts in the air. They reappeared moments later, and this time Jones got the drop on them and marched them into the house at gunpoint. He held them for police who found a loaded revolver on one of the men. (*The Herald*, Sharon, Pa.)

SEPTEMBER 1976

A robber broke through the front door of Frank Davenport's Atlanta, Ga. home, and threatened to beat him until Davenport gave him money. But Davenport reached under the bed for a cal. .38 pistol and fired twice, killing his assailant. (*The Atlanta Journal*, Atlanta, Ga.)

Elmo Ethington's wife telephoned him at home and told him that the Simpsonville, Ky., bank she manages had been robbed. Ethington ran to his car, took the nearest road, and shortly encountered the robber's car. He gave chase, first on the highway and then on foot, subdued the thief at gunpoint, then flagged down a highway patrolman who took the man into custody. (*The Daily Press*, Newport News, Va.)

A cross-country crime spree came to an abrupt halt when an Illinois man attempted to rob Floyd Selleck's Palm Bay, Fla., gas station. The robber entered the station and began firing at Selleck, hitting him in the hand and arm. The station owner's son Arthur returned fire with a cal. .25 automatic, fatally wounding the thief, who was suspected of several car thefts and armed robberies in Illinois. (*Sentinel-Star*, Orlando, Fla.)

A 210-lb. intruder broke into the Chico, Calif., bedroom of Scott L. Cooper and challenged the 135-lb. Cooper to fight for his life. The man then attempted to strangle Cooper, who grabbed a revolver from the nightstand nearby and shot his assailant four times with .38 Special wadcutter rounds. The intruder was convicted of assault and first-degree burglary. (*The Mercury-Register*, Oroville, Calif.)

A Sylmar, Calif., man who grabbed Lauren Rae Birch's purse got a lot more than he bargained for from her husband, William. She drove straight home, then she and William searched for the thief. They spotted him, gave chase and cornered him in a backyard, where Birch covered him with a cal. .22 revolver until police arrived. (*The Valley News*, Van Nuys, Calif.)

A man entered the Lubbock, Tex., grocery store of Weldon Donaghey, 60, pulled a cal. .38 revolver and demanded Donaghey's wallet. After the store owner handed over the billfold, the bandit threatened two other store employees, whereupon Donaghey drew his own cal. .22 revolver and fired six times, seriously wounding the robber, who was also suspected in another grocery store hold-up the same day. (*Avalanche-Journal*, Lubbock, Tex.)

Larry Hardin of Boynton Beach, Fla., was driving his wrecker down a deserted street at 2:30 a.m. when a man began firing at the truck. Hardin grabbed a .357 Magnum revolver, jumped from the truck, and opened fire on his assailant. The latter fled the scene. Hardin then called for police help on his truck's CB radio. (*The Sun-Sentinel*, Ft. Lauderdale, Fla.)

A burglar had just poked his head through the window of Jeff Smith's Danville, Ill., apartment when Smith ordered him to freeze. When the intruder kept crawling through the window, Smith fired once, sending him fleeing. (*The Commercial News*, Danville, Ill.)

A 17-year-old intruder entered the Waynesburg, Ohio, home of Helen Francis and Kathleen Chipko and ordered them to lie down with their hands behind their heads. When the man threatened rape, Francis drew a pistol from under her pillow and fired, killing the youth instantly. (*The Canton Repository*, Canton, Ohio)

A young thief leaped over the counter of Leslie Hicks' Over-the-Rhine, Ohio, grocery store, threatened Hicks' wife with a knife, and began cleaning out the store's cash register. But Hicks reached for his cal. .22 revolver and ordered the would-be robber to drop the money and his knife. As Mrs. Hicks was telephoning the police, the thief and a companion slipped out the front door and escaped. (*The Cincinnati Post*, Cincinnati, Ohio)

OCTOBER 1976

Mary Perrone of Rockford, Ill., arose one morning, noticed a kitchen window had been forced open and then saw a man's hat on the bed in an unused room. Just after she had picked up her .38 revolver, a movement caught her eye, and she turned to confront a masked intruder. The 4ft. 10in. grandmother fired once, hitting the man in the stomach. He leaped through an open window and fled, but was soon caught by police. (*The Morning Star*, Rockford, Ill.)

A gunman entered the Dayton, Ohio, home of Elnora Stone, accosted the owner and shot at her twice with a handgun. Mrs. Stone was able to deflect her attacker's arm and fire her own gun. She mortally wounded the assailant. No charges were brought against Mrs. Stone because, as a Dayton homicide detective stated, "The man was in the bedroom of the house, and she had every right to protect herself." (*The Journal Herald*, Dayton, Ohio)

After repeated burglaries at his Haviland, Kans., pharmacy, Hal Mix installed a silent alarm connected to his home telephone. When the alarm went off one night, Mix summoned two friends and the trio, armed, drove to the drugstore. There Mix and his companions captured three burglars and held them until sheriff's deputies arrived. (*The Wichita Eagle*, Wichita, Kans.)

An intruder had cornered Mrs. Leah Kinser, 70, in the closet of her Springfield, Mo., home and was pounding a hole through the wall when Mrs. Kinser's son arrived. He held the man at gunpoint until police came. (*The News-Leader*, Springfield, Mo.)

Awakened by the sounds of glass breaking in his sister's Cedar Rapids, Iowa, home, Harry Nobel got a .22 revolver and investigated. Entering the dining room, he met a ski-masked burglar carrying a flashlight. Noble fired one shot. That sent the intruder fleeing. (*The Cedar Rapids, Gazette*, Cedar Rapids, Iowa)

THE ARMED CITIZEN

A would-be robber sneaked a pistol in a paper bag into George Fuss' Milwaukee, Wis., coin shop and announced a holdup before drawing the gun. Fuss whipped his own pistol from its holster before the crook could draw. The man fled. (*The Milwaukee Sentinel*, Milwaukee, Wis.)

Rebecca Corey, a Winton, Wash., school teacher, was mowing her lawn when she heard her dog barking inside the house. She entered the home, got a handgun and followed the dog to a bathroom. There she confronted a bandanna-masked burglar and detained him a gunpoint for the police. (*The Wenatchee World*, Wenatchee, Wash.)

When St. Paul, Minn., jeweler Carl Zeglin, 72, was wounded in a robbery two years ago, he vowed he'd never be robbed again. He backed up his words with action recently. When a robber entered his store with a cal. .38 revolver and demanded that the jeweler empty the cash register, Zeglin grabbed his own .38. In an exchange of gunfire, he killed the thug although wounded himself. (*The St. Paul Pioneer-Press*, St. Paul, Minn.)

Kevanlynette Griffin was awakened at 5:25 a.m. by the sound of someone cutting through a window screen of her New Orleans, La., home. After repeatedly warning the intruder to leave, the home-owner reached for her gun and announced she would shoot. When the prowler persisted in his break-in attempt, she fired a warning shot that sent him fleeing. (*The Times-Picayune*, New Orleans, La.)

James Florian, hearing his daughter screaming in the back yard of his Childs, Ariz., home, ran out and saw the child being bitten by a gray fox. Florian began to choke the animal, then his wife arrived with a revolver and killed it. Health officials later theorized the fox had been bitten by a rabid skunk. (*The Phoenix Gazette*, Phoenix, Ariz.)

NOVEMBER 1976

Boat owner Norman Long of Chicago, Ill., was awakened by his wife who heard noises aboard their yacht. Long grabbed a 9 mm pistol and surprised a burglar. When the intruder tried to flee, Long halted him by firing four shots into the air. He soon was arrested. (*The Chicago Daily News*, Chicago, Ill.)

A man walked into the Indianapolis, Ind., gas station operated by Benjamin and Susan Tackett, stuck a knife in Tackett's back and told him to walk toward the cashier's booth where Mrs. Tackett was seated. As the men approached the booth, Tackett broke away and yelled to his wife to call the police and "get the gun." Mrs. Tackett drew a revolver and fired once, killing her husband's assailant. (*The Indianapolis Star*, Indianapolis, Ind.)

A man entered a New Orleans, La., grocery, grabbed store manager Cecil Lee by the throat, cut him across the stomach with a broken bottle and demanded money. When the thug released him so he could get the cash, Lee pulled out a .22 Magnum pistol and shot his attacker twice. Police soon arrested the wounded crook. (*The Times-Picayune*, New Orleans, La.)

Two youths, one brandishing a gun, announced a holdup in Mable Kennedy's Huntsville, Ala., grocery. Instead of giving up her money, Mrs. Kennedy pulled out a revolver and aimed it at the robbers. "They started running and were still running the last time I saw them," Mrs. Kennedy stated later. (*The Huntsville News*, Huntsville, Ala.)

A short time after authorities warned Sedgwick, Colo., residents to be on the lookout for a man sought for a stabbing murder in a nearby town, Bob Price, a local farmer, spotted the suspect. Price got his rifle and held the man at gunpoint in a drainage ditch until police arrived. (*The North Platte Telegraph*, North Platte, Nebr.)

Paul Handy, owner of a Shelburne, Vt., market, had locked up and was walking to his car with the day's receipts when two men on the store's roof ordered him to throw down the money. Instead, he ran into the store and got his gun. Handy fired two shots, and the would-be robbers jumped from the roof and fled into nearby woods. (*The Burlington Free Press*, Burlington, Vt.)

Two women and a man asked Barbara Willis how much money she had in the cash register of her Waco, Tex., drive-in restaurant. Noticing what appeared to be a pistol under one of the women's shirts, Mrs. Willis drew her own cal. .25 pistol from beneath the counter. The trio quickly fled. (*The Waco Tribune-Herald*, Waco, Tex.)

A man entered the lobby of a Brooklyn Park, Md., hotel and asked owner Howard Lawless for a room, then threatened Lawless with a pistol. Lawless drew a revolver from a hip holster and shot and killed the gunman. The slain thug proved to be a convicted felon. On his body police found the wallet of a man who had been murdered earlier that same night. (*The Evening Capital*, Annapolis, Md.)

Awakened about 2 a.m. by noises in his Stallion Springs, Calif., home, Buck Waterstradt turned on his bedside lamp and found two men, one holding a butcher knife, standing over his bed. Throwing back the bed blanket, Waterstradt knocked the knife to the floor, then reached under the head of the bed and pulled out a pistol. Both intruders fled. They later were identified as escapees from a nearby prison. (*The Tehachapi News*, Tehachapi, Calif.)

142

After pumping gas for two men in a Detroit, Mich., service station, Tim Turner, 19, turned to collect and found himself facing two handguns. Turner dropped to the pavement and pulled his own gun. The bandits fled. Turner gave chase, caught one man, and held him at gunpoint until police arrived. (*The Detroit Free Press*, Detroit, Mich.)

DECEMBER 1976

Two robbers armed with knives swam across an inlet to break into the island home of Henry S. Cram near Bluffton, S.C. Holding a knife to his throat, they forced Cram's son, Peter, to lead them to Cram's bedroom. When the crooks shouted through the door for Cram to throw out his gun, the homeowner, a skilled rifle and pistol shot, burst through the door with a cal. .38 revolver at the ready. Peter broke away from the bandit who was holding him, and Cram fired twice, killing both men. A coroner's jury ruled the killings justifiable homicide. (*The Evening Post*, Charleston, S.C.)

Dentist Virgil Menefee of Los Banos, Calif., answered a knock on his front door and was confronted by two robbers, armed with a knife and a toy pistol. As Menefee and his wife struggled with the intruders, Menefee's stepson grabbed a pistol and fired several warning shots, driving the intruders away. (*The Sun-Star*, Merced, Calif.)

Mrs. Louis Romano of North Stonington, Conn., found that burglars had been breaking into her home. So, accompanied by her daughter, she staked out the house with a shotgun. When the two women heard footsteps inside the house, they entered, captured two youthful burglars and held them until police came. (*The Day*, New London, Conn.)

Samuel Coins of Indianapolis, Ind., was "tired of hearing about these guys robbing banks and getting away with it." Spotting a robbery in progress at a local bank, he ran after the thief. He was joined by James L. Snyder, and the pair gave chase in Snyder's car, reaching speeds of 80 to 100 miles-per-hour. When the crook's car hit a light pole and came to a halt, Synder held the robber and an accomplice for police with his licensed cal. .38 revolver. (*The Star*, Indianapolis, Ind.)

A pair of switchblade-armed robbers entered Benjamin Shareff's Brooklyn, N.Y., furniture store and demanded money. When the merchant stalled, they attacked him with the knives. But Shareff's brother-in-law, Herman Salles, was on hand with a cal. .38 revolver, and fired five times, killing one thug, wounding another and a female accomplice. (*The Daily News*, New York, N.Y.)

Armando Chavez and Refugio Arellano of Clint, Tex., were dove hunting when they saw two men entering an acquaintance's house. Knowing the owner was away, they called the sheriff's office and blocked the exits until authorities arrived. (*The Herald Post*, El Paso, Tex.)

A 15-year-old punk strolled into the Richmond, Calif., home of Francine Tiger and began pistol-whipping her and two other women. But Mrs. Tiger was able to break free and reach for a gun hidden in the living room. She fired several times, wounding the youth, who was arrested later when he sought treatment at a local hospital. (*The Tribune*, Oakland, Calif.)

St. Louis, Mo., furniture store owner Thomas R. Bleich had been robbed three times, and didn't plan to be hit again. When a pistol-wielding thief entered his store, Bleisch reached for a cal. .38 revolver. The thug looked away for a second, long enough for the storekeeper to draw the pistol and fire, fatally wounding him in the chest. (*The Globe-Democrat*, St. Louis, Mo.)

A victim of repeated burglaries, Clifford Berg returned to his Loxahatchee, Fla. home one night and found two men in his barn. Berg got a gun and held the burglars at bay until sheriff's deputies arrived. (*The Palm Beach Post-Times*, Palm Beach, Fla.)

After repeated burglaries at his Chicago, Ill., laundry, Thomas Elliot bought two shotguns—one for the store and another for his adjacent home. Awakened by his dog one night, Elliot looked out from his porch to see a burglar leaving the laundry with a load of clothes and his other shotgun. When the laundry owner called for the man to drop the gun, the crook instead whirled around. Elliot fired, killing him. (*The Daily News*, Chicago, Ill.)

JANUARY 1977

A would-be robber was the one who was shocked when he fired an electronic stun gun at Sidney Kerensky of Philadelphia. Only one of the two darts fired from the device connected, and an enraged Kerensky pulled his conventional pistol and fired three times in the air, sending the man fleeing. The stun gun delivers a shock of 50,000 volts, but only if both darts strike the intended victim. (*The Evening Bulletin*, Philadelphia, Pa.)

Angela Winslow returned to her apartment in Chicago's crime-ridden Robert Taylor housing project to find that a hoodlum had raped her roommate and then thrown the woman out the 15th-floor window. She fired at the rapist several times with her cal. .22 revolver, driving him away. The roommate's fall was broken by a canopy and she lived. Police charged Winslow with illegally discharging a firearm then dropped the complaint after the case received national publicity. (*The Tribune*, Chicago, Ill.)

1977

E.M. Beaty, 75, was attacked in the living room of his Charlotte, N.C., home by two armed thugs, one of whom stuck him on the head with a shotgun. Though minus one arm, Beaty managed to draw a cal. .38 revolver and kill one of them. Police believe he may have wounded his other assailant. (*The Observer*, Charlotte, N.C.)

Two young men boarded Alejandro Torres' bus in New York City and refused to pay their fare. When Torres insisted, one leaped behind him and stabbed him in the back. As the pair fled, Torres picked himself up from the bus floor and fired several times with his cal. .38 revolver, wounding one assailant. (*The Daily News*, New York, N.Y.)

A robber's bluff backfired when he pulled a starter's pistol on P.C. Hardman, Kansas City, Mo. The two scuffled for a moment, then Hardman broke loose and drew a pistol from his shoulder holster. He fired twice, wounding his assailant. (*The Star*, Kansas City, Mo.)

Alvin Thompson of Wilshire, Calif., was in the back room of his house when he heard someone breaking down the front door. He reached for a cal. .38 revolver just as the invader crashed into his living room. When the man reached for his belt, Thompson fired, fatally wounding him. (*The Herald-Examiner*, Los Angeles, Calif.)

When a robber entered her San Antonio, Tex., convenience store and demanded money, Kiem Ahn Buentello pretended she didn't understand English. The man became flustered, and Mrs. Buentello used the opportunity to draw a pistol from beneath the counter. The frightened bandit backed out the front door and fled. (*The News*, San Antonio, Tex.)

When a late-night intruder broke into the rural Fowler, Calif., home of Forest H. Smith, 81, neighbors alerted his son-in-law, Roy Garrett. Garrett and his two teenaged sons rushed to the old man's home, where they found the thug holding a knife to Smith's throat. After the man swung at him several times with the knife, Garrett shot him in the shoulder with a rifle, but the powerful crook kept coming. Garrett's younger son then broke a shotgun over the criminal's head, sending him fleeing outside. There, the other son bashed him with a baseball bat, then held the unconscious burglar for sheriff's deputies. (*The Bee*, Fresno, Calif.)

Frank Deece, 70, told a young tough threatening him that he would get a bag of change in the back room of his Ybor City, Fla., photography studio. However, Deece emerged with a cal. .45 pistol instead of the cash. The pair exchanged shots, and the robber was critically injured. Deece was wounded superficially. (*The Tribune*, Tampa, Fla.)

Two panhandlers approached Thad Freeze of Vancouver, Wash., and demanded a handout. When Freeze declined, one produced a knife. When Freeze pulled a cal. .25 automatic, the pair beat a hasty retreat. (*The Oregon Journal*, Portland, Oreg.)

When the first customer of the day at Willie Arrington's Buffalo, N.Y., delicatessen brandished a revolver and demanded money, Arrington dived behind the counter and grabbed a cal. .38 revolver. In the shootout that followed, the robber was killed. (*The Evening News*, Buffalo, N.Y.)

MARCH 1977

A Doberman Pinscher was savagely mauling 10-year-old Vickie Wright of Midland, Mich., when her brother Jamie, 11, appeared with their father's cal. .22 revolver. Young Jamie fired three times, killing the animal. (*The Globe-Democrat*, St. Louis, Mo.)

A parolee from a federal penitentiary broke into the home of Mrs. Beverly Dennis, apparently looking for a narcotics dealer who previously had lived there. When the thug put a knife to her throat, Mrs. Dennis and one of her teenaged sons pushed him away. She managed to grab a gun and fire, sending the crook fleeing. He was later picked up by police. (*The Banner*, Nashville, Tenn.)

When a burglar ran from their aunt's Lake Charles, La., home with a bag of loot, John and Dennis Thigpen armed themselves and gave chase. The thief leaped into a waiting car and tried to make his getaway, but John blew out the vehicle's front tires with his 16-ga. shotgun. The man surrendered himself and a pistol to the pair, who then held him for sheriff's deputies. (*The American Press*, Lake Charles, La.)

A Jacksonville, Fla., grocery store owner ran to James Yankey's truck and shouted that a man was robbing his establishment. Yankey reached for a pistol in his glove compartment and got out of the truck just as the 16-year-old thief emerged from the store. The young hoodlum dropped his loot and waited quietly until police came. (*The Florida Times-Union*, Jacksonville, Fla.)

Tampa, Fla., machinist Phil Moyer was napping when his wife called his attention to two youths who had run up the couple's sidewalk. Moyer grabbed a pistol when the two began rifling a woman's purse. As the pair headed toward a nearby car Moyer made a citizen's arrest, punctuating his action with a warning shot. (*The Tap*, Tampa, Fla.)

George Barber, 75, of Rochester, N.Y., saw three young thugs stab an 80-year-old neighbor when the man's wallet proved to be empty. Barber grabbed a rifle and fired several shots, driving the youths away before they could further harm his neighbor. (*The Democrat and Chronicle*, Rochester, N.Y.)

Jerry Lee Hilliard of Santa Clara, Calif., awoke to find a ski-masked youth standing over his bed, pistol in hand. The thug tied Hilliard up and headed for the room where Hilliard's teenaged daughter was sleeping. But he foolishly left his pistol on a table near the homeowner. Hilliard worked himself free, grabbed the gun and shot the intruder several times. (*The Mercury*, San Jose, Calif.)

Car salvage dealer Isaac Rabb was counting a large sum of cash when a stickup man in a floppy rubber monster mask entered, brandishing a 9 mm automatic pistol. Rabb grabbed a double-barrel shotgun as the man opened fire, and shot him dead at a range of about 4 ft. The would-be robber was later identified as a longtime criminal. (*The American Statesman*, Austin, Tex.)

Two juvenile delinquents on a crime spree entered the Loveland, Colo. trailer home of James R. Love. Convinced the pair planned to use their shotguns on his family, Love attacked with his bare fists, distracting the hoodlums long enough for the home-owner to make an escape to his pickup truck. There, Love reached for a rifle and fired into the air, frightening the young criminals into surrender. (*The Coloradan*, Ft. Collins, Colo.)

Larry Plummer of Spokane, Wash., decided to do a little looking when his son-in-law's car was stolen. Spotting the vehicle in a parking lot, he waited with his pistol and apprehended the jail escapee who had stolen it. (*The Spokesman-Review*, Spokane, Wash.)

Two South Bend, Ind., holdup artists made their final mistake when they picked John Burkhart's pharmacy as their target. The pair entered and one ordered Burkhart to the rear of the store while the other tied James Senior, an off-duty security po-liceman. But the thug apparently failed to notice Senior was armed. The guard quickly freed his hands and fired, killing one crook. As the other rushed to his partner's aid. Burkhart drew an automatic from under his counter and shot him dead. (*The Tribune*, South Bend, Ind.)

David Johnson of Victoria, Tex., walked into a loan office just as a gunman announced a holdup. Johnson ran outside, borrowed a rifle and returned to confront the robber. The thief fled but soon was captured by police. (*The Post*, Houston, Tex.)

APRIL 1977

A lack of expertise in coin dealing was costly to two San Leandro, Calif., burglars. They stole several counterfeit coins from the home of coin dealer Bobby Short. They went the next day to a nearby coin shop to pass the bogus cash. But the shop was Short's: he recognized the coins immediately, drew a pistol, and held the hapless pair until police arrived. (*The Daily Review*, Hayward, Calif.)

Wilma Montgomery, a Chicago, Ill., mother of five, was walking from the bus stop to her home when a man leaped from an alley, dragged her into the gangway of a building and ordered her to lie down. She feigned compliance, but when the man prepared to rape her, she shot him fatally with a legally-registered cal. .38 revolver. Police said the man had a record of sexual assaults. (*The Tribune*, Chicago, Ill.)

Although 19-year-old Rebecca Vigil of Stockton, Calif., had never fired a pistol in her life, when two armed robbers invaded her boy friend's gas station and began to beat him, she took effective action. She first located a hidden cal. .22 revolver and emptied it into one of the crooks, she then retrieved a pistol dropped by the fatally wounded thug, and used it to kill his partner. (*The News-Sentinel*, Lodi, Calif.)

Charles Ware of Barstow, Calif., was in bed reading when he heard noise coming from his bathroom. He armed himself and went to investi-gate. Finding a juvenile burglar rummaging through a chest, he held him for police. (*The Desert Dis-patch*, Barstow, Calif.)

When a stickup man drew a cal. .22 pistol on Betty Milraney, an employee of her East Nashville, Tenn., market dropped behind a counter and se-cretly handed her boss a cal. .38 revolver. Alarmed, the crook opened fire, but Mrs. Milraney replied with a shot to the head, wounding the robber fatally. (*The Banner*, Nashville, Tenn.)

A youthful robber confronted Wesley Krouse of Phoenix, Ariz., at his front door and, armed with a cal. .22 pistol, forced the 72-year-old Krouse to turn over some cash and the keys to his truck. But when the thief pushed the septuagenarian into his bedroom. Krouse grabbed a 12-ga. shotgun and exchanged fire with the bandit, who was killed instantly. (*The Arizona Republic*, Phoenix, Ariz.)

Harry Powell was cutting weeds at his home near Abbeville, S.C. when he heard a roar. A gang of motorcyclists was racing toward his farmhouse. Powell reached it just as the gang surrounded the place. He called out a window, asking what the bikers wanted. When he got no reply, he walked out onto his front porch, armed with a shotgun. The group waited a minute, and then mounted up and raced away. (*The Record*, Ridgeway, Pa.)

When a pair of young thugs invaded Jerome Gaine's West Baltimore, Md., pharmacy, they wer-en't prepared for the spunky resistance of Gaine and his wife Leatrice. One of them pointed a snub-nosed revolver at Mrs. Gaine and demanded cash, but she screamed at him instead. When the startled robber stepped back, Gaine hit an alarm button, grabbed his own cal. .38 revolver and opened fire, wounding one of the pair. Police apprehended him later. (*The Sun*, Baltimore, Md.)

145

THE ARMED CITIZEN

Young Roy Hooker of Richland County, S.C., was left alone with his small brother and sister while the children's mother went on an errand. As soon as Mrs. Hooker left the house, an intruder broke in through the back door, brandishing a stick. But 14-year-old Hooker was not deterred; he grabbed a 12-ga. shotgun loaded with deer slugs and fired, blowing the stick out of the thug's hand. The man fled. (*The State,* Columbia, S.C.)

Two would-be holdup artists picked the wrong target when they tried to rob Walter Williams' St. Joseph, Mo., liquor store. Williams grabbed one robber and, using him as a shield, drew his own cal. .38 revolver and ordered the other criminal to drop his gun. The first robber managed to escape, but Williams marched his comrade to a nearby pay telephone and made him report the crime personally. (*The Gazette,* St. Joseph, Mo.)

Gail Brooks came out ahead when a man tried to rob her Knoxville, Tenn., gift shop. She drew a pistol from beneath the counter and the frightened crook ran, dropping $23 on the floor in his haste. (*The News-Sentinel,* Knoxville, Tenn.)

JUNE 1977

William N. Overstreet was jogging near his Mobile, Ala., home when he spotted three burglars at work on a nearby house. The housebreakers saw him and abducted him at gunpoint. But they didn't count on the reaction of Overstreet's wife Carolyn, who became worried when her husband didn't return home. She jumped into her car just in time to spot Overstreet in the back of the burglar's truck. She gave chase, fired several shots and even rammed the truck with her own car. Finally, the police answered her call over CB radio and stopped the criminals, who surrendered after a brief scuffle. Overstreet was unharmed. (*The News and Observer,* Raleigh, N.C.)

Three holdup men should have several years of prison to contemplate the folly of robbing Mrs. Mildred Woolsey's El Cajon, Calif. coin store. The doughty Mrs. Woolsey not only drove the thugs away at gunpoint, but hounded the local district attorney's office into rearresting the trio after they were released on a minimum bail less than three hours after the robbery. The men now face 10-year minimum sentences for the crime. (*Coin World.*)

Arthur Kilner gave an unruly customer fair warning by blasting him with a fire extinguisher when the man went on a rampage at Kilner's Seattle, Wash. pinball arcade. But the man picked up a heavy stool and advanced on Kilner, who fired a warning shot from his cal. .38 revolver. Even this didn't deter the enraged customer, who kept coming, threatening the arcade manager. So Kilner shot him twice. The man threw the stool, turned over a pinball machine, then collapsed on the floor. (*The Times,* Seattle, Wash.)

A would-be burglar owes his life to some poor shooting by Mrs. Richard Acre of Port Huron, Mich. The burglar broke the glass in Mrs. Acre's front door and was preparing to enter when she grabbed a .44 Magnum carbine and opened fire, nearly destroying the door. The frightened thief ran away. (*The Times Herald,* Port Huron, Mich.)

As an intruder bashed away at the front door of his North Philadelphia, Pa., home, Yancy Sowell gave him several warnings. Finally, as the door broke loose, Sowell fired with a shotgun, killing the crook instantly. (*The Bulletin,* Philadelphia, Pa.)

Charles Dresser and his wife were reading the paper in bed when they heard a loud pounding on their front door. Dresser put on his bathrobe, grabbed a .22 revolver and went to investigate, arriving in the couple's living room just as two would-be burglars burst in. The homeowner fired, hitting one thief. The pair fled, but police later caught the wounded robber. (*The Mercury,* San Jose, Calif.)

Morris E. Whitfield of Fayetteville, N.C., was awakened by the sound of breaking glass. He grabbed a pistol and ran to investigate. He found a would-be burglar in his living room and held the man for police. (*The Observer,* Fayetteville, N.C.)

Baker Robert Burkey of Columbus, Ohio, has been robbed 12 times during the past 27 years; the 13th time was unlucky for a 20-year-old robber. The thief, holding his hand inside his shirt, demanded cash. But Burkey produced a revolver and held the stickup artist for police. (*The Dispatch,* Columbus, Ohio)

JULY 1977

Mrs. Gloria Catrett, a nurse, arrived at her Opp, Ala., home to find three burglars ransacking the place. She drew a revolver from her purse and held the trio, aided by a friend, Mrs. James Mitchell, who rushed to the Catrett home when she heard about the burglars on a police scanner. (*The Opp News,* Opp, Ala.)

A gang of juvenile delinquents was terrorizing a 67-year-old woman across the street from the Oklahoma City home of Noel D. Highfill, 72. Highfill reached for a shotgun, ran into his yard and fired, sending the youthful criminals running. (*The Oklahoma Journal,* Oklahoma City, Okla.)

Sixteen-year-old Cathy Watkins was asleep in her parents' Charlotte, N.C., home when she saw an unfamiliar car back into the garage. She quickly slipped out her window and ran to the home of her grandfather. The grandfather and an uncle armed themselves with shotguns and returned to the Watkins home, where two burglars were filling their car with loot. The pair surrendered quietly. (*The News,* Charlotte, N.C.)

146

When a housebreaker tried to crash into Peggy Monroe's Loda, Ill., home, she phoned police and grabbed a gun from her bedroom. When the intruder fired twice into the house where her four children were sleeping, Mrs. Monroe shot and killed him. (*The Daily Journal*, Kankakee, Ill.)

Chester Iio had been robbed at gunpoint five times in eight years at his N. Harris Co., Tex., grocery. Recently, when two hoodlums broke into the store, Iio slipped up a back stairway into his office, where he reached for a 12-ga. shotgun. He watched through a two-way mirror as the thieves ransacked the cash register. When one broke into his office, Iio fired, killing him instantly. When the other robber blasted at Iio with a pistol, the storekeeper silenced him with another load of shot. Finally, Iio chased the pair's confederate, who tried to escape in a getaway car, and blasted out the vehicle's rear window. (*The Chronicle*, Houston, Tex.)

When 16-year-old Wolfgang Penner entered his Danville, Calif., home, he noticed several items missing and heard noises from another room. He armed himself with a .30-'06 rifle, barricaded his bedroom door and called police. They found five youthful burglars, one of whom was escorted out by Penner. (*The Valley Pionger*, Danville, Calif.)

Eugene Gring's Lancaster, Pa., gas station has been the target of robbers 30 times since 1960. On 27 of those occasions, Gring has captured the crooks. The 30th occasion was much like the others. Gring was awakened by a silent alarm at his home; he alerted his 20-year-old son, and the pair headed for the station. There, they caught the burglars and held them for police. (*The New Era*, Lancaster, Pa.)

Two holdup men, disguised as electric company employees, entered the New York City apartment of Carlos Rodriquez and forced his wife and small son into a rear room. As the two thieves ransacked the place, Rodriquez and a friend, Manual Liriano, unexpectedly walked in. The robbers opened fire, wounding Rodriquez, but Liriano, firing his own legally-registered pistol, killed one thug and wounded the other. (*The Daily News*, New York, N.Y.)

AUGUST 1977

A bandit got away with nothing but a headache when he tried to rob Walter Roempp's Cincinnati, Ohio, grocery. Roempp responded to the man's demand for cash by bashing him with a bottle, then sent him running with a shot from his gun. (*The Enquirer*, Cincinnati, Ohio)

After several robberies at her New Castle, Del., archery range, Joanne Hall decided to set up her own stakeout. When a burglar entered, she levelled a shotgun on the man, who meekly surrendered. (*The Evening Journal*, Wilmington, Del.)

William Hyde, 60, was alone in his Pittsburgh, Pa., furniture store when a gang burst in and began beating him with a shotgun. He blasted the group with a fire extinguisher, then opened fire with an automatic pistol, killing one thug and wounding two others. (*The Press*, Pittsburgh, Pa.)

When a deputy sheriff told Dennis Lemon that an escaped convict was on the loose near Lemon's Vincent, Ohio, home, he armed himself with a .30-30 rifle. When a stranger knocked at 5:30 a.m., Lemon covered him with the rifle while his wife phoned police. The man proved to be the escapee, and was taken into custody. (*The News*, Parkersburg, W. Va.)

NRA Member R. E. Rader, 62, was shaving in his Brentwood, Tenn., home when he saw two young men in his back yard. He went to their car, parked in front, took the license number, had his wife call police, and then waited with a shotgun. He apprehended one of the men, who police later said were burglarizing the neighborhood; the other was found by a police canine unit. (*The Banner*, Nashville, Tenn.)

12-year-old Pamela Thompson was alone in her Baltimore, Md., home when she heard someone breaking in. Since the house had no telephone, she could not summon help. So she loaded a cal. .22 rifle and fired once, hitting the would-be robber, who was later apprehended by police. (*The Sun*, Baltimore, Md.)

When a knife-wielding attacker tried to assault Faye Woodruff of Hamilton, Ga., she bit the man's arm so hard he dropped his weapon. Then she ran to her car and grabbed a cal. .38 revolver. When the thug approached, she shot him in the leg, then held him for police. (*The Enquirer*, Columbus, Ga.)

A bandit who robbed Charlie Speed's Savannah, Ga., bar proved to be short on nerve after Speed turned over a bag full of cash. As the man left, Speed pulled a pistol and fired a round past the thief's head. The crook fainted and had to be revived by police. (*The News*, Savannah, Ga.)

After her Cincinnati, Ohio, apartment was burglarized for the fifth time in a year, 52-year-old Evelyn Jackson decided to purchase a cal. .32 revolver. She got an opportunity to put it to use when a criminal broke in at 4 a.m. one Sunday morning. She ordered the man to halt; when he advanced instead, she shot him several times. (*The Post*, Cincinnati, Ohio)

A New London, Conn., break-in artist was confronted by a chilling sight when he tried to enter the home of Margaret Lord. She heard the man's attempts to open her window, jumped out of bed, and pressed her revolver's muzzle against the glass right under the crook's nose. He fled. (*The Bulletin*, Norwich, Conn.)

THE ARMED CITIZEN

SEPTEMBER 1977

E.H. Thompson was reading in his Richmond, Va., home when he heard noises from his screened porch. He turned out the lights and reached for his pistol. When one of two intruders lit a cigarette lighter, Thompson turned the lights back on, blinding the men. He held the pair for police. (*The Times-Dispatch*, Richmond, Va.)

When Stephen Garrow of Brandon, Vt., saw a stranger emerging from his barn, he sent his wife to call police and grabbed a cal. .22 rifle. He held the man for police, who identified him as a convicted rapist who had escaped from a nearby prison. (*The Free Press*, Burlington, Vt.)

When four burglars broke through the back door of Geneva's Store in rural Stanford, Ky., they got an unpleasant surprise. Owners Julian Farmer and Bobby Yocum were waiting in the store, armed with shotguns. The thieves quickly surrendered. (*The Kentucky Advocate*, Danville, Ky.)

Mrs. Donald A. Edwards of Amherst, N.Y., was roused by the sound of her front doorbell ringing, then heard the sound of someone breaking through a side door. She armed herself with a cal. .22 rifle and apprehended a would-be burglar, whom she held for police. (*The Courier-Express*, Buffalo, N.Y.)

Circuit Judge Gary Black, a former policeman, was being held with three other hostages by a former convict in the Farmington, Mo., courthouse. During the 90 minutes the group was held, a sheriff managed to slip a pistol to Judge Black, who surprised the crook and held him for police. (*The Times*, New York, N.Y.)

Three youthful hoodlums entered the East Liberty, Pa., gas station of Jim Myers and demanded cash. When Myers refused, one began to pistol-whip him. Myers drew his own cal. .38 revolver and opened fire, wounding one thief and sending the others fleeing. (*The Press*, Pittsburgh, Pa.)

When a mugger pressed a cal. .45 automatic to the head of Polish immigrant Zygmunt Soroka in New York City's garment district and ordered him to reach for his wallet, Soroka feigned compliance. But instead of withdrawing cash, he drew his licensed cal. .38 revolver and fired, critically wounding his assailant. (*The Daily News*, New York, N.Y.)

When two thugs robbed his Ewing Township, N.J., store, shot him, and then were released without prosecution, William Thompson vowed he'd never be robbed successfully again. So when a stickup artist entered his business recently, Thompson reached for his cal. .38 revolver instead of the cash register. He chased the crook for three blocks and held him for police. (*The Sunday Trentonian*, Trenton, N.J.)

Cecil Collier, 15, was working with his father in a Wildwood, Fla., vegetable field when a state trooper rushed up and asked them to join a posse searching for three Ohio criminals. The trio had broken through a tollgate and evaded a roadblock formed by CB radio operators. Collier was given a 20-ga. shotgun, and he headed into a nearby thicket. There he found the hoodlums, ordered them to drop their guns, and held them for the rest of the posse. (*The Tribune*, Tampa, Fla.)

OCTOBER 1977

When a convicted murderer who had escaped from a South Carolina prison entered his Fayetteville, N.C., store and demanded money, M.T. Westerfield pulled a cal. .38 revolver instead. Store owner and armed robber shot it out, and the felon was killed. (*The State*, Columbia, S.C.)

A 300-lb former mental patient had stabbed two men to death and was attempting to break through a door to reach two women next to Steve Lennon's Las Vegas, Nev., home when Lennon, hearing the noise, came out to investigate. He challenged the killer, who charged him, brandishing the bloody weapon. Lennon opened fire, killing the slasher instantly. (*The Review-Journal*, Las Vegas, Nev.)

A ski-mask-clad bandit entered George Maguerza's San Antonio, Tex., convenience store and brandished a cal. .38 derringer. He fired a shot at Maguerza, who gave up $35. But as the robber turned to leave, the store manager drew his own .38 revolver and ordered him to halt; when the bandit drew the derringer instead, Maguerza fired, wounding the thug. (*The Light*, San Antonio, Tex.)

Three teenaged hoods found that a 2"x4" scrap of lumber wasn't enough persuasion for a Macon, Ga., store owner. The three broke into the fruit and vegetable stand and began bashing the owner with the beam. But when he reached the cash register and a cal. .38 revolver, the trio fled. (*The Constitution*, Atlanta, Ga.)

Seventy-six year-old J. H. Short saw three youthful thugs preparing to rob his Meally, Ky., grocery. He concealed his own pistol and waited. When the trio entered and threatened Short with a shotgun, he opened fire, wounding one and sending the three fleeing. (*The Daily Independent*, Ashland, Ky.)

Two female members of the non-violent Hare Krishna sect used an unloaded gun to bluff a man who stole their flower van into surrendering. They followed the thief into the San Francisco, Calif., airport's garage and held him for police. (*The Chronicle*, San Francisco, Calif.)

When a young robber entered his Albuquerque, N. Mex., pharmacy and demanded narcotics, Delbert Swindle drew a pistol instead and held the man for police. (*The Tribune*, Albuquerque, N. Mex.)

When a bandit couple entered the Kansas City, Mo., drug store of Robert Kiff and Pat Voight and called for narcotics at shotgun point, the two druggists reached for their revolvers and opened fire. The shotgun-wielding robber fled, knocking his female accomplice to the floor in his haste. Police quickly apprehended the pair. (*The Times*, Kansas City, Mo.)

James Pharpe and a friend were waiting to pick up their wives from church when a pair of young hoodlums began shooting at them. A bullet hit the 75-year-old Pharpe in the stomach, but he managed to pull his own gun and opened fire, killing one robber and driving his companion away. (*The News*, Detroit, Mich.)

An armed robber thought he had frightened William Wienter away from his Portland, Oreg., gas station when he drew a pistol and Wienter fled. But the station owner was only going for his gun; his shots drove the crook away empty-handed. (*The Oregonian*, Portland, Oreg.)

NOVEMBER 1977

Willie Harris, 71, heard the sounds of someone breaking in the back door of his Muskegon, Mich., home. When the intruder tried to burst into his bedroom, Harris leaned against the door and grabbed his 16-ga. shotgun. When the housebreaker refused to leave, Harris poked the gun's twin barrels out the door and fired, killing him. (*The Chronicle*, Muskegon, Mich.)

Dennis Campbell handed over the narcotics a stickup artist demanded; but when the crook left his Birmingham, Ala., pharmacy, Campbell followed with a shotgun. The robber fired twice with a pistol and Campbell replied in kind, causing the man to flee, dropping the drugs and a wig in his haste. (*The News*, Birmingham, Ala.)

When a man jumped from a pickup truck and began to beat a young woman in the parking lot of his Birmingham, Ala. tire store, John Yancy intervened. He drew a pistol and ordered the hoodlum to stop, and the man fled. (*The News*, Birmingham, Ala.)

Ron Cesavice of South Bend, Ind., saw a young car thief pry open the vehicle of a neighbor, Richard Scott. He grabbed a revolver and went to investigate, being joined by Scott on the way. The pair held the youth for police. (*The Tribune*, South Bend, Ind.)

Cynthia Scarborough, a 22-year-old Hawkinsville, Ga., nurse had just dozed off when she heard a crash. She grabbed her cal. .38 revolver and fired a warning shot just as an intruder broke through her bedroom door. The man surrendered in tears. (*The Telegraph*, Macon, Ga.)

A would-be rapist met an untimely end when he attempted to molest an unidentified New Orleans, La., woman cab driver. When the man jumped into the front seat and attacked, she drew a cal. .357 revolver and fired, killing him. (*The Times-Picayune*, New Orleans, La.)

Ralph Festavan watched as a heroin peddler attacked a Shreveport, La., policeman and grabbed the officer's gun. Festavan ran to the patrol car parked nearby and got a shotgun with which he shot and killed the pusher. (*The Post*, Houston, Tex.)

San Diego, Calif., homeowner Jerry Jay survived a toe-to-toe shotgun duel with a robber after the thug broke down his front door. The man opened fire, wounding Jay in the chest and hand. But then Jay grabbed his own double gun and opened fire, killing his assailant. (*The Union*, San Diego, Calif.)

Floyd Bettis arrived at his Anchorage, Alaska, home just as a burglar was leaving with a bag of loot. Bettis chased the man, who leaped into his pickup truck and tried to run the homeowner down. Bettis was saved when neighbors Richard Griffin and Forest Crozier arrived and subdued the housebreaker at pistol point. (*The News*, Anchorage, Alaska)

Mrs. Cleo Ainsworth saw two young thugs attack her husband outside their farmhouse near rural Dora, N.M. After calling for help, she got her husband's pistol and fired a warning shot. The men fled. (*The News-Journal*, Clovis, N.M.)

CHAPTER 6
"THE ARMED CITIZEN" IN TODAY'S SOCIETY 1978 to 1989

FEBRUARY 1978

Two youths entered John Loeffler's South Lake Tahoe, Calif., drugstore, brandished a pistol and demanded drugs and cash. Loeffler filled a pillowcase with prescription narcotics. Then as he handed it to the armed member of the pair, he grabbed the bandit's gun. Loeffler and the robber fought until Loeffler was able to get his own gun and shoot one of his assailants in the leg. He then held both the would-be crooks until the police arrived and took them into custody. (*The Daily Tribune*, South Lake Tahoe, Calif.)

Awakened by her 11-year-old daughter's cries for help, Elizabeth Williams of Birmingham, Ala., investigated and found a burglar inside her home. While scuffling with the intruder, she called out to the child to notify police and get a gun. When the little girl did so, the robber attempted to escape. As he headed for the back door, Mrs. Williams fired twice, wounding the man, then held him until police arrived. (*The Post-Herald*, Birmingham, Ala.)

Arriving home to find his house burglarized, Don Hull of Fremont, Calif., tried to call the police, but got a busy signal. As he put the phone down, the burglar, who had hidden in a back room, appeared, brandishing a knife. Hull got his revolver and chased the man from the house, then ordered him to halt. When the man did not stop, Hull fired and hit him twice. Police arrested the suspect in the back yard of a nearby home. He was charged with burglary and two counts of assault with a deadly weapon. (*The Daily Review*, Hayward, Calif.)

Two armed thugs who forced their way into the rectory of a Philadelphia, Pa., Catholic Church got an unexpected reception. After first terrorizing one of the priests in residence, the gun-waving pair tried to break into the apartment of Msgr. Frederick Moors. Instead of yielding, Msgr. Moors slammed the door in their faces and called, "Jack, get your gun," to his assistant, Fr. John Farry. At the threat of armed resistance, the two crooks beat a hasty retreat. (*The Evening Bulletin*, Philadelphia, Pa.)

A young man in Jacksonville, Fla., who had successfully robbed one motorist, picked the wrong man for his second victim. He stopped Seaboard Coastline Railroad special agent Joseph Loadholtes. Loadholtes carries a gun, and when he saw that he was about to be robbed, he drew it and shot his assailant twice. The wounded suspect fled on foot and police were unable to locate him. (*The Journal*, Jacksonville, Fla.)

Because his San Antonio, Tex., home had been burglarized before, Edwin Jowers was prepared when he heard breaking glass. Placing a whispered call to the police, he armed himself with a shotgun and confronted two burglars. One of the pair, both in their teens, fled, but the other surrendered and Jowers held him until sheriff's deputies arrived. (*The News*, San Antonio, Tex.)

A shotgun-armed assailant accosted Kansas City, Kas., resident Fred Shirley as he was getting into his car, and demanded money. Shirley told the man that his money was in a bag under the car's front seat. He then reached under the seat, got a cal. .38 revolver, and fired, fatally wounding the bandit. (*The Star*, Kansas City, Mo.)

1978

THE ARMED CITIZEN

New York restauranteur Alfred Zerega has an intercom hooked up between his home and his nearby place of business. Hearing noises in the closed restaurant one night, Zerega took his hunting rifle with him and went to investigate. As he entered the building, he confronted three burglars who rushed him. However, they fled when he fired two shots in the air. (*The Advance,* Staten Island, N.Y.)

When Marlene Jacobs noticed three suspicious-looking youths near her New Orleans, La., home, she called police and got her shotgun. A few moments later, the three kicked open her back door and entered, only to find the shotgun-armed woman awaiting them. The hoodlums fled into the arms of police, who were just arriving on the scene. (*The Times-Picayune,* New Orleans, La.)

Alerted by the sound of breaking glass, 75-year-old Cleo Green took a cal. .22 revolver and began searching her Oakland, Calif., home for an intruder. She entered the kitchen in time to find a burglar in the room. When the cornered thug attacked her, she fired three shots critically wounding her assailant. (*The Chronicle,* San Francisco, Calif.)

Mathew Novicki saw two men breaking into a relative's Bristol Township, Ohio, home, so he called the sheriff's office, then armed himself with a shotgun. As the robbers left the house, Novicki fired two warning shots and held the pair until deputies arrived and placed them under arrest. (*The Tribune,* Warren, Ohio.)

The young woman who entered Orange Davis' store in San Antonio, Tex., did not warrant special attention until she pulled a small pistol on the 82-year-old store owner, and demanded cash. Unflustered, Davis stepped behind a meat scale, picked up his own revolver and called for the woman's surrender. She ran. (*The News,* San Antonio, Tex.)

Wayne Brasher of Birmingham, Ala., was hunting with his dog when confronted by a robbery suspect being chased through the woods by police. When the suspect attacked him, Brasher hit the man with his shotgun, and his dog grabbed the culprit by the leg and held on until the police arrived. (*The Post-Herald,* Birmingham, Ala.)

MAY 1978

Pharmacist Jim Rawlinson of Century, Fla., returned to his store late at night. When he was about ready to leave, he heard a noise and turned to see several ceiling panels fall. When a rope was dropped through the hole, Rawlinson pulled out a .38 revolver and ordered the dangling aerialist to come on down. When he refused, Rawlinson shot once. The round was loaded with No. 9 bird shot. "He went up the rope a whole lot faster than he came down," Rawlinson recalled. (*The Tri-City Ledger,* Flomaton, Ala.)

Shawn Stevens, 17, of Cabell County, W. Va., became suspicious when he saw someone he didn't recognize enter his neighbor's house. He called the mother of his neighbor who verified that there shouldn't be anyone in the house. After fetching his father's automatic, he met the mother outside the house. "When she went into the bedroom," Stevens said, "she saw him standing there and started screaming." The intruder kicked the door shut. But Stevens kicked it open and held the robber at bay until the deputies arrived. (*The Herald-Dispatch,* Huntington, W. Va.)

WWI Veteran, Charles Griffen, 80, entered his Jacksonville, Fla., home and spotted three intruders running to the rear of his house. They had knocked down his wife and choked her. While grabbing his shotgun, which he kept near the door, Griffen noticed that his M1 was missing. In the back of his house, he trapped one of the men. Then Griffen heard a noise and turned to see his own M1 in the hands of a robber. "I shot him," Griffen said. "I only got him because he used the sights and I shot from the hip." Two of the assailants fled while the wounded one remained there for the police. (*The Journal,* Jacksonville, Fla.)

Ten years ago Alton, Mo., jeweler John Caperton was robbed of several thousand dollars' worth of diamonds. After that incident Caperton bought a revolver. Recently, a customer he had seen on several occasions entered his store and asked when Mother's Day was. When Caperton turned to check the calendar, his customer turned into an assailant, leaping over the counter and wielding a long hunting knife. Caperton received some superficial wounds before he managed to draw his gun. His second shot killed the robber instantly. (*The Post-Dispatch,* St. Louis, Mo.)

Debra Prince had a feeling that the man who entered her North St. Louis, Mo., food store was not there to buy any food, and she edged toward the side of her counter where her revolver was hidden. The man waited a few minutes, then pulled out his gun and said, "Lady, I hate to do this." "Hate to do what?" Prince replied, raising her own gun and shooting. The thug bolted. He was found a short time later nursing a shoulder wound at his home where the police made the arrest. (*The Globe-Democrat,* St. Louis, Mo.)

Due to a rash of burglaries at a Galesburg, Ill., pizzeria, employee Girolamo Bartolotta spent the night on guard duty. From a back room, he heard someone unlock the door and begin to rifle the cigarette machine. Armed with a small handgun, Bartolotta fired at the floor near where the intruder was standing. He then ordered the would-be thief to pick up the phone and call the police. He did as he was told. Later he was booked on a charge of burglary. (*The Journal Star,* Peoria, Ill.)

Shortly after her husband left for work, Doris Carpenter of Waco, Tex., heard the window of her front door break. A man reached in, unlocked the door and entered the living room. Carpenter closed the door to her bedroom and retrieved a cal. .22 revolver from under the mattress. The intruder kicked in the door, only to find the housewife drawing a bead on him. He beat a hasty retreat. (*The Tribune-Herald,* Waco, Tex.)

Department store security chief and former Texas law officer, Richard Norton, was in New York City on business. As he was opening the door to his hotel suite, he heard running in the hall behind him. He was shoved into his room by two men; one was flashing a knife. Norton carried the fight into the bedroom and managed to get a revolver from his briefcase. Norton fired, mortally wounding one assailant. The other fled. Norton's Texas gun permit was not valid in New York, but a grand jury cleared him of any wrongdoing. (*The Times Herald,* Dallas, Tex.)

Awakened at 3:35 a.m. by loud noises at the front door of her Akron, Ohio, home, 78-year-old Haddie Xenias seized a cal. .22 pistol and went to investigate. She found a man trying to break in and fired three shots that sent him fleeing. Police, responding to her call for help, caught the man in a nearby yard. (*The Beacon Journal,* Akron, Ohio)

David Bigelow was at his home in Chestertown, Md., when he heard some commotion in his living room. Standing in the stairwell, he watched as someone raised a window, crawled through it and walked through the room. Having been the victim of several recent break-ins, Bigelow was prepared. "That's far enough," he said, pointing a gun at the intruder. The would-be burglar stayed, until the police arrived. (*The Kent County News,* Chestertown, Md.)

AUGUST 1978

Awakened by the growling of her dog, Gertrude Ross, 71, of Baltimore, Md., looked up from her bed to see a man in a stocking mask standing in the doorway. The robber demanded money, slapped her and dragged her off the bed. Ross crawled toward a dresser saying she would get her money. Instead, she reached under a piece of furniture, grabbed her gun and fired two shots, one of which struck the assailant fatally in the forehead. (*The Sun,* Baltimore, Md.)

Hearing screams, Perfect Oliver, a retired Army officer, grabbed his pistol, and ran out behind his diner in Hamilton Township, N.J., and came upon a man raping a woman on the sidewalk. Seeing Oliver, the attacker left the woman where she was lying and advanced toward him, whereupon Oliver raised his gun and fired one fatal shot. (*The Daily Advocate,* Dover, N.J.)

In Columbus, Ohio, a passenger grabbed taxi driver Charles Ross by the head, put a knife to his throat, and demanded the day's receipts. He wanted the cabby's watch, too, so Ross reached into his pocket as if to comply. Instead, he drew a .22 and fired into the robber's stomach. When the man slumped over in the back seat, Ross got out of the cab to call the police. On his return, the wounded man attacked him again, hitting him with a wine bottle. Ross fired again, and the robber fell to the street as the police cruiser pulled into view. (*The Dispatch,* Columbus, Ohio)

After ordering soft drinks in L. L. Maready's store in Jacksonville, N.C., the two thugs waited for the clerk to open the register for their change before one of them pulled a pistol and demanded all the money. Maready, the shop owner, sitting nearby, trained a gun on the two and shouted: "I don't have any money." The armed intruder dropped his gun, and both fell to the floor, then crawled out the door and ran to their getaway car. (*The Daily News,* Jacksonville, N.C.)

After George Byrd left his home in North Philadelphia, Pa., two armed men forced their way in and locked Byrd's two daughters, a nephew and a friend of the family in the basement. When Byrd returned a short time later, he, too, was forced into the basement. Byrd quickly retrieved a .30-'06 hunting rifle stored atop a rafter and loaded it. Aiming at a spot where he could hear the men moving the refrigerator above him, he fired killing one of the marauders and forcing the other into a hasty retreat. (*The Daily News,* Philadelphia, Pa.)

A farmer in Idabel, Okla., spotted four escaped convicts walking about 200 yds. from his farm house. He told his wife to call the sheriff, grabbed his rifle, climbed into his jeep and drove in pursuit of the felons. Having heard on the news that the men were armed with a handgun, the farmer stayed out of pistol range and fired a warning shot over their heads, forcing their surrender. The jail birds remained in his custody until the authorities arrived. (*The Tribune,* Tulsa, Okla.)

Armed with a handgun, Joseph Ankenbrandt of Decatur, Ill., encountered two men in his kitchen late at night after he had been awakened by loud noises. While one of the men fled, Ankenbrandt forced the other to lie on the floor until the police could be summoned. (*The Herald,* Decatur, Ill.)

After banging on the door, the bandit, who had waited for Rebecca Rone's husband to leave their home in Clarksville, Ky., pulled out his gun. Watching from behind a curtain, Rone, in an attempt to discourage the gunman, pulled the fabric aside to show him that she, too, was armed with a handgun. Nevertheless, he fired, and Rone, jumping to the side returned fire through the glass and frightened him away. Authorities apprehended the man a short time later. (*The Tennessean,* Nashville, Tenn.)

When Daniel Moore's wife saw three men steal property from their garage and then drive off in a truck, she alerted her husband who grabbed his shotgun and gave chase in his car. The pursuit ended in a parking lot where the thieves apologized and offered to return the belongings. Moore refused, yelling to a bystander to call the police. When the robbers started to drive off, in spite of repeated warnings, Moore fired two rounds into the truck's engine, stopping the vehicle. The police who arrested the three said that Moore had not used excessive force and therefore would not have to face any charges. (*The Commercial-News*, Danville, Ill.)

An elderly widow of Columbus, Ga., heard someone trying to break into her house. She called Forrest Watson, a local gas station proprietor who, due to a recent rash of murders in the area, had asked her to call him *and* the police in case of emergency. Receiving the call, Watson grabbed his gun and arrived in time to see a man removing a screen from the woman's bedroom window. He knocked the intruder to the ground and covered him with his gun until the police arrived. (*The Ledger*, Columbus, Ga.)

"Shoot him, shoot him," one bandit yelled to the other who was struggling with Robert Pittard, a liquor store owner in Little Rock, Ark. Pittard released his hold on the hoodlum's gun and dropped to the floor behind the counter. A bullet struck the display case near Pittard, who jumped up, ran to a rear room and retrieved a 20-ga. shotgun. The bandit who didn't leave by the time the store owner returned received a blast of shot which sent him fleeing. (*The Arkansas Gazette*, Little Rock, Ark.)

NOVEMBER 1978

While in the water at a Bay St. Louis, Miss., beach, Karen Steirwald was assaulted by a man who put a knife to her throat and told her not to move or scream. After she begged him to let her get up and get her towel, the attacker, keeping the knife at her throat, walked her to the beach. Reaching as if for a towel and pushing the knife away at the same time, Steirwald managed to grab her hidden revolver and point it at the man. He slowly backed off and fled with an accomplice. (*The Sea Coast Echo*, Bay St. Louis, Miss.)

There were no customers in a Dallas, Tex., grocery when two women and three armed men came in and announced a holdup. While one of the robbers trained a gun on cashier William Blakemore's fellow worker, Blakemore pulled a shotgun from beneath the counter and opened fire. In the exchange Blakemore sustained a hand wound but still managed to wound two of the men and put the rest to flight. Police arrested the other suspects a short time later. (*The Morning News*, Dallas, Tex.)

Having been raped twice before by the same man, the 51-year-old Los Angeles woman was ready when her attacker broke into her apartment for a third time. Armed since the last assault, the woman drew her handgun when the man entered her bedroom and, following a brief struggle, fatally shot the would-be rapist in the chest. (*The Times*, Los Angeles, Calif.)

Awakened by the sound of breaking glass, Dennis Kinsman of Oxnard, Calif., found three men burglarizing his car behind his home. Kinsman grabbed his pistol and surprised the three who ran off. After a chase, Kinsman apprehended the men at their home a few houses away and held them at gun point until the police arrived. (*The Star Free Press*, Ventura, Calif.)

Fresno, Calif., bus driver Edward Lavelle was awakened by his wife with the news that a young boy was having trouble with a man across the street from their residence. Pocketing a 9 mm pistol, Lavelle went to the distressed youth and asked him if the man was his father or if he wanted to be with him. When the boy answered "no" to both questions, the man released him, allowing the boy to run to Lavelle's side. The kidnapper then advanced, forcing Lavelle to fire two warning shots which put him to flight. He was arrested a short time later. (*The Bee*, Fresno, Calif.)

About the time Myron Sage, vacationing in Crane Lake, Minn., saw the 350-lb. bear above him in the cabin's loft where his daughter had been sleeping, his daughter let out a piercing scream. Sage grabbed his .38 cal. pistol and shot the bear through the throat, causing the animal to fall to the main floor where Sage pumped it full of bullets. Only the bear was harmed. (*The Tribune Chronicle*, Warren, Ohio)

Oklahoma City gas station attendant Robert Jackson sold a customer a pack of cigarettes only a few minutes before he spotted the man trying to steal his car. Jackson stepped outside, holding a pistol, and was nearly run down by the thief, who rammed the car into the station, smashing the front plate glass window. Jackson managed to subdue the outlaw and hold him for the police. (*The Daily Oklahoman*, Oklahoma City, Okla.)

Returning to his Fort Walton Beach, Fla., home, William Moore was alarmed by the absence of his dog. He got a revolver and headed for his bedroom where he confronted an intruder who immediately opened fire on him. After returning fire, Moore ran outside and positioned himself where he could aim at both the door and the bedroom window. From that vantage point he held the burglar at bay until a neighbor called the police and the deputies arrived. (*The Playground Daily News*, Fort Walton Beach, Fla.)

Stanley Scally was working in the early morning hours for a Tampa, Fla., trucking firm when he saw two men breaking into a truck in the parking lot. Scally, armed with a .44 cal. rifle, approached the truck and fired two warning shots into the engine compartment. One of the burglars fled, but Scally held the other captive until the police arrived. (*The Times*, Tampa, Fla.)

Dr. Itzhak Brook heard someone knocking at the back door of his Kensington, Md., home early in the morning; seconds later, there was the sound of breaking glass. Brook grabbed a BB gun from under his bed and went down to the kitchen where he confronted the burglar and held him at gun point until the police arrived to make the arrest. (*The Post*, Washington, D.C.)

Edward Andy, a Lorain, Ohio, hardware store owner, was ready when one of two suspicious customers he'd been watching drew a gun and announced a holdup. The 76-year-old Andy ducked behind a rack, pulled out his nine-shot .22 and fired four times, wounding one of the criminals and causing both to flee. The wounded robber collapsed outside the store where he was arrested while the other escaped. (*The Journal*, Lorain, Ohio)

Salt Lake City grocer Ervin Wilkerson was seated at a table when a man drew a pistol and attempted a robbery at the check-out stand where Wilkerson's wife and son were working. When his son distracted the bandit and caused him to turn around, Wilkerson shot him with a 12-ga. shotgun. (*The Deseret News*, Salt Lake City, Utah)

MARCH 1979

When Ray McDaniel of Charlotte, N.C., drove up to his home and spotted a man climbing out of a window, he shot and killed him. In doing so, he brought to an end the career of a burglar police called "a professional." A search of the dead burglar's house and car turned up a list of 117 names of well-to-do collectors of coins, jewelry, or silver. Local officers were able to solve 20 crimes by matching the burglar's list against crime reports. (*The Winston-Salem Journal*, Winston-Salem, N.C.)

Jose Chavez was walking down a Stockton, Calif., street when one of three young men grabbed him, held a knife to his throat and demanded all of his money. Chavez pulled out a newly purchased pistol and fired five shots at the bandits, killing one of them and putting the others to flight. Chavez was cleared of any wrongdoing in the incident. (*The Bee*, Modesto, Calif.)

Richard Vulliet was awakened at 6:45 a.m. by a loud crash at the door of his Standard City, Ill. tavern. Grabbing his 12-ga. shotgun, he looked up in time to see two men carrying his cash register out the door. Vulliet gave chase, then fired two shots from about 80 ft., and injured one of the bandits. The other, who was later apprehended, had been released from jail on the previous day after doing time in connection with other robberies. (*The State Journal-Register*, Springfield, Ill.)

Joe Robbins was tending his Fort Worth hardware store when an armed man appeared and demanded the contents of the cash register. To facilitate the getaway, the bandit forced Robbins to lie face down so he could bind his wrists. When he put down the pistol, Robbins reached for it. In the struggle for control, an errant shot was fired, which brought a customer running to the scene to lend a hand. When a store employee produced a rifle, the bandit was subdued and later arrested. (*The Morning News*, Dallas, Tex.)

Elmer Benedict, the 65-year-old owner of the Totem Pole Grocery was suspicious of a nervous man who returned to the store for the third time in 10 minutes. Just before closing, the suspect pulled out a pistol and pointed it at Benedict's wife. When he reached across the counter and grabbed money from the cash register, Benedict drew his own pistol and stopped the robber with a shot to the neck. While still conscious, the man admitted he needed money for drugs. (*The Times*, Seattle, Wash.)

When Roosevelt Hastings returned to his San Antonio, Tex., home late at night, he found a car parked in front of the house, his screen door cut, and a panel of glass cut out of his front door. He managed to get a shotgun from the front room just as a man lunged at him with a knife. Hastings killed his attacker with one shotgun blast to the chest. (*The San Antonio Light*, San Antonio, Tex.)

Grace Buckley, an off-duty security guard on Chicago's South Side, was assaulted by an armed man and his accomplice as she climbed from a taxi in the pre-dawn hours. The assailants demanded money, but when driver Eddie Martin could only provide $11.58, they said they would rape the 21-year-old woman. In an effort to trick the assailants, Martin insisted that he be allowed to rape her first since it was his auto. Climbing into the back seat, Martin created some confusion during which Buckley drew her security pistol and killed both bandits. (*The Sun-Times*, Chicago, Ill.)

When Claudia Gray entered her El Paso apartment she was jumped by a man wearing only a stocking mask and a T-shirt. After the attacker had wrestled her to the bed, Gray warned him that she was expecting company. He got up and went to lock the front door, whereupon she grabbed a .22 cal. rifle from beneath the bed and shot him twice. After the police arrived and made the arrest, the previously convicted burglar was sentenced to seven years in the state penitentiary. (*The Times*, El Paso, Tex.)

1979

When two unknown men visited Juan Morales early one morning, he denied them entrance. Returning later, the men forced their way into the house, firing shots, two of which struck Morales' wife in the arm. In the midst of the confusion, Morales produced a .380 automatic with which he returned the fire, killing one man and injuring the other. (*The Herald,* Miami, Fla.)

Timothy Willard, a 22-year-old policeman in South Paris, Maine, was shot to death by a man inside a car parked in the lot of O.D.V. Inc. After gunning down the rookie policeman, the man fired wildly at company president, Robert Carroll. Carroll, an NRA Life member, drew his own gun and killed the man. (*The Sunday Telegram,* Portland, Maine)

An East Naples, Fla. woman heard a tapping at her bedroom window at 1:30 a.m. Looking out and seeing no one, she grabbed her gun and went to investigate. The woman found her suspect squatting among the garbage cans and held him at gunpoint until police arrived to make the arrest. (*The Daily News,* Naples, Fla.)

It was New Year's eve in a Detroit suburb when three men—two of them carrying pistols—broke through a back window and confronted a middle-aged woman in her den. The trio demanded money and inquired as to the whereabouts of her husband. The husband then came out of the bedroom and opened fire with his shotgun. The blast injured one bandit critically and sent the other two scurrying into the arms of nearby police. (*The Free Press,* Detroit, Mich.)

JUNE 1979

Suspicious of a couple who were lingering in his San Antonio liquor store, NRA Life member James E. Moore quietly pocketed his .38. When the couple approached the counter, the woman suddenly pulled a revolver and demanded all the money in the cash register. Her accomplice then took the gun away from her and began to move toward Moore, but was momentarily distracted by the appearance of a delivery boy. Moore quickly drew his own pistol and a gun battle ensued. When the robbers ran from the store, Moore grabbed his .45 from under the counter and gave chase, eventually aiding police in their capture. The couple were later charged in connection with two murders that occurred earlier in the week. (*The News,* San Antonio, Tex.)

When Mrs. Lilly Mahone began hearing noises outside her window in an Atlanta, Ga., apartment complex, she started carrying her .38 cal. pistol to bed. One night she was awakened by the sound of her kitchen window breaking. Rising from bed, the 77-year-old woman confronted a burglar. "What are you doing in my house?" she demanded. When the man made a sudden move, she shot him down and held him captive until police arrived. (*The Constitution,* Atlanta, Ga.)

Leroy Hardnett and Larry Flowers, the owners of the Boogie Shoes discotheque in Toledo, Ohio, were standing in their office when two armed robbers burst through the door. One of the men, carrying a sawed off shotgun, knocked Flowers to the floor. Hardnett then dropped to his knees and begged for mercy, while Flowers drew his .38 and began firing. Hardnett grabbed his .357, and together the two owners killed the intruders before they could get off a single shot. (*The Blade,* Toledo, Ohio)

Mr. and Mrs. Leonard Gantt were at home when a muscular young intruder climbed through their bedroom window one night in St. Petersburg, Fla., and assaulted the elderly couple. He then began to ransack their house. Though his hip had been broken in the attack, the 73-year-old husband reached for his loaded pistol, while his wounded wife pushed a chair against the bedroom door. When the assailant burst through the door, Mr. Gantt shot him in the neck. Police said later that the attacker had been out of prison only a short time after serving 28 months for similar crimes. (*The Times,* St. Petersburg, Fla.)

Manuel Hogan, whose Hartford, Conn., home had already been burglarized four times, reached for his revolver when he heard a crash in his living room one Saturday night. Entering the room, he saw three suspected burglars and ordered them to halt. Instead they fled, and he fired two shots. A fourth burglar then appeared and attempted to flee, but Hogan shot him in the hip and held him captive until the police arrived. The wounded man was charged with second degree burglary and Hogan was charged with first degree assault. Later realizing that the court investigator had erred and that Hogan's life had been endangered, the judge dismissed the case. (*The Courant,* Hartford, Conn.)

Fifty-seven-year-old Louis Armstrong was climbing from his car in Irvington, N.J., when two men approached him, one of them carrying a gun. As Armstrong reached into his pocket, the armed man fired a shot into Armstrong's chest. Armstrong returned the fire, killing the assailant with a shot to the stomach. While Armstrong had a permit to purchase his handgun, a Browning .25 cal. auto, he failed to have a legal permit to carry it. Nevertheless, it appears that charges will not be pressed against him. (*The Herald,* Irvington, N.J.)

Feeling ill, Linda Graham of New Albany, Ind., skipped work on Monday. When her dog began barking at 11 a.m. Mrs. Graham rose from her bed just as a large man was breaking through the kitchen door. The woman immediately picked up a small lever-action .22 carbine, which the intruder believed to be a BB-gun. As the man strode towards her, she fired one shot to his head, killing him instantly. (*The Tribune,* New Albany, Ind.)

Tony Sanford was suspicious when two armed men entered his neighbor's house in Austin, Tex. When he peeked through the back door he saw one of the intruders holding a sawed-off shotgun to the head of a woman. Sanford went back to his house and got his .30-30 rifle, but when he returned the robbers were driving away in a pick-up truck. Sanford fired twice at the tires of the truck and then shot into the back window, killing the driver. The other robber escaped on foot. (*The Herald*, Big Spring, Tex.)

Mrs. Dianne Ryan was on her way to the bank with receipts from the V&E Store in Queens, N.Y., when she was approached by a gunman who ordered her to hand over the money. When she refused, the gunman shot her, grabbed the bag containing $3500, and ran. Frank Martinez, an armed passerby with a permit to carry a pistol, heard the crack of the shot and began to chase the suspect. Joined by other outraged citizens, the mob surrounded the alleged assailant and held him captive until police arrived. (*The Times*, New York)

Maria and Stanley Kushida were forced into a back room of their Rogers Park, Ill., jewelry store by two armed robbers. When Stanley had opened the safe, he reached for a pistol from inside, but one of the robbers knocked him to the floor and began shooting at him. While holding her infant son in one arm, Maria reached under the counter, drew another pistol and began firing at the burglars. One fled and the other was seriously wounded. Police arrived to make the arrest and recover the stolen goods. (*The Sun-Times*, Chicago, Ill.)

SEPTEMBER 1979

The man who held up an Albuquerque, N.M., food store, got a rude surprise. As he approached the fourth checkstand, he found himself face to face with a lady shopper holding a .25 cal. automatic. To enforce her demand that he put down his gun and surrender, the woman told him that she was an undercover policewoman. With that, the thief gave in, dropped his revolver and waited patiently at gunpoint until the real police arrived to make the arrest. Albuquerque police have since offered the housewife a position on the city force. (*The Journal*, Albuquerque, N. Mex.)

Army sergeant Wilford Woodruff, his wife and three of their children were watching TV in the Woodruff's Ft. Gordon, Ga., home when two pistol-wielding thugs smashed their way inside. Sgt. Woodruff immediately grappled with the pair, while his wife got the children out of the way. The kids safe, Mrs. Woodruff got a .44 mag. revolver and went to help her husband. She found him wounded from the fight and opened fire on the bandits, killing one and critically injuring the other. Mrs. Woodruff was declared to have acted in self-defense, and was not charged. (*The Herald*, Augusta, Ga.)

Though the burglar alarm that went off early one morning proved a false one, Waco, Tex., grocer Andy Marquaret decided to stick around. His hunch was correct, for just as dawn was breaking, a man entered the store and headed straight for the cash register. Marquaret, armed with a .22 cal. revolver, confronted the would-be thief, ordering him to stop. When the man failed to heed his warning, Marquaret fired one shot that struck the intruder in the chest, felling him. (*The Tribune-Herald*, Waco, Tex.)

Mr. and Mrs. Michael Dickerson were asleep in their North Nashville, Tenn., home when Mrs. Dickerson was awakened by a prowler, apparently in the bedroom. She awakened her husband, who reached for his .357 Mag. revolver, getting it just in time to meet a lunging attack by the thwarted burglar. Dickerson fired once, felling his assailant. Police did not charge Dickerson in the shooting. "Mr. Dickerson was protecting his life, his wife, and his property," said a police spokesman. (*The Banner*, Nashville, Tenn.)

Ronald Bartnik had just closed his Buffalo, N.Y., tavern and was walking to his car when a young man approached him. "You I am going to kill," said the man, brandishing a knife. Bartnik did not flinch. He drew his licensed .38 cal. revolver and shot his attacker dead. Police, who recovered a knife at the scene, said that the shooting appeared to be justifiable, and turned the case over to the district attorney for routine presentation to the grand jury. (*The Courier-Express*, Buffalo, N.Y.)

The youth who attempted to rob Elmhurst, L.I. podiatrist, Dr. Marvin Lurie, could probably have chosen a better victim. Dr. Lurie, a decorated veteran of WWII combat and an NRA member, is licensed to carry a concealed handgun—and he carries one. When the knife-wielding thug slashed Lurie's arm and demanded drugs, Lurie drew his S & W revolver and shot his attacker. The wounded criminal fled. (*Newsday*, Long Island, N.Y.)

Ming Shiu's Minneapolis, Minn., electronic repair shop had been burglarized twice before, so when three men broke into the store, Shiu was ready. Caught in the shop as Shiu made an early morning check of his premises, the three tried to grapple with the businessman. Shiu eluded their grasp, drew a gun and fired, hitting one of the thugs and forcing all three to flee. (*The Tribune*, Minneapolis, Minn.)

Clifton Williams, a Buffalo, N.Y., armed security guard, returned to his home one evening to find a burglary in progress. Entering the premises, Williams confronted a man who was carrying off his TV set. Instead of surrendering, the thief dropped the set and lunged at Williams, who shot his attacker once, fatally. (*The Post-Star*, Glen Falls, N.Y.)

THE ARMED CITIZEN

Three Clintwood, Va. youths who ransacked a Ford dealership and a movie theater late one night, should have quit while they were ahead. Instead they drove their stolen pickup truck to Carlos Shortt's "Country Store" and began looting that establishment. It was a mistake. Shortt detected the presence of the youths and put a speedy end to their criminal career, by holding the trio at shotgun point until sheriff's deputies arrived to take them into custody. (*Cumberland Times,* Clintwood, Va.)

Charles Hiett was at his home in Portland, Ore., when he was alerted by suspicious noises coming from his garage. Arming himself with a pistol, Hiett investigated. He found a man leaving his garage, with a laundry basket full of food that had been in Hiett's freezer. Caught with the goods, the intruder surrendered and waited quietly for police to arrive and arrest him on a charge of second degree burglary. (*The Oregonian,* Portland, Ore.)

Anthony Lelis was relaxing at his Salt Lake City, Utah, home when he heard a cry for help. Investigating, he found a young woman being assaulted on his front lawn. Lelis called police, then took his .38 cal. handgun and went outside. When a warning shot went unheeded, Lelis fired twice at the would-be rapist, hitting him once and driving him away. Police arrested the man a short distance from the scene. (*The Tribune,* Salt Lake City, Utah)

DECEMBER 1979

James C. Wilson and his wife were asleep in their Fort Lauderdale, Fla., home when a noise near the bed startled them. Assuming that the family dog was restless, Mrs. Wilson reached down to pet it but found instead the unfriendly head of an intruder. Her husband grabbed a pistol from a nearby nightstand and ordered the stranger to surrender. When the man rushed him, Wilson fired and killed him. (*The Herald,* Miami, Fla.)

After two break-ins at his Fallentimber, Pa., general store, Robert McKee began sleeping in back. His vigil ended when, armed with a .357 Mag. revolver, he surprised a trio of would-be burglars. When McKee ordered them to lie on the floor, two obeyed but the third charged him, wielding a large screwdriver. McKee fired and hit his attacker in both legs with a load of birdshot. The three were held at gunpoint until police arrived. (*The Mirror,* Altoona, Pa.)

Dr. Herbert B. Frank was working late at his Philadelphia, Pa., office when two men, one armed with a pistol, waited until the office was empty and then announced a holdup. Frank, who wears a .38 cal. revolver under his smock, drew his gun and fired twice, killing one man and seriously wounding the other. (*The Inquirer,* Philadelphia, Pa.)

When Christie Jones heard a noise inside her Hollywood, Calif., home, she grabbed her .38 revolver and awoke her husband Cliff, who investigated and indeed found someone in the kitchen. When Jones opened the door, the intruder attacked, clubbing him with a pellet pistol and knifing him in the abdomen. Mrs. Jones fired twice but missed, then slipped the gun to her husband, who shot and killed his assailant. (*The Sun,* Las Vegas, Nev.)

Retired policeman Paul Hagerty was surprised to see a man and woman in the hallway of his Roxbury, Mass., apartment and got his revolver. Hagerty confronted the pair and was jumped by the young man. Hagerty managed to fire twice during the struggle and wounded his attacker, who leaped through a window and later was found dead by police. The female intruder, who had previously been convicted of armed robbery and assault, surrendered meekly. (*The Herald American,* Boston, Mass.)

Store manager Marvin Davies was displaying merchandise in a Decatur, Ga., jewelry store when a man leaped over the counter, jabbed a revolver in his side, and ushered him toward the rear of the store. Davies shouted to another employee in back, who grabbed a revolver and shot the would-be robber in the head, mortally wounding him. (*The Constitution,* Atlanta, Ga.)

Pharmacist Russell E. Simpson, Jr., was busy in his Virginia Beach, Va., shop when two men burst inside and announced a robbery. Simpson, a victim of 30 burglaries and robberies during the last 16 years, remained calm and was able to whip out a 12-ga. shotgun, which he fired at the feet of one of the would-be robbers. The man who was shot at managed to escape, but his bewildered accomplice surrendered. (*The Ledger-Star,* Norfolk, Va.)

Shortly after midnight, the Thomas V. Shouses were awakened by the doorbell at their Louisville, Ky., home. Shouse responded and found two women who asked to use the telephone. As the women entered, two male accomplices, one of them armed, burst into the house and demanded money and valuables. Shouse's wife, who had remained upstairs, heard the commotion and fired four warning shots from a .22-pistol; the foursome fled. (*The Courier-Journal,* Louisville, Ky.)

Seventeen-year-old Marsha Gilpatric, hearing a disturbance in the yard of her East Bridgewater, N.H., home, went to investigate, and was viciously attacked by two Staffordshire terriers. Fortunately, Eugene Morgan witnessed the attack and rushed to the defenseless girl's aid. Morgan killed one of the dogs with his .22 pistol, scared away the other. Gilpatric was rushed to a hospital for treatment of wounds to her nose, legs, and arms. (*The Enterprise,* Bristol, N.H.)

When Ted Fiorito pulled into the driveway of his Albion, N.Y., home, he noticed a window had been smashed. Upon further investigation, Fiorito sighted a man inside the house and then secured a shotgun, with which he held the intruder at bay until police arrived. (*The Journal Register,* Medina, N.Y.)

When three masked men, two of them armed, burst into an Irvington, N.J., bank, security guard Johnnie C. Mason reached for his revolver and ducked out of sight. After two of the robbers ran behind the counter, Mason ordered the third, who was standing guard by the door, to surrender. The robber whirled to fire, but Mason shot first and killed him. Mason then turned toward the counter and fired again, mortally wounding the other gunman. The unarmed robber thereupon surrendered. (*The Star Ledger,* Newark, N.J.)

When Rosa Cook heard a neighbor's cries for help, she armed herself, investigated, and found a man trying to force his way into the neighbor's Charlotte, N.C., home. After asking him to leave, Cook fired two warning shots and then, as the hoodlum threatened her and moved closer, fired once again, seriously wounding him. (*The Observer,* Charlotte, N.C.)

Security guard Samuel DeAngelo, Jr., was driving home when he noticed a man armed with a sawed-off shotgun entering a Kernville, Pa., grocery. Stopping in front of the store. DeAngelo drew his revolver and waited. When the robber slowly backed out of the door, DeAngelo ordered him to surrender; the startled robber complied and was held at gunpoint until police arrived. (*The Tribune-Democrat,* Johnstown, Pa.)

JANUARY 1980

1980

Dale Green, a Southern Pacific railroad employee, was working near Picacho Peak, Ariz., when he noticed two unmanned locomotives, coupled back to back, rolling down the tracks. Green grabbed his shotgun and, along with his fellow workers, jumped into a car and gave chase. After 20 miles, the driver pulled alongside the then speeding engines. Green fired several blasts at an air-brake hose and pierced it, causing the air brakes to activate and the $1 million locomotives to grind to a safe halt. (*The Republic,* Phoenix, Ariz.)

When two men entered his Detroit, Mich., market and announced a holdup, owner Tony Haddad was neither amused nor intimidated. He drew his .357 mag. revolver, threw one would-be robber to the floor and then collared the fleeing accomplice. Haddad, who has pulled his gun in self-defense 15 times in 11 months, held the pair at bay until police arrived. (*The News,* Detroit, Mich.)

Awakened by a knock at the door of his Memphis, Tenn., home, which had been burglarized earlier that week, Charles Murrell armed himself. From a window, he saw a man prying at the door with a crowbar. The intruder entered and confronted Murrell, approaching him with the crowbar raised in a threatening manner. After issuing repeated warnings to halt, Murrell fired and wounded the would-be burglar, who was soon taken into police custody. (*The Commercial Appeal,* Memphis, Tenn.)

Steve Menich, a disabled veteran, was sleeping alone at his Ohioville, Pa., home when the burglar alarm sounded. Armed with a pistol, Menich slowly searched the house. When he opened the cellar door, he was attacked by several intruders. Struck on the head and knocked to the floor, Menich still managed to fire several rounds at the intruders, who quickly fled. (*The Beaver County Times,* Beaver, Pa.)

Two men burst into a Wichita, Kans., jewelry store, tied owner Jerry Burnell to a chair, and proceeded to clean out the showcases. Burnell was able to free himself, grab a pistol and fire, mortally wounding one robber. The accomplice escaped unharmed. (*The Beacon,* Wichita, Kans.)

A man broke into the Richmond, Va., home of Brodus Cheatham, crept into the bedroom and demanded cash. Even though Cheatham complied with the demand, the thief punched him in the face. At that, Cheatham grabbed a .38 cal. revolver from under the bed and fired, seriously wounding his attacker, who fled but was later arrested by police. (*The News-Leader,* Richmond, Va.)

F. Russell Sprung was working at his Tucson, Ariz., car wash when he saw a man clutching a paper bag fleeing from a nearby bank. Sprung jumped into his pickup and pursued the suspected robber, who ducked into an apartment complex and emerged riding a bicycle. After drawing his revolver and ordering the man to stop, Sprung forced him off the road and, with the help of a bystander, managed to subdue the knife-wielding bandit until police took him into custody. (*The Daily Star,* Tucson, Ariz.)

A San Jose, Calif., woman was attacked by a would-be rapist who had entered her house through an unlocked window. The woman managed to break free, grab her revolver, and hold her assailant at gunpoint while she called police. (*The Mercury News,* San Jose, Calif.)

Shortly before 1 a.m., James Phillips, who lives above his optometrist father's Westfield, Mass., shop, heard someone smash the office door, grabbed his .22 cal. rifle and searched the premises. He found a man who claimed he had broken into the office to have his glasses repaired. Phillips marched the intruder at gunpoint to the nearest police station. (*The Daily News,* Springfield, Mass.)

159

Responding to a knock at the door of his Louisville, Ky., home, James F. Freeman was confronted by an armed man who ordered him and five friends to lie on the floor and then demanded cash. When Freeman's wife went into another room to get the money, the gunman followed. Freeman hurriedly found his revolver and greeted the robber with a burst of gunfire, wounding him in the side. The robber managed to escape with the cash but was later identified by Freeman at a hospital and arrested. (*The Courier-Journal,* Louisville, Ky.)

Gary Gentry, night manager of a Nashville, Tenn., liquor store, was alerted by a customer that a suspicious man was prowling around an adjacent market. Armed with a pistol, Gentry investigated and spied a man inside the market holding a knife to a clerk's throat. Gentry ordered him to drop the weapon and fall to the floor; the hoodlum obeyed and was held at gunpoint until police arrived. (*The Tennessean,* Nashville, Tenn.)

Cecil Perkins was sleeping in the back room of his Niagara Falls, N.Y., restaurant when he was awakened by the sound of shattering glass. After arming himself with a 16-ga. shotgun, Perkins discovered three would-be burglars and fired a warning shot. Two thieves fled but the third surrendered and was held at gunpoint until police arrived. (*The Evening News,* Buffalo, N.Y.)

A man armed with a pistol burst into a National City, Calif., food store and demanded money from the clerk, Basim Younan. Owner Nizar Habib Younan, working in the back room, found his revolver, came out firing and seriously wounded the would-be robber. (*The Star-News,* National City, Calif.)

Cheryl Thom, who lives above her West Bend, Wis., music store, heard suspicious noises shortly after midnight. Armed with a shotgun, she investigated and surprised an intruder, whom she ordered to leave. He did just that. (*The News,* West Bend, Wis.)

APRIL 1980

A man walked into an Atlanta, Ga., television repair shop, whipped out a pistol, and announced a robbery. Store clerk Frank Brand, who was carrying his own pistol, outdrew the gunman and fired. The wounded robber fled but was later apprehended by police. (*The Journal,* Atlanta, Ga.)

Timothy Lamprey, a police officer, was awakened by the doorbell at his Fairview Township, Pa., home. As he reached for a bathrobe, Lamprey heard someone break a window and come inside. When the intruder, a 17-year-old boy, eased into the bedroom, Lamprey grabbed his service revolver and apprehended him. (*The Evening News,* Harrisburg, Pa.)

After repeated break-ins at his John's Island, S.C., feed and liquor stores, William Brunson decided to conduct his own stakeout. He left the stores temporarily and returned to find three men standing in front of several broken store windows. Brunson held the trio at gunpoint until a passing police detective stopped to make the arrests. (*The Evening Post,* Charleston, S.C.)

When a burglar returned to a Marysville, Calif., jewelry store to make one final haul, he didn't expect to run into Daniel P. Burk, an employee who had been sleeping in the store since the earlier break-in. Burk watched silently as the thief forced open the skylight, threw down a rope, and lowered himself onto an 8 ft.-high partition. Burk then switched on the lights and held a shotgun on the would-be burglar until police responded. (*The Appeal-Democrat,* Marysville, Calif.)

Two men, one carrying a crowbar, entered a Norwich, N.Y., motorcycle shop, approached the owner's son, and asked to see an item from a wall display. When owner Loren Frink walked into the room and saw his son being beaten with the crowbar, he drew his pistol and fired. The would-be robbers fled unharmed but soon were arrested. (*The Sun-Bulletin,* Binghamton, N.Y.)

Awakened by the cries of her 6-year-old daughter, a Baytown, Tex., woman spied a male intruder hiding beside her bed. The woman grabbed a pistol she kept under her pillow, took the child in her arms, and ran into the next room. When the intruder followed, she shot him. The wounded man fled, but police found him hiding in some nearby bushes and wearing only a pair of socks. (*The Chronicle,* Houston, Tex.)

When Ernest Wright was awakened by the sound of a tractor-trailer coming to a halt outside his Corona, N. Mex., ranch house, he armed himself with a shotgun and investigated. When the driver kicked in the kitchen door and walked inside, Wright asked him to leave, then retreated to the hall. The intruder threw a crowbar at Wright, who fired one shot, hitting his attacker in the chest. State police found the wounded man inside the truck. (*The Lincoln County News,* Carrizozo, N. Mex.)

Dwayne Mahan was in the bedroom of his Paramount, Calif., home when someone knocked at the front door. His wife responded and found a woman who asked to use the phone. As the women talked, two men, one with a handgun and one with a knife, forced their way inside and ransacked the house. Mahan grabbed his shotgun and confronted the trio. When the gunman shot at him and missed, Mahan returned fire, wounding him and causing the male accomplice to flee. The woman surrendered peaceably. (*The Independent,* Long Beach, Calif.)

When J. C. King decided to leave work for a few minutes to stop by his Lake Wales, Fla., home, he found a burglar lugging an outboard motor out of the garage. As King drove up, the thief dropped the motor and ran, but King reached for his .22 cal. rifle and ordered him to stop. The burglar complied with King's demand and was held at gunpoint until deputies arrived. (*The Ledger*, Lakeland, Fla.)

When 89-year-old Fred Green saw a man leaving one of his vacant San Antonio, Tex., rental houses, he called police, found his pistol, and confronted the intruder, who started toward him in a threatening manner. When his warnings to halt were ignored, Green fired a shot near the would-be burglar's legs and thus persuaded him to wait peaceably until police arrived. (*The Daily News*, Amarillo, Tex.)

A bandit armed with a pistol walked into a Sacramento, Calif., liquor store and robbed its owner of cash, liquor, and cigarettes. As the robber was leaving the store, he fired a shot at the owner but missed. The owner then pulled his own pistol and shot the gunman in the chest, killing him instantly. (*The Sacramento Bee*, Sacramento, Calif.)

Walter Jackson was sitting in his car outside a Pontiac, Mich., market when a man wearing a ski-mask jumped into the car, pulled a gun, and ordered Jackson to drive home. Once inside the house, the gunman ransacked the bedroom and slugged Jackson in the mouth. At that, Jackson pulled a revolver from under the bed pillow and shot his assailant in the jaw. (*The Oakland Press*, Pontiac, Mich.)

JULY 1980

When two men rang the front doorbell of Jonathan Sargent's Toledo, Ohio, home, Sargent, who was in a garage behind the house, entered through the back door. One man went to the rear of the house, walked inside, and demanded Sargent's wallet. When the intruder attacked him, Sargent called for help, and a resident in an upstairs apartment joined the scuffle. Sargent slipped into the kitchen, got his pistol, and when the tenant broke free, shot the would-be robber to death. The accomplice fled uninjured. (*The Blade*, Toledo, Ohio)

A man and woman walked into a Phoenix, Ariz., jewelry store and began looking at rings. When the man pulled out a pistol and struck store owner Mirko Culibrk over the head with it, Culibrk went for his own revolver. As the man tried to leap over the counter, Culibrk fired, hitting the robber with two loads of birdshot. The female assailant fled; her companion died soon after arrival at a local hospital. (*The Arizona Republic*, Phoenix, Ariz.)

When two armed men entered his Mira Mesa, Calif., coin shop and announced a robbery, owner Roy Collins drew his revolver and exchanged shots with the gunmen. One robber fled, but the other grappled with Collins, pointed a gun at his head and threatened to kill him. At that, Collins's wife, who had secured her own pistol, shot the would-be robber, critically wounding him. (*The Union*, San Diego, Calif.)

Awakened by pounding at the front door of his Dade County, Fla., home, George Daubert peered through a peep hole, saw two men trying to break in, and found his revolver. When the intruders forced their way inside and were standing in the foyer, Daubert ordered them to freeze. As one man lunged at him, Daubert fired and wounded him. Both intruders fled, but the wounded man collapsed at a nearby corner and died soon after at a hospital. (*The Herald*, Miami, Fla.)

After repeated burglaries at his Pleasant Grove, Tex., used goods store, owner Ernest Graf and his 15-year-old son started sleeping in the office. Awakened by noises on the roof. Graf armed himself with his shotgun and waited. When the would-be burglar was half way down a rope he had secured to the skylight, Graf switched on the lights and held him at bay while his son called police. The intruder, it turned out, was wanted for three Dallas-area murders. (*The Times Herald*, Dallas, Tex.)

When a neighbor called to report intruders in the garage of her Indianapolis, Ind., home, Gladys O'Brien set off the burglar alarm, found her pistol, and investigated. Accompanied by the neighbor, O'Brien surprised two men inside the garage and held one at bay until police arrived; the other intruder fled. (*The Palladium-Item*, Richmond, Ind.)

A man entered a Waterbury, Conn., liquor store, snuck up on owner Frank Tuttolo, and slugged him on the back of the head. The attacker then shoved Tuttolo to the floor, threw the cash register on him, and began punching him in the face and groin. Tuttolo was able to reach a pistol under the counter and fire several shots. His assailant, wounded in the neck, fled but was later apprehended by police. (*The Republican*, Waterbury, Conn.)

Seventy-six-year-old Wilma Hamilton was working outside her Tampa, Fla., home when a man demanding money grabbed her by the neck and threatened her with a concrete block. The robber ushered Hamilton into the house, released the choke hold, and started searching for cash. Hamilton then took a revolver from a drawer and chased her assailant through the house. When he stopped to threaten her with the block still in hand, Hamilton fired and wounded him. The would-be robber fled but was later arrested. (*The Times*, Tampa, Fla.)

THE ARMED CITIZEN

Greta Young walked inside her Baltimore, Md., apartment and was confronted by a 14-year-old intruder armed with a knife and a meat cleaver. When Young tried to run to safety, the youth forced her into a bedroom and demanded money. Young then pulled a revolver from under the mattress and shot her assailant to death. (*The Sun*, Baltimore, Md.)

A man and woman entered a Blackwood, N.J., jewelry store and asked to see some gold rings. When owner Anthony Travia set a ring tray on the counter, the man pulled a handgun and demanded all the jewelry. Travia whipped out his own revolver and in an exchange of gunfire killed the gunman. The accomplice was held at bay until police arrived. (*The Bulletin*, Philadelphia, Pa.)

Jorge Linan had just closed his San Jose, Calif., liquor store and was putting a money bag in his car when a man wearing a ski mask and carrying a sawed-off shotgun approached and demanded the money. When Linan backed out of the car, he came up with his revolver instead of the money bag and shot the gunman to death. (*The Mercury*, San Jose, Calif.)

Cy Cohen was working behind the counter of his Topeka, Kans., cutlery when a man who claimed he had a gun approached him and announced a robbery. As Cohen opened the cash register and put the money on the counter, he drew his own pistol. The would-be robber beat a hasty retreat. (*The Daily Capital*, Topeka, Kans.)

OCTOBER 1980

When a Perry, Fla., woman refused to admit a stranger who asked to use her bathroom, he forced entry, and attempted to rape her at knife point. The woman retreated to a bedroom, grabbed a .22 revolver, and shot her assailant as he broke into the room. As the wounded man fled, the woman pursued and shot at his fleeing auto, which piled into a tree. Deputies said that the mortally wounded rapist, an ex-convict, was driving a stolen car and was a suspect in an earlier rape and possible child molestation incident. (*The Democrat*, Tallahassee, Fla.)

Alton Altizer heard the sound of breaking glass about 3 a.m. at the gun store in the same building with his Arnoldsburg, W.Va., apartment. Altizer called state police, then he went outside to investigate. When Altizer hailed a man carrying three rifles from Bartlett's Gun Store, the man spun in his direction, and Altizer fired his 12-ga. shotgun. The burglar, a recently released three-time escapee from the state penitentiary, was dead at the scene. Police said a stolen car with 18 handguns taken from the store was parked nearby. (*The Inter-Mountain*, Elkins, W. Va.)

Two men accused in the kidnap-rape of a 20-year-old woman in the Boston area were apprehended by police after an Andover, Mass., resident, Henry Lebensbaum, pumped six rounds into their escaping auto. The woman, kidnapped from in front of a Boston night spot and then sexually assaulted, escaped screaming from the car in Andover. Lebensbaum, who came running to her aid, put one of his bullets through a tire. The pair was arrested after abandoning the car. (*The Eagle-Tribune*, Lawrence, Mass.)

When an armed robber threatened to kill three fellow employees and the manager of a suburban Dallas supermarket as they lay at gunpoint on the store's floor, clerk Kathy Carter whispered a prayer and killed him with a single shot from a pistol concealed in her cashier's booth. (*The Times Herald*, Dallas, Tex.)

Mr. and Mrs. Roy Shock were suspicious when a young man came to their isolated New Paris, Ohio, home, awakening them to use a telephone. Minutes later, the man returned to their door and attempted to drag Shock outside. When a second man came through the door with a shotgun and attempted to get a bead on her struggling husband, Mrs. Shock fired at him with a handgun. He fled and later was found dead nearby. Shock's assailant also fled, but later surrendered to authorities. (*The Daily News*, Dayton, Ohio)

Corbin, Ky., motel operator Ray Miracle came upon state trooper James Phelps attempting to subdue two drunken occupants of a stopped auto and, carrying his revolver, went to the officer's aid. At that point, another car stopped and one of two men inside levelled a gun on Trooper Phelps. Seeing Miracle's drawn gun, however, they hastily drove off. Kentucky State Police rewarded Miracle with their highest civilian honor. (*The Times-Tribune*, Corbin, Ky.)

Seventy-year-old Baxter Blagg was preparing to retire when a man climbed through the bedroom window of his Salupa, Okla., home and aimed a revolver at his head. When his wife rushed through the room, distracting the intruder, Blagg was able to snatch his .38 from beneath a pillow. He fired and fatally wounded his assailant, who turned out to be an escaped convict. (*The Tribune*, Tulsa, Okla.)

Home with her children while her police officer husband was on duty, Lorelei Mehler heard a prowler outside her Bay Shore, N.Y., home. After calling police, she discovered a kitchen window had been opened. She fetched an M1 rifle from a bedroom in time to smack the burglar as he came through the window and then pursued him outside, showering him with blows. Two arriving policemen arrested the culprit. (*Newsday*, Long Island, N.Y.)

162

After his Kennewick, Wash., auto garage had been burglarized on two consecutive nights, owner Bradford Smith decided to sleep in the office. Shortly after midnight a burglar entered the office, pried open the money drawer, and found a note that read "GOTCHA." Smith then pumped a shell into his shotgun and held the would-be burglar at bay until police arrived. (*The Post-Intelligencer,* Seattle, Wash.)

Bob Bennett was behind the counter in his East Greenwich, R.I., coin and stamp shop when a robber wearing a halloween mask demanded money. Bennett grabbed his .32 cal. pistol, and in an exchange of fire was wounded in the forearm. The would-be robber fled, but police soon arrested a man seeking treatment for two bullet wounds. (*The Journal-Bulletin,* Providence, R.I.)

Two young men entered 95-year-old Maude Riffe's North Denver, Colo., home shortly after midnight, and one of them pressed a gun to her head and demanded money. When she could offer only her Social Security check, the pair left empty-handed, only to return minutes later. This time, however, the homeowner greeted them at a window with her double-barrel shotgun. They fled and didn't return. (*The Rocky Mountain News,* Denver, Colo.)

Plano, Tex., attorney M. G. Davis was entering a savings and loan when warned that a man at the drive-in window had a bomb. Davis, a former intelligence officer, rushed across a hallway and grabbed a .38 from his office. He then raced outside and confronted the fleeing suspect, who surrendered only after Davis fired a warning shot in the air. (*The Morning News,* Dallas, Tex.)

FEBRUARY 1981

When John Woolman responded to a knock at the door of his Porter, Ind., home, a man threatened his life and demanded entry. Woolman refused to admit the man and went for his revolver. In the meantime, the man had broken down the front door and entered the living room. When the intruder again threatened and advanced toward him. Woolman fired a shot that wounded him and then summoned police. (*The Tribune,* Chesterton, Ind.)

Two deer hunters taking target practice about six miles from the Montana State Prison recently apprehended three escaped convicts who had eluded a massive manhunt for two days. Ron Collins, an ex-guard at the prison, and Graham Blacklock spotted the three hiding in sagebrush and held them at gun-point until authorities could arrive. (*The Missoulian,* Missoula, Mont.)

Three armed men entered a Santa Barbara, Calif., jewelry store, ordered manager Steven Brooks and two customers to lie on the floor, and began smashing into display cases. When owner Robert Bryant, who saw the robbery on closed-circuit TV, started down a stairs to the show room, a robber fired on him. Bryant killed two robbers with his shotgun, but was wounded by the third man. At that point store manager Brooks pulled his own pistol and fatally wounded Bryant's attacker. (*The News-Press,* Santa Barbara, Calif.)

St. Louis, Mo., restaurateur Gus Kircher started carrying a gun in his restaurant after he was robbed of $600. A week later a robber accosted Kircher and two female companions in an alley as they returned to the restaurant. The robber put a gun to the one woman's head, demanded money, and pulled the trigger four times. It didn't fire. Kircher pushed the gun aside and shot the robber twice, fatally wounding him. Police found two unfired rounds in the deceased's revolver. (*The Post-Dispatch,* St. Louis, Mo.)

Forced by an armed robber to kneel on the floor at the rear of his Phoenix, Ariz., pharmacy and then knocked unconscious, Robert Wells recovered enough to crawl to a hidden handgun. Returning to the front of the store, Wells confronted his assailant, fired one shot, and wounded the robber who was soon arrested. (*The Gazette,* Phoenix, Ariz.)

1981

NRA Life member Richard Willard awoke to the sounds of someone rummaging about his Woolwich, Maine, home. Armed with a pistol, he entered his living room and confronted an intruder who threw a chair at him. Willard fired one shot that sent the man crashing through a door in a hasty retreat. (*The Newspaper,* Wiscasset, Maine)

An unidentified woman clad only in panties heard a glass door shatter in her suburban Cincinnati home. Picking up a .32 revolver, she went to investigate and encountered an intruder in the hall. She screamed and levelled the gun at the man, who fled and eluded a police search. (*The Enquirer,* Cincinnati, Ohio)

Entering his law office in Bangor, Maine, attorney Peter A. Anderson, an NRA Life member, found a burglar hiding behind his desk. Anderson drew his licensed .357 Mag. revolver, ordered the intruder to stay where he was, and called police. The man, who was armed with a knife, was a suspect in other burglaries. (*The Daily News,* Bangor, Maine)

Three 16-year-olds entered the tiny Towers Book and Card shop operated by 68-year-old Murray Elpern and his wife in the Bronx. One came behind the counter and pressed a 9 mm pistol to Elpern's head. When Mrs. Elpern pressed an alarm, another vaulted a counter and grabbed her. With the gun-wielder distracted, Elpern drew his licensed .38 revolver and shot him. A second robber lunged at Elpern and was shot, while the other one surrendered and was held for police. (*The Daily News,* New York, N.Y.)

Alone at home while her husband was elk hunting, Doris Walls shot a 33-year-old who she said broke into her Hermiston, Ore., residence and attempted to rape her. The suspect, wounded in the shoulder by a .30-30 round, was charged with burglary and attempted rape. (*The Hermiston Herald,* Hermiston, Ore.)

Atlanta, Ga., jeweler Bob Jordan, working at his repair bench, looked up to see two men holding guns on his wife and his associate. A veteran of numerous robbery attempts, Jordan dove for a back room as one gunman shot twice. Coming up shooting, Jordan fatally wounded one robber with his .380 semi-automatic and chased the other one from the store. (*The Constitution,* Atlanta, Ga.)

Norma and Eduardo Ortega returned to their Miami, Fla., home to find two burglars ransacking their belongings. One burglar fled the house when Mrs. Ortega found her pistol and fired, but the other hid in a bathroom. He was spread-eagled on the living room floor when police arrived. The second suspect, a juvenile, was arrested later. (*The Herald,* Miami, Fla.)

Jim Gardner was asleep in his Wixom, Mich., apartment when he heard a knock at the door. Finding no one there, Gardner returned to bed, only to then hear noises at his second floor balcony door. Armed with his revolver, Gardner opened the drapes and watched a would-be burglar back over a railing, tumble to the ground and flee. (*The Spinal Column,* Novi, Mich.)

MAY 1981

Robert Teumer was taking an afternoon nap when his son ran in, shouting that a pair of intruders had entered their Hammond, Ind., home. Grabbing a shotgun, Teumer ran to investigate and chased the pair out a side door. The Teumers jumped in their car and caught up with one of the housebreakers, holding him for police. (*The Times,* Calumet, Ill.,)

A stickup man had been plaguing convenience stores in the Salisbury, Md., area, so when Robert Brown saw a man fitting the robber's description approaching his store, he reached for a gun. When the would-be robber pulled a pistol from his coat, Brown drew his own gun and the criminal fled. (*The Daily Times,* Salisbury, Md.)

City Councilor Albert L. "Dapper" O'Neil was leaving a Boston, Mass., restaurant when he encountered an old friend, William Vaughn, a probation officer from Dorchester, Mass. Vaughn had been attacked by a mugger with a knife, and had shot the thug, who fled. O'Neil and Vaughn took off in pursuit, chasing the criminal for a few blocks and holding him for police with their licensed revolvers. (*The Herald-American,* Boston, Mass.)

When he saw three robbers speeding away from a grocery store near his El Paso, Ark., service station, Jim Smith grabbed a .44 Mag. revolver and a 12-ga. shotgun and gave chase. He pursued the trio for several miles, eventually catching one stickup man and holding him for police. "I'm a Christian and I go to church," Smith said, "but I don't want people running over us." (*The Arkansas Gazette,* Little Rock, Ark.)

"Give me all your money or I'll blow your head off," was the command of an armed robber who walked up to John Gregg's Denver, Colo., gas station pay booth. Gregg dived for the floor of the booth and opened up with a .45 cal. automatic through the wall. The robber and an accomplice fled empty-handed. (*The Rocky Mountain News,* Denver, Colo.)

A would-be burglar got a nasty shock when he tried to rob George Highsmith's Terre Haute, Ind., home. Highsmith fired warning shots at the criminal, who ran for his life. (*The Tribune,* Terre Haute, Ind.)

Gary Boozer had suffered two burglaries at his Metaline Falls, Wash., pharmacy and was in no mood for more. When a silent alarm alerted him to a break in, Boozer grabbed a gun and caught two culprits with cash and drugs. (*The Daily Chronicle,* Spokane, Wash.)

A gas thief shouldn't have pushed his luck after he escaped Guy Bolin, who was guarding his Center Point, Tex., service station with a shotgun. But the man returned a bit later to retrieve his car, which he'd forgotten in his haste to get out of range of Bolin's smoothbore. The second time around, Bolin caught and held him for police. (*The Paper,* Center Point, Tex.)

A Lynchburg, Va., housebreaker suffered the ultimate indignity when he was caught trying to enter Buford Thornhill's home. The armed homeowner forced the sneak thief to call police and report the crime himself. (*The News,* Lynchburg, Va.)

John and Deby Matthews were asleep early one morning in their Las Cruces, N. Mex., home when they heard the sounds of cabinet doors opening and closing. John leaped from bed and tackled the intruder, while Deby grabbed a 12-ga. shotgun and followed behind. They held a youthful housebreaker until police arrived. (*The Sun-News,* Las Cruces, N. Mex.)

Burglars had broken into Dean French's Cedar Flats, Wash., home a dozen times within a year, so one morning he pretended to leave for work, and then surreptitiously returned to keep watch for housebreakers. His patience was rewarded when he captured an 18-year-old burglar at gunpoint. (*The Daily Olympian,* Olympia, Wash.)

Jennifer Ivy had stopped at a cafe near her Chelan, Wash., home to get a soft drink to go. She hadn't driven far when a would-be rapist jumped from the back seat into the front next to her. As the thug slashed at her with a knife, she slammed on the brakes, grabbed a .22 pistol, and opened fire. The assailant beat a hasty retreat, along with two accomplices who were following in another car. Chelan County Sheriff Larry Hively said of the incident, "having the gun in her possession seems to have saved her from considerable harm." (*The Post-Intelligencer,* Seattle, Wash.)

A trio of young thugs, after kidnapping a San Francisco woman, forced her to drive them to the San Rafael, Calif., jewelry store of Tony Spitaleri. When they dragged their hostage into his store and demanded cash, Spitaleri responded by drawing a gun. The surprised hoodlums then beat a hasty retreat. (*The Independent-Journal,* San Rafael, Calif.)

Two farm equipment thieves made the mistake of picking the Oley Township, Pa., property of Daniel Levengood on which to ply their trade. As the pair loaded equipment onto a truck, Levengood and his son arrived with a shotgun and held them for police. (*The Eagle,* Reading, Pa.)

Two holdup men, one brandishing a knife, tried to extract money from Al Hewitt at his Buffalo, N.Y., liquor store but had a quick change of heart when Hewitt reached under the counter and produced a gun. They fled empty-handed. (*The Evening News,* Buffalo, N.Y.)

AUGUST 1981

Gladys Kastensmith, 77, was awakened by the sounds of someone trying to break into her Phoenix, Ariz., home. Her .38 revolver in hand, she found a man trying to enter by crawling through her doggie door. When the man refused to leave, the great-grandmother fired three shots into a wall that sent him backtracking. Unbelieveably, the intruder returned and again attempted to wedge his way through the small opening. Police arriving at the scene found the man lodged in the door and staring into a revolver being leveled at him from a nearby rocking chair. (*The Arizona Republic,* Phoenix, Ariz.)

When he received a phone call from an elderly neighbor saying that a man was trying to break in her bedroom window, George Underwood, a retired Holly Springs, N.C., sheriff's constable, knew what to do. Grabbing a rifle, he ran to the house and found a young man attempting to break in through a kitchen door. When the man refused to stop breaking the glass door, Underwood shot him in the leg. The would-be intruder then fled, only to be apprehended by police minutes later. (*The Times,* Raleigh, N.C.)

Brian Berg arrived at his Racine, Wis., home to hear glass breaking in a rear hallway. Seeing an arm appear through the broken glass, Berg grabbed his handgun and then chased a startled would-be burglar from the house. When the man refused to stop, Berg fired warning shots that brought him to a halt. Berg then escorted the culprit to a neighbor's house where police were called. (*The Journal Times,* Racine, Wis.)

Three men entered a Macon, Ga., restaurant, and one pointed a sawed-off rifle at proprietor Archie McBride and demanded cash. Instead of complying with the demand, McBride pulled out a pistol and shot the gunman once in the stomach. The three bandits fled, but the wounded man died the following day at a local hospital. A coroner's jury ruled that McBride had acted justifiably. (*The Constitution,* Atlanta, Ga.)

Donna Stotts, a janitor at a Oklahoma City church, arrived at 3 a.m. to clean floors when she was attacked by a rapist, who slashed her with a switch-blade knife. Wiping the blood from her eyes, she pulled a .32 cal. automatic and put the attacker to flight. "If he had've come any closer I probably would have shot him," she said. "But I hated to kill anybody in a church." (*Friday,* Oklahoma City, Okla.).

Robert Green was inside the camper parked in his Wichita Falls, Tex., driveway when he spotted a man breaking into a neighbor's house. He grabbed his pistol, ran to the house, and confronted the burglar as he emerged from a side door. Green held the man until police arrived. (*The Record News,* Wichita Falls, Tex.)

Buffalo, N.Y., welfare worker Mary Guidice was working at her desk in the Rath County Office Building when a recipient, enraged by the news that he would have to fill out some forms to receive benefits, began beating a welfare examiner. Guidice pulled her licensed pistol and subdued the attacker. (*The Evening News,* Buffalo, N.Y.)

Awakened by the sound of the front door screen of his Virginia Beach, Va., home being pushed in, Thomas Smith picked up a shotgun and began to search the house. He found a man in the dining room and asked what he was doing there. When the intruder approached, Smith retreated, asking him to leave. The man instead made a threatening gesture and kept coming, and Smith fired, killing him. (*The Ledger-Star,* Norfolk, Va.)

A man entered Irv Huppin's Portland, Oreg., pharmacy, displayed a handgun, and threw a bag on the counter, yelling "hurry up and get the stuff." Huppin, who had been robbed three times in the preceding six months, drew a handgun from his back pocket and began firing. The wounded thief beat a hasty retreat. (*The Oregonian,* Portland, Oreg.)

THE ARMED CITIZEN

An unidentified Rawlins, Wyo., woman was awakened about 4 a.m. by noises at the front door of her home. Thinking it might be her husband, she shouted out his name but got no response. When she approached the door armed with a shotgun, a man who had been trying to jimmy the door open with a screwdriver quickly fled. (*The Daily Times,* Rawlins, Wyo.)

Seeing a man carrying a purse run across a nearby yard, Kenneth Luigs went to investigate and found an elderly female neighbor lying on the sidewalk in front of his Evansville, Ind., house. Luigs comforted the mugging victim, then grabbed a rifle, got in his car, and drove around hoping to find the attacker. He soon spotted the suspect and made a citizen's arrest. (*The Press,* Evansville, Ind.)

Larry Womack was inside his Austin, Tex., service station when he heard screams coming from behind a nearby building. Picking up his .357 Mag. revolver, Womack ran to the scene to find a rape in progress. One warning shot sent the assailant fleeing, and after Womack checked the condition of the young victim, he set off in pursuit. He apprehended the suspect and then held him for the police. (*The American-Statesman,* Austin, Tex.)

Awakened by noises coming over the intercom burglary system he rigged up between his house and his Murray, Nebr., service station, Jim Gruber picked up a shotgun and ran to investigate. Two burglars fleeing from the store were brought to bay by warning shots from Gruber's 12-ga. (*The Journal,* Lincoln, Nebr.)

NOVEMBER 1981

Mary Markham was willing to hand over cash to two criminals who burst into her Mount Clemens, Mich., liquor store. But when one robber put a pistol to her son's head and his partner opened fire on her husband, she had to take action. Grabbing a pair of pistols, she loosed a fusillade of shots at the crooks, killing both. A police officer on the scene noted that one robber was hit three times and the other five, commenting, "that's pretty good shooting from two hands—for anyone." (*The News,* Detroit, Mich.)

In seven years of facing criminals at his Glendale, Calif., jewelry store, Ed Kovacs has been held up four times, but has never lost a dime to robbers. The criminals, on the other hand, have suffered two dead and two wounded. In the most recent incident, a trio of criminals entered and demanded loot. Kovacs hauled out a .38 instead, killing one shotgun-armed robber, wounding a second, and holding the third inside the store with the help of an electric lock. Kovacs said World War II service in Italy taught him "if someone points a gun at you, shoot him." (*The Times,* Los Angeles, Calif.)

One holdup man was killed and his partner wounded when they tried to rob the Miami discount store of Vincent Molina and Gerardo Fojo. As the robbers demanded cash, one of Fojo's brothers began flinging soft drink bottles at the pair. In the confusion, Fojo and Molina grabbed their own guns and opened up, killing one robber and putting the other to flight. He was pursued by two passers-by in a CB radio-equipped cars, who chased him to a nearby hospital. (*The Herald,* Miami, Fla.)

"You wouldn't use that, now honey," a would-be burglar said as he advanced on Linda Gulleege in her Phoenix, Ariz., home. Her reply was a warning shot from a .44 revolver that sent the man fleeing. (*The Gazette,* Phoenix, Ariz.)

When a man-woman team of holdup artists made their second raid on his West Seattle, Wash., pharmacy in a week, it was too much for Bill Shuey. He armed himself with a pistol and gave chase, running the woman robber to ground and holding her for police. (*The Times,* Seattle, Wash.)

A Union Township, Ohio, housebreaker got a humiliating shock as he tried to exit the home of 14-year-old John Martino. Martino and four young chums were waiting for him armed with BB guns. The youngsters held the red-faced burglar for police. (*The Community Journal,* Clermont Co., Ohio)

Ben Grisar was leaving his Brooklyn, N.Y., ice cream store when he was set upon by five muggers. Although severely beaten, he managed to pull his licensed .38 cal. revolver and open fire, wounding one and sending the rest fleeing. (*The Post,* New York, N.Y.)

Newburgh, N.Y., homeowner Dale Southwell heard the sounds of forced entry into his home and investigated, armed with a .22 rifle. He found a pair of youthful housebreakers stealing his wife's purse. He demanded they freeze, and when they didn't, managed to get off a single shot before the rifle jammed. Police apprehended the 15-year-old suspect as he sought medical attention for a bullet wound in his legs. The youth was on probation for an earlier crime—pistol-whipping and robbing an elderly woman. (*The Times-Herald Record,* Newburgh, N.Y.)

Thelma Kouba, 85, suffering from shock, had to be removed from her home by ambulance, after a neighbor's pet bear tried to break into her Garwin, Iowa, home. The result was kept from being worse by her son George, who shot the bear twice, slowing it down enough for a game warden to deliver the coup de grace. (*The State Journal and Register,* Springfield, Ill.)

An armed robber announced with a glazed look that he was going to kill Nashville, Tenn., convenience store cashier Betsy Harris. Harris managed to distract the criminal long enough to draw her own .38 revolver and open fire, wounding her assailant. (*The Banner,* Nashville, Tenn.)

Freddie Malone watched from his wheelchair as a criminal walked out of his Houston, Tex., home carrying his televison set. But he wasn't going to let the man beat him up, too. As the crook advanced he pulled a pistol and fired once, killing the attacker. (*The Post,* Houston, Tex.)

Warren Redmond, 87, handed over money to a 15-year-old delinquent who invaded his Louisville, Ky., home. But when the young criminal began to beat him, Redmond grabbed a .44 Mag. revolver and fired once, killing the assailant. (*The Times,* Louisville, Ky.)

The operator of a 48-ft. yacht owned by noted defense attorney F. Lee Bailey was ready for action when a boatload of pirates attacked the craft north of the Bahamas. Paul Roadman of Needham, Mass., returned the brigands' fire with a .30 cal. rifle, forcing them to break off their attack. When the Coast Guard inquired by radio whether he needed help, Roadman, hoping the criminals were listening, replied that he "had enough ammunition to start a war." The pirates disappeared. (*The News & Courier,* Charleston, S.C.)

When he heard the sounds of forcible entry at his family's St. Paul, Minn., home, 11-year-old Craig Tschida grabbed a 20-ga. shotgun and went to investigate. A masked burglar took one look at the armed youngster and beat a quick retreat out the nearest window. (*The Dispatch,* St. Paul, Minn.)

MARCH 1982

Steven and Marion Winn were stopped at a Miami, Fla., traffic light when an elderly woman in the car next to them began to gesture frantically for help. The Winns gave chase and followed the car for some distance before it abruptly stopped. Winn pulled his .38 cal. revolver as a pair of kidnappers bolted from the car. The woman and a friend had been sitting in the back seat of the car waiting for their husbands when the criminal pair jumped in and drove off. (*The Herald,* Miami, Fla.)

John C. Fletcher was working in his Pewaukee, Wis., gun store when he heard a hammering on one of the building's walls. He grabbed a .357 Mag. revolver and went to investigate. He found a would-be burglar trying to pound his way into the store. (*The Freeman,* Waukesha, Wis.)

Kahlil Gibran was seeing two guests out the front door of his Boston home when he decided to watch them walk down his block. As the pair strolled down the street, Gibran, a sculptor and godson of the famous mystic poet of the same name, saw a young man start walking after them. Gibran retrieved his licensed pistol and gave chase, catching up just as the criminal began poking one of his friends with a 7″ knife. Gibran held him for police. (*The Herald-American,* Boston, Mass.)

Retired postal clerk Clark Goodwin, 68, saw a pair of men leave his next-door neighbor's house and try to break into the neighbor's car. When he challenged them, one man fired at him with a .22 cal. pistol. Goodwin opened up with his own pistol, routing the two. The next-door neighbor was found severely beaten and rolled up in a carpet. Police speculated that the criminals planned to return and kill him. Goodwin was honored by the St. Louis Grand Jury Ass'n for his action. (*The Globe-Democrat,* St. Louis, Mo.)

Minnie Storer and her husband, both 77, returned to their Sacramento, Calif., trailer home one evening to find a youthful burglar inside. When the hoodlum began to beat her husband, Mrs. Storer pulled a .38-cal. revolver from a chair and fired, hitting the assailant in the abdomen. (*The Union,* Sacramento, Calif.)

Liem Nguyen, formerly of the South Vietnamese army, made use of his training when he saw a strongarm robbery in progress. The San Jose, Calif., resident grabbed an M1 carbine from the trunk of his car and fired two warning shots. The robbers, who had taken a bag of money from a store clerk on her way to a night depository, dropped their loot and ran. (*The Mercury,* San Jose, Calif.)

Connie Albritton had been robbed five times in one year, and had decided that she wasn't going to let it happen again. After a criminal robbed her at knifepoint inside the Tampa, Fla., bar where she worked, she followed the man into a parking lot, leveled a .25 automatic and held him for police. (*The Tribune,* Tampa, Fla.)

A pair of thugs started beating Woodrow Wilson Glanton of Newark, N.J.; they took his wallet, his money and his car keys. But the 69-year-old Glanton drew a .25 automatic and opened fire, hitting one of the criminals in the chest, killing him. The other robber was wounded by an irate relative of the dead man when he reported the crime and killing. (*The Star-Ledger,* Newark, N.J.)

Joseph Hodson, 73, was reading a newspaper in his rocking chair when a young robber entered his Indianapolis, Ind., home. The intruder ripped Hodson's phone from the wall and began to ransack the house. Hodson armed himself with a double-barreled shotgun and, when the robber charged him, loosed a single blast that killed the criminal instantly. (*The Star,* Indianapolis, Ind.)

The instincts gained from enduring five robberies in 10 years told Louis Anderson that something was wrong when three men entered his Oakland, Calif., tavern. After one demanded cash and bashed him on the head, Anderson drew a derringer and shot him twice. The doughty barman then pulled a 9 mm automatic and shot it out with the three criminals, wounding two and being hit three times himself. Anderson, who had killed an armed robber three years earlier, said he would keep his establishment open: "It's my business ain't it? The rest didn't run me out." (*The Tribune*, Oakland, Calif.)

When an armed robber pointed a .22 pistol at him and demanded money, Tulsa, Okla., liquor store owner Thomas Shaw reached instead for a .357 Mag. revolver. He opened up and hit the criminal once in the head and three times in the chest, killing him on the spot. The robber had a criminal record dating back to 1942 and had killed a man in 1952. Police called the dead man "an 11-time loser." (*The Tribune*, Tulsa, Okla.)

An armed robber pointed a pistol at Hamilton, Ohio, grocer William Hieb and demanded cash. As the criminal rifled his cash register, Hieb grabbed a .38 cal. revolver and opened fire; hitting him three times. The robber tried to flee in a waiting car, but died before he got far. (*The Enquirer*, Cincinnati, Ohio)

Edward Martin started to get nervous when a customer began to fidget and move to the center of the back seat of his cab. The St. Louis cabbie's fears were confirmed when the man reached over the seat, stabbed him and demanded cash. Martin responded by firing his .25 automatic, hitting the criminal three times. The man, who was linked to other cab holdups, died of the wounds. (*The Post-Dispatch*, St. Louis, Mo.)

JUNE 1982

Rev. Martin Jarreau was asleep in the rectory of St. Ann's Catholic Church in Miami when he heard strange noises. He grabbed a .38 cal. revolver and went to investigate. He found a would-be burglar trying to exit via a bathroom window. Fr. Jarreau held the man, who had a long criminal record, for police. (*The Herald*, Miami, Fla.)

American Airlines flight attendant Teresa Quinn saw a man sneaking into a neighbor's garage near her Dallas, Tex., home. Armed with a revolver, Quinn confronted the man and held him for more than 20 minutes before police arrived. Police accused the man of setting six separate fires in North Dallas homes; he had already been convicted of setting fire to two homes and four automobiles and was out on bond. A fire investigator said of the intrepid stewardess "we need more folks like her." (*The Morning News*, Dallas, Tex.)

Dennis Gray had kept a rusty old .38 in his hall closet for almost 30 years, long enough for the ammunition to start to corrode in the cylinder. But when a burglar broke down the door of his San Diego, Calif., home, the gun did its part. Gray opened up, hitting the criminal in the neck and putting him to flight. (*The Tribune*, San Diego, Calif.)

A youthful hoodlum leaped over the counter of Alma Harris' South San Diego, Calif., restaurant and attacked her. As he tried to strangle her with a telephone cord, she grabbed a revolver and shot him four times. The assailant fled, but only made it about a block before collapsing. (*The Union*, San Diego, Calif.)

Frank Rock heard someone breaking into his Racine, Wis., home. He grabbed a .22 rifle and went to investigate. He found a youthful burglar just inside a bedroom window. Despite the homeowner's order to freeze, the intruder tried to dive out the window. Rock fired once, hitting him in the buttocks. Police caught up with the would-be burglar at a nearby hospital. (*The Journal-Times*, Racine, Wis.)

Palm Beach, Fla. blue jeans wholesaler Charles Bradley decided to stand guard at his warehouse, armed with a 12-ga. shotgun. His patience paid off when he heard a pair of burglars stuffing jeans into the trunk of their car. When his order to halt was unheeded, Bradley fired, injuring one thief. Both burglars were later captured by police. (*The Post*, W. Palm Beach, Fla.)

Israel Abel was fed up with the robberies his Miami jewelry store had suffered and was ready for action when five armed robbers stuck up his place and tried to kidnap his sister. The sister fainted as one robber tried to take her from the store, giving Abel the chance to grab a gun from under the counter and open fire. One criminal was killed, while the other four fled for their lives. Abel's sister was unharmed. (*The Ledger*, Lakeland, Fla.)

C. H. Meadows, 83, awoke to find an intruder choking his wife. When the Longview, Tex., householder tried to intervene, the criminal threatened him with a butcher knife. When the intruder began ransacking the house for loot, Meadows grabbed a .410 shotgun and opened fire, hitting the assailant in the shoulder and putting him to flight. (*The Herald Zietung*, New Braunfels, Tex.)

Ward Yont, 17, was cruising a Phoenix, Ariz., street in his pickup truck when he saw a young hoodlum snatch a purse from an old woman and run. Yont pursued the criminal for several blocks, both in the truck and on foot, before catching him and holding him for police with his .38 cal. revolver. A police officer on the scene said, "I wish we had more citizens in town who would get involved like that." (*The Gazette*, Phoenix, Ariz.)

When her dog began barking, Cecilia Cates decided to retrieve her .22 cal. rifle from the bedroom of her Moon Lake, Fla., trailer and investigate. Suddenly an intruder attacked her with a razor, inflicting severe cuts on her arms. She managed to get off a single shot from the rifle that hit the man in the thigh, putting him to flight. (*The Tribune*, Pasco, Fla.)

A criminal who had just broken into his Cincinnati, Ohio home had a rifle pointed at 79-year-old W. P. Henry. But when Henry's 18-year-old granddaughter momentarily distracted the assailant, Henry had time to draw a .38 cal. revolver from under his pillow and open fire, hitting the intruder three times and putting him to flight. Asked whether he'd continue to sleep with the gun under his pillow, Henry said, "I tell you, it's dangerous to sleep without it." (*The Enquirer*, Cincinnati, Ohio)

An armed robber should have taken Alton Treace's advice when the San Jose, Calif., shop owner told him, "play it cool; I've got a gun here and I'm calling the police." But the criminal, claiming to have a gun of his own, advanced on the 64-year-old Treace, who opened fire, dropping the intruder in his tracks. (*The Mercury*, San Jose, Calif.)

An apparent case of mistaken identity cost a Livermore, Calif., man his life when he tried to break into the home of Vietnam veteran James Golden. Golden was roused at 3 a.m. by pounding on his front door. He grabbed a 9 mm automatic and opened up as the door crashed in. Police speculated that the intruder, who was hit five times, was a drug dealer who mistook Golden's house for that of a confederate. (*The Valley Times*, Pleasanton, Calif.)

SEPTEMBER 1982

Chuck Madison, 73, has to have oxygen to move around and suffers several other ailments of old age. But he was more than a match for a pair of robbers who crashed into his Phoenix, Ariz., trailer. Although one criminal broke Madison's hand and a rib, Madison managed to retrieve a .32 cal. pistol and open up, wounding his attacker and putting the pair to flight. Police quickly caught the wounded robber. (*The Arizona Republic*, Phoenix, Ariz.)

Joseph Dean of Winchester, Calif., and Wendell Knighton of McGill, Nev., were stopped at a rest area near Jackpot, Nev., when they saw a man shoot a sheriff's deputy. As the criminal advanced on his car, Dean grabbed a pistol, rolled under the vehicle and exchanged shots with him. Knighton, sitting in his own car, opened up, too. In the fusillade, the criminal was killed with no injury to bystanders. Meanwhile, Knighton's wife and sister-in-law gave first aid to the fallen deputy, probably saving his life. (*The Daily Free Press*, Elko, Nev.)

Lottie Eldridge, 60, had hunted for years near her Ossippee, N.H., home, so gun-handling was nothing new to her. But she took on bigger game than deer or bear when she spotted a pair of burglars at work on a nearby home. She called police, then retrieved her .38 cal. revolver. She apprehended one burglar and held him for police, who said her action helped a crack a two-state antique burglary ring. (*The Daily News*, Bangor, Maine)

A pair of con artists tried to pull the classic "pigeon drop" scam on an unidentified Highland Park, Mich., woman as she emerged from her bank. But the 66-year-old woman pulled a revolver instead and replied, "I read about you in the newspaper; you ain't getting my money." The flim-flam men fled so quickly they forgot their "roll," a wad of newspaper wrapped in a $5 bill. (*The News*, Detroit, Mich.)

Sherry Davis flushed a would-be burglar from her parents' Daytona Beach, Fla., home as she was checking it for storm damage. She got a neighbor, William Coveney, who grabbed a .30 cal. rifle and held the man for police. (*The Morning Journal*, Daytona Beach, Fla.)

Dan Heffron had already handed over a bag of narcotics to an armed robber, but the youthful criminal still had a .32 revolver pointed at his face. So Heffron reached under the counter of his Littleton, Colo., pharmacy and pulled a .45 revolver. The druggist shot the robber once, then pursued him to a nearby gas station where he held him for police. (*Rocky Mountain News*, Denver, Colo.)

Karen Sargeant had warned the intruder who broke into her Seminole, Fla., home several times to stay back. But when he kept advancing on her, she fired her .32 once, killing him. "She gave him every chance and was in fear of her life," a police official said. "As far as we're concerned, it was a justified shooting." (*The Times*, St. Petersburg, Fla.)

Tonya Baugess heard someone breaking into the Boomer, N.C., home where she was staying, grabbed a .38, and hid in an upstairs closet. After the intruder ransacked the downstairs, he approached her hiding place. Baugess opened the closet door and fired, killing him. No charges were filed against Baugess, because, as one police officer said, she was justified in shooting the criminal, since she had "run as far as she could go and had to hide." (*The Journal-Patriot*, N. Wilkesboro, N.C.)

Rev. Charles White, 67, thought the man who had come to his Philadelphia church wanted counseling. But what he really wanted was cash, he said, as he drew a gun on the Baptist clergyman. But the cleric pulled a .25 instead of loot and killed the would-be robber with a shot to the chest. (*The Tribune*, Chicago, Ill.)

169

A holdup artist pointed a small automatic at Cindy Branford and demanded the contents of the till at her Anchorage, Alaska, gas station. But she pulled a .357 Mag., not cash, and the criminal took to his heels. (*The Daily News,* Anchorage, Alaska)

A Mobile, Ala., robber picked the wrong target when he pulled a knife on cabbie Charles Herman. Herman surrendered his cash, but when the criminal tried to exit the cab, he pulled a gun, pistol-whipped the man and shot him in the arm. (*The Press,* Mobile, Ala.)

"Give me all your money or I'll kill you," the armed robber demanded. But Melinda Wilson pulled a .38 from under the counter of her Waco, Tex., gas station and opened fire instead, critically wounding the criminal. She told police she was sorry she had to shoot the robber but "I didn't want to die." (*The Tribune-Herald,* Waco, Tex.)

Leona Atkinson, 75, was in her Memphis, Tenn., home with an elderly friend when a trio of thieves began to remove her window air conditioner. She drove the three away by firing warning shots from her .38. (*The Banner,* Nashville, Tenn.)

Fred Belile, 13, was at home with his two sisters when a masked intruder tried to force his way into the Nicholville, N.Y., home. The youngster fired a warning shot, but when the housebreaker kept coming, he loosed a 20-ga. shotgun blast that killed the criminal. (*The Register-Star,* Hudson, N.Y.)

A group of hog rustlers had to beat a hasty retreat when neighbors warned Lucerne, Ind., farmer Herd Crimmins that thieves were loading his hogs onto a truck. The doughty farmer, armed with a .357 Mag., rammed the criminals' truck with his own pickup. They fled, shoving hogs out the tailgate as they went. (*The Pharos-Tribune,* Logansport, Ind.)

DECEMBER 1982

Under the bed was no place to hide for a burglar in Reading, Pa. Returning home from an evening out, Mrs. Basilino Cruz heard a noise in the bedroom. She called to her husband to get his gun. "Don't shoot!" the intruder cried out and surrendered. Police came and took him away. (*The Eagle,* Reading, Pa.)

Alerted by the sounds of someone breaking into his Godfrey, Ill., home, Victor Calhoun took up his .44 cal. handgun and positioned himself behind a kitchen wall. He hollered a warning, whereupon the invader yelled back, "I'll shoot." Calhoun, 68, and his assailant then traded gunfire before the intruder fled from the house. (*The Telegraph,* Alton, Ill.)

A jogger stepped into the Miami Lakes, Fla., real estate office of Gerri Fontanella, inquired about a townhouse and locked the door when she turned around. After ordering her to disrobe, he stabbed her in the stomach, then forced her into a back room. When he looked away, Fontanella was able to unstrap a small pistol secured to her ankle and fire a shot that grazed the assailant. The man fled but was later apprehended and charged with several counts, including attempted first-degree murder. (*The Herald,* Miami, Fla.)

A man entered Wilbur Bury's LeRoy, Ill., home and proceeded to bludgeon him with a wooden hoe handle. Despite a broken wrist, Bury reached for a nearby handgun and fired three shots, driving off his assailant. (*The Journal,* LeRoy, Ill.).

An armed man barged into a Virginia Beach, Va., country club as a bingo game sponsored by the Norfolk (Va.) Fraternal Order of Police was breaking up. Announcing a robbery, he pointed a gun at off-duty policeman Robert Wheaton. When they subsequently exchanged shots, fellow officers Joseph Monaghan and Roger Pederson also returned fire, wounding the gunman. (*The Ledger-Star,* Norfolk, Va.)

Linda Curtis was walking home from work when a man over-powered and dragged her into a construction site off an Evanston, Ill., street. As he began to assault her, Curtis, a police officer, pulled her service revolver from her purse, shot and killed him. (*The Tribune,* Chicago, Ill.)

Entering through a slashed screen, a knife-carrying intruder struggled with an unidentified Columbus, Ohio, woman, then raped her twice while her young children slept in the next room. When the attacker fell asleep, the woman was able to get a pistol from the closet and shoot him. Naked and bleeding, the rapist staggered from the residence and was arrested shortly thereafter. (*The Advocate,* Newark, Ohio)

John Hofmaster answered an early morning knock at his Westmoreland, N.Y., door to be shoved aside by a man who scuffled with him until he managed to get the keys to the family car. Hofmaster broke free, retrieved a .45 semi-automatic and fired a single shot through the car's window as the thief tried to run him down. The bullet hit the man in the left arm, preventing his escape. (*The Daily Press,* Utica, N.Y.)

An armed robber confronted Columbia, S.C., liquor store operator Kyle Roberson and told him to get on the floor. Unsatisfied with the operator's slow compliance, the gunman squeezed the trigger twice, but his revolver misfired. Roberson, who had a pistol tucked under his belt, came up firing and killed the would-be robber, who it turned out was an ex-convict out of jail on bond. (*The State,* Columbia, S.C.).

A would-be robber brandishing a piece of broken glass demanded all the money in the cash register of a Rock Hill, S.C., convenience store. Clerk Regina Moore countered with a drawn revolver and forced the man to lie facedown on the pavement outside while she sent her son to get the police. (*The Evening Herald*, Rock Hill, S.C.)

Confined to a wheelchair, Sergy Bublikow of Rochester, N.Y., was unable to summon authorities after he'd shot and killed one of a trio of housebreakers that invaded his home. Bublikow retaliated with shotgun blasts after one intruder threw a five-pound horseshoe that struck his wheelchair. The telephone wires had been torn down and the invalid was isolated with the body until a neighbor returned home six hours later. (*The Democrat and Chronicle*, Rochester, N.Y.)

Having fallen asleep watching television in his Santa Paula, Calif., home, Robert Moore was awakened by a pair of housebreakers glowering over him. One man stabbed Moore twice in the abdomen, but the homeowner managed to call for his wife to summon the police and then retrieved a handgun from a bedroom nightstand. When he saw one burglar approaching, blade ready, he fired one shot that dropped the man. His partner had already fled the scene. (*The Star Free-Press*, Ventura, Calif.)

Awakened by a crashing sound, Eula Luffman discovered a man had shattered a door of her Danville, Va., home and was stalking through the house. She retrieved a handgun from the bedroom and confronted the man in the living room. Luffman, 69, warned him to stop but he continued to approach, and when he reached out for her, she shot him. Police linked the dead man to the rapes of several elderly women in the area. (*The Register*, Danville, Va.)

A 60-year-old man was working on his car in front of a Madera, Calif., senior citizen housing project when he was suddenly attacked from behind by a hammer-swinging assailant. Driving by the scene, David Brown stopped his vehicle, leveled his licensed handgun at the attacker and held him until authorities arrived. (*The Tribune*, Madera, Calif.)

JANUARY 1983

1983

A teller in an Indianapolis, Ind., bank called out to Joseph Ernst when a man claiming to have a pistol and a bomb was about to get away with a bagful of stolen money. Ernst, a uniformed sheriff's deputy, tackled the man. As they grappled on the floor, the robber tried to get to Ernst's sidearm. But Samuel Hatcher, who'd worked with the deputy years before, halted the struggle by drawing a licensed handgun and holding it to the robber's head. (*The Star*, Indianapolis, Ind.)

Phil and Lena Mae Gray have been frequent theft victims at their home and junkyard near McDonald, Tenn. A couple of years ago, she caught a pair stealing parts—and held them at gunpoint for police. So she didn't hesitate when she spied two men siphoning gas from her husband's dump truck. After calling the sheriff, she loaded her shotgun and trained it on the thieves until officers came to take them into custody. (*The Daily Banner*, Cleveland, Tenn.)

As he was locking his San Francisco, Calif., grocery for the night, Gene Hui saw four young men charging him. He jumped into his pickup, but the gang closed in and yanked the grocer and a waiting friend to the street. Beating Hui with a bottle, a pair of the thugs tried to wrest a briefcase containing the day's receipts from him. But Hui countered with a drawn derringer and shot and injured them. Police arrested two suspects shortly thereafter when they sought treatment at a local hospital. (*The Chronicle*, San Francisco, Calif.)

A masked man with a shotgun blew open the front door of Mark McClenahan's Wichita, Kans., home and went straight to the bedroom. Roused by a roommate bringing him a .22 rifle, McClenahan fired and hit the intruder after being struck on the head with the shotgun. The attacker fled and was taken into custody when he sought treatment at a nearby hospital. (*The Eagle-Beacon*, Wichita, Kans.)

John Marker of North Toledo, Ohio, was returning home from work when two men, one bearing a knife, confronted him as he parked his car. Marker, holder of a handgun identification card, thwarted the apparent robbery attempt by snatching a handgun from a garage shelf and firing a round at the would-be bandits. They fled, but one man was later identified after seeking treatment at an area hospital. (*The Blade*, Toledo, Ohio)

From his residence in rural Ripley County, Mo., James Junior Dean heard strange noises coming from his adjacent package store. While his wife called the sheriff's office, Dean armed himself with a shotgun and investigated. He discovered the front door had been forced by a juvenile burglar whom he held until authorities arrived. (*The Ozark Graphic*, Doniphan, Mo.)

A masked man strode into a Detroit tavern and announced a holdup by firing a gunshot into the ceiling. He then shot owner Harold Gibson in the leg. Gibson's wife Florence drew a handgun from behind the bar and returned fire. The wounded bandit fled and was found dead in a nearby alley. (*The Free Press*, Detroit, Mich.)

THE ARMED CITIZEN

A young man attempted the armed robbery of a Woodland, Calif., gas station by jumping onto the counter and flashing a 9″ knife. The bandit demanded the cash reciepts, but he was thwarted when 71-year-old clerk David Baumbach drew a revolver from beneath the counter. Warding off a slash and receiving a stab wound to his left hand, Baumbach fired a shot that sent the robber running to the waiting car. (*The Daily Democrat,* Woodland-Davis, Calif.)

As NRA Life Member Rex Burroughs drove away from a Lander, Wyo., restaurant, two men pulled up, blocked his car, and demanded money at gunpoint. When the driver yelled "kill him," his partner aimed and pulled the trigger. The gun failed to fire, and Burroughs was able to draw his own revolver and shoot the gunman. The robbers then sped off. (*The Wyoming State Journal,* Lander, Wyo.)

A man carrying two guns entered the Houston, Tex., barber shop owned by Lewis Warren, Sr. and asked to use some barber tools to remove cartridges from his gun. Warren refused. Later that evening, the gunman returned, kicking in the glass door and announcing that he would slay the barber. Warren, 69, was able to pull his own gun first, shoot and kill the intruder. (*The Post,* Houston, Tex.)

Vera Stark and her mother were asleep in their Wichita, Kans., home when a lone gunman broke in and made his way to their bedroom. Stark's 86-year-old mother called to alert her to the man crawling across the floor, and she sat up in bed. The man stood, pointing his gun at her. After his gun went off, shooting her in the hand, she retrieved a handgun from the nightstand, and fired twice, killing the assailant. (*The Eagle-Beacon,* Wichita, Kans.)

A man stepped up to the checkout counter of a Providence, Ky., pharmacy with a tube of salve. When the clerk rang up the sale, the man pulled a gun and told her to stay quiet. He then ordered pharmacist Jim Scott to come to the counter. When Scott obeyed, the robber fired a shot his way. The bullet missed, but the druggist, having taken up a pistol, returned two rounds which mortally wounded the gunman. (*The Sunday Courier and Press,* Evansville, Ind.)

Late-night noises outside the bedroom window awakened Gary Whipple of Houma, La. Investigating, he discovered two persons prowling around the rear of his home. When Whipple yelled and the prowlers ran toward him, he fired a warning. One man surrendered, dropping to the ground while his accomplice escaped. The homeowner held the man at bay for police, who caught the other shortly thereafter. (*The Daily Courier,* Houma, La.)

APRIL 1983

A man and two women entered a Largo, Fla., diamond brokerage. After forcing the owner to the floor at gunpoint, one of the women accosted employee William Seabrook, striking him on the head with a crowbar. Though dazed, he removed a revolver from a desk and confronted the would-be robbers. They fled the premises, pursued by Seabrook, who apprehended the male bandit and one female accomplice. (*The Sun,* Clearwater, Fla.)

Discovering his Ludlow, Mass., home ransacked, Leon Allore was confronted by a pair of robbers. One thief grappled with the homeowner, then fled. The second man then jumped into a waiting car and began backing out the driveway, pinning Allore between the open car door and a stone wall. Allore retaliated, firing a pistol round that wounded the driver. A suspect was soon arrested at an area hospital. (*The Morning Union,* Springfield, Mass.)

An intruder bashed through the door of David Gerken's home near Elwood, Nebr., struck Gerken with a sawed-off shotgun, then bound him and his wife. The gunman threatened to kill the couple if they moved while he left the house, but Gerken, 74, slipped his bonds, readied a shotgun and warned the man against re-entry. When answered by a shotgun blast, Gerken returned fire, and the intruder fell back through the door. The gunman managed to drive away, but collapsed shortly thereafter in a nearby restaurant. (*The World-Herald,* Omaha, Nebr.)

Wailing sirens and barking dogs roused Joey Cumia to witness two men run into a shed on the ranch at which he works near San Juan Capistrano, Calif. While his wife phoned authorities, Cumia confronted the trespassers and held them at gunpoint. The two were the subjects of a police manhunt and later were charged in connection with a spree of burglaries. (*The Times,* Los Angeles, Calif.)

Disturbed by noises in the night, a Huntsville, Ala., woman got up to find a man going through her house. At gunpoint, he demanded money and threatened to kill her, then forced her into the bedroom. He repeated the demand to her husband, Willard Shelton, who tossed some bills toward the thug. When the intruder insisted they hand him the cash, Shelton reached for a gun and fatally shot him. (*The Times,* Huntsville, Ala.)

Noticing several household items disturbed upon returning to her home near Seaford, Del., Mrs. George Mortimer stepped outside to await her husband. After he arrived and had taken up a .22 rifle, they searched the house and discovered a would-be burglar hiding under a bed. Ordered to leave, the intruder instead lunged at the woman, but was stopped when Mortimer shot him in the leg. (*The Morning News,* Wilmington, Del.)

Dairy store operator Loren Ditsch of South Bend, Ind., was faced at his checkout counter by a holdup man wielding a handgun and demanding cash. Ditsch stalled, and in the process, the criminal was distracted by store customers. Seizing a pistol, Ditsch fired two rounds that mortally wounded the would-be robber. (*The Tribune,* South Bend, Ind.)

Left alone to mind the family store, Lise Lessard of Montreal was confronted by a knife-wielding man who demanded the store's money and threatened her. But when he reached to help himself to the cash register contents, Lessard picked up a pistol from beneath the counter and shot him. The would-be thief ran, but was arrested with a suspected accomplice shortly thereafter. (*The Gazette,* Montreal, Quebec)

A panhandler approached Timoteo Castillo in the parking lot of a Dallas laundry, punched him and stole his wallet. Apparently dissatisfied with the $12 it contained, he demanded more, knocked the 74-year-old Castillo to the ground and began stabbing him with a screwdriver. The elderly victim plucked a revolver from his pocket and fired a warning that only intensified the attack. He then struck the thug with several shots that sent him fleeing to a nearby hospital. (*The Times-Herald,* Dallas, Tex.)

Members of the Albert Cross family awoke to discover a pickup parked by an open barn door on their farm near Conway, N.H. When Larry Cross flipped on an outside light, the truck sped away. A slain heifer was left behind. About 15 minutes later, the farmer's son saw three men run up the road and into the barn. Cross grabbed a rifle and followed, cornering the would-be rustlers, two of whom carried axes. They surrendered immediately. (*The Carroll County Independent,* Center Ossipee, N.H.)

Two men appeared unexpectedly at the residence of Raleigh, N.C., attorney Karl Knudsen, seeking to finalize a jewelry purchase. Rather than a check, the attorney was handed a burglary note and both visitors produced handguns. Knudsen tried to stall, and managed to seize a hidden pistol. After trading shots that dropped one thief, Knudsen fired on the other just as he prepared to shoot the homeowner's 10-week-old daughter. Both intruders were killed. (*The News & Observer,* Raleigh, N.C.)

A Memphis restaurant patron witnessed the armed abduction of an elderly couple as they were forced into their car at gunpoint by a man who got into the back seat. After following them several blocks, Timothy Jewell parked behind the car after it had turned into a driveway. The kidnapper left the vehicle and approached Jewell's pickup, pointing his pistol and ordering Jewell out. But as he stepped back, Jewell displayed a pistol and the would-be abductor fled. (*The Press-Scimitar,* Memphis, Tenn.)

JULY 1983

Entering through a roof-top skylight, two men ransacked a Warrington, Fla., bowling center. After vandalizing the pinball machines, they began kicking in the office door, awakening 71-year-old proprietor L. H. Felton, who slept therein. He retrieved a shotgun, and, as the vandals smashed through the door, fired a blast that set them to flight. One intruder, however, turned and charged Felton again, but was stopped and killed by a second round from the shotgun. (*The Journal,* Pensacola, Fla.)

Idaho Falls, Idaho, furniture store owner Nick Vrontikis responded when the store's burglar alarm activated one evening. As he stood, armed with a pistol, in the darkened establishment, the shopkeeper heard noises coming from the back room. There, among some mattresses, Vrontikis discovered an intruder and held him at gunpoint until police arrived. (*The Post-Register,* Idaho Falls, Idaho)

Carolyn Bennett had her reading interrupted by noises late at night in her Tice, Fla., home. She picked up a gun before investigating, then discovered a masked man in the hallway. Bearing a knife, he threatened to kill her. Instead, when he advanced, she shot him dead. Police said the man recently had been paroled from a Florida prison. (*The News-Press,* Ft. Myers, Fla.)

The occupants of a Waterbury, Conn., cafe were accosted by a pair of armed men and forced to lie on the floor. With his accomplice posted by the door, a pistol-wielding hoodlum removed money from behind the counter and took cash from the customers and owner. One patron began arguing, and as a scuffle ensued, the owner retrieved a revolver. Firing three shots, he drove the would-be robbers from his establishment. (*The Republican,* Waterbury, Conn.)

Because he hadn't heard anything from his guard dogs, Justice of the Peace Cameron Gray of Grand Prairie, Tex., was hesitant when his wife told him an intruder was in their home. Nevertheless, after grabbing a .38 cal. revolver, he found the prowler in the kitchen. Judge Gray ordered him to get on the floor, but he began backing toward the door. Gray cut the escape short by firing a warning shot. The intruder surrendered immediately. (*The Daily News,* Grand Prairie, Tex.)

As he switched off the television set, Hugh Gallup heard the stairs creaking in his Missouri Valley, Iowa, home. Gallup armed himself with a pistol, then was faced by a masked man waving a knife. The homeowner fired two warning shots, but the invader kept moving toward him. With more shots, Gallup dealt the thug a mortal injury. The dead man was later identified as having been recently released on parole from an Iowa prison. (*The Register,* Des Moines, Iowa)

THE ARMED CITIZEN

A masked, gun-wielding bandit entered a Taunton, Mass., pharmacy, shoved a female clerk to the floor and demanded money and drugs. Pharmacist Thomas Hall reacted by drawing a .38 revolver from under the counter, firing and wounding the gunman, who was soon hospitalized in police custody. (*The Sun Chronicle,* Attleboro-N. Attleboro, Mass.)

A knock at the door of Dorella Claypool's Odenton, Md., home brought a man who forced his way into the house. Flashing a knife, the assailant insisted the woman give him her money. Claypool backed into the bedroom, managed to grab a pistol and told him to leave. The would-be robber fled immediately. (*The Evening Capital,* Annapolis, Md.)

A pair of armed bandits split up as they entered a Jacksonville, Md., pharmacy. While one gunman stalked to the prescription counter, the other tried to detain a 13-year-old girl leaving the store. The girl's companion freed her, and they ran across the street and informed John Yarema and off-duty policeman Harold Wertz of the holdup. One suspect surrendered to Wertz and the other jumped into a getaway car where a third hoodlum was waiting. When the car began to pull away after Yarema ordered them out, Yarema fired a blast that injured the driver and sent the vehicle out of control. (*The Sun,* Baltimore, Md.)

Something seemed suspicious when Joseph Girgenti arrived to find an unfamiliar van parked outside his Methuen, Mass., home. Then he spotted a man exiting the house through a bathroom window. He ordered the burglar to stop, informing him that he was armed. Girgenti displayed his gun and used it to hold the man for authorities. (*The Eagle-Tribune,* Lawrence, Mass.)

OCTOBER 1983

A would-be rapist awoke Claudine Hale in her Baltimore apartment, grabbed her by the throat and threatened to harm the children sleeping in the same room. Hale struggled with the assailant, then managed to reach a handgun, which she used to halt the attack. He fled after being shot, and a suspect was found dead nearby. Baltimore authorities declined to press charges against the woman. (*The Evening Sun,* Baltimore, Md.)

After two earlier visits, a man entered a Bell Gardens, Calif., furniture store and, displaying a gun, forced proprietor Raymond Nitkin into a back room. Shoved aside when the gunman was distracted by the presence of two young employees, the shopkeeper ducked behind a refrigerator and drew his own gun. An ensuing exchange of gunfire dropped the gunman. Police later identified the injured man as an escaped convicted murderer. (*The Times,* Los Angeles, Calif.)

Newspaper carrier Farley Johnson had previously accommodated a local man by giving extra papers, but when he had none to spare and refused, the man assaulted him. The thug departed, then returned with a rifle to Johnson's house where he fired several rounds through the front door. Police came, but unable to locate the gunman, left the Birmingham, Ala., neighborhood. Soon, the assailant resurfaced and shot at Johnson, who was carrying his father's shotgun. The young man returned fire with a blast that critically injured the attacker. (*The News,* Birmingham, Ala.)

Roused by his 15-year-old daughter's screams, a Carbondale, Ill., man grabbed a pistol, then confronted an intruder who was attempting to leave the girl's room. When ordered to lie on the floor, the assailant instead moved on the father. A pistol round to the leg halted his advance. Police later identified and arrested a suspect. (*The Daily American,* West Frankford, Ill.)

When Richard Vallejos awakened to the sounds of a window being broken in his Tucson, Ariz., home, he secured a pistol and lay on the floor next to his bed. An intruder made his way through the house into the bedroom and, upon spotting the homeowner, pulled a gun from his belt. Vallejos fired first, striking the prowler in the arm and chest. The man died shortly thereafter at a nearby hospital. (*The Citizen,* Tucson, Ariz.)

Visiting New York City to settle her late brother's estate, Roberta Leonard was set upon by eight muggers. The 67-year-old Alabama native, who walks with a cane, had been mugged on her prior visit to New York and this time drew a revolver from her purse. The gang fled. Charges filed against Leonard for violating the city's permit law were eventually dropped when the grand jury failed to return an indictment. (*The Daily News,* New York, N.Y.)

Leaving her disabled husband, Grace Edenholm grabbed a revolver before answering a pre-dawn pounding at the door of their rural Rockcastle County, Ky., home. When she cracked the door, a young shotgun-toting criminal pushed his way in, backing her across the room until she stopped him with a fatal gunshot. "If I start running because some hoodlums say, 'I'm going to bother you,' then I don't feel I'm really an American," said the 67-year-old woman. ". . . As long as we call this a land of liberty, we have to . . . fight for the liberty." (*The Courier-Journal,* Louisville, Ky.)

A Stratham, N.H., resident who had sustained five previous burglaries readied a shotgun and concealed himself after noticing a car repeatedly driving by his home. When a youthful, knife-wielding housebreaker climbed through a window, the homeowner confronted him and held him until police arrived. Two suspected accomplices were arrested in the incident. (*The News-Letter,* Exeter, N.H.)

While sitting on his porch, Roe Watson of Detroit was approached by a young man asking to see his son. Watson, 70, invited the caller into his home. Once inside, the man produced a gun, robbed the elderly resident of several hundred dollars and ordered him into a chair. As the robber talked on the phone, Watson pulled his own gun, fired and mortally wounded the invader. The prosecutor's office classified the shooting as justifiable homicide. (*The News,* Detroit, Mich.)

A would-be housebreaker ripped the telephone lines from her home and threw rocks through a window, but Ella McReynolds, 69, of Hopkinsville, Ky., held him off by firing a pistol through the shattered pane. Brothers Roy and John Cozac, who were target shooting nearby, rushed to the disturbance and held the culprit at gunpoint until a state trooper arrived. (*The New Era,* Hopkinsville, Ky.)

FEBRUARY 1984

Andre Dufour, coowner of a Montreal convenience store, was making coffee in the back room when he heard glass breaking out front. When he investigated, a man armed with a hammer charged him. Dufour shot the attacker with the store's licensed revolver, and the man stumbled out the door and down the street. He was later arrested and charged with burglary. (*The Gazette,* Montreal, Quebec)

Victor Malcom, a Florida condominium developer, was taking a bath when a man wielding a hammer appeared in the doorway and demanded money. Wet and naked, Malcolm was hit several times as the battle raged through the house. Malcolm was finally able to retrieve a hidden gun and shot the man, killing him. (*The Times,* St. Petersburg, Fla.)

Philadelphia store manager Rubin Martinez, 45, defied a would-be armed robber, saying: "If you want the money, you'll have to get it yourself." When the criminal attempted to open the cash register, Martinez drew a revolver, precipitating a "Mexican standoff" for a moment before the gunman dropped his gun and raised his hands. (*The Bulletin,* Philadelphia, Pa.)

Frederick Glaeser of Baltimore, Md., was in his backyard when a shotgun-wielding neighbor walked up and threatened to kill him. He had minutes before shot and seriously injured a 13-year-old neighborhood boy and his younger sister as they watched him from their doorway. He levelled the gun at Glaeser and pulled the trigger, but the gun misfired. Glaeser ran for his own gun and, after a shotgun blast came through his kitchen window, killed his assailant with a single shot. No charges were filed. Both children were recovering in area hospitals. (*The Evening Sun,* Baltimore, Md.)

As Linda Woodward put her child into the car at a Knoxville, Tenn., service station, three men accosted her. One man demanded she surrender her car keys, then stabbed her in the side with a knife when she refused. Despite the injury, Woodward continued to struggle with the bandits, and, when she was able to withdraw a pistol from her purse, they took off running. (*The News-Sentinel,* Knoxville, Tenn.)

A Seguin, Tex., nurse, awakened when something bumped her bed, discovered a man wearing a stocking over his head. He threatened to kill her and her young son if she did not submit to him. Pretending to get a tissue from the nightstand, she instead extracted a pistol and shot him. The would-be rapist grappled with the woman, trying to turn the gun on her, but she stopped the attack, seriously injuring him with two more shots. (*The Express,* San Antonio, Tex.)

1984

A 16-year-old Orlando, Fla., girl awoke to find a man undressing in her bedroom. When the man grabbed her and said he had a gun, the girl said she, too, had a gun and was going to get it. The threat startled the man so much that, pants dropped to his ankles, he backed off and attempted to escape out a window. But he got caught in the window, which the girl and her mother held shut on him. When police arrived, he was dangling helplessly from the window. (*The Daily Tidings,* Ashland, Oreg.)

Stephen Todd, 41, was alone in his Berkeley, Calif., home when the doorbell rang about 10 p.m. Suspicious of the caller, Todd armed himself with a .38 revolver before answering. When he opened the door, several men burst inside, knocked him to the floor, and began beating him, apparently trying to subdue him before burglarizing the house. But Todd was able to draw his gun and fire five shots. The attackers fled, but one later died of a bullet wound and one was arrested and listed in critical condition at a local hospital. Todd was not charged. (*The Chronicle,* San Francisco, Calif.)

An armed robber pointed a pistol at Phillip Hackwith, an off-duty San Diego police officer, and demanded his wallet. Saying he kept his wallet in his sock, Hackwith bent over, drew his .38 cal. service revolver and shot the man in the neck and shoulder. (*The Tribune,* San Diego, Calif.)

Robert Joe Wade was at work in his father's Rock Hill, S.C., liquor store when a customer leaped over the counter and beat him over the head with a metal object. Wade managed to fend off the attack long enough to grab a gun from beneath the counter and fire several shots, critically wounding his assailant. No charges were filed against Wade. (*The Evening Herald,* Rock Hill, S.C.)

Nellie Fox, 87, was babysitting her five grandchildren near Inglewood, Calif., when her former son-in-law telephoned and threatened to kill her and her daughter. He had broken into the house earlier in the week and made a similar threat. Alarmed, Fox immediately called police to report the phone threat. But before they arrived, the man broke into the house through the front door, and was killed with a blast from Fox's 12-ga. shotgun. She was not held in the incident. (*The Daily Breeze,* Los Angeles, Calif.)

Edgar Macias, 18, and his mother were working in their family grocery store in Miami, Fla., when three armed robbers entered, demanding cash. Macias quickly grabbed a pistol and shot one robber, while his mother opened up on the other criminals. Two men, one wounded, were later captured and held in connection with the attempted robbery. (*The Morning Advocate,* Baton Rouge, La.)

Three men drove into Bernard Jordan's parked vehicle in a Gary, Ind., parking lot. After an argument the three pulled away but returned moments later. Witnesses saw one of them get out and point a shotgun at Jordan. Jordan, however, had enough time to draw a .45 automatic and fire first. He then fired at a second man about to attack him with a wrench. Both assailants died, and the shooting was ruled self-defense. (*The Post-Tribune,* Gary, Ind.)

Shirley Gill, 90, of Lakeland, Fla., was relaxing in her living room when she heard noises at the back of her house. She went to her bedroom, got a revolver, and investigated the disturbance. When she spotted a man running in the hallway, she fired. The shot missed but forced the intruder to flee out the back door. (*The Ledger,* Lakeland, Fla.)

Floyd C. Yaw, 75, had just left a Birmingham grocery store when he was approached by a man with a gun who demanded money. When Yaw refused, the criminal shot him in the chest. But Yaw was able to pull his own gun and disable his assailant with a shot. The would-be robber was arrested, and Yaw was treated at a nearby hospital. (*The News,* Birmingham, Ala.)

MAY 1984

A Houston businesswoman was changing a flat tire when two men pulled over to assist. But, instead of offering help, they forced her into their car at gunpoint, blindfolded her, and took her to an apartment. The men were not aware their victim had hidden a pistol inside her belt before starting to change the tire. When they removed the blindfold, the woman drew the pistol and fired two shots, hitting neither man but sending both running. One was later arrested, and police were searching for the other. (*The Houston Post,* Houston, Tex.)

When an armed man entered his Mar Vista,Calif., store and demanded the money in the register, clerk Vaclav Fara handed over the cash. But as the robber turned to get away, Fara pulled a gun from behind the counter and ordered him to stop. The robber whirled and raised his gun to fire, but Fara fired first, killing the man with two shots. The shooting was ruled justifiable homicide. (*The Los Angeles Times,* Los Angeles, Calif.)

In an effort to discover how his home security system had been defeated recently, Tulsa, Okla., surgeon R.W. Goen, Jr., staked out his home. The phone rang, followed a bit later by the doorbell, and Goen heard someone enter and identify himself as an employee of the security company. The man then walked straight into a bedroom and began pilfering pain killers. Goen levelled a semi-automatic rifle at the man, forced him to lie on the floor, tied him up, and summoned help. (*The Tulsa Tribune,* Tulsa, Okla.)

Just 15 days after he had been robbed by an armed man, Armand Fortin was alone in his Montreal convenience store when two men entered, pulled knives, and held them to his throat. Fortin quickly yanked out a handgun and fired two shots, killing both assailants. Both men were found to have long criminal records. (*The Gazette,* Montreal, Quebec)

Recently released from the hospital following a heart attack, Herman McBroom, 81, was resting in his Port Orchard, Wash., home when a man broke in, entered the bedroom, and demanded money. The intruder struck McBroom in the face several times, breaking the elderly man's glasses and cutting his forehead. While the man rifled the dresser drawers, McBroom retrieved a .25-cal. handgun. When the assailant moved to attack once again, McBroom shot him in the neck, forcing him to flee. A suspect was arrested at a nearby hospital. (*The Bremerton Sun,* Bremerton, Wash.)

A 70-year-old New York City resident was on his way home when an assailant grabbed him from behind and threw him down a subway stairwell. The elderly man, though dazed, drew a licensed .38-cal. revolver as the mugger was lifting his wallet and fired twice, hitting the thug both times. Police later arrested a suspect as he sought treatment for gunshot wounds at a local hospital. (*The New York Post,* New York, N.Y.)

Jonathan Hall, 29, of Fitchburg, Mass., answered an urgent knock at his door and found a neighbor and her two children pleading for protection. The woman's husband, ranting that he was going to kill the family, had chased them from their home with a rifle. Hall quickly put the family in a back room, then sat by the door with a .357 Mag. revolver until police arrived and arrested the husband. (*The Sentinel and Enterprise,* Fitchburg-Leominster, Mass.)

William Kesler, 29, of Bristol Twp., Pa., obligingly admitted two acquaintances into his apartment but then had to fight them off when they attempted to rob him. One man wielded a knife, while the other punched Kesler and sprayed him with teargas. Kesler, who was on crutches because of knee surgery, got to a handgun and fatally shot one attacker. The other was arrested later. Police said Kesler would not be charged. (*The Burlington County Times*, Burlington Co., N.J.)

A 16-year-old Riverside, Calif., girl was walking to school when a pickup truck carrying three people pulled up behind her. One man jumped out and began chasing the girl, catching her when she tripped and fell. The man began beating the girl and pounding her head into the dirt. A passing motorist saw the attack, pulled over, and tried to stop the attack by threatening the assailant with a baseball bat. When that failed, he got a handgun from his car, whereupon the attacker immediately ran for the truck and was driven away. (*The Press-Enterprise*, Riverside, Calif.)

Disabled former security officer Roy Howard, 47, of Orangeville, Calif., heard his doorbell ring repeatedly, but couldn't get there in time to answer it. He looked out the window and discovered two people sneaking around to the back door. A moment later they entered the house and headed for Howard's gun cabinet. Howard grabbed a rifle from another room and held the two at bay until the sheriff came and arrested the two 16-year olds. (*The Sacramento Union*, Sacramento, Calif.)

A 25-year-old Winter Park, Fla., woman was outside her home when a man suddenly jumped out of the bushes and attacked her, tearing at her clothes and threatening to rape her. When the victim's roommate heard the disturbance, she came running to the scene with a .44 Mag. revolver and fired a shot into the ground, frightening the man away. (*The Orlando Sentinel*, Orlando, Fla.)

Shattering glass alerted Allegan, Mich., resident DeWitt Jordan, 41, to an intrusion late at night. Taking a 12-ga. shotgun to investigate, he discovered a man inside his home shouting threats. During an ensuing struggle the shotgun went off, killing the burglar. No criminal charges would be filed against Jordan, police said. (*The Grand Rapids Press*, Grand Rapids, Mich.)

AUGUST 1984

Fountain, Colo., grocer Shirley Melton was working in a back room when a man carrying a long-bladed knife entered the store. When she asked "What have you got there?" the man whirled and raised the knife. Melton drew her handgun, cocked it, and leveled it at him. After a brief stand-off, the man turned and ran out of the store. (*The Gazette Telegraph*, Colorado Springs, Colo.)

San Antonio, Tex., convenience store owner Gil Garza had just told a man the price of an item when the customer showed a derringer and demanded money. Garza responded by drawing his .357 Mag. and putting it to the man's chest. He was about to call police when another customer entered the store. The would-be holdup man took advantage of the interruption and fled. (*The Light*, San Antonio, Tex.)

Betty Ross, Boise, Idaho, was dozing in a living room chair when her dog awakened her about 2 a.m. She saw an intruder enter the house through a back door and start toward a bedroom. Ross slipped into the room through a side door and picked up a rifle. Switching on the lights, she met the man face to face and ordered him out. The man fled, but a suspect was arrested minutes later. (*The Idaho Statesman*, Boise, Idaho)

Phillip Borelli, co-owner of a Hempstead, N.Y., auto dealership, noticed two men asking his brother Anthony, the other proprietor, about the price of a truck. Suddenly, one pulled an unidentified weapon and struck Anthony on the head, knocking him to the ground. Phillip pulled his licensed revolver and fired, sending the two attackers fleeing. (*The Newsday*, Long Island, N.Y.)

George Shamoun, a Royal Oak, Mich., merchant, was outside his store when he saw an armed woman, disguised as a man, holding a gun on his wife and demanding money. Shamoun slipped inside, but the assailant noticed him, turned, and pulled the trigger. When her gun misfired, Shamoun drew his own pistol and killed the woman. No charges have been filed against him. (*The Free Press*, Detroit, Mich.)

Nashville, Tenn., resident Bruce Metcalf was buying gasoline at a local market when he witnessed two armed robbers holding up the store. Realizing they'd been seen, the pair burst outside and opened fire on Metcalf. But Metcalf drew his own gun, returned fire, and killed one, a fugitive prison escapee. The other robber fled. (*The News-Sentinel*, Knoxville, Tenn.)

When a barking dog awakened him, Gardena, Calif., resident Gary Kindle grabbed a gun and investigated. Finding a man crawling on the floor toward his children's bedroom, Kindle ordered him out. When the intruder ignored the command and moved toward the bedroom, Kindle fired twice, fatally wounding him. (*The Herald Examiner*, Los Angeles, Calif.)

St. Albans, W. Va., grocer Norma Bryan had just rung up a sale for a customer when the man pulled a gun and reached for the cash drawer. Bryan quickly drew a shotgun from under the counter and ordered the man "to get out and get out now. He just looked at me strange and walked out," she said. (*The Daily Mail*, Charleston, W.Va.)

A would-be rapist had bound an Oklahoma City woman with telephone cord and was ransacking her apartment in search of liquor when she freed herself and grabbed a 12-ga. shotgun. When he returned to her room and ignored her warning to leave, she fired once, hitting him in the chest and putting him to flight. (*The Daily Oklahoman,* Oklahoma City, Okla.)

Alerted by the sound of breaking glass, a Watts, Calif., man and his wife discovered an armed burglar standing in front of a broken window. The home-owner, who is partially paralyzed, had armed himself, and a struggle ensued. The resident's gun discharged during the fight, and the burglar was killed. The resident was not charged. (*The Times,* Los Angeles, Calif.)

A rapist had attacked a Cincinnati, Ohio, woman once, but, when he crashed through her door, a month later, she was waiting with a .38 cal. revolver. She fired at the assailant, who fled. (*The Enquirer,* Cincinnati, Ohio)

When the sound of breaking glass awakened him about 3:35 a.m., a Cleveland, Ohio, resident armed himself with a revolver and investigated. When a burglar suddenly jumped at him, the homeowner fired, killing him. Police said the resident was in fear for his life and would not be charged. (*The Plain Dealer,* Cleveland, Ohio)

After a pair of would-be armed robbers entered his North Dade, Fla., carpet store, the owner drew his own gun. A struggle followed, and the owner fatally shot one of his assailants. The other made his escape. (*The Herald,* Miami, Fla.)

An Eureka, Mich., resident was asleep at home when a brick suddenly crashed through one of his windows. The homeowner, who had been burglar-ized seven times, robbed at gunpoint twice, and pistol whipped once, armed himself and investi-gated. He confronted a pair of burglars entering his home and fired five shots, killing one of the men instantly and forcing the other to flee. (*The News,* Detroit, Mich.)

When her ex-boyfriend broke into her home and threatened her with a shovel, Teresa Johnson of Wichita, Kans., got to a .22 cal. pistol and shot her attacker in the stomach. Johnson has not been charged. (*The Eagle-Beacon,* Wichita, Kans.)

When jewelry salesman Phillip Sutton answered the door of his N. Wilkesboro, N.C., motel room, an intruder armed with a straight razor lunged at him. Sutton opened fire with his .38, hitting the criminal in the head and killing him. Police said the would-be slasher was wanted for automobile theft, firearms larceny and moonshining. (*The Journal-Patriot,* N. Wilkesboro, N.C.)

NOVEMBER 1984

After hearing radio bulletins that two fugitives responsible for wounding four persons were loose in the area, Lewis Run, Pa., resident William Huber armed himself as a precaution and kept an eye out the window. His vigilance paid off when he spotted a man trying to steal his three-wheeled recreational vehicle. Huber fired a shot over the man's head, and the fugitive, accused of a long list of violent crimes in the area, surrendered. "I'm a pacifist," said Huber, "but I have my kids to protect. We're all avid hunters and the entire family knows how to handle firearms." (*The Pacific Stars and Stripes,* San Francisco, Calif.)

A 33-year-old Seattle, Wash., woman was in bed late at night when she heard noises in another part of the house. A man suddenly entered her bedroom, saying he'd kill her if she didn't keep quiet. Pulling a pistol she keeps hidden near the bed, the woman fired twice, killing the man with a shot to the chest. (*The Post-Intelligencer,* Seattle, Wash.)

When a pair of robbers sprayed Mace into the face of Columbus, Miss., motel owner Bill Hall, Hall thwarted the latenight robbery attempt by pulling a small-caliber handgun and firing at his attacker. The man died from a chest wound, but his female accomplice escaped. (*The Commercial Dispatch,* Columbus, Miss.)

When a pistol-wielding holdup man gave him a note demanding cash, jewelry store owner Mike Young of Los Altos, Calif., responded by pulling his licensed .38 cal. revolver and ordering the man to drop his gun. The would-be robber loosed a barrage of shots, none of which hit Young, and then pulled a knife. Young returned fire, hitting the man at least once. Wounded, the man collapsed outside the store and died later. The shooting was ruled justifiable homicide. (*The Town Crier,* Los Altos, Calif.)

Mike Martinez, a clerk at a San Antonio, Tex., convenience store, was closing up when, in a mirror, he noticed a man coming up behind him, gun drawn. As the man put the gun to Martinez' back, the store clerk grabbed a hidden .25 cal. automatic, whirled, and fired a single shot. Wounded in the chest, the man died at the scene. (*The News,* San Antonio, Tex.)

Mary Brooks of Chattanooga, Tenn., must have looked like an easy mark behind the counter of a bait and tackle shop where she works. But when a would-be thief brandished a knife and demanded money, she shut the cash register drawer and grabbed her .38 cal. handgun. In his haste to escape the feisty 62-year-old grandmother, the man went *through* the store's glass front door. Though cut badly, he got away with assistance from a female accomplice. (*The Times News,* Kingsport, Tenn.)

Awakened by the sounds of a window being broken, San Antonio, Tex., homeowner Lowell Salyer took his .357 Mag. revolver to have a look around. Spotting an intruder inside his home, Salyer yelled "hold it!" but had to fire when the man turned on him. Salyer's second shot killed the man. Police recommended a ruling of justifiable homicide. (*The Sunday Express-News,* San Antonio, Tex.)

A 73-year-old resident of the High Sierras thought it would be safe to spend the night in his pickup while en route to a friend's home in Los Angeles. After pulling off the street in the city's Wilshire district and going to sleep in the truck bed, he was jumped by a pair of robbers. Despite being beaten, kicked and choked, the old man managed to pull a pistol and fire several times, killing one attacker and wounding the other. No charges were filed against the traveler. (*The News,* United Press International, Shelbyville, Ind.)

Alerted by early-morning noises in his Oklahoma City, Okla, residence, off-duty policeman Steve Pistole got his .357 Mag. service revolver and checked his daughter's bedroom. He found a man clad only in a shirt and socks on the 9-year-old girl's bed. Firing several times, Pistole killed the intruder. The officer's daughter was treated for bruises to the head suffered during the attack. (*The Times,* Oklahoma City, Okla.)

Hearing a disturbance, service station manager Alvin Burris of Dallas, Tex., entered the station office and found an armed man taking money from a female clerk. The robber ordered Burris and the woman to crouch behind the counter and struck Burris on the head. While the robber rifled the cash drawer, Burris' assistant slipped him a pistol. Burris fired several times, prompting the man to drop the money and his gun as he fled. The robber was arrested at a nearby hospital when he sought treatment for gunshot wounds. (*The Morning News,* Dallas, Tex.)

"I think if this happened a lot oftener, there wouldn't be so many robberies," said Lomita, Calif., city councilman Harold Hall after an armed robber's attempt to rob Hall's paint store ended in death for the criminal. The thief ordered Hall to lie on the floor, but while he rifled the cash register, the storeowner grabbed a .38 cal. revolver and opened up, fatally wounding the bandit. (*The Mercury,* San Jose, Calif.)

Hearing someone breaking through the double dead-bolted front door of his Silver Lake, Calif., home, late at night, a 78-year-old man pulled an M1 carbine from storage. His niece, attacked by the intruder, broke free, took refuge in the bedroom, and locked the door. The assailant continued his attack, but the elderly uncle shot him twice, killing him, as he attempted to break down the bedroom door. (*The Tribune/News,* Whittier, Calif.)

MARCH 1985

Hearing noises at a rear door, a Houston, Tex., convenience store owner was about to investigate when an armed man burst inside and shot him. Reaching under a counter, the owner retrieved a handgun and fired two shots. The attacker fled, but police found the man dead a few blocks away. (*The Chronicle,* Houston, Tex.)

A Simpson County, Miss., woman was accosted in her driveway by a man armed with a knife and sawed-off rifle. He forced her into the house and ordered her to strip and lie down. Just then, several barking dogs distracted the would-be rapist long enough for his victim to grab her husband's .44 Mag. revolver and shoot. Police apprehended and charged the wounded suspect with robbery and attempted rape. (*The Daily News,* Jackson, Miss.)

Maritza Gonzalez twice yelled warnings to a man attempting to force entry through a window in her Miami, Fla., home, but the intruder continued his attempt to enter, threatening to kill her. Gonzalez finally stopped him with a shot from her .25 cal. handgun. Police said the wounded man had a history of sex offenses and psychiatric treatment. (*The Herald,* Miami, Fla.)

When Orlando, Fla., grocer Herbert Wise, an ex-policeman, saw a customer readying a gun, he warned, "Whatever you're going to try, I advise you against it." But the man ignored the advice and pulled his pistol, catching it against the edge of the counter. That gave Wise all the time he needed to reach for his own pistol and fire two shots. The wounded thief was taken into custody at a hospital. (*The Herald-Tribune,* Sarasota, Fla.)

Charleston, W. Va., convenience store owner Carol Thomas was at the counter when three masked men entered and demanded money. When one of the trio put a gun to her head and repeated the command, Thomas yelled for her husband, distracting her assailant long enough for her to grab her handgun. When they saw her gun, the three burst out of the store. A passerby got a partial license number, and state police promptly collared three suspects. (*The Daily Mail,* Charleston, W. Va.)

A couple was in bed watching television in a Ft. Worth motel when three men broke through the door and demanded money. Although the assailants carried guns and clubs, the male guest grabbed his own gun and shot two of them fatally. The third man fled. The dead men were both ex-convicts, and one carried a billfold taken in a recent robbery. (*The Times-Herald,* Dallas, Tex.)

1985

179

Atlanta druggist Bynum "Doc" Perkins was busy behind the counter when a man approached and pointed a pistol at him, saying, "This is a holdup." Perkins a victim of multiple robberies over the years, drew his .38 cal. handgun and shot the man twice. The would-be robber escaped, but a wounded suspect was arrested later by police. An Atlanta detective commented, "I think you'll see more and more of this because people are getting fed up with being robbed." (*The Journal,* Atlanta, Ga.)

A 14-year-old Dallas boy saved the life of Carolyn Lewis, who was staying with his family after leaving her husband a few days earlier. Awakened by a disturbance before dawn, the boy heard Lewis scream and found the estranged husband attacking her with a hunting knife. The boy tried unsuccessfully to subdue the man, then got a .22 cal. rifle and shot him fatally. Police said no charges will be filed against the youngster. (*The Morning News,* Dallas, Tex.)

When a 26-yr.-old Sacramento, Calif., woman answered her front door, two men sprayed her with Mace, tied her up, and began ransacking her home. While the thieves were looting her possessions, the woman freed herself and retrieved a pistol. One of the men was shot once when he lunged for her and again during a struggle. Both robbers fled, but a man seeking help for gunshot wounds at a local hospital was considered a suspect. (*The Union,* Sacramento, Calif.)

Gynell Smyre, 65, of North Philadelphia, Pa., used a .38 cal. pistol to defend herself against a man who broke into her home, threatened and finally shot her. Police found the intruder dead inside the residence. Smyre was hospitalized in intensive care. The shooting was ruled justifiable homicide. (*The Times,* Reading, Pa.)

San Antonio, Tex., resident Diane Garcia refused entry to three suspicious-looking men who demanded to see her husband. Instead of leaving, the group began kicking at the front door. But Garcia fired her 12-ga. shotgun, wounding one of the men. All three were arrested shortly. (*The Light,* San Antonio, Tex.)

Hearing screams from the hallway outside her St. Louis apartment, Monica Jones found a man brutally assaulting a naked 12-year-old girl. When the child broke free and fled into Jones' apartment, her assailant began battering the door. He finally burst through, only to be confronted by Jones, who was holding a shotgun purchased after an earlier assault against her by the same man. Jones held the assailant until police arrived. (*The Post-Dispatch,* St. Louis, Mo.)

After ordering store employees to lie on the floor, a gunman handed Wylam, Ala., pharmacist Joe Gandy a pillowcase and demanded he fill it with drugs. While doing so, Gandy lifted a pistol and fired. In an exchange of gunshots, the robber was fatally wounded. (*The Birmingham News,* Birmingham, Ala.)

JUNE 1985

Like everyone in his family, six-year-old Jimmy Roland had been taught firearms safety. When a masked man recently held his mother at knife point outside their home near Bethel, Okla., Jimmy levelled an empty rifle and yelled, "Let my mommy loose!" The man demanded that Jimmy put down the rifle, but instead the youngster cocked it, giving his mother the chance to break away. The assailant fled, but a suspect and two accomplices soon were arrested and charged with attempted burglary and assault with a deadly weapon. Speaking of Jimmy's bravery, Sheriff Paul Abel said, "The amazing thing is, it was no big deal to him. I'm real proud of that kid." (*The World,* Tulsa, Okla.)

John Kreilach, a 73-year-old Cleveland resident with a heart condition, was reading when two men began pounding on the front door of his home. When Kreilach refused to admit them to use his telephone, one kicked in a storm door glass and the other smashed through a front window. Kreilach fired a pellet pistol to drive off the intruders. (*The Plain Dealer,* Cleveland, Ohio)

Manuel Ferreira, 87, answered a knock at the door of his Fall River, Mass., home to two men who asked to use the phone. Once inside, they grabbed him and demanded money at knifepoint. Ferreira went to the bedroom for his wallet, but returned instead with a pistol in hand. The would-be robbers fled. (*The Herald News,* Fall River, Mass.)

Gary Martins was napping in his Van Nuys, Calif., home when he was startled by a noise. Suspecting a burglar, he armed himself with a pistol and went into his living room, where the intruder lunged at him. Martins fatally shot him. (*The Daily News,* Van Nuys, Calif.)

Walter Courts, a former World War II P.O.W. from Mesa, Ariz., was preparing to shower in his motor home when a man with a pistol entered, bound and robbed him and started driving the vehicle. Courts untied himself, got a gun and told his abductor to get out. The man jumped out while the motor home was still moving. (*The Gazette,* Phoenix, Ariz.)

Samuel Deas retrieved a pistol from beneath the counter of his mother's Denver liquor store and wounded a gun-wielding man who demanded money. Deas was not charged. (*The Post,* Denver, Colo.)

Rev. James Teamer of Charlotte, N.C., and his wife, awakened by a disturbance, discovered the lights were not working. After arming himself with a pistol, the 77-year-old Teamer confronted four intruders entering through a rip in the porch screen. Teamer told them to leave, but one advanced and the elderly cleric shot and wounded him. The intruders fled, but were arrested later. (*The News and Observer,* Raleigh, N.C.)

Don Gladden, an ACLU lawyer and gun control advocate, was alone in his previously burglarized Fort Worth weekend home when a burglar attempted to enter through a hole made in a wall by thieves a day earlier. Gladden fired a shotgun loaned to him by a neighbor and wounded the man. "I don't think guns are the solution, but circumstances were such that I was forced to shoot," Gladden said. (*The Morning News,* Dallas, Tex.)

A Tucson, Ariz., woman was home alone when an intruder walked into her house. When she tried to escape, he forced her into a dark bedroom. She grabbed a gun near the bed and fired. Thinking he had fled, she began to cry, but he grabbed her again. During a struggle she fired another shot, and this time the would-be rapist fled. (*The Daily Star,* Tucson, Ariz.)

Willie James Moreland was working the night shift in an Atlanta gas station when a hold-up man drew a gun. Moreland tried to wrestle the man's gun away, and it discharged. The assailant then fled out the door, turning and aiming at Moreland, who had grabbed his own pistol and with it fatally wounded the man. (*The Journal,* Atlanta, Ga.)

A neighbor alerted Charles Keppler that a person had entered his Shelby Center, N.Y., barn on his farm property. Armed with a pistol, Keppler investigated and held a knife-toting intruder for the police. The intruder was charged with burglary. (*The Daily News,* Batavia, N.Y.)

Barbara Jackson picked up her rifle when she was awakened by a man in her bedroom. The man lunged at her and she shot and killed him. Police said the man was free on bond after a previous arrest for sexual assault. (*The Sun,* Gainesville, Fla.)

A Poughkeepsie, N.Y., homeowner armed himself with a pistol when the sound of a window being forced open awakened him. He confronted a burglar in his kitchen and held him until police arrived. (*The Journal,* Poughkeepsie, N.Y.)

A Lindale, Tex., woman stepped outside her rural home and was grabbed by a masked assailant who forced her back into the house and cut off her clothing with a knife. During the struggle, the woman managed to grab a pistol kept near the bed and fired two shots. The would-be rapist fled immediately. (*The Morning Telegraph,* Tyler, Tex.)

Margarita Washington was working in her Omaha, Nebr., store when a masked man entered, pulled a gun and demanded money. Washington retrieved a pistol, and the man ordered her to drop it. Instead, she fired a shot that sent him fleeing. "If I had let him get away with it, I might as well close up," she said later. (*The World-Herald,* Omaha, Nebr.)

SEPTEMBER 1985

Dino Starn awoke to find a man climbing through the bedroom window of his New Jersey home. "He picked the wrong window," said Starn, who, for the second time in two years, used a handgun for protection. He shot once at the intruder, who was apparently hit in the arm and ran. Starn had previously used the gun to capture two burglars in his home. (*The Press,* Atlantic City, N.J.)

A burly intruder burst into the San Antonio home of lawyer Andrew Carruthers and fired a shot from a .45 auto that whizzed by Carruthers' wife's head. Carruthers picked up his M1 carbine, and after a struggle, twice wounded the gunman, who was later arrested. (*The Express-News,* San Antonio, Tex.)

Two armed men who had just committed a robbery gained entry into the home of Servado and Maria Elorza in rural Reedley, Calif. One of the intruders, threatening to kill the couple, followed Mrs. Elorza into a bedroom. Her husband grabbed a pistol and fatally wounded the man. The other intruder fled. (*The Exponent,* Reedley, Calif.)

Wilbur Logan heard a noise at the back door of his Detroit home, picked up a shotgun, and investigated. The 66-year-old homeowner found an intruder attempting to force open an iron security gate at the home. When the burglar lunged at him, Logan fired, fatally wounding the man. Logan was released after questioning by police. (*The News,* Detroit, Mich.)

Paulette Nelson and a teen-aged daughter had been accosted by a neighbor before and, when the club-wielding man smashed into her San Leandro, Calif., home, she was ready. Nelson confronted the man with a revolver purchased the day before. When he rushed forward, she fired. The intruder started toward Nelson's 79-year-old mother, but collapsed, mortally wounded. (*The Daily Review,* Hayward, Calif.)

Despite being warned, a prowler who had been banging on a window of Gary Junghans' Junction City, Kans., home burst through the door. As the intruder approached the bedrooms where Junghans, his wife, and son were, the homeowner repeatedly told him to stop, with no results. Junghans picked up a gun and fired once, wounding the man, who was held until police arrived. (*The Daily Union,* Junction City, Ks.)

"He demanded I give them all the money or he would shoot me," Denver jeweler Ronaldo Quintana said. But instead, the store owner pulled a pistol and opened fire on the gunman as his two accomplices headed for the door. The would-be robber dropped the gun and ran; he was later arrested and hospitalized with multiple gunshot wounds. (*The Rocky Mountain News*, Denver, Colo.)

Stopping by for breakfast at his parents' Cleveland home, Darrell Mathews saw an unfamiliar truck parked in their driveway, then saw a man carrying furniture from the house to the truck. Mathews walked quietly up to his parents' bedroom, notified them that a robbery was in progress and asked to borrow their pistol. He went back downstairs, captured the robber and held him for the police. (*The Daily Banner*, Cleveland, Ohio)

Harold and Doris Doster were behind the counter of their Hartwell, Ga., convenience store when a man approached and pointed a pistol at Mr. Doster. Mrs. Doster drew a revolver from behind the counter and, in an exchange of fire, wounded the gunman. He escaped but a suspect was later arrested The suspect had recently been paroled after serving 10 years for murder committed during an earlier robbery. (*The Sun*, Hartwell, Ga.)

A Newton, Mass., man heard noises on his fire escape about 1 a.m. and investigated with pistol in hand. As he looked out the window, he saw a prowler with a chisel raised, apparently poised to attack. The gunowner fired warning shots, then detained the would-be burglar for the police. (*The Tab*, Newton, Mass.)

A Lake Station, Ind., woman walked from her yard to her house one morning and was attacked by a man who had sneaked into her home. The man had cut the telephone line and had a pair of handcuffs ready, but his intended victim was able to struggle free and reach her shotgun. Seeing the gun, the assailant ran off. (*The Post-Tribune*, Gary, Ind.)

An intruder entered a Live Oak, Fla., woman's home, and was attempting to rape her. But she managed to struggle free, grabbed a pistol, and opened fire. The would-be rapist escaped, but a suspect with four gunshot wounds turned up later at a nearby hospital. (*The Suwanee Democrat*, Live Oak, Fla.)

A Carthage, Tenn., woman, alone in her home, was startled by an intruder in the middle of the night. She picked up her husband's deer rifle and confronted the uninvited visitor. "She gave him till the count of three to get out," a sheriff's department spokesman said. "At the count of one, he hit the door." A suspect was soon arrested. (*The Banner*, Nashville, Tenn.)

DECEMBER 1985

The neighbor was drunk, threatening to kill 68-year-old Loretta Arnold with a butcher knife. Police said it was self defense when the Mesa, Ariz., woman killed her attacker with a single pistol shot after he lunged at her. (*The Tribune*, Mesa, Ariz.)

Grover Vincenzo Martino and a policeman were staking out Martino's Hackensack, N.J., store following a rash of thefts, when an intruder appeared with a meat cleaver. With the weapon raised the man charged the store owner, who stopped him with a gunshot to the shoulder. (*The Record*, Hackensack, N.J.)

After being burglarized twice, James Obleton began carrying a pistol and checking his Benning Hills, Ga., home before leaving. Opening the door to his den, he was confronted by a burglar with a metal bar raised, ready to strike. Obleton warned the man but was forced to shoot, fatally wounding the intruder. (*The Ledger*, Columbus, Ga.)

Awakened by banging on their door, Billie and Doris Lee saw a man burst into their Benson, N.C., home and grab a broom. The intruder attacked the couple, but the homeowner killed his assailant with a gun. The death was ruled a justifiable homicide. (*The Herald*, Smithfield, N.C.)

Awakened about 1:30 a.m. by the sounds of a burglar breaking into her Sarasota, Fla., apartment, Norma Lilly grabbed a rifle. As her bedroom door slowly opened, she opened fire, disabling an intruder who was taken into police custody. (*Herald-Tribune*, Sarasota, Fla.)

The stranger had threatened the woman with rape and allegedly was trying to make good the threat as he broke into her Buffalo, N.Y., home. As he struggled with the woman's husband, trying to stab him, she opened fire with a rifle, wounding the intruder. (*The News*, Buffalo, N.Y.)

"He was either drunk or crazy," police said of the man who came to the Chewalla, Tenn., home of Geraldine Wilbanks. The stranger tried to force his way into the house, and refused to leave until Wilbanks felt compelled to fire two shots that sent him running. (*Independent Appeal*, Selmer, Tenn.)

Startled by bricks smashing through his living room window, Kenneth Hinson investigated and was struck in the face by several pellets from a shotgun fired from outside his Henderson, Tex., home. Hinson grabbed his own shotgun just as the armed assailant crashed through the door. In an exchange of shots. the intruder was killed. The dead man had been sought by police in connection with an earlier armed robbery.(*The Morning Telegraph*, Tyler, Tex.)

When a shotgun blast tore open the front door of his Mankato, Kans., home, Bob Newell armed himself and ran to investigate. Newell confronted a man, and in an exchange of gunfire, critically wounded the intruder. (*The Daily Call*, Beloit, Kan.)

Approaching an Ontario, Calif., liquor store counter, a robber brandished a gun and demanded cash. The quick-acting clerk reached down and retrieved not money, but a revolver. The store employee fired and wounded the gunman. A suspect was arrested 20 minutes later at a hospital. (*The Daily Report*, Ontario, Calif.)

Returning home just before midnight, a Harrisburg, Penn., woman found a burglar removing a stereo from her living room. Drawing a pistol she held the man while she called the police. The intruder was charged with burglary. (*The Patriot*, Harrisburg, Penn.)

A 83-year-old St. Petersburg, Fla., man awoke to his wife's screams and found an assailant pinning her to her bed attempting to rape her. The homeowner pulled a pistol from beneath his pillow and fired two shots that sent the attacker fleeing. (*The Evening Independent*, St. Petersburg, Fla.)

Two masked and knife-wielding robbers held their ground when Irondequoit, N.Y., store clerk Rosemary Tambe produced a pistol and ordered them out. But when the resolute woman fired a warning shot, they fled. (*The Times-Union*, Rochester, N.Y.)

The burglar had tied-up Jim and Bonnie Pence and was ransacking their Newton Falls, Ohio, home. With a handgun he had stolen from Pence, the burglar entered the room where the couple lay bound, only to find that the homeowner had freed himself and obtained a shotgun. The intruder was killed instantly. (*The Tribune*, Warren, Ohio)

Staying late in his Chicago store one night, George Perez watched as five men smashed a window and entered the shop. The store owner drew his registered handgun and ordered the men to leave, but instead they advanced menancingly. Perez then fired and chased them off. One would-be burglar still clutching stolen goods was found dead outside. Police said Perez acted in self-defense. (*The Sun-Times*, Chicago, Ill.)

Awakened in the night, a Gulfport, Miss., man found an intruder attempting to rape his wife. He struggled with the man and was stabbed, but his wife managed to grab a gun and chase off the attacker. A suspect was later arrested. (*The Daily Herald*, Gulfport, Miss.)

Willie Griffin had forced a robber out of his Florence, Calif., store and was phoning police when the man returned. As the robber came at him with a piece of steel pipe, the shopkeeper mortally wounded him with a single shot from his handgun. (*The Times*, Los Angeles, Calif.)

JANUARY 1986

Stopped at an Elko, Nev., gas station Betty Gibson watched in disbelief as a truck driver twice rammed the family van, then pointed a shotgun at her husband and pulled the trigger. The gun apparently misfired, giving Gibson time to grab a revolver and fire at the stranger, who drove off. A suspect was arrested later. (*The Bee*, Sacramento, Calif.)

Hearing a commotion, Mike Kopp ran from the shower, grabbed his handgun and caught a burglar breaking into his Redding, Calif., motel. Kopp told the man to sit down while he called police; the intruder took a seat. (*The Record-Searchlight*, Redding, Calif.)

Hearing a commotion in back of his apartment, a St. Louis homeowner directed his wife to call police while he investigated with a gun. As he walked to a door it burst open, and an armed intruder rushed toward him. Though warned, the intruder would not stop and was killed by a single shot. Police said the burglar had multiple felony convictions. (*The Post Dispatch*, St. Louis, Mo.)

An 81-year-old Hope, Ark., man had been pistol-whipped and robbed before, so he was ready for the three burglars as they tried to climb through his window at 5 a.m. A bullet from Johnny Holmes' rifle went through one burglar's arm and into the chest of another, killing him. (*The Gazette*, Texarkana, Ark.)

Crouching in the bedroom of her Sacramento, Calif., apartment, Judith Scott heard burglars break down two doors as they tried to elude police who interrupted their burglary of her adjoining video store. As they approached her room, Scott opened fire and wounded one. The burglars were arrested. Scott, who had been robbed and her store burglarized previously, had taken a firearms course offered by Sacramento police. (*The Union*, Sacramento, Calif.)

A would be burglar knocked loudly on the Damon, Tex., house in midafternoon and, thinking no one was home, forced open a door. The intruder was met by a housewife, who wounded him with her rifle. He and three waiting accomplices fled; four suspects were later arrested. Two of the men were on parole from burglary sentences. (*The Herald-Coaster*, Rosenberg, Tex.)

1986

After robbing a Philadelphia grocery, the armed robber began leading clerk Helen Rispo away at gunpoint. As they passed a counter, Rispo reached down, grabbed a handgun, and shot the thief in the chest, fatally wounding him. (*The Daily Times,* Clifford Heights, Penn.)

Preparing to open his Canton, Ohio, tavern, Paul Krueger heard a strange noise at the rear of the tavern and investigated with gun in hand. He found burglars prying open a back door and held them until police arrived. (*The Repository,* Canton, Ohio)

Hearing a crash, Valerie Donaldson grabbed a gun and opened her bedroom door to find four masked and armed men who had burst into her Seattle, Wash., apartment. One burglar fired, wounding her in the stomach, but Donaldson shot and killed one burglar and sent the others running for cover. (*The Chronicle,* Spokane, Wash.)

Returning home from work just before midnight, an Henrico, Co., Va., man heard a voice behind him announce, "this is a stickup." The intended victim, who had been held-up a month earlier, drew a handgun, spun around and shot his armed assailant. The robber fled, but a wounded suspect was soon arrested. (*The News-Leader,* Richmond, Va.)

Three men pretended to be browsing but didn't fool Tulsa, Okla., pharmicist Jim Sawyer. Sawyer secretly picked up his pistol, and when one of the men drew a gun, the store owner wounded him and held all three for police. Sawyer, 72, said his "sixth sense" has helped him foil three robberies in 10 years. (*The World,* Tulsa, Okla.)

Awakened by the sounds of a burglary, the Houston, Tex., homeowner called police and grabbed a shotgun. When two armed intruders burst into his bedroom, the man opened fire, killing one and sending the other fleeing. Police said they found a pistol next to the slain man's body. (*The Post,* Houston, Tex.)

"Come on, let's get her—she is here by herself," a man called out to an accomplice after breaking into a Kingsville, Tex., house. Unable to reach her husband on the telephone, the woman got a gun, fired, and killed the intruder with a single shot. (*The Record,* Kingsville, Tex.)

When a man walked into the Hatch, N. Mex., gift shop and turned the open/closed sign around, owner Jeanie Taylor knew something was amiss and grabbed a gun. The man leaped over the counter and began beating the 73-year-old woman, but she stopped the attack with a shot to her assailant's chest. (*The Sun-News,* Las Cruces, N. Mex.)

Hearing his door crash in, El Paso, Tex., resident Thomas Reed picked up a shotgun. He confronted two intruders and fired when one attacked him with a metal object. One intruder was wounded and hospitalized; his accomplice was arrested for burglary. (*The Times,* El Paso, Tex.)

APRIL 1986

The 58-year-old Garden Grove, Calif., homeowner, crippled by emphysema, looked like an easy target. But even though the man was dependent on an oxygen bottle, he managed to grab a pistol and kill the burglar who crawled in his kitchen window. (*The Herald-Examiner,* Los Angeles, Calif.)

"If you move one step, I'll blow you out," shouted Houston store clerk Mohammed Ali, getting the drop on an armed robber about to make his escape. The frightened pistol-packing thief dropped his own gun, which discharged as it hit the floor, shooting its owner in the mouth. He was held for police. (*The Chronicle,* Houston, Tex.)

A knife-wielding man and his gun-toting accomplice demanded all the receipts from Patrick Brennan's Colchester, Vt., store. All the shopkeeper presented them, though, was the muzzle of a revolver. The panicked robbers dove to the floor, crawled out the door, and fled. (*The Herald,* Rutland, Vt.)

Answering his doorbell, San Juan Capistrano, Calif., resident Craig Tantalo was jumped by two masked armed robbers. Tantalo started to give them cash, but when they threatened to shoot his dog, the angry homeowner grabbed a pistol and shot one intruder in the groin. The dog chased the other off. (*The Register,* Orange County, Calif.)

As Carrie Carter watched in horror, one burglar began ransacking her daughter's home next door while an accomplice walked across her yard and through her front door with a club. But the 64-year-old Cleveland, Tex., woman was ready, levelling her gun and wounding the man. Both burglars were later arrested. (*The Advocate,* Cleveland, Tex.)

The brash gunman was only after one thing in the Portland, Oreg., pharmacy, and ordered owner Meredith Fisher away while he cleaned out the till. He didn't notice when the pharmacist picked up a gun and set off an alarm as he sidled out the back door. Pharmacist Fisher returned, aimed his revolver carefully and twice wounded the robber as he tried to empty a cash register. (*The Oregonian,* Portland, Oreg.)

The sound of shattering glass in her Kankakee, Ill., home prompted the 19-year-old woman to fetch her revolver as she called for help. While on the phone, she was confronted by an intruder, who was scared off by two shots. (*The Daily Journal,* Kankakee, Ill.)

After loitering in the Philadelphia bookstore for an hour, a "customer" pulled a gun and began gathering the store's money. But, as a customer walked in, distracting the gunman, clerk Bobbie Lee Nesbit pulled his own gun from a shelf and wounded the robber four times. (*The Daily News,* Philadelphia, Pa.)

Two armed and masked men strolled into Margarette Lattimore's Brentwood, Fla., store, but then lost their cool. One began stammering and suddenly fired a shot, grazing the clerk's head. She dove for a .45 auto and opened fire, missing the robbers but sending them fleeing for their lives. (*The Journal,* Jacksonville, Fla.)

As James Beam walked over to the counter of his Dallas liquor store, he suddenly realized the "customer" had a gun pointed at the clerk. The robber opened fire as Beam dove behind the counter and came up shooting. The store owner was uninjured; the robber was killed. (*The Times-Herald,* Dallas, Tex.)

Stepping up to their apartment door, a Chicago couple was accosted by a stranger who demanded money. The assailant began beating the husband until the victim pulled a gun and shot the robber in the face. No charges were filed against the husband. His assailant was hospitalized. (*The Tribune,* Chicago, Ill.)

"I don't have no money," Birmingham, Ala., resident Dock Brazzle told the intruder. But it only enraged the stranger, who shot the 75-year-old apartment dweller in the chest. Brazzle had hold of his own pistol by then, however, and killed the burglar with a single shot to the head. Brazzle said the same man had robbed him earlier. (*The Post-Herald,* Birmingham, Ala.)

Police had just left after two intruders were chased from Fran Foster's Houston, Tex., home. The 76-year-old Foster heard a scream and ran to the next room, where he found one burglar was back, stabbing his wife. Foster, though severely beaten, managed to shoot the assailant four times. Both he and Mrs. Foster recovered; the burglars were imprisoned. (*The Post,* Houston, Tex.)

The young Galleria, Tex., woman awoke to hear a stranger stalking through her townhouse. She picked up a .38 and went to her bedrooom door, where the intruder appeared and lunged at her. After she fired, the burglar fled, but he was found dead a few blocks away. (*The Chronicle,* Houston, Tex.)

The masked intruder had once gotten the drop on him, so the Renton, Wash., homeowner was ready the second time. Returning home with his revolver in hand, the man found the armed stranger inside waiting for him. Both men opened fire; the wounded burglar was arrested several blocks away. (*The Times/Post-Intelligencer,* Seattle, Wash.)

JULY 1986

"Give me all your money or I'll kill you," snarled the thief, his hand hidden in a coat pocket. As the robber vaulted the convenience store counter, Norristown, Pa., store clerk Dennis Leppert grabbed his own gun and killed the robber. The dead man was a suspect in a series of recent robberies. (*The Times-Herald,* Norristown, Pa.)

Alerted by the sound of smashing glass in his Jeanerette, La., home, Harlan Lucas fetched his pistol and investigated. He confronted a burglar who lunged and struck him with a tire iron, but stopped the attack by killing the burglar with several shots. (*The Daily Iberian,* Iberia, La.)

After browsing in the Houston, Tex., store, the man suddenly pulled a gun, put it to clerk Johnny Hong's head, and demanded cash. The clerk complied but, fearing for the safety of his 2-year-old son on the floor beside him, grabbed a pistol and opened fire. The child was fine, but the robber was found dead outside. (*The Post,* Houston, Tex.)

Awakened by her dog's barking, Tracy Strawn picked up a revolver and stepped outside her bedroom just in time to see a man's head poking around a corner in her apartment. The young Lubbock, Tex., nurse fired just as the intruder charged. She managed to get off one more shot before he overpowered her, but that was enough. The wounded burglar fled and was arrested nearby. (*The Evening Journal,* Lubbock, Tex.)

The armed robber had surprised the elderly couple in their Oklahoma City, Okla., garage, beating the man and threatening to kill them both. But the tables were turned when neighbor James Owen, hearing the commotion, arrived with pistol in hand. He wounded the burglar, who was later arrested, and was credited with saving the lives of his neighbors. (*The Daily Oklahoman,* Oklahoma City, Okla.)

Joe Gonzalez looked up from the counter of his Daytona Beach, Fla., grocery just in time to see a man pull a pistol and start shooting. Both Gonzalez and his wife grabbed handguns of their own, however, and wounded the would-be robber. Arrested at a hospital, the man is a suspect in two murders in an earlier robbery. (*The Sentinel,* Orlando, Fla.)

Harry Thompson was awakened as two of his children leaped across his bed, terrified. "Daddy, there are two men climbing into our room," one said. Thompson picked up a handgun and confronted one burglar who, despite a warning shot, came at him until the homeowner wounded him and held him for police. Thompson said he is disabled after being mugged seven times in four years. (*The Chronicle,* San Francisco, Calif.)

185

On his knees with a robber's gun at his head, Denver restaurant manager Bruce Cluster thought he was a dead man. But when the crazed, screaming thief set his gun down for a moment, Cluster saw his chance. He dove for his own .357 Mag. and fired until the advancing assailant fell dead. (*The Rocky Mountain News,* Denver, Colo.)

The shadowy figure kicked a box out of the way and kept coming, despite Cincinnati store owner Bob Cotter's warning to stop. Cotter had no option but to level his shotgun, wounding the late-night burglar with a blast of birdshot. (*The Enquirer,* Cincinnnati, Ohio)

As the Spanaway, Wash., woman investigated noises in her home, an assailant suddenly leaped out, struck her on the head with a hammer, and attempted to rape her. She managed to recover, however, and drove off the intruder with a handgun. (*The News-Tribune,* Tacoma, Wash.)

The burglar thought he had it made. The phone lines were cut, he'd broken into the mobile home undetected and he had the 67-year-old woman trapped alone in her bedroom. What he hadn't planned for was the pistol Romelia Martinez of Albuquerque, N.Mex., used to shoot him in the chest. (*The Tribune,* Albuquerque, N.Mex.)

It took several armed robberies to finally persuade Brooklyn store owner Mikail Kats to buy a handgun for protection. It came in handy when three robbers, one armed with a gun, walked into the store and demanded cash. Kats gave one bandit $100, then a .25-cal. slug in the chest. The wounded robber later died, and his alleged partners were arrested. (*The Daily News,* New York, N.Y.)

Bursting into the Flat Creek, Ky., home, the masked robber pointed a gun at the horrified family and demanded drugs and money. Homeowner Walter Peach grabbed a handgun and killed the intruder. Police arrested an alleged partner. (*The Herald-Leader,* Lexington, Ky.)

He had just opened the store for the day, so Birmingham, Ala., pharmacist William Camp hadn't yet taken off the gun he carried to work. That was unfortunate for the robber who walked in and stuck a pistol in Camp's face; in the ensuing shootout, the robber was critically wounded, but Camp was unhurt. The robber was free on bond for two earlier robbery charges, police said. (*The News,* Birmingham, Ala.)

The intruder had already raped the young mother at knifepoint in the presence of her children, and was leading her to another room. While he was distracted, the Lemon Grove, Calif., woman grabbed a handgun. As the rapist approached her with the knife, she fired once, wounding him critically. (*The Daily Californian,* Berkeley, Calif.)

OCTOBER 1986

Posing as a package carrier, a man forced his way into Charisse Gross' Baltimore, Md., home, drew a handgun and demanded money and jewelry. The gunman herded the 28-year-old woman upstairs to her son's bedroom, where he attempted to tie up the boy. While he was distracted, Gross slipped away, grabbed her .38, and fired at the intruder, striking him. The man fled and a suspect was arrested later by authorities. (*The Sun,* Baltimore, Md.)

Retired Troy, N.Y., police officer William Gilley and his wife were relaxing on a boat dock when a man approached, saying he had a gun and wanted their money. The 68-year-old Gilley said he had to get his wallet from his van, but pulled a handgun from under the seat instead and held the would-be robber for police. (*The Record,* Troy, N.Y.)

Hearing a prowler in the store in front of his Dayton, Ohio, home, Joe Hurlburt armed himself and went to investigate. The electronic repair shop owner confronted an intruder and kept him covered with the gun while phoning police. "Here's your free ride downtown," Hurlburt told the burglar when police arrived. (*The Daily News,* Dayton, Ohio)

Rickie Curtis was on the phone to police after hearing someone attempting to gain entrance to his Alderson, Okla., home. But when an intruder kicked in the front door, Curtis dropped the phone and went for his .38. When the man started toward him, the homeowner fired, killing the man. (*The News-Capital & Democrat,* McAlester, Okla.)

Hearing noises in her apartment at 2 a.m., a South Side Chicago, Ill., woman got her handgun and found a man crawling through her kitchen window. She shot the intruder once, killing him. No charges were filed against the woman. (*The Tribune,* Chicago, Ill.)

Waking to find a light on in his Sarasota, Fla., home, Frank Falato called out for his mother, who was staying at his home. Discovering an intruder trying to escape the house, the homeowner tackled the man. In the meantime, his wife got a .22 pistol and handed it to Falato, who held it at the man's head until police arrived. (*The Herald-Tribune,* Sarasota, Fla.)

A Chula Vista, Calif., couple on a weekend fishing trip along the Mexican border was menaced by 10 men, some armed with knives. When the men split into two groups and circled John Spizale's camper, he got his .45 pistol. One of the men pointed at his gun, asking, "Bullets?" Spizale replied that the gun was indeed loaded and that he was prepared to use it. The group then left, and the Border Patrol said the gun's presence probably saved the couple. (*The Star-News,* Chula Vista, Calif.)

When a Myrtle Grove, Fla., woman heard noises in her garage, she loaded her gun and walked to the kitchen, turning on the lights. Suddenly, the 58-year-old woman heard a male voice cry out, "She has a gun as big as her." The would-be thieves fled the premises. (*The News Journal*, Pensacola, Fla.)

Breaking in through a kitchen window, a knife-wielding intruder walked into the bedroom of Nancy Tomlinson's Macon, Ga., home. The man, his pants unzipped, advanced despite the 33-year-old woman's warnings. She snatched her 20-ga. shotgun from beside the bed and killed the man with a single blast. (*The Telegraph*, Macon, Ga.)

A 64-year-old Glendale, Ariz., man was awakened by his doorbell ringing and went to the door, seeing a stranger outside. When the prowler moved away from the door, the homeowner got his .22 revolver. After again ringing the doorbell the intruder kicked down the door. The alarmed resident opened fire, and the man fled. A suspect with gunshot wounds was later questioned by police at a local hospital. (*The Gazette*, Phoenix, Ariz.)

Off-duty Detroit, Mich., policeman Robert Winbourn was attacked by three would-be robbers, one of whom was armed with a gun. Winbourn drew his service revolver, exchanged fire with the gunman and wounded him. The other two men escaped. (*The News*, Detroit, Mich.)

After a heavily armed gunman broke into Jeremy Sterger's Wilton, Calif., home, killed his brother and his father's girlfriend and wounded his father, the 14-year-old boy ran to his room. Turning off the lights, the boy got his .22 revolver and took cover behind his door. When the intruder entered, the youth fired three times, downing his assailant. His father arrived and shot the man once more with a .22 rifle, killing the gunman. No charges were filed against the Stergers. (*The Union*, Sacramento, Calif.)

Raped in her bed while her unsuspecting husband worked outside in the garage, a 62-year-old Fort Worth woman grabbed a handgun and tried to telephone police as the rapist ransacked her home. The phone was dead. When the intruder marched her husband into the kitchen at gunpoint, the woman exchanged shots with the rapist, putting a shot in his head as he wrestled her husband. Seriously injured, the criminal fled and was apprehended by police. (*The Fort Worth Star Telegraph*, Fort Worth, Tex.)

A man asking to use the telephone at a Bayside, Oreg., woman's apartment walked in and pushed her down on a couch and began ripping her clothes off. Breaking free, the 21-year-old woman grabbed her .22 revolver and pointed it at the assailant, saying she knew how to use it. The would-be rapist fled. (*The Press Herald*, Portland, Oreg.)

FEBRUARY 1987

A Dania, Fla., man was prepared when he heard someone prying open the window of his home, the fifth intrusion in two months. Kirtley Estes, who is confined to a wheelchair, had been beaten and robbed in previous break-ins; but when he heard the man prying at his window with a hatchet he fired. A wounded suspect was arrested at a local hospital and charged with armed burglary and aggravated assault. Estes was not charged. (*The Herald*, Miami, Fla.)

A New Orleans, La., woman was getting out of her car when accosted by two armed robbers demanding money. Instead of giving them money, the 34-year-old woman pulled a gun and fired at her assailants. Two wounded suspects were detained by police at a local hospital. (*The Times-Picayune*, New Orleans, La.)

Thomas Wright answered a knock at his Jacksonville, Fla., motel room door, and was accosted by two men, both armed. Wright, 68, managed to reach a pistol he had on a dresser, fire, and shoot one of his attackers. Both assailants fled, but a wounded suspect was arrested at a hospital and charged with attempted robbery and attempted murder. (*The Florida Times-Union*, Jacksonville, Fla.)

While Patrick Kelly was getting ready to make a delivery from his dairy truck in Pensacola, Fla., two men approached and stood behind him. Without saying a word, one struck Kelly with a tire iron, but the truck driver whipped out a pistol and fired on his assailants. One assailant was slightly wounded, and Kelly chased him down and held him for police. An accomplice was later picked up by police, and both were charged with attempted robbery. (*The News Journal*, Pensacola, Fla.)

When 16-year-old Brian Urbanek saw a man approach his family's Cedar Rapids, Iowa, home, he woke his mother and grabbed his .410 shotgun. As he loaded, he heard his mother yell and ran downstairs to find her grappling with the knife-wielding intruder. After several warnings, Urbanek fatally shot the man. A juvenile court judge found the youth innocent in the slaying, saying the boy was only trying to protect his mother. (*The Register*, Des Moines, Iowa)

William Schroeder thwarted a robbery attempt at his Caledonia, Wis., bar when a man entered shortly after closing time and demanded money, pulling a pistol from his pocket. Schroeder responded: "I have a shotgun and will blow your head off." The armed man fled the bar. (*The Times Journal*, Racine, Wis.)

1987

THE ARMED CITIZEN

A man entering a Dallas, Tex., ice cream store had a coat draped over his arm, as if hiding a gun, and demanded money from the register. The cashier pulled a handgun and said, "Tonight we are going to shoot each other because I have a gun, too." The would-be robber fled the shop empty-handed. (*The Times Herald*, Dallas, Tex.)

Kee Kim's wife was behind the counter of their Philadelphia, Pa., grocery store when a man armed with a knife attempted to rob the store. After the intruder grabbed her, Kim, who was in an aisle, drew his registered .38 and shot the man. Following a struggle, the grocer killed the would-be burglar. Police said the shooting was self-defense. (*The Inquirer*, Philadelphia, Pa.)

During a robbery of his Palmer, Mass., jewelry store, Richard Theriault's wife and a clerk were assaulted by a man wielding an electronic stun gun. Hearing the commotion, the owner armed himself and confronted the armed intruder on a staircase. Theriault raised his pistol and shot the man, killing him. (*The Morning Union*, Springfield, Mass.)

A vacationing Texas policeman and his wife were parked on a New Orleans, La., street looking at a map when they were approached by three men. The trio walked away after asking Rudolpho Salazar for the time, but one returned with a gun when Salazar got out of his car. The gunman tried to rob him and threatened his life. The policeman waited for the would-be burglar to repeat the demand several times, then drew a .25 cal. pistol from his pocket and fatally wounded the gunman. (*The State-Times*, Baton Rouge, La.)

Karen Lampkin was watching television in her Kansas City, Kans., home when a youth broke in the front window, apparently intent on burglarizing the house. She shot and killed the intruder. A judge ruled that "she had every right to use force to terminate the unlawful entry into her home." (*The Times*, Kansas City, Kans.)

An Estacada, Oreg., store owner took a .38 revolver with him when he went to investigate noises in his shop. Beryl Hartsock saw two burglars loading cigarettes into a box and told them to freeze. One of the men fled, but the proprietor detained the other intruder until police arrived. (*The Oregonian*, Portland, Oreg.)

Eugene Thompson of Augusta, Ga., was awakened in the middle of the night by the sound of glass breaking in his home. He saw one man outside a rear window and heard a second man kicking his bedroom door and demanding money. When the intruder burst through the door, the 52-year-old homeowner fatally shot him. Authorities ruled the shooting self-defense. (*The Chronicle, Herald*, Augusta, Ga.)

Awakened by noises in her Los Angeles, Calif., home, a 70-year-old widow picked up her .38 and started for the living room. She confronted an ex-convict armed with a screwdriver at the bedroom door and opened fire, killing the intruder. (*The Times*, Los Angeles, Calif.)

MAY 1987

While opening a Lubbock, Tex., truck parts store, Wayne Higgins heard a dog barking and looked out to see a masked man in the window. The employee went into an office to get a handgun as the man entered the store. Higgins yelled that he had a gun, and the intruder opened fire. Higgins returned fire, and following the exchange the man fled. (*The Avalanche-Journal*, Lubbock, Tex.)

An office worker leaving her Harris County, Tex., office building was accosted by a man who tried to rob her. At first, she struggled with her assailant, but then agreed to give him jewelry. Instead, she drew a gun from her purse and fatally shot her attacker. The man was on parole for robbery and theft. (*The Chronicle*, Houston, Tex.)

Timothy Clark awoke to the sound of someone breaking into his Memphis, Tenn., townhouse. Attacked by the intruder, Clark called to his wife, and she brought him a .22 rifle. During the struggle, the resident wounded his assailant but the intruder continued the attack. Clark fired once more, fatally wounding him. (*The Commercial Appeal*, Memphis, Tenn.)

A Milwaukee, Wis., bartender was alone with a customer who came behind the bar and beat her with a bottle and a pool cue. The man began rifling the cash register, and threatened the woman bartender, who reached for a gun and wounded her assailant. He then fled. (*The Journal*, Milwaukee, Wis.)

Dennis Donovan was talking to a customer in a Portland, Oreg., convenience store when an armed man wearing a ski mask burst through the door. "This is for real, hit the floor," the man shouted, and he began firing. Donovan reached for a .357 Mag. under the counter and shot back, forcing the robber out the door. It was not known if the intruder was hit. (*The Oregonian*, Portland, Oreg.)

Sacramento, Calif., apartment manager Joseph Harshaw was told to evict a tenant. The tenant came to Harshaw's apartment, and, after the men talked awhile, the man pulled a butcher knife. The manager's cousin wrestled the man outside, and Harshaw ordered him off the property. When the knife-wielder came at Harshaw, who was armed with a .357 Mag., the manager warned him off. When the man continued to advance, the Vietnam veteran fired when his assailant was about 3 ft. away, fatally wounding him. (*The Bee*, Sacramento, Calif.)

188

Rex Sims was awakened early in the morning by a noise at his screened porch and the sound of his dog barking outside his Bonita Springs, Fla., home. Arming himself with a handgun, the resident went to his back door, where he saw a naked man trying to break in a sliding glass door. Sims went outside and held the man at bay while his wife called authorities. (*The Daily News,* Naples, Fla.)

After robbing a Fort Wayne, Ind., pizza store, a stickup man attempted to rob Scott Collier's liquor store. When the man came in wearing a mask and his hand shoved in a pocket, the store owner grabbed a shotgun and forced the would-be robber to lie on the floor. Collier frisked the man and called police, who booked the man on two counts of armed robbery. (*The News-Sentinel,* Fort Wayne, Ind.)

Seventy-year-old Eric Christian stepped onto the porch of his Louisville, Ky., home to check a bird feeder when he was attached by an armed masked man. His 72-year-old wife tried to lock the door, but the man caught her and dragged the elderly couple into the backyard. Alerted by the noise, two neighbors, one armed with a handgun, came to see what was happening. When confronted by one neighbor, the attacker ran to the front of the house where he met Jeff Tafel. The intruder shot at Tafel, who returned fire and killed the man. Tafel was not charged. (*The Courier-Journal,* Louisville, Ky.)

At a Cleveland, Ohio, doughnut shop a knife-wielding robber ordered two female clerks to lie on the floor. When he ordered Bonnie Kerkhoff to hand over her purse, she complied but produced a .38 revolver from it and fired at the intruder, wounding him. Police charged a wounded suspect with aggravated robbery. (*The Plain Dealer,* Cleveland, Ohio)

A Bridgeport, Conn., resident went to help two men who said their car had broken down near his home. But when his wife saw the pair strike her husband with a hammer, she came out of the house firing a .38. She struck one of the assailants, and two suspects were arrested at a local hospital where the injured man sought medical treatment. (*The Evening Post,* Bridgeport, Conn.)

Shu Kun Lee was alone in his Jersey City, N.J., stationery store when a man walked in, pulled a revolver and demanded money. As the proprietor began walking to the back of the store, the gunman struck Lee with the gun. The intruder began to take the money, and Lee grabbed his licensed .38, warning the man to stop. When the criminal replied he was going to take the money and then shoot Lee, and then turned his gun toward him, the owner fired, wounding the man. With the aid of a customer, Lee held the wounded suspect for police. (*The Jersey Journal,* Jersey City, N.J.)

Celester Thompson saw three men start to break into her Tulsa, Okla., home and figured she was about to be robbed. She woke her son and the pair armed themselves and hid in the bathroom. When the first of the burglars entered the home, the mother and son captured the intruder and held him for police. The accomplices fled. (*The World,* Tulsa, Okla.)

An intruder forced his way into Connie Peoples' Georgetown, La., home and began threatening her and a 16-year-old babysitter. When the man entered her bedroom, Peoples killed him with a single blast from a 16-ga. shotgun. (*The Town Talk,* Alexandria, La.)

AUGUST 1987

Two men were waiting for Leonard Freidberg, a 47-year-old taxi driver from Jacksonville, Fla., dispatched to an early morning fare. After the cab took the two to their destination, the duo assaulted Freidberg with a small pistol. Freidberg picked up his own .357 revolver and fired, mortally wounding one of his attackers. The slain robber had an extensive prior arrest record. The taxi driver was not charged. (*The Democrat,* Talahassee, Fla.)

Chester Blanchard was in the kitchen of his Stark County, Ohio, home when he heard his back door being forced. A masked and hooded intruder entered and fired at Blanchard. The 61-year-old homeowner responded by grabbing a handgun and opening fire, seriously wounding his attacker. Blanchard, the victim of a burglary two weeks prior, said, "He must not have been able to see anything except straight ahead, which probably saved me." (*The Beacon Journal,* Akron, Ohio)

A man entered Jim Barr's La Habra, Calif., jewelry store to ask for directions. But when an accomplice entered and pulled a gun, Barr grabbed a .38 revolver from a shelf only to come under fire from the two robbers in the store and two others outside, who smashed a window with a sledgehammer. After the store owner emptied his revolver, the robbers fled. (*The Register,* Orange County, Calif.)

A Salt Lake City, Utah, homeowner was disturbed late at night by knocking at his door. After telephoning police, the homeowner armed himself and answered the door. An armed man standing in the door fired at the resident, who returned fire. In the ensuing struggle the homeowner fatally wounded the man. (*The Tribune,* Salt Lake City, Utah)

A 78-year-old Crestwood, Ala., widow heard a noise at her back door and saw a man cutting a hole in her screen door. After recognizing him as a man who had raped and robbed her previously and a suspect in a series of rapes, she drove off the intruder with gunfire. (*The News,* Birmingham, Ala.)

THE ARMED CITIZEN

A paroled convicted murderer, fleeing from sheriff's deputies from three Texas counties following a three-day crime spree, ran afoul of the armed citizens near Magnolia. When one resident fired a .357 at the fugitive after hearing the screams of a neighbor, the man sought refuge at another home. The homeowner brandished a hunting rifle, and the parolee fled into the brush, where he was apprehended by police. (*The Chronicle*, Houston, Tex.)

An armed man walked into a Sherman Oaks, Calif., liquor store and demanded that the customers and a front clerk lie down on the floor. A teenage clerk working in the rear armed himself with a handgun, and, in a confrontation with the intruder, fatally wounded him. Police said the case would be treated as a justifiable homicide. (*The Daily News*, Van Nuys, Calif.)

When an armed man attempted to rob Salvatore Caruso's San Diego, Calif., shoe repair shop for the second time, the 61-year-old owner decided to fight back. While handing money to the robber with his left hand, Caruso fired a .38 revolver from his right, wounding the armed man. The wounded man was held by police on suspicion of armed robbery. A preliminary investigation showed Caruso was justified in shooting the robber. (*The Union*, San Diego, Calif.)

An armed holdup man invaded the Miami, Fla., apartment of 50-year-old Lamar Johnson. When the intruder turned his back on Johnson to demand money from another resident, Johnson seized the chance to grab a shotgun from her bedroom. The resident then fired her shotgun at her assailant, who fled the apartment, only to be arrested by police nearby. (*The Herald*, Miami, Fla.)

An elderly Grass Valley, Calif., couple was awakened at 3 a.m. by the sounds of a break-in. Jay McLeod armed himself with a handgun. After two masked men attacked him and his wife, Inez, the badly injured homeowner fired at his assailants, who fled. (*The Union*, Grass Valley, Calif.)

Alice Teamer, a 39-year-old resident of northwest Detroit, Mich., was upstairs in her home at night when a man banged on her front door, demanded to be let in, and then crashed through her front window. Teamer reached for a rifle and fired, mortally wounding the intruder. (*The Free Press*, Detroit, Mich.)

An inmate who had escaped from a correctional facility near Birmingham, Ala., was captured for police by resident Gordon Rickles. While watching a television report of the escape, 47-year-old Rickles heard his dog barking outside. Noticing his dog was holding at bay a suspicious man armed with a large stick, Rickles grabbed a carbine and, with other armed neighbors, held the escapee for police. (*The Post-Herald*, Birmingham, Ala.)

Linda Henderson had received phone calls from a stranger who said he intended to "come over." When two men began to batter down the door of the 53-year-old woman's North Houston, Tex., apartment, Henderson immediately phoned the police. As the door was kicked in Henderson fired several shots from a .38 revolver, fatally wounding one intruder. The other intruder escaped. No charges were filed against Henderson. (*The Chronicle*, Houston, Tex.)

NOVEMBER 1987

When her daughter frantically told Sandra Valencia that a burglar was breaking into their Harris County, Tex., home, the fact that the 26-year-old mother was in the shower didn't slow her response. Telling her daughter to call police while she grabbed her revolver, Valencia confronted the intruder in the kitchen. When the burglar hefted a barstool, the housewife lifted her revolver and fired, fatally wounding the criminal. (*The Chronicle*, Houston, Tex.)

Noticing the back door of his Lake Charles, La., store was open in the early morning hours, Von Ned took his pistol along as he investigated, having been burglarized previously. Confronting two burglars, the storekeeper ordered the pair to stop; when they continued to advance Von Ned fired, killing one burglar and setting the other to flight. The other man was later arrested by police, who said both men were free on bond from other charges. (*The American Press*, Lake Charles, La.)

At first, William Tolbert thought the early morning noise in his Ensley, Ala., home was only his dog scratching at the window. But when he heard the noise again, the homeowner quickly armed himself. He discovered an armed man entering his home and ordered the man to lay down his weapon. The man refused, and Tolbert opened fire, wounding the burglar. Police disclosed the man was sought on warrants for burglary and rape in two earlier incidents. (*The Post-Herald*, Birmingham, Ala.)

Norris Hamilton, a 77-year-old resident of St. Louis, Mo., was getting into his car when a holdup man shoved him against the vehicle and began to go through his pockets. Hamilton drew a handgun from another pocket and shot and killed the robber. Police said the dead holdup man had a criminal record. (*The Post-Dispatch*, St. Louis, Mo.)

Recognizing a shotgun-wielding robber as the man who had held up his Houston, Tex., store less than a month earlier, a convenience store clerk decided twice was enough. Instead of handing over the cash, the clerk drew a pistol, fired, and then held the wounded man for police. A suspect was charged with two counts of aggravated robbery. Investigators believed the suspect was connected with several other area robberies. (*The Chronicle*, Houston, Tex.)

190

Awakened when her dog began barking, a 101-year-old St. Clairsville, Ohio, woman quickly phoned police to report someone had cut off her electricity and was trying to break into her house. Deputies dispatched to the scene found the elderly homeowner holding a juvenile suspect at bay with a .32-20 revolver dating from before the turn of the century. The suspect was taken into custody. (*The Times-Leader,* Martins Ferry, Ohio)

When Mamie Thornton awoke in her Birmingham, Ala., home, she found a man's hand over her mouth. Bending back one of her attacker's fingers to make him release his grip, the 87-year-old jumped out of bed and ran for her revolver. Firing a shot in the direction of the intruder, the elderly homeowner forced her assailant to flee the premises. (*The News,* Birmingham, Ala.)

Two strangers were met at gunpoint by Lloyd Carter of Gretna, La., after the homeowner heard the two kick down his front door. Carter confronted the two burglars and ordered them to leave. The pair continued to advance into the house, however, and Carter opened fire, mortally wounding one man. The other culprit fled. (*The Times-Picayune,* New Orleans, La.)

Carol Earp of St. Petersburg, Fla., knew there was something wrong when she arrived home from work early one day. Taking up her pistol, the woman moved slowly through her house, checking each room. As Earp approached her bedroom, a bandana-masked man with a knife appeared in the doorway. Firing twice, Earp wounded the knife-wielder. A wounded suspect was charged with armed robbery. (*The City Times and Independent,* St. Petersburg, Fla.)

U.S. Fish and Wildlife Service biologist B.J. Schmitz was puzzled when the geese she was studying about 185 miles northwest of Fairbanks, Alaska, began stirring. Glancing up, she found a grizzly bear about 15 ft. away digging roots. The bear charged as Schmitz pumped a shell into her 12-ga. shotgun's chamber. Her shot from the hip took the grizzly in the head, killing it instantly. "What if I hadn't had my gun?" Schmitz reflected afterward. (*The Times,* Seattle, Wash.)

Sid Bowden and Grey Hemmett of Baton Rouge, La., teamed up after Bowden's son noticed two suspicious men trying to get into a neighboring house. After notifying police, Bowden reached for his shotgun and Hammett grabbed his revolver. The duo then took up vantage points around the house to prevent the burglars from leaving. Police later arrested three suspects on burglary charges. When asked why he and his neighbor had taken action. Bowden replied, "If we hadn't taken action, they would have been back again tonight." (*The Morning Advocate,* Baton Rouge, La.)

Alerted by the sound of his front door being kicked in, Lexington, Ky., resident Bernard McCarthy armed himself. When a knife-wielding burglar burst into McCarthy's residence, the homeowner warned he would shoot. As the man continued to threaten him with a knife, McCarthy fired, wounding him. Charges of first-degree burglary were placed against the man. (*The Herald-Leader,* Lexington, Ky.)

MARCH 1988

When her landlord forced his way into her Salt Lake City, Utah, home and began beating her friend over a dispute involving automotive repairs, Michele Hansen grabbed her .44 Mag. handgun and repeatedly ordered him to leave. When he instead lunged at her, Hansen fired, killing him. A circuit judge dismissed charges against Hansen, who went into labor after the shooting and gave birth to a son later the same evening. (*The Tribune,* Salt Lake City, Utah)

Fort Ann, N.Y., resident Arthur Stiles had been burgled in 1984 and $33,000 was stolen. Three years later, one of the same burglars, who had been given a one-year prison sentence, returned to "mastermind" a second burglary attempt. This time, however, Stiles was armed and ready when two burglars entered his kitchen, wounding one of the intruders. For his effort in the second burglary, the "mastermind" got a five- to 10-year sentence in state prison. (*The Post-Star,* Glen Falls, N.Y.)

After surprising a thief trying to run off with the cashbox from his Dingmans Ferry, Pa., restaurant, Robert Edwards retrieved a handgun from his office and held the intruder at gunpoint while he phoned police. But when the thwarted thief began smashing furniture and threatened Edwards with a broken chair, the restaurant owner fired twice, wounding the man. Charges of aggravated assault and theft against the suspect were dropped as a result of plea bargaining, but the man pled guilty to making terroristic threats. (*The Wayne Independent,* Honesdale, Pa.)

Roy Dieffenderfer of Monroeville, Ohio, and his wife were at home when two armed men barged in, demanding money. Handing over his cash, Dieffenderfer indicated that he needed to go to a bedroom to get more. But once inside the room, the resident armed himself with a .357 Mag. revolver and, in an exchange of gunfire in which Dieffenderfer himself was wounded, killed one of his attackers. The local prosecutor ruled the incident a justifiable homicide. (*The Journal,* Lorain, Ohio)

1988

Gunsmith Roy Hinton was working in the back of a San Antonio, Tex., shop when two armed robbers used a stolen pickup truck to smash the front window. Investigating with shotgun in hand, Hinton was fired on by the intruders. Returning fire, the gunsmith drove off his attackers. Co-owner Dell Toedt commented, "It shows what a citizen can do to protect his property." (*The Express-News*, San Antonio, Tex.)

Stephen McDermott, a Quincy, Mass., college student, was studying alone in his parents' house when he heard voices downstairs. Grabbing a rifle, McDermott went to the stairs and, confronting a stranger, fired down the stairs. Two burglars, one with a minor wound caused by a bullet ricochet, fled the house. The local district attorney announced that legal action was not anticipated against McDermott in the incident. (*The Patriot Ledger*, Quincy, Mass.)

After his release from prison, a "cat burglar" returned to a senior citizens' complex in Seal Beach, Calif., to continue a series of break-ins that had numbered his own parents among the victims. When the burglar scaled a wall early in the morning and headed for a house, a 76-year-old resident opened fire with a handgun. The wounded suspect fled and was later arrested by police. (*The Press-Telegram*, Long Beach, Calif.)

Hueytown, Ala., resident Jadie Bailey was awakened by his wife after she saw an intruder in their upstairs bathroom. Armed with a pistol, Bailey went to investigate. When he turned on a light, the burglar opened fire. Wounded, Bailey returned fire, forcing the man to smash through a window in his escape. The suspect later arrested by police at a county hospital was thought to have been responsible for a string of regional burglaries. (*The Post-Herald*, Birmingham, Ala.)

The first time Jose Barrios was held up, the Miami, Fla., resident lost his left eye to an assailant's bullets. But the second time Barrios was ready with his own revolver when a pair of armed robbers tried to stick up his market. When one robber demanded cash at gunpoint, Barrios drew and fired, wounding the man, who fled. Two suspects were arrested on armed robbery and related charges. (*The Herald*, Miami, Fla.)

After a pistol-toting robber held up a neighboring San Diego, Calif., store and wounded the owner's son, barber Freddie Orlando armed himself with a pistol and cornered the man in an alley. Ordering the armed robber to drop his gun, Orlando then made the man lie spread-eagled on the ground until police arrived. Police said the suspect taken into custody had been recently released on parole. (*The Union*, San Diego, Calif.)

After a string of neighborhood burglaries, a group of four Beaumont, Tex., residents armed with shotguns, handguns, and bats pursued a burglary suspect to an overgrown field. Police and residents then joined forces to capture the suspect, who had set some dry grass on fire to elude pursuit. A police detective later commented, "In the rush, we didn't have time to get their names, but we really appreciated it." (*The Enterprise*, Beaumont, Tex.)

A man had followed Naomi Owens from a Birmingham, Ala., shoe store and then forced his way into her car by pretending to have a gun. The pretense vanished when Owens drew her own .38 revolver from her pocketbook, and, in a struggle with the assailant, mortally wounded him. No charges were brought against Owens. (*The News*, Birmingham, Ala.)

JUNE 1988

Miami, Fla., cabdriver Mark Yuhr had just delivered his fare when the passenger pulled out a pistol and screamed demands for money. Instead, as the robber looked away momentarily, Yuhr, who was recently licensed for concealed carry under a new Florida law, reached for his own .45 and opened fire, killing his assailant. The man had an extensive criminal record that included armed robbery, firearm violations and the attempted first-degree murder of a police officer. Police said, "This sends a major message to the rest of the robbers out there." (*The Herald*, Miami, Fla.)

As two men began kicking down the door of his St. Louis, Mo., house, Robert Reed armed himself. Opening fire when the two intruders entered his residence, Reed wounded one of the pair. Both fled, but police later arrested a suspect at a nearby hospital. Reed, 70, said, "If I hadn't had a gun maybe I'd be in bad shape. They could have knocked me off." (*The Post-Dispatch*, St. Louis, Mo.)

Two robbers held Lou Marks and his daughter at knifepoint in their St. Petersburg, Fla., home. Marks, 84, distracted the men by offering to show them jewelry in another room. One drawer contained diamonds, and, as one robber began stuffing them in his pockets, Marks drew a handgun from another drawer and fired, wounding one assailant and sending the other to flight. "I don't feel a bit of remorse," Marks said. "They weren't going to let me live." (*The Times*, St. Petersburg, Fla.)

Lexington, N.C., resident Blaine Springer arrived home to find a pair of burglars had broken into his home. When one of the housebreakers pulled out a pistol, Springer retreated to a neighbor's to phone police, but when the intruders made their own retreat, the homeowner followed and took the duo captive with a shotgun. Police said both suspects had also been charged with breaking and entering, and larceny in connection with another recent burglary. (*The Journal*, Winston-Salem, N.C.)

When his wife was critically wounded and maimed in their Clyde, Wis., house by three escapees from a detention home armed with a shotgun, Harold Morris, 62, drove them off with shots from his revolver. Morris, who recently underwent triple bypass surgery and has an artificial leg, managed to get his wife to a neighbor for assistance after realizing the attackers had cut the phone lines. All three fugitives were arrested after a search effort that involved officers from four county sheriff's departments. (*The State Journal,* Madison, Wis.)

When a stranger began pounding on her front door, then flung himself through her bay window, a 53-year-old Los Angeles, Calif., woman reached for the .38 revolver she kept in the house and opened fire. The mortally wounded intruder dove back through shards of glass in his efforts to escape. Police said no charges will be brought against the woman. (*The Times,* Los Angeles, Calif.)

Eleven-year-old Todd Knight of Switzer, S.C., was home alone after school for the first time when two "rough looking" men broke in through a window. Realizing he had no way to escape, Knight loaded his .22 rifle, a Christmas gift, and when the two intruders spotted him as they were ransacking the house, the boy opened fire, killing both burglars. The county sheriff's department, calling the shootings justifiable, said both men had records. (*The Herald-Journal,* Spartanburg, S.C.)

A Spokane, Wash., woman, confronted by a burglar in her home, opened fire with her pistol, sending him fleeing. Police used a dog to follow the trail of the fugitive, charging a suspect later arrested by sheriff's deputies with first-degree burglary. (*The Spokesman-Review Chronicle,* Spokane, Wash.)

Hearing noises in the basement of his Collinsville, Ill., house, Thomas Williamson went to investigate, taking along his .357 Mag. handgun. Fearing for his life when he discovered a burglar trying to conceal himself on the stairs, the homeowner fired once, killing the intruder. Authorities said no criminal charges would be sought against the resident, stating Williamson was "protecting himself and his dwelling." The dead man had just completed a prison sentence for burglary. (*The Intelligencer,* Edwardsville, Ill.)

When Jennie Crowder of San Antonio, Tex., woke to find an intruder "doing something with her bra" in her closet, the 44-year-old NRA Life Member got her handgun from a nightstand, turned on the lights and ordered the man into the living room while she phoned police. A suspect charged with burglary of a habitation with intent to commit sexual assault was found to have Crowder's money and diamond rings in a trouser pocket. (*The Express-News,* San Antonio, Tex.)

Previous break-ins at his Germantown, Pa., home prepared Mark Robin for an early morning burglary attempt. Firing his revolver, 49-year-old Robin sent the intruder to flight. Police arrested a wounded suspect who was later charged with burglary, criminal trespass and attempted theft. (*The Inquirer,* Philadelphia, Pa.)

Two men who broke into a Hartford, Conn., home made the mistake of waking the sleeping owner. The resident grabbed a gun and opened fire, killing one intruder and forcing the other to flee through a glass window. No charges were filed against the homeowner. (*The Courant,* Hartford, Conn.)

SEPTEMBER 1988

Michael Salerno of Phoenix, Ariz., was showering when he heard his dogs barking. Taking up his 9 mm handgun, Salerno investigated and found an armed burglar in his kitchen with a cocked revolver. Firing, the homeowner mortally wounded the intruder. Police said the slain man had Salerno's wallet in his possession. (*The Republic,* Phoenix, Ariz.)

Orlando, Fla., Mayor Bill Frederick was at a restaurant cash register when someone rushed in and said a woman was being assaulted in a car outside. Frederick and another patron rushed to her rescue, pulling the man off the woman and out of the car. The assailant came up swinging a long screwdriver he had allegedly used to assault his estranged wife, and then fled. Mayor Frederick retrieved a police-issued handgun from his city car, jumped in another good samaritan's truck and pursued. The man came to bay when the mayor fired a warning shot in the air. Police charged the man with aggravated battery and attempted murder. (*The Tribune,* Tampa, Fla.)

Awakened by his dog's growls, Savannah, Ga., resident Dennis Warren reached for his handgun and went to his bedroom door. Discovering a man advancing toward him in the hallway, Warren announced he was armed and ordered the intruder to stop. But, as Warren backed into his bedroom, the burglar lunged at him, and the resident fired. He then held the wounded man at gunpoint while his wife summoned police, who charged the man with burglary. (*The Evening Press,* Savannah, Ga.)

When a knife-wielding man broke into his ex-girlfriend's home and assaulted her, neighbors Fred and Mary Harrell answered the girl's mother's cries for help. As the nude attacker confronted a group of neighbors in the front yard, he knocked down Fred Harrell and tried to slash him. Harrell's wife retrieved the shotgun her struggling husband dropped and killed his assailant. Police, who were tracing the slain man's record, said the slaying appeared justified. (*The Herald,* Miami, Fla.)

Terrorized by a burglar who had forced open the front door of her Tifton, Ga., house and threatened her life in the middle of the night, 92-year-old Clara McKelvin then had her pistol taken by the assailant. But when the man made his way to another room, McKelvin grabbed another handgun and opened fire. The dead burglar's body was later found a short distance from McKelvin's residence. (*The Herald,* Albany, Ga.)

A Clint, Tex., homeowner armed himself after his shouts brought no reaction from a man he found trying to force open a sliding glass door into his home. When the homeowner went outside to confront the stranger, the man raised a shovel threateningly and the homeowner fatally shot him. The confrontation followed an earlier incident when the man went beserk on a Greyhound bus, shattering its windshield with his head, authorities said. (*The Times,* El Paso, Tex.)

Suspicious when he heard a noise outside and noticed a helicopter circling his Lawndale, Calif., neighborhood, Jack Baugh armed himself with a pistol and went into his back yard to investigate. Discovering a man in hiding, Baugh held the man, later identified as a burglary suspect, until sheriff's deputies arrived. (*The Daily Breeze,* Torrance, Calif.)

Attempting to rob a Zephyrhills, Fla., grocery store, a man broke a bottle on the floor and threatened the clerk with it. As the robber demanded that the clerk open the cash register, her husband stood up in the back of the store with his registered handgun. The intruder ran out the door, jumped in a car and fled. (*The Times,* St. Petersburg, Fla.)

With his wife screaming at an intruder hiding in their Bismarck, N. Dak., home, Hal Peterson grabbed an unloaded revolver from a gun cabinet and ordered the man out. When the stranger lunged at him, Peterson slapped his hand away with the gun barrel, then stepped back and cocked his pistol. The man fled. Police captured a suspect a short distance away, recovering a $5,000 ring belonging to Peterson's wife and charging the individual, who had been released from jail the day before, with two felony counts of burglary. (*The Tribune,* Bismarck, N. Dak.)

Two men, armed with an axe and a handgun, burst into a Jericho, N.Y., residence and disrupted a four-man gin rummy game. After extorting valuables from the cardplayers, one robber ordered his accomplice to tie the men up and threatened to burn down the house. At that point one player, Allan Fishman, a retired New York City police officer, drew his licensed handgun and opened fire, wounding one bandit and sending the other to flight. No charges were brought against Fishman. (*Newsday,* Long Island, N.Y.)

Hearing noises near the back door of her Cumberland County, N.C., home, Grace Easterling armed herself with a rifle. When a man broke in through the front door and started down a hallway toward her, the 74-year-old woman warned the stranger that if he didn't get out, she would shoot. He didn't, instead shining his flashlight in her face, so Easterling fired. The intruder fled. (*The Observer-Times,* Fayetteville, N.C.)

Miami, Okla., motel owner Oba Edwards witnessed two policemen struggling with a man they were attempting to arrest and saw the man wrest away one officer's revolver, shoot and kill him. Edwards armed himself and fired a shot that allowed the remaining officer to recover his partner's revolver and fatally wound the attacker. The dead man was on probation for assault of a Texas police officer. (*The Daily Oklahoman,* Oklahoma City, Okla.)

DECEMBER 1988

Kings Mountain, N.C., store owner Jack Barrett had been sleeping at his business to protect it from burglars. Late at night the lights and phone went out and the owner heard glass breaking. Armed with two guns, Barrett caught an intruder halfway through the broken window. The shopkeeper kept one gun on the man and fired the other into the air to attract the attention of passing cars. After a two-hour stand-off a deputy sheriff arrived to take the man into custody. (*The Citizen,* Asheville, N.C.)

Taking a day off from his landscaping job, Tom Pleasant was relaxing in his Lodi, Calif., home when a man and a youth tried to gain entry. Pleasant armed himself with a handgun, and when the intruders entered the kitchen, he surprised them. The man broke from the house, but the resident was able to catch the youthful offender and hold him for police. (*The News-Sentinel,* Lodi, Calif.)

When a 6-year-old girl was kidnapped from in front of her Denver, Colo. home, her relatives went to the police to report it. They then conducted a search of their own, spotting a van that fit the description of the kidnapper's vehicle. The girl's aunt, Marla Big Horse, flagged the van down and saw her niece inside. Big Horse, armed with a handgun, ordered the man out of the vehicle, freed her niece and held her kidnapper for police. (*The Rocky Mountain News,* Denver, Colo.)

Jackson Watkins was watching television when he heard someone remove a third-floor window at his North Philadelphia, Pa., home. Watkins, armed with a handgun, went upstairs where he was charged by an intruder. The 72-year-old homeowner fired a single shot, killing his attacker. No charges were filed against Watkins. (*The Inquirer,* Philadelphia, Pa.)

Roy Kitchen, a retired Texas City, Tex., construction worker, was awakened from an afternoon nap by a loud pounding at his door. When he heard someone kicking in the door's wooden panel he grabbed his handgun and investigated, finding a man crawling through a hole in the door. Kitchen, 65, fired once, killing the intruder. The slain man was twice paroled on separate burglary convictions, according to authorities. (*The Chronicle*, Houston, Tex.)

Tammy Stuart looked out the window of her Murfreesboro, Tenn., home in the middle of the night and saw a man rummaging through the family car. She woke her husband, who got his deer rifle. Joseph Stuart ordered the man to lie on the ground until police arrived. "We're always glad to have the help of the public," the local sheriff said. "But they should weigh each situation." (*The Daily News Journal*, Murfreesboro, Tenn.)

When a youth wandered into Neva Clark's Baltimore, Md., grocery store and began looking over the candy counter, the owner asked what he wanted. The youth replied he wanted money, and pulled what later turned out to be a BB gun. Pretending to comply, Clark reached for his own revolver and came up firing. The wounded would-be robber was apprehended by police and faces three charges. "I wanted to make sure I got the first shot," the 81-year-old shopkeeper said. "I beat him to it." Clark was not charged in the shooting. (*The Sun*, Baltimore, Md.)

A 19-year-old Los Osos, Calif. woman allowed a man in her home after he asked to use the phone. Once inside, however, he attempted to rape her. Breaking free from her assailant, she ran to her bedroom and picked up a shotgun. The would-be rapist fled the house. (*The Telegram-Tribune*, San Luis Obispo County, Calif.)

Confronted by a knife-wielding man on the stairway of her Englewood, Colo., apartment building, a 25-year-old woman was forced into her apartment where the man tried to rape her. She managed to barricade herself in the bedroom, but her attacker broke through. The pair struggled until the woman was able to get hold of her handgun and shoot her assailant. Police said the man could face charges of attempted murder and attempted rape in addition to kidnapping. (*The Post*, Denver, Colo.)

Nervous from a recent break-in at their Detroit, Mich., home, Isadore Holly's wife woke him in the early morning hours because she heard noises. The 85-year-old homeowner armed himself and went to investigate, finding an intruder in the house. Holly fired a shot into the floor to warn the man away, but he continued to advance. The resident fired again, critically wounding the man. (*The News*, Detroit, Mich.)

Ernest Johnson III heard noises coming from the garage of his Virginia Beach, Va., home and armed himself as he went to investigate. The junior high school assistant principal found a prowler in the kitchen and told the man to halt. The intruder ran toward Johnson, who fired his handgun once, fatally wounding the prowler. The city prosecutor declined to prosecute the homeowner, saying the shooting was self-defense. (*The Virginian-Pilot*, Norfolk, Va.)

Linda Fincher thought the man who approached her in a Pensacola, Fla., parking lot was going to help her get her wheelchair out of the car. Instead, the man grabbed her purse and ran to a waiting car. Fincher and a bystander gave chase in their cars, cutting off the fleeing vehicle. Fincher pulled her revolver and aimed it at the driver; the passenger, who'd snatched the purse, tossed it back to Fincher, saying, "It's all there." The thieves escaped, but the 28-year-old woman got back the purse containing $400. (*The Times*, St. Petersburg, Fla.)

JANUARY 1989

Donald Orr's 17-year-old daughter awoke to find a large, knife-wielding man clearing items off her dresser. She lay quietly until the intruder left, but Orr's wife heard the man moving around and woke her husband. The homeowner armed himself with a handgun and found the prowler in the kitchen. Orr ordered the man to stop but when he continued toward the children's bedroom the resident fired. The wounded suspect was expected to be charged with armed robbery. (*The Daily News*, Naples, Fla.)

Eleven-year-old Jason Green, the son of a Houston, Tex., police officer, was home sick when a woman rang the doorbell of his home. Not recognizing the woman, whom police later believed to be casing the residence, the boy called his mother. Later the boy heard noises in the house and hid in his bedroom, but he came out armed with his father's shotgun to find a burglar removing valuables from the house. The child told the man to stop, but when the boy heard his mother pull up and, fearing she might be harmed, he fired. Green's mother, hearing the shot, burst into the house firing her revolver. Both mother and son hit the burglar, killing him. (*The Post*, Houston, Tex.)

1989

Hearing someone pounding on the front door of his Blacksburg, Va., home screaming "I'm going to kill you," the homeowner, James Bishop, armed himself to defend his wife and 6-year-old daughter. When the man finally broke in, Bishop confronted him. After the man again repeated his threat to kill the family, the resident shot once and wounded the intruder; police arrived shortly and took the man to the hospital. (*The Times & World News,* Roanoke, Va.)

Returning to work after hours at a scrap metal company in North Little Rock, Ark., employee Gerald Hall found a number of aluminum radiator cores stacked at the front gate. When two men in separate cars drove into the parking lot and got out, Hall ordered them to stop. The men began running, but the employee fired his handgun into the air. The pair stopped. Both were later arrested and charged with burglary. (*The Arkansas Gazette,* Little Rock, Ark.)

A man pounding at the door of Henry Lewis' Fort Myers, Fla., home asked to use the phone. Lewis refused, and the man crashed through the front door wearing underwear over his head and socks on his hands. The intruder began chasing Lewis, who retreated to a bedroom where he grabbed a gun from a nightstand and shot his assailant. Police later arrested the wounded man on burglary and robbery charges; Lewis was not charged. (*The News-Press,* Fort Myers, Fla.)

When the doorbell rang at Doug Ferdig's Aurora, Colo., home he thought it was a salesman. But when he looked out the window, he saw a man walking around the side of the house. Ferdig armed himself with a pistol and dialed 911. As he talked to the dispatcher he heard noises coming from the upstairs. The 41-year-old mailman rushed up and confronted an intruder coming out of the master bedroom where his wife was sleeping. When the man did not stop, Ferdig fired, wounding the intruder—a man whose police record included several arrests on burglary and related charges. (*The Post,* Denver, Colo.)

A Chattanooga, Tenn., gas station employee had been sleeping at the business because of a previous burglary. When a man broke into the station in the early morning hours, the employee surprised the burglar and after an altercation fired at him with a shotgun. The wounded suspect was charged with two counts of burglary. (*The News-Free Press,* Chattanooga, Tenn.)

An 89-year-old Ft. Wayne, Ind., woman was talking on the phone when the line went dead. Later she heard noises and thought someone was trying to break in. So she headed out the door to a neighbor's home to call police. But, as she opened the door, a man wearing a black hood pushed her back into the house. Her 91-year-old husband heard the commotion and grabbed a shotgun. The hooded man told the husband to get back, but when the resident continued to advance, the hooded man fled. "The gun saved us," the woman said. "Boy did he run." (*The News Sentinel,* Fort Wayne, Ind.)

Two men had broken through the screened porch of Melvin Hogg Jr.'s home in Jacksonville, Fla. When the homeowner saw one forcing his way through the window, he shot and killed the intruder. The other fled. The slain man was recently let out of prison, nearly half the sentence of his burglary conviction suspended. Ruling the shooting justifiable, the assistant state's attorney said: "People have the right to protect their property and their home. I've got a lot of sympathy for a homeowner who feels his life is in danger." (*The Times-Union/ Journal,* Jacksonville, Fla.)

Susan Galewick was home alone when she observed a man unfastening a window screen at her Orange, Calif., residence. She quickly called 911, then grabbed her husband's pistol just as the intruder appeared at the bedroom door. The 24-year-old woman pointed the gun at him, and he pleaded with her not to shoot him before fleeing. The man, who had a lengthy criminal record, was shortly arrested. "I want other women to know at least a gun is good protection," Galewick told the press. (*The Register,* Orange County, Calif.)